Identity and Religion in Palestine

PRINCETON STUDIES IN MUSLIM POLITICS

Dale F. Eickelman and Augustus Richard Norton, Editors

Diane Singerman, *Avenues of Participation: Family, Politics, and Networks in Urban Quarters of Cairo*

Tone Bringa, *Being Muslim the Bosnian Way: Identity and Community in a Central Bosnian Village*

Dale F. Eickelman and James Piscatori, *Muslim Politics*

Bruce B. Lawrence, *Shattering the Myth: Islam beyond Violence*

Ziba Mir-Hosseini, *Islam and Gender: The Religious Debate in Contemporary Iran*

Robert W. Hefner, *Civil Islam: Muslims and Democratization in Indonesia*

Muhammad Qasim Zaman, *The Ulama in Contemporary Islam: Custodians of Change*

Michael G. Peletz, *Islamic Modern: Religious Courts and Cultural Politics in Malaysia*

Oskar Verkaaik, *Migrants and Militants:* Fun, *Islam, and Urban Violence in Pakistan*

Laetitia Bucaille, *Growing up Palestinian: Israeli Occupation and the Intifada Generation*

Robert W. Hefner, editor, *Remaking Muslim Politics: Pluralism, Contestation, Democratization*

Lara Deeb, *An Enchanted Modern: Gender and Public Piety in Shi'i Lebanon*

Roxanne L. Euben, *Journeys to the Other Shore: Muslim and Western Travelers in Search of Knowledge*

Loren D. Lybarger, *Identity and Religion in Palestine: The Struggle between Islamism and Secularism in the Occupied Territories*

Identity and Religion in Palestine

The Struggle between Islamism and Secularism in the Occupied Territories

LOREN D. LYBARGER

PRINCETON UNIVERSITY PRESS PRINCETON AND OXFORD

Published by Princeton University Press, 41 William Street, Princeton,
New Jersey 08540

In the United Kingdom: Princeton University Press, 3 Market Place,
Woodstock, Oxfordshire OX20 1SY

Library of Congress Cataloging-in-Publication Data

Lybarger, Loren D., 1964–
Identity and religion in Palestine: the struggle between Islamism and
secularism in the occupied territories / Loren D. Lybarger.
p. cm.—(Princeton studies in Muslim politics)
Includes bibliographical references and index.
ISBN-13: 978-0-691-12729-3 (hardcover : alk. paper)
ISBN-10: 0-691-12729-8 (hardcover : alk. paper)
1. National characteristics, Palestinian. 2. Islam—Palestine.
3. Arab nationalism—Palestine. 4. Islam and politics—Palestine.
I. Title.
DS113.6.L93 2007
956.95'3—dc22 2006019001

British Library Cataloging-in-Publication Data is available

This book has been composed in Sabon Typeface

Printed on acid-free paper.∞

pup.princeton.edu

Printed in the United States of America
1 3 5 7 9 10 8 6 4 2

For Olivia

Contents

Foreword

SCHOLARS and journalists have written on the politics of the Palestinians of the occupied West Bank and Gaza, but often their writings seem only a few steps from yesterday's headlines. With the exception of Laetita Bucaille's recent *Growing Up Palestinian* (2004), few recent writings on Palestine and Palestinians reveal what makes younger Palestinians "tick" in terms of political ideas, loyalties, and conceptions of the nation and its goals. Allusions to shifting political identities, often glossed with an anecdote or two, are commonplace in the literature, but we have lacked a systematic discussion. Palestinian pollsters now provide longitudinal data on political opinion, but their work leaves mostly unexamined the underlying shifts in political perspectives and identities that undergird expressed opinions. Important studies of Palestinian elites, organizational politics, and associational life are available, but none of them succeed to the degree that Loren D. Lybarger has in *Identity and Religion in Palestine* in revealing how Palestinian men and women relate to politics.

This book is a product of fieldwork under arduous conditions. While the author is modest about the challenges that he faced, we are certain that without his stamina and courage this manuscript would not have been completed. In all, the author spent six years in the Occupied Territories: three in the 1980s in the West Bank, two in the Gaza Strip in the early 1990s, and one in both West Bank and Gaza from 1999 to 2000. Lybarger's command of Arabic is reflected throughout the text as he helpfully but unobtrusively adds colloquial terms and phrases that lend further authenticity to his commentary and conclusions.

Lybarger's frame of reference begins in the mid-1980s when many Palestinians drew lessons from Israel's failed invasion of Lebanon, continues through the first Intifada that began in 1987 and the turbulent 1990s including the launching and subsequent erosion and collapse of the "peace process," and finally encompasses the early years of the twenty-first century, when the prospects for a negotiated solution to the Israeli-Palestinian conflict seemed as distant as ever. As Lybarger shows, the new generation of twenty-, thirty-, and forty something Palestinians drew new conclusions, not only concerning their changing political milieu, but their understanding of religion and the nature of their society. This is not to say that the Palestinians of the West Bank and Gaza are isolated from events and ideas in the region. Palestinians are shown to be constantly comparing and reflecting on developments in other settings, such as Hizbullah's notable recent successes in Lebanon.

The humiliation of living under occupation is ever present in Palestinian society, and all of Lybarger's interlocutors feel the weight of the occupier's structure of control. The new generation of Palestinians often embrace the delineation of a definitive Palestine state comprised by the West Bank and Gaza, but they are deeply skeptical of Israel and its intentions, and not less so about the United States. For many the lessons of recent history underline the imperative of further struggle rather than quiescence. At the same time, Lybarger provides ample evidence that Palestinians are trapped neither by dogma nor fanaticism, contrary to some popular stereotypes in the U.S. media in particular.

As the January 2006 elections dramatically illustrated, Islamist politics have become mainstream in Palestine. Islam has been reconfigured as an alternative rationality, a riposte to nationalists and their periodic hostility to faith. Palestinian voters were not merely voting for Hamas to chastise Fatah for its failures. They were also reflecting realignment in political attitudes and a skepticism that the painful compromise that so many Palestinians were willing to accept vis-à-vis Israel would not be on offer. While Lybarger did not anticipate the rise to power of Hamas, no one reading his lucidly written volume would be much surprised by the victory.

While many younger Palestinians remain committed to Fatah and groups further on the left like the Popular Front and the Communist party, there has been a striking migration from more nationalist groups to more self-consciously religio-nationalist groups, notably Hamas and Islamic Jihad. While these alignments are no more permanent in Palestine than anywhere else, these shifting loyalties are more than a tactical swing occasioned by a single election. As Lybarger argues, we are witnessing profound reconstructions of what it means to be a Palestinian and, for that matter, what it means to be a Muslim (or a Christian) in Palestine today.

This foreword is an appropriate time to note that Augustus Richard Norton has joined Dale Eickelman as the "Muslim Politics" series coeditor. We also take this opportunity to thank James Piscatori of the University of Oxford, who cofounded the series with Dale Eickelman in 1994 and served as coeditor through the end of 2004. Discussions with James Piscatori over the years helped shape critical thinking in a challenging field for which intellectual boundaries are as contested as political ones. Ever generous with colleagues, students, and others, James continues to offer us an inspiring model of academic commitment and friendship.

Augustus Richard Norton
Dale F. Eickelman

Preface

THIS BOOK explores how Palestinian political identities have changed since the mid-1980s. It focuses, in particular, on the competition between the Islamist movements—Hamas and Islamic Jihad—and the secular-nationalist factions associated with the Palestine Liberation Organization (P.L.O.). The account charts how this competition has shaped the life orientations of individual activists from across the social and political continua. What results is a complex, bottom-up portrayal of the diverse directions in which Palestinian attitudes have recently been evolving in response to a crisis-ridden peace process, the continuing occupation, and a persisting violent resistance.

The concerns and questions that animate this book flow from my long personal encounter with Palestinians and their daily struggles under occupation. This encounter began two decades ago when, after my graduation from college in 1986, I volunteered with the Mennonite Central Committee, a relief and development organization, to teach English in Bayt Jala, a town adjacent to Bethlehem. I had been in the West Bank for only a year and four months when the first Intifada broke out in December 1987. With my neighbors and colleagues I found myself swept up into the collective effervescence of the first weeks. Normal, daily life was turned on its head as we huddled hourly around radios to hear of the latest clashes or the next *nidā'* or *bayān* (communiqué) from the United National Leadership of the Uprising laying out the program of strikes and other collective actions to be taken in the coming week. The excitement and sense that a profound change was underway were palpable everywhere. Curfews, strikes, clashes, and marches fed an upsurge in patriotic fervor. Communities came together in new initiatives—house schools, "victory gardens," tax refusal, neighborhood committees of all sorts—designed to replace the Israeli occupation with new forms of local and national control. I took part in a clandestine house school as an English teacher, at one point ducking out of a home with my students as an Israeli foot patrol approached. Soon, however, the costs of this collective nonviolent resistance began to mount. Homes were demolished by army sappers. Students, including my own, were imprisoned and injured. Others were killed. A friend, the eldest son of the cook at our school, was shot dead at close range at an army checkpoint. After the Israelis ordered all schools shut down, I began work with the Palestine Human Rights Information Center in Jerusalem. I helped collect data on army abuses, traveling the length and breadth of the West Bank with the center's fieldworkers. I saw not only the suffering but also the immense pride that everyday Palestinians everywhere had in their newfound empowerment.

I left the West Bank in 1989 for M.A. studies in teaching English as a foreign language at the American University in Cairo, Egypt. The U.S.-led war to oust the Iraqi army from Kuwait occurred during this period. I visited the West Bank and Gaza Strip upon conclusion of the war, noting how Israel's total closure and curfew of the Occupied Palestinian Territories during the war had effectively fractured what remained of the Uprising. Reduced to despair, many Palestinians openly voiced support for Saddam Hussein's defiant stand and his willingness during the war to lob missiles at Tel Aviv. Two years later, with my degree in hand, I headed to the Gaza Strip to take charge of an English-language program that prepared Palestinian professionals for advanced training in the United States. I spent two years in Gaza, deepening friendships there, especially in the pseudonymously named Karama Refugee Camp, one of the communities I describe in this book. This was a period of political implosion among the Palestinians. The Uprising in tatters, tensions mounted among the factions, especially between Hamas, the dominant Islamist faction, and Fatah, the main P.L.O. movement. Israeli repression continued to intensify with undercover assassination units operating at will. At the same time, the United States, flush with its victory in Kuwait, mounted a diplomatic initiative to inaugurate a "new global order" in the Middle East. The Madrid peace negotiations began in 1992, leading a year later to the surprise announcement of a deal hashed out between Israel and the P.L.O. during secret talks in Oslo, Norway.

Just before Oslo was announced in September 1993, I returned to the United States to take up graduate studies in Muslim-Christian relations at the Lutheran School of Theology at Chicago. In 1995, I shifted gears again, beginning doctoral work in the sociology of religion and Islam at the University of Chicago's Divinity School. Three years on, as I searched for a dissertation topic, I found myself going back to the momentous events that had propelled me into my studies in the first place. Several questions, disciplined by my exposure to sociological methods, began to take form. What had actually taken place in Palestinian society during the late 1980s and 1990s, and what had been the long-term consequences for my friends and neighbors? Why had some Palestinians rejected the P.L.O. to embrace new affiliations—especially Islamist-oriented ones—during the first Intifada? And how had the increasing tension between Islamist and P.L.O. groups developed during my time away and with what ultimate impact? This book attempts to answer these questions.

The stories and analyses presented here come primarily from a year of fieldwork carried out in the Bethlehem urban area and in Karama Camp in the Gaza Strip between September 28, 1999, and September 28, 2000. As it turns out, my interviews and observations provide a record of what Palestinians were thinking and feeling about the direction in which their society was moving on the eve of the collapse of the Oslo Peace Process. The very day after I departed Bethlehem, the Oslo interregnum disintegrated into a protracted fit of guerrilla attacks, bombings, and devastating military reprisals that have come to be known as the al-Aqsa Intifada.[1]

The fieldwork employed participant-observation and life-history interviews to document the process through which individuals from across the social, religious, and political spectra came into and articulated their identities. Interviewees represented the entire range of political factions, religious communities, age groups, geographical locations (towns and refugee camps), and economic and social classes. The more than eighty tape-recorded conversations consisted of in-depth life histories that explored an individual's social and political trajectory from family of origin to school and work experience and mobilization, or lack thereof, into the factions. Most of these interviews were with individuals who matured politically during the first Intifada. These individuals were in their twenties and thirties when I interviewed them in 1999–2000. I also drew from detailed journals of my daily interactions, visits to homes, and experiences at rallies and ceremonies.

The Bethlehem area, with its mix of town, village, and refugee camp as well as its concentration of mostly middle-class Christians, presented itself as an ideal location for documenting the life histories of individuals from diverse backgrounds. Yet because of its high degree of pluralism, a sole focus on Bethlehem would have skewed the broader conclusions of the research. Consequently, the fieldwork included a more monolithically Muslim and impoverished working-class setting, a Gaza Strip refugee camp that I have named Karama. The choice to rely on the already familiar settings of Bethlehem and Karama admittedly may have prevented consideration of other locations that might have shifted or modified my conclusions. However, my previous connections to these places provided me with an established network, a level of trust that would have taken months, if not years, to build elsewhere, and a depth of knowledge of local conditions that might otherwise have been much weaker.

Comparatively little ethnographic and sociological research of the sort presented here has been done on Palestinian political identities. This is

[1] The name Palestinians have given to this latest uprising reflects its origins in the initial riots that occurred when soon-to-be prime minister Ariel Sharon went to al-Haram al-Sharif (the "Noble Sanctuary," also known as the Temple Mount) in a provocative electioneering tactic that dramatized and reinforced long-standing Israeli claims to the entirety of Jerusalem.

surprising given all that has been written on the Israeli-Palestinian conflict in the Middle East. The late Edward Said, perhaps the most eloquent and erudite spokesperson for the Palestinians until his untimely death in 2003, observed ironically that while "a huge body of literature has grown up, most of it polemical, accusatory, denunciatory . . . for all the writing about them, Palestinians remain virtually unknown." He went on to say:

> Especially in the West, particularly in the United States, Palestinians are not so much a people as a pretext for a call to arms. It is certainly correct to say that we are less known than our co-claimants to Palestine, the Jews. Since 1948, our existence has been a lesser one. We have experienced a great deal that has not been recorded. Many of us have been killed, many permanently scarred and silenced, without a trace. And the images used to represent us only diminish our reality further. To most people Palestinians are visible principally as fighters, terrorists, and lawless pariahs. Say the word 'terror' and a man wearing a *kaffiyah* and mask and carrying a *kalachnikov* immediately leaps before one's eyes. To a degree, the image of a helpless, miserable-looking refugee has been replaced by this menacing one as the veritable icon of "Palestinian."[2]

This image of Palestinian-as-terrorist has shifted somewhat since Said wrote those words during Israel's 1982 invasion of Lebanon. The signing of the Declaration of Principles between Israel and the P.L.O. on the White House lawn in September 1993 transformed the Western image of Palestinians from terrorists and fighters into diplomats and peace-seekers. Despite the subsequent collapse of the agreement, U.S. president George W. Bush has spoken openly of the need to establish a Palestinian state—the content and limits of which remain, nevertheless, worryingly vague. In the wake of the defunct peace process, the world has come to divide Palestinians between pragmatists and radicals. The pragmatists are the "good Palestinians" because they are willing to accept a truncated territorial compromise, one fashioned largely in accord with Israel's strategic and ideological interests. The radicals are the masked guerrillas and bombers who reject such compromise and seek to shift the balance of power in the Palestinians' favor by reviving the armed struggle. Increasingly, these radicals have been folded into the image of a new global menace, the Muslim terrorist bent on sowing mayhem in European, American, and Israeli cities. Both caricatures—pragmatist and radical—distort the complex textures of Palestinian politics. Their deployment as interpre-

[2] Edward W. Said, *After the Last Sky: Palestinian Lives*, with photographs by Jean Mohr (New York: Pantheon Books, 1985, 1986; reprint, New York: Columbia University Press, 1998), 4, emphasis in the original (page reference is to the reprint edition).

tive rubrics forces understanding of Palestinian actions into a much too simplistic dichotomy. The rubrics fail to explain precisely because they ignore the internal dialectics of Palestinian history and culture and instead subject Palestinian motivations to an externally imposed yardstick of political rationality—whether what Palestinians do is good for Israel, or the international order, for example.

This book takes a different approach. It is a sustained attempt to listen carefully to Palestinians and interpret their choices within a framework informed by historical context, ethnographic observation, and sociological theory. My intent is not to speak on behalf of Palestinians, but rather to report on and interpret what I have directly encountered through my experience of living among them and reflecting on the dynamics that have shaped their contemporary condition. In this endeavor, I seek to apply a disciplined scholarly perspective that resists ideology in the interest of truth—truth always conditioned by the observer's historical and social location, his relation to power, the accidents of his life course, and the choices for alignment that flow from prior political commitments, experiences, and values. This truth is a reflexive one—seeking understanding of the other and of the self. If I use interpretive frames and methods drawn from sociology and religious studies to make sense of Palestinians, the irreducible complexities of Palestinian life also challenge these analytical structures. This interaction between analytical frame and empirical reality leads ideally to more precise concepts and thus a more profound understanding of the forces that have formed not only the contemporary Middle East but also the global political order. My deepest hope is that this more nuanced understanding might lead to empathy and the crafting of better, wiser policies that assist Palestinians to achieve, finally, a viable state of their own in their ancestral lands. A durable peace in the Middle East requires no less than such an outcome.

Acknowledgments

SEVERAL INDIVIDUALS and organizations have supported me in researching and writing this book. I wish first to thank my mentor, Martin Riesebrodt, for his invaluable guidance and encouragement at every stage. He has inspired me profoundly through his example of disciplined and creative scholarship. I also recognize Rashid Khalidi, Patrick Gaffney, and the two anonymous external reviewers of this monograph for their careful reading and criticism.

I wish to acknowledge, as well, Robert Burton, Bruce Grelle, and Joel Zimbelman for reading multiple chapter drafts, engaging me in stimulating conversation, and providing key assistance in applying for grants. I would also like to express my sincerest gratitude to Tom Abowd, Tom Borchert, Kelly Chong, Muna Hamza, Doug Ierley, Mary Ellen Konieczny, Heather McClure, Adnan Mussallam, Paul Powers, Bernard Sabella, and Graham Usher. I owe a particular debt of gratitude to my editor at Princeton University Press, Fred Appel, for his unflagging support in moving this manuscript toward production. I would also like to thank Sara Lerner and William R. Hively for their expert attention to detail in shepherding this manuscript through its final stages.

In Palestine, several individuals have contributed immeasurably to helping me understand the issues that are the focus of this book. Among them are my longtime friends Abu Ahmad, Abu Tariq, and Abu Jiriyis—men who spent countless hours with me discussing "the situation." What understanding I have of the Palestinians and their struggle I owe in large degree to them.

Alongside friends and colleagues, several organizations have provided me with invaluable financial support. The foundation of this book rests on a year of fieldwork in the West Bank and Gaza Strip made possible by a Fulbright-Hays Doctoral Dissertation Research Abroad Fellowship. Subsequent write-up and revision received the support of a number of other grants, including the Henry Luce Foundation Fellowship in Theological Studies; the MacArthur Scholars Fellowship through the Council for Advanced Studies on Peace and International Cooperation at the University of Chicago; and the Research and Creative Activities Grant of California State University, Chico.

Throughout my research and writing the support of family has been crucial. My parents, Lee and Connie Lybarger, have inspired me through their passionate interest in other cultures and their commitment to social justice at home and abroad. My sister, Kathryn Lybarger, sister-in-law,

Nina Ackerberg, and brother, Lowell Lybarger, have also shared these concerns in their own activism, art, and scholarship. I treasure the bonds we have forged among us. I have also received loving support from my parents-in-law, Thomas V. and Annemarie Abowd, and from my brothers- and sisters-in-law: Elizabeth, Gabrièle, Michael, Jemma, Paul, and Tom. I owe all of them my deepest thanks.

I reserve my sincerest and most profound gratitude for my wife, Mary Abowd. She has sacrificed her own interests at key junctures to enable me to pursue this project and has read every word of this manuscript, commenting expertly on its content and form. She has been a most loving companion in every sense.

Finally, this book, while it has drawn heavily from the input of others, remains my sole responsibility. I hope that it does some justice to the experiences of those who gave so graciously of their time to help me comprehend their lives.

Note on Transliterations

All transliterations from Arabic follow the guidelines provided in the style sheet of the *International Journal of Middle East Studies*. The first instance of a transliteration within any given chapter is rendered in italics and thereafter in nonitalic form. Proper nouns and transliterations in book titles are not given diacritic markings. Included within this category is the title of Islam's holy book, the Qur'an. Commonly used spellings of widely familiar names are adopted instead of literally transliterated (Sinai, not *Sīnā'*, for example). Exceptions include instances in which there is no consensus on an English rendering; in such cases, the more literal transliteration is adopted, for example, Nasir instead of Nasser or Nasr. All translations from Arabic into English are my own unless indicated otherwise.

Chronology of Events

1948 Civil war in Palestine; Britain ends its mandate, Israel declares independence, Arab states declare war against Israel; Israel gains control of 77% of British Mandatory Palestine; Jordan and Egypt hold the West Bank and the Gaza Strip respectively, Jerusalem divided; 600,000–900,000 Palestinians displaced, not allowed to return.

1956–1957 Suez War begins when Israel, supported by Britain and France, attacks Egypt.

1964 Egypt and other Arab states establish Palestine Liberation Organization (P.L.O.).

1965 *Fatah* (founded in 1959 by Yasir ʿArafat and others) conducts first guerrilla action against Israel.

1967 June (Six Day) War begins when Israel attacks Egypt, claiming it is acting preemptively; Israel occupies West Bank, Gaza Strip, Egyptian Sinai, and Syrian Golan Heights, expands Jerusalem boundaries, and extends Israeli law over East Jerusalem; U.N. Security Council Resolution 242 calls for withdrawal of Israeli troops from territories newly occupied.

1968–1970 Israel begins building Jewish settlements in the Occupied Territories; P.L.O. adopts goal of a democratic secular state in all of Mandate Palestine; ʿArafat named P.L.O. chairman; War of Attrition between Israel and Egypt, Syria.

1970 Civil war between Jordanian army and Palestinians; P.L.O. expelled from Jordan, moves to Lebanon.

1973 October (Yom Kippur/Ramadan) War begins when Egypt seeks to regain by force Egyptian land that Israel captured in 1967; U.N. Security Council Resolution 338 calls for cease-fire and comprehensive peace conference.

1974 Arab League declares P.L.O. the sole legitimate representative of Palestinian people; ʿArafat addresses United Nations, which grants P.L.O. observer status in 1975.

1977 Likud wins Israeli elections, Menachem Begin becomes prime minister; Egyptian president Anwar Sadat visits Jerusalem and addresses the Israeli Knesset; negotiations begin between Israel and Egypt.

1978 Temporary Israeli invasion of southern Lebanon; Begin, Sadat, and U.S. president Jimmy Carter sign the Camp David Accords.

1979 Begin and Sadat sign Israeli-Egyptian Peace Treaty in Washington, D.C.

1980 Palestinian *Islamic Jihad* movement founded as a Muslim Brotherhood/Islamic Collective splinter, attracts some Islamist-oriented activists away from Fatah.

1982 Israeli invasion of Lebanon; P.L.O. evacuated from Beirut to Tunisia.

1987–1993 First Palestinian Intifada, or Uprising, against the Israeli occupation in the West Bank and Gaza Strip.

1988 *Hamas* founded as Islamic Collective front organization but soon replaces the collective as primary Islamist movement; declaration of the State of Palestine at the Palestine National Council meeting in Algiers.

1991 U.S.-led coalition defeats Iraq; international Arab-Israeli peace conference in Madrid.

1993 Israel and P.L.O. sign Declaration of Principles (the "Oslo Accords") on interim self-government arrangements.

1994 Cairo Agreement on implementation of the Oslo Accords; ʿArafat establishes Palestinian Authority in Gaza.

1995 Oslo II Accords establish three types of control in the West Bank (Area A: direct Palestinian control; Area B: Palestinian civilian control and Israeli security control; Area C: Israeli control); Rabin assassinated.

1996 First Palestinian elections for president and parliament result in ʿArafat victory; Palestinian suicide bombings in Jerusalem and Tel Aviv; Israeli "Grapes of Wrath" operation against Lebanon; Binyamin Netanyahu elected Israeli prime minister.

1997 Hebron Protocol divides West Bank city of Hebron into Israeli and Palestinian areas.

1998 Wye River Memorandum; P.L.O. renounces anti-Israel clauses in P.L.O. charter.

1999 Ehud Barak elected Israeli prime minister; Sharm al-Shaykh Memorandum.

2000 Clinton-led Camp David II summit and negotiations end in failure; new Palestinian Uprising (al-Aqsa Intifada) begins, sparked by Ariel Sharon's visit to al-Haram al-Sharif/Temple Mount.

Identity and Religion in Palestine

CHAPTER ONE

Islamism and Secular Nationalism

During the past two and a half decades, Palestinian political identities have undergone significant changes in response to war, occupation, uprising, and a failed peace process. These massively destabilizing events have created profound uncertainties that have weakened once dominant forms of secular nationalism and opened up paths for new collective identities, especially resurgent Islamic, or "Islamist," ones. In this book, I use the terms "secular nationalism," "secular nationalist," and "secularist" to refer to a type of political orientation that envisions the national collective as sharing a common language (Arabic), a set of key historical experiences (e.g., the 1948 and 1967 wars, among other significant events), and a territorially bounded space demarcated by the borders of the former British Mandate in Palestine, what is today the West Bank, Gaza Strip, and Israel (see map, fig. 1). For secular nationalists, the nation includes adherents of multiple religions: Muslims and Christians, primarily, but even Jews. Secular nationalism, or secularism, in this sense, bases itself not so much on the repression or restriction of religion, though some left-secularists would demand this, but rather on its integration within a multiconfessional framework. Secular nationalists, generally, seek a nonreligious democratic state, even if this state will make various concessions to the customary legal practices of the different religious communities. This state is seen to encompass members of diverse constituencies, religious and otherwise, who possess the same rights under a single constitution. The Arabic term most commonly used by Palestinians to refer to secularist orientations is *ʿalmānī* (secular). It is often applied to adherents of the leftist/Marxist factions. Those in the mainstream Fatah movement, which constitutes the core of what I have termed the secular-nationalist sphere, would be careful to distinguish between a strict ʿalmānī secularism that insists on the privatizing or abandoning of religious practices (the leftist variant) and a soft secularism that integrates religion as part of a multiconfessional national identity (the Fathawi alternative).

By "Islamist," conversely, I mean activists and movements whose orientations align with the ideology of politically resurgent Islam. Such orientations, referred to in the Palestinian setting as *al-tayyār al-islāmī* (the Islamic [political] tendency), draw on key symbols, discourses, and

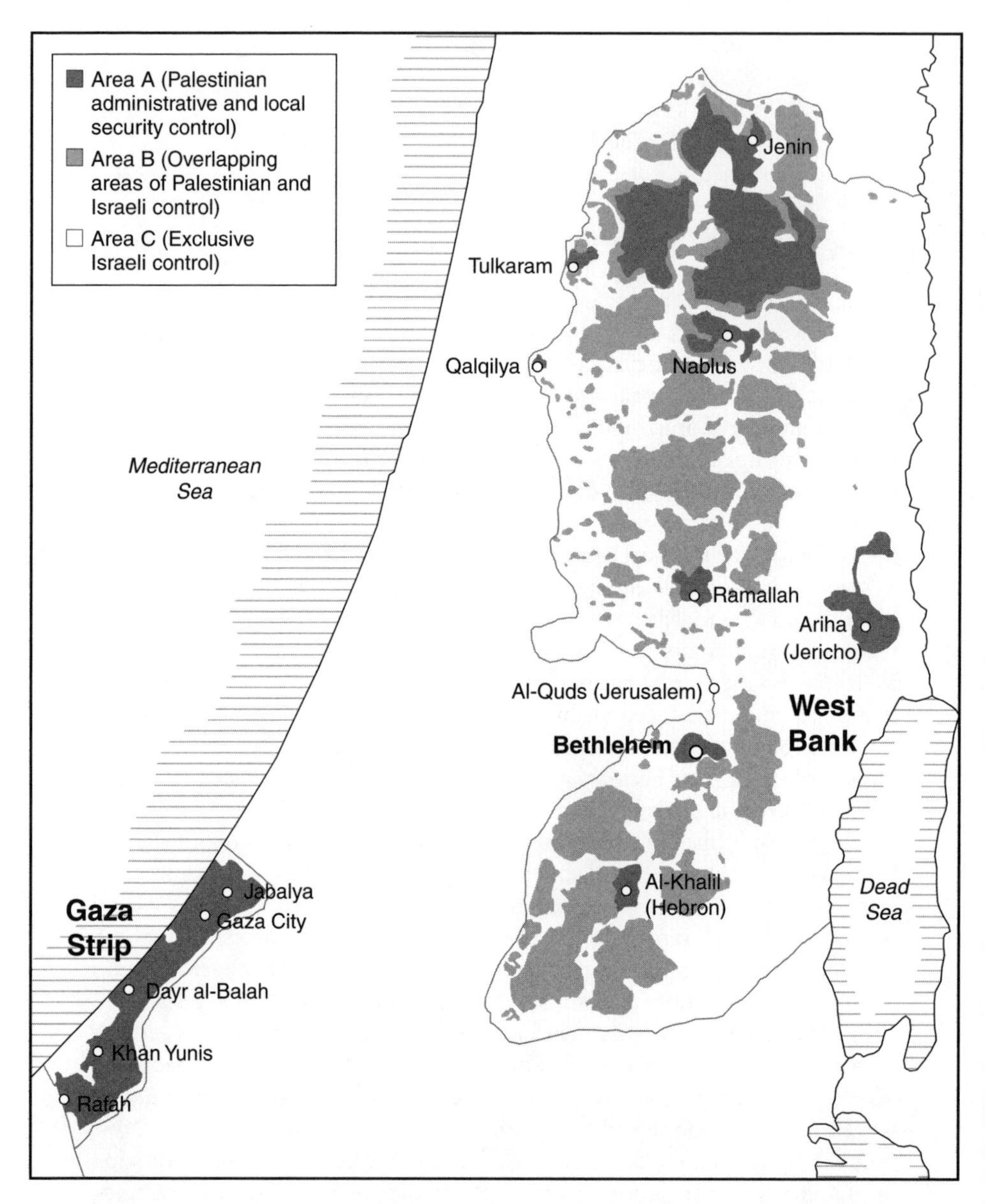

Figure 1. Geopolitical map of the West Bank and Gaza, October 1999. Adapted from Applied Research Institute, Jerusalem, http://www.arij.org/atlas/maps/Geopolitical%20Map%20of%20the%20West%20Bank%20and%20Gaza,%20October%201999.gif.

narratives of the Islamic religion—such as the notions of *jihād* (the "effort" to lead a pious life, establish a society based on the precepts of *sharīʿa*, the "religious law," and defend and expand the boundaries of Islam, militarily), *umma* (worldwide Islamic community), and *khilāfa* (caliphate), among others—to reinterpret the meaning and goals of national political resistance and solidarity. The objective of Islamists is some form of sharīʿa-based state and society within the boundaries of what is now Israel, the West Bank, and the Gaza Strip in their entirety. As Islamists have moved into the political mainstream, by becoming elected representatives on town councils and, in January 2006, gaining an overwhelming majority in the Palestinian Legislative Council, for example, they have modified their objectives, proposing the idea of a long-term *hudna*, or truce, with provisional borders between the yet-to-be-established Palestinian state and present-day Israel as delimited by the 1948 armistice lines. Because ending occupation and achieving a territorially bounded state are its primary objectives, Islamism, in the Palestinian setting, becomes a type of religious-nationalism. By using the term "Islamist," this book distinguishes between those for whom Islam has come to mean a specific type of religio-political identity and those for whom Islam may instead be a personal religious (Islam*ic*) orientation or practice existing alongside, or integrated within, a type of multiconfessional secular nationalism.[1]

The principal struggle within Palestinian society lies between what I am calling the Islamist milieu—at the center of which is the Islamic Resistance Movement, Hamas, literally meaning "Zeal," the acronym for *ḥarakat al-muqāwama al-islāmiyya* (the Islamic Resistance Movement), principally, but also the much smaller Islamic Jihad movement—and the secular-nationalist milieu anchored primarily by Fatah, meaning "Opening" or "Conquest," the reverse acronym for *ḥarakat al-taḥrīr al-filasṭīnī* (the Palestinian Liberation Movement), the dominant faction in the Palestine Liberation Organization. Vying to define and control the collective Palestinian fate, these movements and their associated sociopolitical milieus have so far proven incapable of overtaking or absorbing one another. The consequent competition and division have created the conditions for a multidirectional reformulation and reorganization of political identities. Activists who came of age under these conditions have fashioned new conceptions of collective belonging that selectively integrate elements from both sides of the cultural-political divide. This book documents these new forms of political identity and explores the social processes that have given rise to them.

[1] On the highly debated and complex definitions of secularism and Islamism, see the collection of essays in John L. Esposito and Azzam Tamimi, eds., *Islam and Secularism in the Middle East* (New York: New York University Press, 2000), and Talal Asad, *Formations of the Secular: Christianity, Islam, Modernity* (Stanford, CA: Stanford University Press, 2003).

SITUATING SECULAR NATIONALISM AND ISLAMISM IN THE PALESTINIAN SETTING

The tension between secular nationalism and Islamism among Palestinians has attracted sustained scrutiny among journalists and scholars specializing in the Palestinian-Israeli conflict and the politics of the Middle East, generally. Among journalists, the close-to-the-ground perspectives that have typified the work of Graham Usher and Amira Hass have been particularly influential in shaping the analyses of this book. Drawing on extensive interviewing and long experience of living in Gaza and the West Bank, both authors use rich, multilayered analyses to situate the Islamist-secularist dialectic within the vicissitudes of the broader Palestinian struggle against the occupation.[2] In similar fashion, this book utilizes life-history interviews and direct observation to place Islamist-secularist competition within the wider context of Palestinian nationalism, the Israeli occupation, and the self-rule arrangements of the Oslo period. To comprehend Hamas and the Islamic Jihad, one must understand Fatah and the secular-nationalist milieu that it anchors as well as the general dynamics of repression and resistance that have so profoundly shaped Palestinian life under Israeli domination. With Usher and Hass, thus, I argue that Islamism, while it emerges from a very particular cultural-political milieu within Palestinian society, nevertheless must be understood as a dimension of Palestinian nationalism. What distinguishes this book from journalistic accounts such as those of Usher and Hass is its sustained interpretation of the Palestinian situation as an instance of broader processes—particularly, those of generational change—that shape individual and collective political identities in chronically destabilized societies.

Alongside journalistic accounts, several academic studies have explored the history, ideology, organizational structure, and social setting of Islamism and its relationship to Palestinian nationalism. These works have documented the historical background of Islamism, beginning with Muslim Brotherhood political activism in the 1930s and 1940s; the

[2] Cf. the following articles by Graham Usher: "What Kind of Nation? The Rise of Hamas in the Occupied Territories," chap. in *Dispatches from Palestine: The Rise and Fall of the Oslo Peace Process* (London: Pluto Press, 1999), 18–33; "The Islamist Challenge," chap. in *Palestine in Crisis: The Struggle for Peace and Political Independence after Oslo* (London: Pluto Press, 1995), 25–34; and, among other pertinent articles, "The Politics of Atrocity"; "Fatah, Hamas, and the Crisis of Oslo: Interviews with Marwan Barghouti and Ibrahim Ghoshah"; and "The Meaning of Sheikh Yassin," chaps. in *Dispatches from Palestine*, 83–87, 136–144, and 166–168, respectively. Also, Amira Hass, *Drinking the Sea at Gaza: Days and Nights in a Land under Siege*, trans. Elana Wesley and Maxine Kaufman-Lacusta (New York: Metropolitan Books, Henry Holt and Co., 1996, 1999).

retrenchment and "culturalist"[3] reorientation of Brotherhood structures during the era of secular pan-Arabism and P.L.O. nationalism in the 1950s through the early 1980s; and the revitalization of a more activist Islamism toward the end of the 1970s and into the 1980s and 1990s. They have also focused on the formation of Islamist networks in the mosques and universities in response to similar mobilization processes in the secular-nationalist milieu. A number of other studies have looked at the ideology of Hamas and Islamic Jihad, its connections to the broader Islamist intellectual currents in the region, and its implications for decision-making processes within the Islamist movements and for Palestinian state-building, in general, during the period of the now defunct Oslo Peace Process. These studies have emphasized the range of ideological tendencies within Hamas, particularly, noting that movement leaders demonstrated an ability to think and act pragmatically when confronted by the prospect that Oslo might succeed. From yet another perspective, there is nearly a decade of survey research on public attitudes toward the various political factions. These valuable data show, not surprisingly, that support for Fatah/P.L.O. relative to Hamas/Jihad fluctuated in accordance with public sentiments toward the peace process and the prospects for achieving meaningful statehood and basic personal and collective security. In periods when the Oslo Process appeared capable of succeeding, especially at the time of the 1996 presidential and Legislative Council elections, support for Fatah tended to increase while that of Hamas remained constant or declined. Conversely, when the Oslo Process began to implode in the late 1990s, collapsing finally under the weight of new violence at the end of 2000, the situation became reversed, with Hamas/Jihad gaining in popularity and the P.L.O. factions, especially Fatah, remaining steady or even losing support.[4]

[3] By "culturalist" I mean a focus on cultural Islamization and a corresponding de-emphasis of direct political activism. During the 1970s and early to mid-1980s, the Muslim Brotherhood engaged in missionary activities in an effort to reorient Palestinians away from secular nationalism toward an Islamic religious outlook. The sway of secularism within the culture, not the occupation, was identified as the primary threat.

[4] Ziad Abu-Amr, *Islamic Fundamentalism in the West Bank and Gaza: Muslim Brotherhood and Islamic Jihad* (Bloomington and Indianapolis, IN: Indiana University Press, 1994); Beverley Milton-Edwards, *Islamic Politics in Palestine* (London: Tauris Academic Studies, 1996); Khaled Hroub, *Hamas: Political Thought and Practice* (Washington, DC: Institute for Palestine Studies, 2000); Abd al-Fattah Muhammad El-Awaisi, *The Muslim Brothers and the Palestine Question, 1928–1947* (London: Tauris Academic Studies, 1998); Glenn E. Robinson, "Hamas and the Islamist Mobilization," chap. in *Building a Palestinian State: The Incomplete Revolution* (Bloomington and Indianapolis, IN: Indiana University Press, 1997), 132–173; Andrea Nüsse, *Muslim Palestine: The Ideology of Hamas* (Amsterdam: Harwood Academic Publishers, 1998; reprint, London: Routledge Curzon, 2002); Shaul Mishal and Avraham Sela, *The Palestinian Hamas: Vision, Violence,*

Several key assumptions, some of which I share, underlie these diverse studies. First, Islamism is presumed to comprise a separate sphere with its own unique history and ethos stretching back to the 1930s. Second, the collective commitment to resistance forged during the first Intifada ultimately impelled Islamists to shed their culturalist activism and embrace a more militant, antioccupation posture. The acceptance of Islamism beyond its core constituencies, as the argument goes, resulted from the perception that Islamists were finally contributing to the general *national* struggle against Israel. Third, as Abu-Amr states: "While Islamic groups have had their own appeal, activities, and followings, setbacks of the Palestine Liberation Organization (PLO) have translated into additional influence for these Islamic groups."[5] This latter supposition grounds the sociological and survey analyses that view the changes in the fortunes of Hamas/Jihad as oscillating inversely with those of Fatah. The same presupposition informs the literature on the history of the P.L.O. These works, generally, have interpreted Islamist successes, instrumentally, as the consequence of P.L.O. failures to articulate a coherent positive ideology beyond the lowest-common-denominator commitment to armed struggle and national liberation. The P.L.O.'s extensive use of patronage to co-opt support from diverse constituencies in the West Bank and Gaza Strip, moreover, worked against building a collective purpose that went beyond the interests of clan, status group, religion, and region. The Islamists filled the gap with a comprehensive ideology dedicated to a transcendent ideal.[6]

This book offers a different vantage point. Drawing on extensive interviews with activists from across the political and social spectrum, I argue that Islamism and P.L.O. nationalism ("secular nationalism"), while analyzable as separate spheres with distinguishable institutions, symbols, and styles of discourse, practice, and sociability, have in reality undergone significant long-term transmutations as individuals across the political continuum have crossed over milieu boundaries and selectively

and Coexistence (New York: Columbia University Press, 2000); Bernd Schoch, *The Islamic Movement: A Challenge for Palestinian State-Building* (Jerusalem: PASSIA, 1999). For Khalil Shikaki's survey research, see the data and analyses posted at http://www.pcpsr.org.

[5] Abu-Amr, *Islamic Fundamentalism in the West Bank and Gaza*, xv.

[6] For two varying perspectives on the P.L.O. that nevertheless converge on a critique of the limitations of its authority structure and decision-making processes, see, among other studies, Yezid Sayigh, *Armed Struggle and the Search for State: The Palestinian National Movement, 1949–1993* (Oxford: Oxford University Press, 1997), and Barry Rubin, *Revolution until Victory? The Politics and History of the PLO* (Cambridge, MA: Harvard University Press, 1994). See also the opening chapters of Jamil Hilal, *Al-nizam al-siyasi al-filastini ba*ʿ*d Oslo: Dirasa tahliliyya naqdiyya* [The Palestinian Political System after Oslo: An Analytical Study] (Beirut: Institute for Palestinian Studies, 1998).

drawn from both types of orientation to articulate new forms of political-cultural solidarity. These changes reflect a deeper, intrinsic reworking of inherited attitudes in response to the persisting destabilization of political life. With the weakening of the P.L.O. and the rise of the Islamist movements, the collective Palestinian narrative has become unraveled into multiple threads. As a metaphor for the current Palestinian plight, "unraveling" suggests not a neat splitting into opposing blocs but rather a complex process of unwinding and rewinding of narratives into new patterns with new strands of experience.

Palestinian society, as reflected in the perspectives of my interlocutors, does not fall neatly into two camps, Islamist or secular nationalist. This is not to say that these two blocs do not exist as real, competing formations within society; they do exist, and the findings of this book will build on, and deepen, the helpful work of already existing studies that document the history and ethos of the Islamist and secular-nationalist milieus. At the same time, however, what has remained unexamined is how diversely situated individuals at the ground level have negotiated the competing ideological claims of these formations. This missing ethnographic perspective reveals a far more complex picture, one in which individuals adapt and creatively recombine overlapping orientations into novel expressions of collective belonging. Thus, while this book employs the standard categories of "Islamist" and "secular nationalist," its results point beyond these rubrics toward new trajectories of political identity. The consequent payoff is a much more complex and grounded understanding of the multiple directions in which Palestinian politics are presently moving.

PALESTINIAN ISLAMIST MOBILIZATION IN REGIONAL PERSPECTIVE

The Palestinian case, as described in this book, also yields new and contrasting perspective at the regional level. Islamic religious revitalization in other parts of the contemporary Middle East occurs not as part of a general national liberation struggle in search of statehood but rather as an expression of a countercultural identity and corresponding politics of protest within already established nation-states. Much like conservative evangelical Christians in the United States, or Jewish fundamentalist movements in Israel, Islamism in these other settings identifies a perceived crisis of values within the nation and attempts to address this crisis through a retrieval of a more "authentic" religious past that is felt to have been elided both by the established bearers of religion (the scholars, or *ʿulamāʾ*) and contemporary secularized society, generally. This retrieval occurs through, among other ways, creation of parallel institutions (separate schools, social service agencies, etc.), deployment of alternative symbols of legitimacy ("Islamic" styles of dress and comportment, Qur'anic references in slogans and discourse, banners colored in green, the Prophet Muhammad's color, and so on), and direct action through party-political activism. When repressed by the state, as occurred, for instance, in Iran before 1979, in Egypt, and in Algeria, Islamists have often waged violent campaigns against governments. The purported goal of these struggles has been to reorient state and society toward a more thoroughgoing "piety-mindedness," that is to say, a more profound sense of Islamic identity rooted in the reformation of cultural practices, legal structures, and governing institutions according to the religio-legal ethic of the sharīʿa.[7]

The Palestinian case is different. Certainly, Palestinian Islamism, like Islamist movements elsewhere, does constitute an identifiably distinct "subculture," one that possesses its own networks, symbols, and discourses that separate it from the broader culture imbued with P.L.O. nationalism. Palestinian Islamists also share with other similar movements in the region a sense that the nation is headed in the wrong direction and requires redirection toward a sharīʿa-based order. Still, the occupation and the collective struggle against it have been decisive for shaping a distinctive Palestinian variant on Islamism—a point that is often downplayed or passed over in comparative studies. In their book *Muslim Politics*, for instance, Dale Eickelman and James Piscatori emphasize the competition between state and Islamist civil society actors concerning the proper interpretation of key legitimating religious symbols and discourses.[8] The cases to which they refer most frequently—Algeria, Iran, Egypt, Pakistan, Nigeria, among others—are all instances in which Islamists comprise protest movements within established, postcolonial

[7] The literature on Islamist movements in the Middle East and beyond is immense. A valuable introduction, one that places Islamist activism in relationship to other contending loyalties and broader social-political processes, is Dale F. Eickelman and James Piscatori, *Muslim Politics* (Princeton, NJ: Princeton University Press, 1996). See also the very helpful case studies in Bruce B. Lawrence, *Shattering the Myth: Islam beyond Violence* (Princeton, NJ: Princeton University Press, 1998). Another useful study that surveys the multiple modes of Islamist activism is John L. Esposito, *The Islamic Threat: Myth or Reality?* 3rd edition (New York: Oxford University Press, 1999). For a social movement perspective, see the case studies in Quintan Wiktorowicz, ed., *Islamic Activism: A Social Movement Theory Approach* (Bloomington, IN: Indiana University Press, 2004). On book-centered religio-legal orientations and how they contrast with other forms of religious revitalization, see Martin Riesebrodt, *Pious Passion: The Emergence of Modern Fundamentalism in the United States and Iran*, trans. Don Reneau (Berkeley, CA: University of California Press, 1993), 15–20. The term "piety-mindedness" comes from Marshall Hodgson, *The Venture of Islam: Conscience and History in a World Civilization*, vol. 1, *The Classical Age of Islam* (Chicago; University of Chicago Press, 1974), 247–256 and 315–358.

[8] Eickelman and Piscatori, *Muslim Politics*, 18–21.

nation-states. Islamist movements in these settings thematize a range of grievances among the middle- and lower-middle classes and rural segments of the population. The issues at stake have to do not only with fairer distribution of resources and opportunities but also with cultural values and styles of life that are felt to be threatened or devalued by the secularizing policies of governments and the secularized elites that control them. The authors tend to analyze the tensions between Hamas and the P.L.O. in the Palestinian setting within this framework of postcolonial struggles. They refer, for instance, to Hamas's successes in winning elections against P.L.O.-associated candidates in various professional and student associations during the early 1990s.[9] Their immediate point is that these elections give evidence of the youthfulness of Islamist movements; however, this analysis is set within a wider discussion of transnational similarities in Islamist politics. The implication of this broader context appears to be that the P.L.O. and its successor structure, the Palestinian National Authority, are analogous to established secular governments elsewhere in the Middle East, and that the grievances expressed through Hamas's ideology and activism are parallel to those mobilized by other Islamist movements elsewhere.

This assumption may mislead, however, precisely because the struggle for statehood remains unfinished for the Palestinians. This fact has imposed on Islamist politics in the Palestinian setting the necessity of framing issues in terms of the collective effort to achieve independence. As long as Islamists refused to heed this political reality, they failed to gain the mass support needed to contend effectively against the P.L.O. The emergence of the Islamic Jihad and Hamas just prior to and during the first Intifada transformed Islamism into a viable alternative vehicle for collective Palestinian political identity primarily because these movements, unlike their immediate predecessors, placed priority on liberating the homeland (*al-waṭan*) from Israeli domination. This shift required a reinterpretation of core ideological principles, strategy, and tactics among the new generation of Islamist activists. The most important ideological shift was to subordinate the goal of reviving the umma, the worldwide Islamic community, to a seemingly more limited objective—the retrieval of the nation's patrimony.[10] Granted, the new leaders did continue to speak of the larger effort to revitalize the Islamic

[9] Ibid., 112, 172.

[10] In secular-nationalist parlance, the terms "al-waṭan" (homeland) and "al-umma" (nation), the latter term being drawn from the Islamic religious context, indicated a continuum of Arab national solidarity. The "waṭan" referred to the particular national territory of a particular Arab people, while "umma" indicated the collective Arab nation. Among Islamists, a similar continuum existed but with a different valuation. The "waṭan" denoted a particular ethnic/national group within the larger *Islamic* community, i.e., the umma.

umma, but their principal focus had become the liberation of Palestinian territory and the creation, in that territory, of a territorially bounded Palestinian state as the first and necessary step of the worldwide Islamic revolution. It was this focus, and their demonstrated willingness to sacrifice their lives and treasure for it, that gave Islamists credibility within the wider society. The result: Islamism became "Palestinianized"; and, simultaneously, as Islamists established their nationalist credentials and attracted mass backing, proponents of mainstream Palestinian nationalism increasingly began to integrate Islamist themes into their imaginary.[11]

I would thus nuance Bruce Lawrence's conclusion that the appeal to jihād has ultimately been self-defeating for Islamist movements, including in the Palestinian case.[12] The Palestinian situation actually shows the opposite: that the turn to violent jihād as a form of *nationalist* resistance succeeds in making Islamism an accepted and successful, if not yet dominant, alternative form of collective *Palestinian* identity. This is not a novel point. Several of the writers mentioned earlier have noted the importance of the first Intifada, or Uprising, in radicalizing the Palestinian Muslim Brotherhood and definitively reorienting the Islamist milieu, as a whole, toward the nationalist struggle.[13] The question that has received less attention has been the impact of this reorientation on the identities

[11] Olivier Roy has advanced a similar argument about Islamism, generally. In his view, Islamism has everywhere failed to achieve its strategic goal of instituting a transnational political entity, a revived "umma," and instead has either fragmented into a collection of diverse movements focused on specific national concerns or transmuted into an amorphous and rootless internationalism that attracts alienated youth (e.g., second-generation immigrants in European cities or the newly urbanized in majority Muslim states). He notes the role, in this process, of the failure of Islamist ideologies to adequately and accurately comprehend the factors that have given rise to, and sustain, the nation-state system regionally and internationally; the concomitant Islamist failure to articulate a viable alternative to this system; and the generally successful strategy of states of co-opting Islamist symbols and rhetoric and repressing violent revolutionary groups. While his arguments are generally convincing, Roy nevertheless does not seem to take into sufficient consideration the possibility that the modern nation-state, and the diverse societies in which this political form has become manifest, might be undergoing an internal, bottom-up politico-cultural Islamization even as Islamist movements increasingly become "nationalized." Whether this internal Islamizing process leads to a new transnational political entity—a kind of Islamic Community similar, say, to the European Community—that replaces or significantly transforms the current nation-state system remains unclear, but it is also too soon to write the obituary of Islamism as a political force. Attempts to take control of, and overthrow, the nation-state system may have failed to date, but Islamization in its multiple political and social forms continues to be a vibrant and evolving phenomenon. See Olivier Roy, *The Failure of Political Islam*, trans. Carol Volk (Cambridge, MA: Harvard University Press, 1994).

[12] Lawrence, *Shattering the Myth*, 174.

[13] See, among others, Usher, "What Kind of Nation?" 18–20; Milton-Edwards, *Islamic Politics in Palestine*, 145–151, notes the Islamic movement's lethargic response to the Intifada, initially, but attributes the slowness to Shaykh Yasin's desire to proceed cautiously;

of activists in both the Islamist and secular-nationalist settings since that key turning point of the first Uprising.

The period of the Oslo Peace Process, in which a quasi state under the control of the senior P.L.O. leadership came into existence, shifted the context of Islamist activism from the struggle for independence to the dynamics of state building. It was perhaps during this period that Palestinian Islamism came into greater parallel with Islamist movements elsewhere. Under Oslo, Hamas and Islamic Jihad activists began to reinterpret the meaning of their activism in ways that oscillated between preserving the emphasis on national liberation (i.e., the still unfinished struggle with Israel) and becoming a political party that could mobilize the broad discontent of refugees and other groups that felt excluded from influence and power in the new order coming into existence in the form of the Palestinian National Authority. This book explores these shifting circumstances and dynamics, tracing their effects not only on the identities of Islamist activists but also on the orientations of individuals embedded within the more dominant multiconfessional secular-nationalist sphere.

Perhaps the closest regional parallel to the Palestinian type of Islamism is the Hizbullah movement in Lebanon. Although Shiʿi in orientation, Hizbullah's successful guerrilla struggle against Israel has served as an inspiration and model for continuing militancy among the Sunni Palestinian Islamists. Many of the younger heads of Hamas and Islamic Jihad, the ones leading the current "al-Aqsa Uprising," actually came into direct contact with Hizbullah and its Iranian advisers after the Israeli government, on December 17, 1992, expelled some 408 Islamist activists to Marj al-Zahur, a barren hilltop situated in Israel's former "security zone" in southern Lebanon.[14]

Hizbullah got its start during Israel's 1982 invasion of Lebanon, a campaign that, according to initial Lebanese police reports of the time, left approximately nineteen thousand Lebanese and Palestinians dead, the vast majority of them civilians,[15] and ended in the expulsion of the P.L.O. from Beirut and the setting up of a long-term Israeli occupation in the Shiʿi[16] southern part of the country. Like the Palestinian Islamists, Hizbullah's

she also notes the need to "catch up with the nationalists and Islamic Jihad," 4ff.; Abu-Amr, *Islamic Fundamentalism in the West Bank and Gaza*, 68, also identifies a multiplicity of factors leading to the creation of Hamas, including the desire to wrest initiative and position away from the secular-nationalist factions.

[14] Milton-Edwards, *Islamic Politics in Palestine*, 158.

[15] Noam Chomsky, *The Fateful Triangle: The United States, Israel, and the Palestinians* (Boston, MA: South End Press, 1983), 223, citing Lebanese police statistics compiled during the invasion.

[16] The term "Shiʿi" (Shiite) is the adjective form of "Shiʿa," a collective noun referring to the Shiʿi community, in general.

credibility within the wider society rests on the perception that it has acted patriotically on behalf of the Lebanese nation against an external enemy. Israel's unilateral withdrawal from its "security zone" in 2000 greatly amplified the stature of the Shiʿi guerrilla movement both nationally and regionally. Like most Arabs in the Middle East, Palestinians viewed Israel's retreat as vindicating Hizbullah's tactics of armed resistance.

While Hizbullah has had multiple influences on Palestinian Islamists, the movement differs from Hamas and the Islamic Jihad in at least one crucial respect: in addition to being a guerrilla force fighting Israel, Hizbullah has also become, alongside AMAL (a parallel Shiʿi political movement that predated Hizbullah), the primary vehicle for advancing the specific communal interests of the Lebanese Shiʿa. As such, it seeks to increase the influence and power of the Shiʿa vis-à-vis other non-Shiʿa competitors—such as the Maronite Christians, Druze, and urban Sunni Muslim communities—by mobilizing its constituencies through its extensive network of charitable associations and representing them in Parliament. Although pan-Islamist in its ideology, Hizbullah is primarily one political party among many others that advocates the interests of a particular religious-ethnic community within the existing multiconfessional structure of the Lebanese state and its politics. Palestinian Islamism, by contrast, comprises a national movement that contends with the P.L.O. to define the content and direction of the Palestinian collective, as a whole. Its orientations have become diffuse within the society, integrating into Palestinian nationalist sensibilities and, in so doing, transforming, and becoming transformed by, these sensibilities. Such a transformation, largely the consequence of the unique conditions of the Palestinian struggle for statehood against Israel, is absent in the Hizbullah movement. Hizbullah is Shiʿa-identified and like all other major political formations in Lebanon remains, as such, communally oriented and sectarian.[17]

A second important regional comparison is with the Muslim Brotherhood in Egypt. The connections between Egyptian and Palestinian Islamism are direct and long-standing. Egyptian Muslim Brotherhood missionaries established branches in Palestine during the 1930s. The Brotherhood had mobilized mass discontent against the British occupation in Egypt; its activism in the Palestinian setting was an expression of its pan-Islamic and anticolonialist sympathy with Palestinian nationalists in their struggle against British control and Zionist colonization of the "Holy Land." Traveling up and down the Nile River, the founder of the

[17] On the politicization of the Shiʿa of Lebanon, and on Hizbullah specifically, see Fouad Ajami, *The Vanished Imam: Musa al Sadr and the Shia of Lebanon* (Ithaca, NY: Cornell University Press, 1986), and Amal Saad-Ghorayeb, *Hizbu'llah: Politics and Religion* (London: Pluto Press, 2002).

Brotherhood, Hasan al-Banna, made Palestine a mobilizing cause by preaching to his constituents on the duties of jihād and collecting funds from them to support the purchase of weapons. In 1948, Muslim Brotherhood volunteers fought against Zionist forces in the war that led to the creation of Israel. After the war, Brotherhood cells continued in the Gaza Strip to organize clandestine attacks across the Egypt-Israel armistice lines. The reputation of the Brotherhood as a militant force initially attracted Yasir ʿArafat and Khalil al-Wazir ("Abu Jihad"), cofounders of the Palestinian Liberation Movement (Fatah), to become members for a brief period. Gradually in the aftermath of 1948, but especially following the 1967 war, in which Israel occupied the West Bank and Gaza Strip, the Brotherhood in the Palestinian areas became independent of the parent movement in Egypt; nevertheless, ties of affinity remained. The founders of Hamas (most prominently, the late Shaykh Ahmad Yasin) and of the Islamic Jihad (the late Fathi Shikaki and Shaykh ʿAbd al-ʿAziz ʿAwda, primarily) were all trained in Egyptian universities at different points in time and during their tenures came into contact with Muslim Brotherhood activists and members of other, more militant Brotherhood spin-off formations in Egypt.[18] The increasing radicalism of Egyptian Islamism during the 1970s, along with the successful revolution in Iran, provided inspiration and a model especially for the Islamic Jihad.[19]

Despite the direct organizational ties in the early period and the ongoing affinities since then, the unique circumstances of the Israeli occupation and the concomitant struggle for independence and statehood have caused Palestinian Islamism to diverge in significant respects from its sister movements in Egypt. Unlike the Egyptian case, Palestinian Islamism, especially after the period of radicalization in the mid- to late 1980s, reversed the logical progression from cultural Islamization to Islamic

[18] Yasin actually encountered Brotherhood activists in the Shati Refugee Camp in Gaza, where he grew up after becoming, at twelve years of age, a refugee with his family during the 1948 war. Yasin never formally studied the classical religious sciences, preferring instead to seek certification as a schoolteacher at the Ain Shams University in Cairo during the 1950s. Following Nasir's crackdown on the Brotherhood in 1966, he distanced himself from the movement while nevertheless maintaining his basic commitment to its goals. He quietly began to preach and teach at a mosque near his home in Shati, seeking to revitalize the much-marginalized Muslim Brotherhood movement. In 1969–70, he helped form, and became head of, a small committee that spearheaded the revival by focusing on social and cultural work. Gradually, he drew around him a small core of younger activists who resonated with his message of Islamic revival as a response to the post-1967 Palestinian condition. Eighteen years later, this younger nucleus would provide the central leadership of Hamas. Milton-Edwards, *Islamic Politics in Palestine*, 98–102.

[19] Chapter 3 will go into more precise detail concerning the connections between Egyptian Islamism and Palestinian Islamist activism, and the influence of the former on the latter. For references on these issues, see the citations listed therein.

revolution that Islamist ideologues, such as the influential Egyptian writer Sayyid Qutb, had mapped out. Deeming Egyptian state and society to be a new *jāhiliyya*—the period of polytheistic "ignorance" that medieval Muslim scholars thought to have typified human history before the arrival of Islam—Qutb had advocated a spiritual and social withdrawal of "true Muslims" into segregated subcultures as a first step toward creating an Islamized vanguard, a first instantiation of a revived Islamic consciousness. With these vanguard formations in place, a new generation thoroughly imbued with Islam would rise up to lead a mass revolt against the secular state. The Palestinian Islamist movements that appeared in the 1980s, especially the Islamic Jihad, drew on this vanguard idea but redirected the objective of struggle away from internal social transformation and toward the Israeli occupation. In a significant departure from earlier Muslim Brotherhood orientations that, like their Egyptian counterparts, identified a secularizing society as the primary problem, the Islamic Jihad, and later Hamas, argued that the road to a revitalized Islamic umma, the transnational Islamic community, passed through Jerusalem. In making this shift, these movements brought Islamist structures and ideology into direct parallel with P.L.O. nationalism and, in so doing, transformed Islamism into a live option for patriotic activism that could also be construed as genuinely Islamic. The new Palestinian Islamism, in a sense, identified an alternative and more dangerous jāhiliyya, that of the Israeli state. The problem of the internal jāhiliyya, represented by the P.L.O. and secular nationalism, generally, receded into the background as the new Islamist activists engaged in direct action against the Israeli occupation. Today, Palestinian Islamists seek to represent the entire nation, and, as a consequence, the unfinished business of liberation and state formation has become their primary concern.

GENERATION DYNAMICS WITHIN SOCIAL MOVEMENTS

In addition to providing an important typological distinction relative to other forms of Islamism in the Middle East, Palestinian Islamist mobilization raises critical questions for theories of social movements, generally. Social movement theory is only just beginning to be applied to Islamism in the Middle East. The initial attempts look promising, especially in their stress on regional comparisons.[20] These early studies, however, have generally replicated the biases in favor of structural analysis

[20] See, for instance, Marwan Khawaja, "Resource Mobilization, Hardship, and Popular Collective Action in the West Bank," *Social Forces* 73, no. 1 (September 1994): 191–220, and the case studies, including the one on Hamas by Glen E. Robinson, in Wiktorowicz, *Islamic Activism*. See also Asaf Bayat, "Revolution without Movement, Movement without

that have typified much of social movement research as a whole. Consequently, they tend to stress the determinative role of independent external variables such as network formation, institutional process, and event dynamics in shaping individual and collective behavior. Cultural factors—discourses, practices, value orientations, ideologies, for example—are seen, in this approach, to be subsidiary, dependent, or derivative effects of these more basic structural dimensions. Recently, however, this attitude has undergone sustained criticism as sociologists have come to develop a more sophisticated concept of culture as an independent causal factor in the formation of social milieus and movements. A particularly influential corrective reconceptualizes the relation of culture to structure through the metaphors of "toolbox" and "framing." In this approach, narratives, discourses, symbols, and the other dimensions of culture are viewed as resources that social movement "entrepreneurs" draw upon (i.e., as if from a toolbox) to construe (or "frame") issues in such a way as to make them resonate with specific constituencies. Achieving such resonance aids the effort to mobilize groups in one direction or another. Cultural factors thus become a part of the causal explanation. Still, the structural bias remains intact in these approaches because cultural resources continue to serve as an annex to institutional processes. Culture is treated as a passive reservoir of meanings, metaphors, signs, and symbols that leaders can draw upon at will to recruit and mobilize followers in response to competition from other movements, the state, and so forth.[21]

I take a different approach in this book. Building on Anne E. Kane's work, I argue that cultural factors do not merely emerge from, reflect, or serve structural processes (network formation, constituency mobilization, large historical transition) but rather can shape these very processes in their own right. More precisely, I see culture and structure as interrelated. Position within networks, institutions, and events certainly can determine consciousness. But consciousness is also constituted by inherited

---

Revolution: Comparing Islamic Activism in Iran and Egypt," *Comparative Studies in Society and History* 40, no. 1 (January 1998): 136–169, and David A. Snow and Susan E. Marshall, "Cultural Imperialism, Social Movements, and the Islamic Revival," *Research in Social Movements, Conflicts and Change* 7 (1984): 131–152.

[21] The literature on social movements is gigantic. For references to the major works and an important critique of the structural biases in social movement theory, see Mustafa Emirbayer and Jeff Godwin, "Network Analysis, Culture, and the Problem of Agency," *American Journal of Sociology* 99, no. 6 (May 1994): 1411–1454. For recent work in the cultural analysis vein, see Ann Swidler, "Culture in Action: Symbols and Strategies," *American Sociological Review* 51 (April 1986): 273–286; Anne E. Kane, "Theorizing Meaning Construction in Social Movements: Symbolic Structures and Interpretation during the Irish Land War, 1879–1882)," *Sociological Theory* 15, no. 3 (November 1997): 249–276; and Anne W. Esacove, "Dialogic Framing: The Framing/Counterframing of 'Partial-Birth' Abortion," *Sociological Inquiry* 74, no. 1 (February 2004): 70–101.

sociopolitical orientations, discursive and symbolic formations, practices, and ideals that possess their own logic and that interact dialectically with institutions and events. Structural processes such as institutional collapse might occasion crises of orientation that then call forth reinterpretations of received attitudes and methods. But this process of reinterpretation is itself subject to the inherited limits on the range and logic of the symbols, discourse, and narratives that have become embedded within a given social context. While new symbols, discourses, and narratives can emerge from critical reflection and recombination, the changes that result will always occur in dialectical relation to what has come before. This process, moreover, is multidirectional, occurring potentially at many different levels of social aggregation. Meanings are not the preserve of a single actor; hence, not just leaders but also followers will engage in the reinterpretation process. The novel forms of affiliation and concomitant new conceptualizations for action that evolve from this multiplex revision are thus the result of tensions and negotiations among leaders and followers. These tensions/negotiations often end in the formation of unforeseen subtendencies and splinter groups. This differentiation can lead either to the emergence of a new, shared narrative through "symbolic fusion" or to the development of multiple narratives through symbolic fragmentation. In either case, cultural processes appear to be partially autonomous and capable of creating the conditions for the emergence of new structures.[22]

Several key questions arise from the methodological starting point that I am elaborating here: How and under what conditions do individuals at different social levels rethink or reappropriate inherited memories and orientations to make sense of the present? What is the relationship between these acts of reappropriation and the forging of new kinds of group memory and solidarity? What role, in particular, do collective symbols and narratives play in creating the cognitive and emotional ties of these new memories/solidarities? Through what social processes are the expectations, sentiments, and moral obligations of solidarity that are embedded within collective symbols and narratives absorbed within the hearts and minds of individuals? And, finally, how do memories/solidarities actualize themselves at different levels of social aggregation and in different situations?

[22] Kane, "Theorizing Meaning Construction in Social Movements," 249–276. The multilevel, multidirectional process of symbolic/discursive/narrative revision that I outline here receives a much more detailed discussion in Kane's article. Kane stresses "symbolic fusion" (or "hybridization," to use the term adopted in this book) as the normal outcome of "discursive tension," while I view fragmentation to be an equally likely outcome, at least in the Palestinian case.

Adopting these questions as guideposts, I trace in this book the new discourses and narratives that are emerging among individual Palestinians as they negotiate the polarized terrain of Islamist/secular-nationalist competition. These new forms of sociopolitical consciousness represent fluid reworkings of inherited symbols and interpretations that connect with the key moments of crisis in collective Palestinian experience. These moments have been numerous. Despite a general consensus rooted in basic P.L.O. nationalism, the meanings of these events have always been contested, especially when a new crisis crops up. The importance of crises in generating new interpretations raises additional questions: How do such events produce changes in individual and collective orientations? What is the vehicle through which these changes happen? And what are the effects of these changes in consciousness on how individuals associate with one another?

The answer I propose to these questions rests on the concept of sociohistorical generations. Destabilizing events create generations, and it is within the structures of a generation that new forms of meaning and association emerge. But what exactly are "generations," and what produces them? How does the generational process lead to the production of new cultural meanings? And how do these new meanings give rise to novel forms of solidarity?

In a seminal essay, Karl Mannheim, a Hungarian sociologist who was active between the world wars, suggested that a generation was similar to a socioeconomic class.[23] Class position defined individuals by their common objective location within the economic and sociopolitical structures of their society. Class situation was objective in the sense that it shaped the outlook and mannerisms of individuals regardless of whether or not they were aware of or acknowledged their actual position within the class hierarchy.[24] Like class, the sociohistorical generation was a "location phenomenon." It shaped the orientations of a broad group of individuals who may or may not have had actual, direct interaction with one another and who might or might not have been aware of their shared position. In contrast to class, however, a generation's identity was given not by the socioeconomic structure but by a unique combination of demographic and historical factors. Generations came into existence as a social phenomenon through the interaction of the "rhythm of birth and death" with institutionalized modes of socialization that perpetuated shared patterns of speech, movement, thought, and desire. Socialization

[23] Karl Mannheim, "The Problem of Generations," chap. in *Essays on the Sociology of Knowledge*, ed. Paul Kecskemeti (London: Routledge & Kegan Paul, 1952), 276–320.

[24] Ibid., 289.

practices reduced the disruptive effect of birth and death by crystallizing past experience and inculcating it within new members of society, thus creating a sense of intergenerational continuity. Destabilizing historical experiences, however, could undermine this sense of connectedness by causing inherited orientations to appear irrelevant or problematic, thus opening up spaces for the revival of marginalized or "forgotten" discourses and practices.[25]

The shared experience of a moment of social destabilization stamped a generation with its peculiar sense of "fate," through which all later experience got filtered. Destabilization was the necessary catalyst that initiated the process of forming actual generation identities.[26] Rapid change did not so much wipe the slate clean as it created perceptions of a radical disjunction between inherited attitudes and lived reality. Old ways appeared not to work. In the crisis of orientation that ensued, received ideals and those who supported them faced the possibility of rejection and replacement. The social codes that comprised collective, institutional identities thus could become fluid and reorderable.[27] This work of reordering occurred principally among young adults. Because youth had not yet crystallized a basic life orientation, they were more capable of seeing circumstances as new, critically evaluating inherited narratives, and adopting alternative models in response to conditions of crisis and upheaval.[28]

The experience of upheaval and consequent reevaluation and reconstruction of inherited orientations would then become definitive of the identity of the segment of youth undergoing the process. All later experience of this group would be filtered through the memory of the originating trauma and meanings attached to it. It is the possession of this mem-

[25] As Mannheim puts it: "The continuous emergence of new human beings . . . facilitates reevaluation of our inventory and teaches us both to forget that which is no longer useful and to covet that which has yet to be won." Ibid., 295. For a fuller discussion of how destabilizing events can undermine inherited orientations and create new ones, see William H. Sewell, Jr., "A Theory of Structure: Duality, Agency, and Transformation," *American Journal of Sociology* 98, no. 1 (July 1992): 1–29, and "Historical Events as Transformations of Structures: Inventing Revolution at the Bastille," *Theory and Society* 25, no. 6 (December 1996): 841–881.

[26] Mannheim, "The Problem of Generations," 302–304. Mannheim comments in this regard: "We shall therefore speak of a *generation as an actuality* only where a concrete bond is created between members of a generation by their being exposed to the social and intellectual symptoms of a process of dynamic de-stabilization." Emphasis is in the original.

[27] Ibid., 299–302.

[28] Ibid., 296–298; Charlotte Dunham, "Generation Units and the Life Course: A Sociological Perspective on Youth and the Anti-war Movement," *Journal of Political and Military Sociology* 26, no. 2 (Winter 1998): 137–155; and Howard Schuman and Jacqueline Scott, "Generations and Collective Memories," *American Sociological Review* 54 (June 1989): 359–381.

ory, rooted in a shared experience of upheaval, that is most important to the analysis of generations. Beyond merely constituting a statistically identifiable "cohort," historical generations—or "strategic generations," to borrow Bryan Turner's phrase—comprised a self-conscious collective whose actions become socially and politically significant, especially in the creation or revision of national identities. The historical importance of such entities could be measured in the impact they had on subsequent generations. The "Intifada" generation, I argue, constitutes a strategic generation in this sense. Exposure to the Uprising and its aftereffects marks the cohort of youth undergoing the trauma of this period with a distinct set of orientations. These orientations have profoundly revised Palestinian identity in various ways during the subsequent post-Intifada period.[29]

Generations, however, especially in the Palestinian case, were rarely, if ever, homogeneous entities with uniform perspectives. Within generations, conflict could occur when opposing narratives developed of the common historical event that had called a particular generation into existence. The social tendencies that became the vehicles for these conflicting interpretations constituted what Mannheim called "generation units."[30] At the core of every unit were cultural and political groups that had articulated specific ideological programs. Some groups would have greater institutional strength and thus be more successful in articulating the hopes and fears accompanying an emerging historical moment; these groups would generalize their particular interpretation of events, embedded within the narratives and symbols of distinct sociopolitical milieus, to individuals and groups beyond their immediate sphere. Others not directly affiliated with these groups/milieus would nevertheless absorb their orientations. Generation units became significant historical forces to the extent that they achieved this wider effect. The concept of generation units enables us to develop a more coherent theory of change within social movements by linking structural processes (network formation, institutional location, large historical events) to cultural ones (interpretation of symbols, articulation of discourses, authoring of narratives). Generation units are the vehicles for culturally reimagining and institutionally reconstituting movements and milieus.

[29] Bryan S. Turner, "Strategic Generations: Historical Change, Literary Expression, and Generational Politics," in *Generational Consciousness, Narrative, and Politics*, ed. June Edmunds and Bryan S. Turner (Lanham, MD: Rowman & Littlefield Publishers, 2002), 15–18.

[30] On the definition of generation units relative to generations, as a whole, Mannheim writes: "Youth experiencing the same concrete historical problems may be said to be part of the same actual generation; while those groups within the same actual generation which work up the material of their common experiences in different specific ways, constitute separate generation units." Mannheim, "The Problem of Generations," 304.

GENERATIONAL TRANSFORMATION AND PALESTINIAN NATIONAL IDENTITY

In the Palestinian case, a series of crises has produced a number of generational shifts. These changes occurred as evolutions and disjunctions within the milieu structures and accompanying narratives and symbols through which Palestinians have formed and expressed their political identities. The process was open-ended, often leading to surprising new departures; but each development grew out of, or in reaction to, the social and political formations and symbolic repertoires of earlier periods. Major social upheaval coincided with the main shifts. These events created structural uncertainty and, in so doing, provided the conditions for the emergence of new networks and orientations. The new forms of organization and consciousness marked the boundaries between generations. Figure 2 provides a flowchart detailing the historical development of the main Palestinian political formations and their opposing milieus.

At least three main generational shifts mark the evolution of the current Palestinian sociopolitical field. The first one occurred after the War of 1948, the event that brought the State of Israel and Palestinian dispossession simultaneously into existence. Prior to 1948, two main groups characterized Palestinian society: landless (tenant) farming peasants and the landowning notable classes.[31] The 1948 war had two main effects on

[31] For background on pre-1948 society in Palestine, see Butrus Abu-Manneh, "The Husaynis: The Rise of a Notable Family in 18th Century Palestine," chap. in *Palestine in the Late Ottoman Period: Political, Social, and Economic Transformation*, ed. David Kushner (Leiden: E. J. Brill, 1986), 93–108; ʿAdil Mannaʿ, *Aʿlam filastin fi awakhir al-ʿahd al-ʿUthmani, 1800–1918* [The Distinguished Personalities of Palestine of the Late Ottoman Period, 1800–1918] (Jerusalem: Jamʿiyyat al-Dirasat al-ʿArabiyya, 1986); Albert Hourani, "Ottoman Reform and the Politics of Notables," chap. in *Beginnings of Modernization in the Middle East: The Nineteenth Century*, ed. William R. Polk and Richard L. Chambers (Chicago: University of Chicago Press, 1968), 41–68; Rashid Khalidi, *Palestinian Identity: The Construction of Modern National Consciousness* (New York: Columbia University Press, 1997); Baruch Kimmerling and Joel S. Migdal, *Palestinians: The Making of a People* (Cambridge, MA: Harvard University Press, 1993, 1994), 64–123; Uri M. Kupferschmidt, *The Supreme Muslim Council: Islam under the British Mandate for Palestine* (Leiden: E. J. Brill, 1987); Ann Mosely Lesch, *Arab Politics in Palestine, 1917–1939: The Frustration of a Nationalist Movement* (Ithaca, NY: Cornell University Press, 1979); Phillip Mattar, *The Mufti of Jerusalem: Al-Hajj Amin al-Husayni and the Palestinian National Movement* (New York: Columbia University Press, 1988); Muhammad Y. Muslih, *The Origins of Palestinian Nationalism* (New York: Columbia University Press, 1988); Yohoshua Porath, *The Emergence of the Palestinian-Arab National Movement, 1918–1929* (London: Frank Cass, 1974), and Porath, *The Palestinian-Arab National Movement, 1929–1939: From Riots to Rebellion* (London: Frank Cass, 1977); and Ted Swedenburg, *Memories of Revolt: The 1936–1939 Rebellion and the Palestinian National Past* (Minneapolis: University of Minnesota Press, 1995).

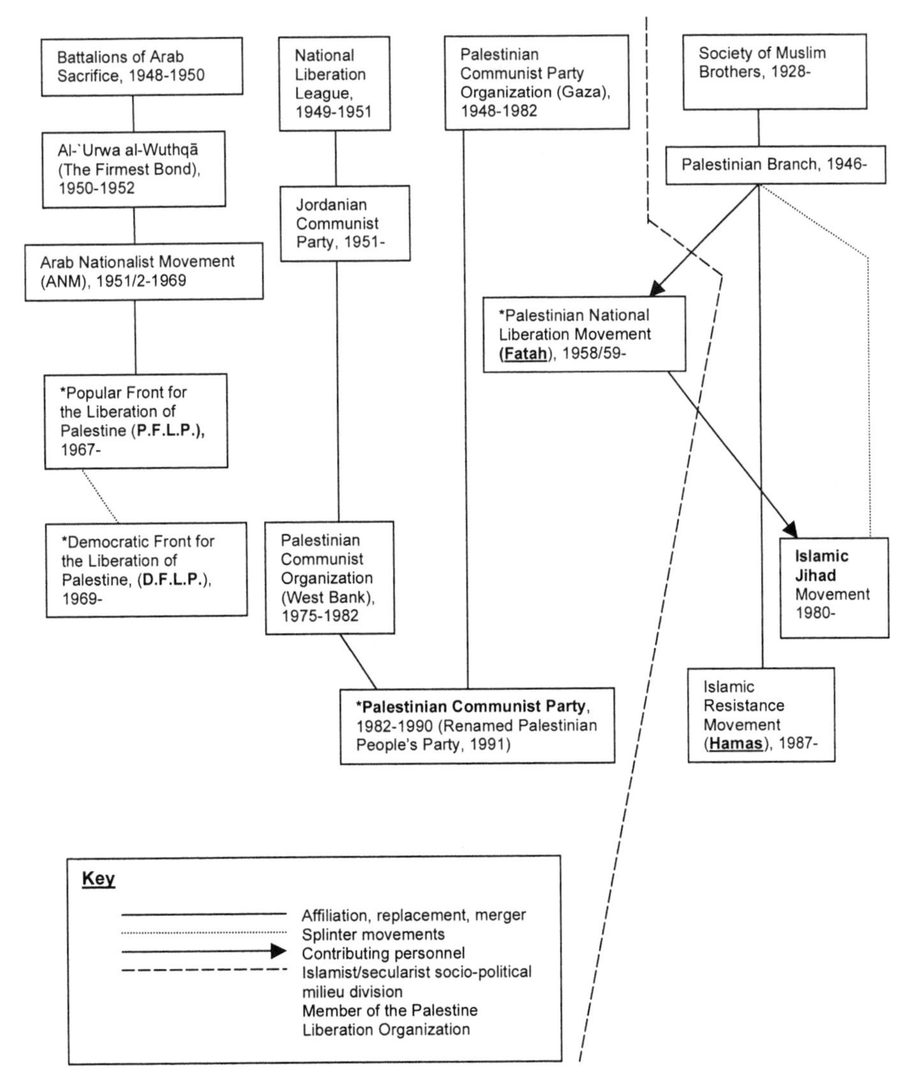

Figure 2. Evolution of secular-nationalist and Islamist factions. Adapted from Yezid Sayigh, *Armed Struggle and the Search for State: The Palestinian National Movement, 1949–1993* (Oxford: Oxford University Press, 1997, 1999) xlii–xliii.

these groups. First, it discredited the leadership of the notables. In their place, there arose a new generation of university-educated leaders from the nonlandowning merchant and small-business classes who were forced from their towns and neighborhoods along with the tenant farming communities during the war.[32] Individuals such as the late Yasir ʿArafat, cofounder of the Fatah movement, and George Habash, cofounder of the Popular Front for the Liberation of Palestine, represented this trend. Educated at Cairo University and American University of Beirut, respectively, they met other activists on these campuses who had undergone similar experiences. The student organizations they formed became the basis for new political movements that would reforge Palestinian national identity in the exile (*al-ghurba*).

The second effect of the war was the synchronic split within this new generation of nationalists. The main division lay between those who advocated a pluralistic Palestinianism that looked back to the "customs and traditions" of village and town life, and those who called for a secular pan-Arab revolution across the region. The leaders of both tendencies had common social origins in the lower-middle to mid-middle classes; after the 1948 debacle, they all underwent transitions in their social class identities as they entered the universities and became members of the new professional elites.

The founders of the Fatah movement, the core of the first tendency, articulated a form of nationalist consciousness that coincided with the ethos of the lower-middle classes—groups with origins in small towns or villages that had shifted into the business and professional classes (small-shop owners and traders, government employees, teachers, etc.). This ethos stressed the importance of the *ʿādāt wa taqālīd* (the customs and traditions) of the recently lost peasant and village past. Fatah's founders reflected this orientation in their symbols and discourse. They adopted stylized forms of peasant costume (ʿArafat's kūfiyya scarf, e.g.); invoked the ties of family and religion, Muslim and Christian, as the foundation of national solidarity; and apotheosized the peasant-as-heroic-guerrilla who rose up to avenge and reclaim the land. Unlike the pan-Arabists, they emphasized a strictly Palestinian nationalist orientation, viewing the liberation of the Palestinian homeland as the royal road to Arab unity. At the same time, the founders of Fatah consciously cultivated the image of the Third World revolutionary who had discarded the customs

[32] On the formation of the new national movements after 1948, see Helena Cobban, *The Palestinian Liberation Organisation: People, Power and Politics* (Cambridge: Cambridge University Press, 1984); Kimmerling and Migdal, *Palestinians;* Sayigh, *Armed Struggle and the Search for State*; William B. Quandt, Fuad Jabber, and Ann Mosely Lesch, *The Politics of Palestinian Nationalism* (Berkeley, CA: University of California Press, 1973); and Rubin, *Revolution Until Victory?*

and traditions of the peasant past in favor of the "revolution" that would create an up-to-date bureaucratic nation-state; they signaled this orientation by wearing Western-style suits or military fatigues with pens in breast pockets and pistols in hip holsters. Fatah's and, after 1967, the P.L.O.'s fusion of these different and divergent symbols and discourses into a more or less coherent Palestinianism served ideologically to integrate the diverse constituencies—shop owners, town dwellers, villagers, university students, and the new professionals—that comprised the Palestinian refugee population after the Nakba (Disaster) of 1948.

In contrast to this "right," hybrid form of nationalism that predominated in Fatah, a second, competing "left" segment among the new generation moved more resolutely in a strictly secularist direction. Drawn to the ideals of pan-Arabism and the rhetoric of Marxist revolution, these members of the emerging professional classes (medical doctors, teachers, writers, and so on), many of them from displaced merchant and landowning families, and many of them Christians, embraced an Arab unity founded on the concept of a desacralized Islamic cultural heritage that all groups shared, the Arabic language, and anticolonialism. They formed the Movement of Arab Nationalists (M.A.N.) and supported Jamal ʿAbd al-Nasir's rise to power in Egypt. The movement's founders theorized that once "revolutionary" pan-Arab regimes had replaced the "reactionary" pro-West and pro-capitalist kingdoms (e.g., in Jordan, Iraq, Saudi Arabia), a war of liberation against Israel would become possible.

The generation that founded Fatah and M.A.N. created the main structures of what I term the "secular-nationalist milieu." This milieu underwent two subsequent changes, first in the aftermath of the 1967 war and then in the decade between the Israeli invasion of Lebanon in 1982 and the end of the first Intifada and start of the Oslo Peace Process in 1993. One of the main shifts was the integration of the right and left tendencies that had been institutionally represented in the separate Fatah and M.A.N. structures. The 1967 war ended with the complete defeat of the Egyptian, Jordanian, and Syrian forces and the Israeli occupation of the Sinai desert, Gaza Strip, West Bank, and the Syrian Golan Heights. It was a humiliating defeat for Nasir and the pan-Arabist cause. In the aftermath, the Fathawi stress on independent decision-making, armed struggle, and national liberation above all other considerations increasingly resonated among Palestinians. Fatah attracted hundreds of recruits through its highly touted, but largely ineffective, armed actions. The M.A.N. responded by embracing Fatah-type nationalism, carrying out its own spectacular operations (airplane hijackings, guerrilla raids), and renaming itself the Popular Front for the Liberation of Palestine. The P.F.L.P. joined the P.L.O.—which Fatah took over in 1968–69—and functioned within it as a counterforce to Fatah.

These shifts coincided with the creation of an independent P.L.O. base in Lebanon and the concomitant emphasis on guerrilla attacks against Israel launched from the "outside." The *fidā'ī* (one who sacrifices his or her life), his (sometimes her) face masked in the peasant kūfiyya (checkered scarf), became the symbol of this resurgent Palestinian identity. So did the images, captured in poster art, of the militant peasant rising from the ground with rifle in hand or, alternatively, of the peasant woman dressed in a *thawb* (embroidered dress) holding on to her children as she remained rooted to her land. The fighter and militant peasant represented the virulent "outside"; the woman, the passive and steadfast "inside" awaiting liberation. Such symbols tapped into patriarchal notions of honor and the necessity to redeem it when it became violated. These ideas had been part of the ethos of village and small-town life and continued as values within the refugee communities. Religious strictures, Muslim and Christian, reinforced these orientations in various ways. The nationalist reformulation, however, produced a secularized patriarchalism, symbolically linking "honor" to the "people's revolution" as the P.L.O. incorporated the left and adapted its rhetoric within the context of Fathawi Palestinianism.

Alongside this transfiguration of patriarchal discourse, the P.L.O. also created a meritocracy that empowered refugees and women, in particular, to become educated and pursue careers as movement bureaucrats. The P.L.O. became, in Yezid Sayigh's terms, a protostate in exile modeled on the single-party bureaucratic states, especially in the Egyptian form, that had come into existence in the Arab world with the demise of colonialism. As such, it sought to fashion new forms of solidarity by prioritizing the creation of "revolutionary consciousness" in the younger generations through education, professionalization, and military training.

The second main effect of the 1967 war was the reconstitution of the Muslim Brotherhood in Palestinian society.[33] The Brotherhood, as mentioned earlier, had been active as a guerrilla force during and immediately after the 1948 war but then went into abeyance with the rise of Nasir, pan-Arabism, and the Fatah-controlled P.L.O. The activists who undertook to revitalize the Brotherhood after the 1967 war explicitly rejected participation in the P.L.O., insisting that nationalism was contrary to Islam and that Palestinian suffering would end only with a return to religion. Accordingly, they emphasized missionary outreach and charity in an effort to reorient the wider culture. Avoidance of explicit antioccupation activities helped the revitalizing effort steer clear of Israeli repression. In-

[33] The following discussion draws on Abu-Amr, *Islamic Fundamentalism in the West Bank and Gaza*; Hroub, *Hamas*; Milton-Edwards, *Islamic Politics in Palestine*; Mishal and Sela, *The Palestinian Hamas*; and Nüsse, *Muslim Palestine*.

deed, Israel saw the Brotherhood as a potential force for undermining the P.L.O. in the Occupied Palestinian Territories and assisted its reemergence by issuing its charities licenses and allowing it space to organize. The main significance of the efforts of these new Brotherhood activists lay in the formation of an extensive, mosque-based social service network. This base would eventually provide the necessary structural foundation for the Hamas and Islamic Jihad movements. A similar institutionalization process, it should be noted, occurred in the secular-nationalist milieu as P.L.O. factions, principally the left but increasingly Fatah after the 1982 Israeli invasion of Lebanon, established their own social and political networks. These groups enjoyed greater legitimacy than the Brotherhood because of their basic nationalist orientation. By the 1980s, to identify as Palestinian was to be a supporter, passive or active, of the P.L.O.

In the 1980s, major political upheaval would again play a role in generating structural and ideological shifts in both the Islamist and the secular-nationalist milieus as they had taken form in the post-1967 period. The destruction of the last independent P.L.O. base in Lebanon during Israel's 1982 invasion and the outbreak of the first Intifada some five years later shifted momentum away from the old founding P.L.O. leadership, now in distant exile in Algeria and Tunisia, toward a new generation of activists based in the "inside" (the occupied West Bank and Gaza Strip). A diachronic split thus took form within the secular-nationalist milieu, particularly within Fatah, between the outside "old guard" and inside "young guard" leaderships.[34] This split would deepen during the Oslo period (1993–2000), creating the conditions for a resurgent militancy as the young guard attempted to assert control of the secular-nationalist movement as a whole. Among the Islamists, a similar diachronic dynamic emerged; but instead of a split, the older leadership embraced a more militant posture in response to the mass upheaval of the first Uprising and the rise of radicalized younger activists seeking an Islamic-nationalist option. The Islamic Jihad, which appeared in the early 1980s as a small underground armed movement, was a precursor of this shift, serving notice to the wider Islamist movement that a failure to embrace a more militant stance could lead to political irrelevancy for yet another generation. The formation of Hamas indicated that the older leadership had drawn the appropriate conclusions from the rise of the new militants and the spreading mass ethos of resistance that the first Intifada created.

[34] Khalil Shikaki coined these terms. See Khalil Shikaki, "Old Guard, Young Guard: The Palestinian Authority and the Peace Process at a Cross Roads" (Ramallah: The Palestinian Center for Policy and Survey Research, November 1, 2001), and, by the same author, "Palestinians Divided," *Foreign Affairs* (January/February 2002): 89–105.

The appearance of Hamas also signaled a *synchronic* split within the Intifada generation. The Islamists had finally arrived as an independent political force. By refusing subordination to the P.L.O.-associated United National Leadership of the Uprising, Hamas and Islamic Jihad imposed a fundamental political and cultural divide within Palestinian society. This division took form in the Intifada generation and deepened during the Oslo Peace Process (1993–2000). The progressive installation of the Palestinian National Authority in most of the Gaza Strip and designated areas of the West Bank during the Oslo period was a major factor in the entrenchment of the Islamist-secularist division. The P.N.A. became a vehicle primarily for the old-guard Fatah leadership that had returned from exile under the Oslo arrangement to reestablish dominance over both the secular-nationalist "young guard" and the Islamist groups that had emerged during the first Intifada. While they largely succeeded, at least until the current al-Aqsa Intifada, in co-opting the new guard, the P.N.A.'s leaders failed in either integrating or isolating the Islamists. This is not to say the Islamists escaped Oslo unchanged. Violent repression in the mid-1990s did force Hamas and Islamic Jihad into temporary quiescence, and the 1996 elections did encourage Islamist leaders to consider party-political transformation. Still, these adjustments reflected adaptation to new conditions, not a diminution in Islamist cultural or political strength, per se.

By the end of the Oslo period (1999–2000), the secularist-Islamist tensions had created a fluid situation in which the old political identities were up for grabs. Activists across the political spectrum—at least those with whom I interacted—were reinterpreting the inherited symbols, discourses, and narratives of Palestinian nationalism and Islamism in an effort to make sense of, and develop responses toward, the new Oslo order and the dynamics it had set in motion. By 1999–2000, this process had given rise, at least among my interlocutors, to a range of new sociopolitical orientations with the potential for engendering new avenues of affiliation and action. This book is an effort to map the directions in which these emerging orientations were moving and to trace the social processes that had produced them. The result is a complex account that deepens understanding not only of the particular Palestinian context but also of the relationship between events, generations, and the cultural and historical forces that transform social movements and political identities, generally.

CHAPTER TWO

The Secular-Nationalist Milieu

It was a hot, bright afternoon in July 2000. Perspiration soaked my forehead as I climbed the stairs of the Red Crescent Society in Bethlehem. On the second floor, I walked up to a desk, gave my name to the receptionist, and sat down. Within minutes, a twenty-four-year-old woman dressed in fashionable black miniskirt, black heels, and crisp white blouse appeared in the lobby, shook my hand, and invited me into her smartly appointed office. Her long black hair cascaded over her shoulders as she took her seat behind her desk. A computer hummed behind her. From all appearances, ʿAbir fit the picture of the young, hip professional—a figure whose debut in the West Bank and Gaza Strip had coincided with the establishment of the new Palestinian National Authority. She had been a teenage activist with the Fatah movement during the first Intifada but then went on, with a P.L.O. scholarship, to get a B.A. degree from Bethlehem University in sociology and social work. Immediately after graduating, she found employment, also with the help of her political faction, as a "social statistician" with the Red Crescent—the counterpart of the Red Cross in the Middle East. Ensconced in a professional career, she seemed to be breaking with traditional middle-class expectations of early marriage and the life of a housewife. She also clearly had shunned the scarf and long coat of the Islamist movement, choosing instead a fashionable "Western" look. All these indicators placed her squarely in the secularist milieu. Yet, as she described her life path to me, these first impressions gave way to a more complex portrait.

ʿAbir initially joined Fatah after trying and rejecting the Marxist Popular Front for the Liberation of Palestine. She explained this transformation, saying she "just didn't feel at ease with the Popular Front's ideas." The Popular Front activists she hung around with thumbed their noses at religious and social conventions by conspicuously eating in public during Ramadan, drinking alcohol, and getting together for unsupervised parties or trysts with members of the opposite sex. This provocative behavior made ʿAbir uncomfortable. Referring to how she did not dress according to customary religious expectations (*sharʿī*), she stated: "It may not seem from the outside that I pray and fast . . . but, I take account of what is proper and required of me." She separated herself from the Popular Front because she "wasn't prepared to give up our customs and traditions [*ʿādātnā wa taqālīdnā*]."

Several other Fathawis and former-Fathawis-turned-Islamists recounted similar initial loose affiliations with leftist-nationalist factions such as the Popular Front, Democratic Front, or Communists early on in their activist careers. All of them had subsequent negative reactions to what they viewed as hostility and contempt among these groups for the "customs and traditions." Fatah, by contrast, seemed to be a middle ground, a structure and culture that integrated the ethos of home and neighborhood with, as my interlocutors put it, the "modern" (*ʿaṣrī*—a term that can also mean "advanced" and "up-to-date," with all the teleological implications of the English term "modern") and "progressive" (*taqaddumī*) identity of the Palestinian "revolution." This integration depended fundamentally on a pragmatic, pluralist ambiguity: As ʿAbir put it, Fatah concerned itself with "political issues," leaving individuals free to practice their particular religious traditions as they saw fit. "Fatah," she continued, "says it's secular but it's not really. . . . We say we want to separate religion from the state but then we Fathawis are the first ones to tell you that our religion says such and such." Coinciding with, and reinforcing, this ideological pragmatism was a social and political network that linked multiple social constituencies—refugees, small-shop owners, villagers, urban elites, school and university youth, Christians and Muslims, and so on—with the P.L.O. faction structures. This combination of an extensive network and patronage system with an ideologically flexible pragmatism served Fatah and the P.L.O. well: by the 1980s, Fatah had become the dominant element in the secular-nationalist milieu, both in the diaspora and the Occupied Palestinian Territories. As such, it presented itself as the quintessential expression of Palestinian identity. "One is Fatah by nature and then one changes," ʿAbir told me, meaning that to be a Palestinian was ipso facto to embody, consciously or unconsciously, the Fatah sensibility. All other tendencies on the continuum—from Marxist to Islamist—were simply variations on this core identity. By joining Fatah, ʿAbir was, in her mind, simply reverting to origins.

At the same time, in spanning so many different constituencies, in trying to be all things to all people, Fathawi nationalism contained potential cleavages. These tensions would actualize in the confrontation with the Islamist movements during and after the Intifada and in the drive by older, formerly exiled Fatah leaders following the signing of the 1993 Oslo Declaration of Principles to impose their dominance through the Palestinian National Authority. Both sets of tensions were generational in character. The first type was synchronic, dividing the cohort of activists who emerged during the first Uprising into parallel secularist and Islamist units. This division resulted from the emergence of Hamas as a competing countermovement that placed pressure on Fatah and the wider secular-nationalist milieu that it anchored. Hamas attracted proto-Islamists with nationalist sympathies—a group that, in an earlier time, would have aligned with Fatah by default. Hamas's emergence had the additional effect of dividing younger, Intifada-generation Fathawis internally into a variety of subtendencies that revised received Fathawi nationalist themes in ways that more consciously integrated religious identity. Such revisions parried Islamist criticisms of Fatah, the P.L.O., and the Palestinian National Authority as antireligion. They also created ambiguities in the "secular" identity of Fathawi nationalists among this younger generation. Where religion began and ended was a key theme in the discourse of my informants from this group. The second tension was diachronic, segregating older Fatah leaders whose orientations were forged on the "outside" from younger Fatah activists who grew up under the Israeli occupation on the "inside." These diverse tensions—the synchronic one with Hamas and the diachronic one within Fatah—had their sources in the historical unfolding of the Fathawi milieu.

THE ETHOS OF FATHAWI NATIONALISM

Since its emergence as the main embodiment of Palestinian nationalism in the mid- to late 1960s, Fatah has served as a primary vehicle for status advancement among the middle to lower-middle classes and proletarianized refugee communities both in the areas occupied by Israel after 1967 and in the exile.[1] Fatah arose from the rubble of the discredited and defeated leadership of the landowning, urban "notables" (*al-aʿyān*) as represented by al-Hajj Amin al-Husayni, the head of the pre-1948 independence movement. Husayni was from a prominent Jerusalem family, as were the other major leaders of the time. These families controlled the religious endowments and other main political and economic institutions under the Ottomans and then the British. Both the 1936–39 peasant rising and the 1948 debacle seriously undermined the authority of this group.

In contrast to the pre-1948 leadership, Fatah's founders by and large were university students from lower-middle-class to mid-middle-class

[1] As the main competitors of Fatah from the 1960s through the 1980s, leftist groups such as the Popular Front for the Liberation of Palestine played an important role in shaping Palestinian secular nationalism. These groups never achieved dominance of the broader national movement, however; thus, to comprehend what secular nationalism means in the Palestinian context, it is crucial to place primary focus on Fatah. Discussion will turn to the leftists, nevertheless, in chapter 4 as the analysis takes up Islamist-secularist tensions in a Bethlehem-area refugee camp.

families that had lost everything in the war that led to Israel's formation. Yasir ʿArafat, originally known as Muhammad ʿAbd al-Ra'uf al-Qidwa al-Husayni, was from a middle-class family distantly related to al-Hajj Amin. He was a twenty-year-old engineering student at Cairo University when the war broke out and reportedly joined a Muslim Brotherhood cell that fought in the Gaza Strip. Khalil al-Wazir (nom de guerre: Abu Jihad), another founder, who was assassinated by an Israeli undercover squad in Tunis in 1988, fled Ramla with his family in 1948 as a thirteen-year-old. He set up a substantial armed group three years later and then also joined the Muslim Brotherhood only to leave the movement in disgust with what he saw as its timidity and disarray. Salah Khalaf, a third important founding member, who was assassinated by the Abu Nidal group during the faction feuds of 1991, became a refugee in Gaza when his family fled Jaffa aboard an overcrowded ship. All three of these men would later meet at Cairo University through the Palestine Students Organization, of which ʿArafat became president in 1952.[2]

With the founding of Fatah and its subsequent takeover of the P.L.O. in 1968–69, the revitalized liberation movement developed into a burgeoning bureaucracy replete with military and civil wings that provided stateless Palestinians with a vital sense of national cohesion in the midst of the new nation-states that had emerged in the Middle East in the 1950s and the 1960s. These new bureaucratic structures coincided with and accelerated the evolution of new status classes, especially professionals. Fatah and the P.L.O. were particularly adept at channeling the youth of the proletarianized refugee and emerging lower-middle and mid-middle classes into their ranks by establishing student associations and youth wings such as the Shabiba organization and distributing scholarships and jobs to graduates.[3] Moreover, although leadership remained predominantly in the hands of men, Fatah and the P.L.O. as a whole nevertheless developed elements of a meritocracy, enabling women to gain professional employment as teachers, movement bureaucrats, and even military officers. Participation in the national struggle became, for women, a basis for demanding gender equality in a range of institutional settings. The General Union of Palestinian Women evolved as part of

[2] Helena Cobban, *The Palestinian Liberation Organisation: People, Power and Politics* (Cambridge: Cambridge University Press, 1984), 21–35; Yezid Sayigh, *Armed Struggle and the Search for State: The Palestinian National Movement, 1949–1993* (Oxford: Oxford University Press, 1997), 80ff.; and Baruch Kimmerling and Joel S. Migdal, *Palestinians: The Making of a People* (Cambridge, MA: Harvard University Press, 1993, 1994), 212–214.

[3] Other important groups such as the Movement of Arab Nationalists (*ḥarakat al-qawmiyyīn al-ʿarab*) had also focused on youth, mimicking Zionist and fascist paramilitary organizing methods. Sayigh, *Armed Struggle and the Search for State*, 73 and 80–87.

Figure 3. P.L.O. "martyrs." These charcoal drawings depict well-known figures in Fatah and other P.L.O. factions, some of whom lost their lives during the 1970s and 1980s. Foremost among them are Khalil al-Wazir and the novelist Ghassan al-Kanafani, second and third from the left, respectively, along the top row. The three women in the bottom row, none of whom wear any form of *ḥijāb* head covering, include Dalal al-Mughrabi, second from the left, and perhaps the most famous (or infamous) female *fidā'iyya*, Layla Khalid, fourth from the left. The drawings served as campaign propaganda for the Fatah-associated student movement (Shabiba) during the 1999 elections for Bethlehem University's Student Council. Author's photograph.

this process and was allotted seats alongside the students', engineers', workers', and writers' unions on the Palestine National Council.[4]

In creating these structures, the founders of Fatah and the P.L.O. adapted the models of single-party state organization that took root in Iraq, Syria, and Egypt. Jamal ʿAbd al-Nasir, the Egyptian colonel who came to power in the Free Officers' Coup of 1952, was especially influential in the political tutelage of ʿArafat and his colleagues. Nasir's crackdown on the Muslim Brotherhood within months of the coup ended whatever flirtation existed between the Islamists and the nascent Palestinian liberation movement; moreover, in setting up the all-encompassing

[4] Cobban, *The Palestinian Liberation Organisation*, 10–14.

"Liberation Rally" as a single party that aimed to incorporate every political tendency in Egypt within the newly nationalized state bureaucracies and military, Nasir provided Fatah and the P.L.O. with a blueprint for the evolution of Palestinian protostate structures in exile. Nasir's role was actually quite direct: it was with his sponsorship of the initiative of Ahmad al-Shuqayri—a lawyer and former minister of the All Palestine Government of 1948 whom Nasir supported for selection as Palestine's representative to the League of Arab States—that the Arab League decreed the establishment of the Palestine Liberation Organization, approved its charter, and recognized the reestablishment of the Palestine National Council as the highest decision-making body of the P.L.O. Initially, the P.L.O. was heavily weighted toward traditional elites—the landowning notables, mayors, village heads, "men of religion" (*rijāl al-dīn*—muftis, imams, priests, etc.), and so on. Only later, after Fatah took over the organization in 1968–69, did it become a main conduit for advancing the interests of the refugees and new professionals, too.[5]

The state-bureaucratic and liberation-movement dimensions of Fatah and the P.L.O. gave rise over time to two ideal-typical identity-authority styles: the *wazīr* (pl. *wuzarā'*: bureaucrat, government minister) and the *fidā'ī* (pl. *fidā'iyyūn*: "one who sacrifices himself" for his country, e.g., a "freedom fighter" or "partisan"). The two types often combined into one: P.L.O. leaders such as ʿArafat and Khalil al-Wazir (Abu Jihad) not only posed for photographs while sitting behind desks and holding pens but also appeared in military fatigues with gun holsters at their waists. The model was ubiquitous in the Arab Middle East in the 1960s and 1970s. Nasir was the quintessential example. He projected himself as the revolutionary army officer of humble provincial origins who championed the cause of the downtrodden Arab masses through heroic leadership at the helm of government. Arafat would emulate this model as P.L.O. chairman and then president of the Palestinian National Authority, meticulously cultivating himself as the preeminent symbol of collective Palestinian aspirations above and beyond the factions and the P.L.O. itself.

Embedded within ʿArafat-as-symbol, and in the wazīr and fidā'ī authority types that it combined, were two basic principles: armed struggle

[5] Sayigh, *Armed Struggle and the Search for State*, 93–104. The P.L.O. under Fatah actually served to bridge the new movement bureaucrats and the older elites. Fatah's nonideological emphasis on liberating the homeland and its romantic apotheosizing of the pre-1948 peasantry (its ties to the land and its "customs and traditions") provided the symbolic and narrative skeleton for this bridge. Note also that the single-party model has continued to be influential in the formation of the Palestinian National Authority. On this point, see Jamil Hilal, *Al-nizam al-siyasi al-filastini baʿd Oslo: Dirasa tahliliyya naqdiyya* [The Palestinian Political System after Oslo: An Analytical Study] (Beirut: Institute of Palestinian Studies, 1998), 20–26.

Figure 4. Yasir ʿArafat and Khalil al-Wazir. The Fatah-associated student group, Shabiba, produced these posters in the lead up to the Bethlehem University Student Council elections in 1999. The posters depict Yasir ʿArafat in military attire and Fatah cofounder Khalil al-Wazir. Author's photograph.

and independent decision-making. Fatah's identity took form historically as a rejection of the pan-Arabist and Marxist approach of its main competitor, the Movement of Arab Nationalists (*ḥarakat al-qawmiyyīn al-ʿarab*). Against the M.A.N.'s insistence on merging the struggle to liberate the homeland with the effort to create Arab nationalist governments, regionally, Fatah pursued independent armed actions, arguing that successful and courageous demonstrations of the Palestinian will would awaken a nationalist spirit within the various Palestinian communities and rally the Arab masses to put pressure on their governments to be supportive. In the aftermath of the 1967 war, Fatah's highly publicized guerrilla attacks inspired Palestinian youth to travel from the newly occupied West Bank and Gaza Strip to Jordan to join the "revolution." Watching this transpire, M.A.N.'s leadership reconfigured their organization, naming it the Popular Front for the Liberation of Palestine. They abandoned their earlier insistence on a wider Arab revolution and instead adopted Fatah's tactics, indeed going beyond them to hijack airplanes and bomb Israeli businesses abroad to win adherents away from Fatah.

The stress on armed action and institutional independence succeeded largely because it was inclusively pragmatic: Fatah and the P.L.O., after Fatah's takeover of it, subordinated the supranationalist ideologies (pan-Arabism, Marxist revolutionism, etc.) to a baseline solidarity that put the liberation of the Palestinian homeland above all other dogmatic considerations. Such pragmatism enabled Fatah to encompass a wide variety of individuals and groups ranging from secular leftists to the more traditional and religiously oriented. Fathawism—and by extension P.L.O. nationalism—was a type of secular nationalism to the extent that its ideology subordinated religious notions of collectivity (e.g., the Islamic conception of the *umma*) to a common ethnic-national identity spanning regional, religious, and clan-based solidarities. It did not exclude or negate these solidarities but rather sought to integrate them within a larger, strictly Palestinian Arab vision of the nation. Palestinians, in this view, were Muslims and Christians and even Jews, villagers and townspeople and refugees, members of different clans, Jerusalemites and Hebronites, Gazans and Galileans; but, above all, they were a people linked to a geographical area defined by the ill-fated British Mandate and bound together by the shared experience of expulsion and occupation. They were an educated and democratic people linked to the peasant past, to be sure, but building their own modern state in exile in anticipation of their return to their homeland. Finally, they were a "revolutionary" people, like other Third World oppressed groups (the Algerians, the South Africans, the Cubans, the Vietnamese, the Irish, and so on) who were engaged in protracted armed struggles to overcome colonialism. By the mid-1980s, P.L.O. institutionalization had made this basic multiconfessional, nationalist orientation normative among Palestinians everywhere.

Fathawism, thus, provided Palestinians with a broad canopy that defined them as a national group; yet, under the Fathawi roof, other kinds of solidarities and diverging historical experiences continued to persist or emerge to give the national cloak multiple contrasts. One of the most important contrasts evolved from the different historical experiences and geographical settings of the "outsider" (the exile) and "insider" (those living in the Occupied Palestinian Territories). Outsiders generally tended to equate "the organization" (i.e., the P.L.O. and its factions) with the nation, whereas insiders had a much more diffuse sense of a broader society, separate from the movement, as the main bearer of national identity. The faction as a form of political-social organization was certainly central for insiders, but it was not the sole, defining mode of integration. Especially in the West Bank, where town and village institutions had remained relatively intact through the 1948 and 1967 wars, "insiders" were also shaped by patriarchal clans, religious associations, the ethos and networks of the village or small town, neighborhood clubs and committees, and so on. Arguably, prior to 1987, insiders still had not formed a coherent sense of collective national identity. The first Intifada (1987–93), at least its first year or two, changed this situation. Submerging particularities of all sorts in a wave of mass mobilization, it forged a new and profound sense of the collective as a single national whole that included but exceeded the factions and the P.L.O. Institutionally, this new conception manifested itself in the multiple interfactional neighborhood associations that sprang into existence as experiments in self-government. These experiments gave rise to a sense of unity reflected in a popular song of the time whose refrain declared: "Don't tell me which faction/And, don't ask me about my religion/My soil is of this land/And, my name is Palestinian Arab."[6]

The Islamist groups such as Hamas, while sparking intragenerational tensions with P.L.O. partisans, shared also in this general outlook: the more they were seen risking their lives at the barricades, the more the Islamists were accepted and accommodated as part of this broader, mobilized society, even as their vision of a "Muslim Palestine" fundamentally challenged core aspects of the pluralist Fathawi-P.L.O. outlook. Thus, in contrast to outsiders, whose identities were shaped much more profoundly by integration into P.L.O. structures and the struggle to establish an independent national existence in host countries such as Jordan and Lebanon, insider identities took form through complex, crosscutting socialization in churches, mosques, neighborhood associations, clan-based structures; integration into P.L.O. factions or the Islamist movements; collective subjection to the occupation; and mass participation in a prolonged, violent societal uprising against that occupation. A closer examination of social backgrounds, factors of mobilization, and conceptions of solidarity among my interlocutors will shed light on how these historical, social, and geographical factors shaped contrasting orientations at the individual level within the Fathawi milieu, in particular.

SOCIAL BACKGROUNDS

The majority of the Fatah activists whom I interviewed were from the middle to lower-middle classes and refugee groups that have historically comprised the movement's base. Three main groups were most prominent: (a) individuals from families that were part of the landowning elite but then lost everything in 1948; (b) individuals from families that

[6] The lines in Arabic were, "*lā itqūlī ayy tanẓīm/wa lā tas'alnī ʿan dīnī/anā turābī min al-arḍ/wa ismī ʿarabī filasṭīnī.*" The song was recorded by Mustafa al-Kurd on his album *Awlād filasṭīn* [Children of Palestine] (Nazareth, 1988), sound cassette.

engaged in tenant farming, sharecropping, or subsistence agriculture—the so-called *fallāḥīn,* or "peasants"; these groups formed the vast pool of skilled, semiskilled, and unskilled labor in the massive refugee camps after 1948; and (c) individuals from lower-middle-class families that occupied the trades, shopkeeping, and lower-level bureaucratic positions in the towns and villages of the West Bank. While coming from diverging backgrounds, individuals from all these groups began to have access, especially after 1967, to secondary, vocational, and advanced education through the United Nations Refuge Works Agency (U.N.R.W.A.) schools and the new national universities that were established in or near the major urban centers of the West Bank and Gaza Strip after the 1967 war. The consequent emergence of a much-expanded professional class occurred concurrently with the rise to prominence of the Fatah-dominated P.L.O. in the 1970s. The P.L.O. factions established a strong presence in these new institutions through student and faculty associations and through scholarships that enabled youth from refugee camps, villages, and small towns to get advanced degrees and certificates either in the national universities or abroad in Europe and the United States. After their studies, many of these individuals found jobs in P.L.O. agencies abroad or various faction-based associations and unions in their home communities. Fatah and the P.L.O. thus facilitated a generational shift from village and camp settings to the new professionalizing milieus among the groups of activists that came of age during and after the 1967 war.

Sabr, a twenty-eight-year-old resident of a Bethlehem-area refugee camp, exemplifies this process as it occurred among descendants of the first type of group, the former landowning elite. In particular, her path reflects the formation of the wazīr type—the modern revolutionary bureaucrat. Sabr became an activist as a teenager during the first Intifada. Despite the Israeli-imposed school closures, she graduated from high school in the early 1990s and then received P.L.O. scholarships to pursue bachelor's and master's degrees at Birzeit University, the premier Palestinian postsecondary institution. Having moved up the ranks in the Bethlehem-area Fatah movement, she was being groomed for higher-level offices in the Palestinian National Authority and for service as an adviser to the P.L.O.'s negotiating team. She was planning in 2000 to pursue a Ph.D. in international relations in the United States.

Sabr's grandparents had been large landowners in a village just to the west of Jerusalem. A soccer stadium and blocks of Israeli-only apartments had since been built over the bulldozed ruins of the village. Sabr's grandfather had been the *mukhtār* (pl. *makhātīr*), the village elder and patriarch. He had owned a lot of land and a large house but lost everything in the 1948 war. Her grandmother also came from a prominent rural family. Her grandmother's father had been a *shaykh* (pl. *shuyūkh*: a respected elder or leader who might also be someone accorded respect for his piety and religious knowledge). He had owned land, too, and received tribute from sharecropping peasants in the surrounding villages. During the British Mandate, such figures mediated between villages and the authorities. "The family had servants [*ʿabīd*, sing. *ʿabd*: literally, "slaves"], which is something that is shameful," Sabr said, self-consciously. Sabr's grandmother had inherited some of her father's status, becoming renowned in her own right as an overseer and skilled mediator. During the 1948 war, she had been able to salvage much of her transportable wealth (gold jewelry) and used it, according to Sabr, to help her husband purchase weapons for the resistance and later to put her children through private schools in Bethlehem. Sabr's father had gone to the Latin Catholic Terra Sancta School and eventually became a lifelong administrator in U.N.R.W.A. Her mother also had received a high school education, and a diploma in mathematics from the U.N.R.W.A. Teacher's College in Ramallah. She then began teaching math in the U.N.R.W.A. schools in Bethlehem-area refugee camps. Her mother's brother had studied in a university in Spain but cut short his training in medicine in 1982 to join the P.L.O.'s resistance effort in Beirut, where he was killed. The family lived in a relatively spacious home on the edge of the small refugee camp to which the grandparents had originally fled.

As she described her upbringing, Sabr spoke of the importance of her grandmother and her aunts. "My grandmother was a very strong woman and she influenced me a lot," Sabr told me. "She is the one who poured into my ears all the time the issue of being kicked out of the village." Sabr saw her grandmother as a "superwoman." She could ride a horse and fire a gun, and she waited until she reached a relatively late age to get married. She supervised peasants who worked the family's fields before 1948 and held the family together financially after the expulsions, making sure her children received education. The daughter of a respected shaykh, the grandmother was also known for her ability to mediate and provide advice. Songs were sung about her at village weddings in the area. And she was the only woman in her village who smoked cigarettes. During the occupation and then the Intifada, she joined her daughter and granddaughter in confronting soldiers who would come to search the family's home. Sabr also pointed to her aunts as role models. "My aunts joined Fatah in the 1970s," she told me. "They were active and were imprisoned and tortured by the Israelis." Her mother, too, was a Fatah supporter, although she never became an official member of the movement. For Sabr, these women, including her grandmother, were examples of the "modern," liberated female; they were women who were strong decision-makers and courageous activists. Unafraid of breaking with patriarchal traditions, they forged new roles, providing Sabr with important models for her own unconventional path.

Yet Sabr and her family also demonstrated a continuing adherence to inherited ways. When I visited Sabr's home, her father and mother both would take time out to perform the prayers required of Muslims five times per day. Her mother, when I met her, wore an embroidered *fallāḥī* (peasant) dress but nothing over her head. Sabr, by contrast, wore modest Western-style clothing—long-sleeved blouse and midlength skirt or dress pants—and no scarf. Still, despite this more "up-to-date" look, Sabr, who was unmarried when I got to know her, was always very careful to appear correct and proper in her relationship with me. When she came to my home for her tape-recorded interview, she had her brother drive her and then made sure we were introduced. During our meeting, she preferred for my wife to be in attendance. She also told me that she was a practicing Muslim. "Do you pray and fast?" I asked her. "Yes, I do all that," she replied, "I believe in god. . . . If I never find a companion in life, I will always find god." She was quick to distance herself from Islamism, however. She told me: "I don't believe in people who exploit religion to accomplish political, financial, or economic interests. I am happy when Hamas does a military operation against the Israelis . . . at least they are doing something . . . but their other ideas, especially how they think of women and their role and how to organize society, are things I do not accept." Sabr was a "modern" and "liberated" woman, but one who, like ʿAbir earlier, took into account what was "proper and required" of her without at the same time acquiescing in the conceptions of female piety and place purveyed by the Islamists.

Sabr's story highlighted how P.L.O. faction structures provided women with life chances other than those of marriage and childbearing that typified traditional patriarchal orientations and practices. In so doing, the factions created conflict between young women and their parents and communities. ʿAbir (the activist mentioned at the start of this chapter), for instance, had to contend with the fears of her mother and father, who worried not only for her safety but also for her social reputation. It was not proper for young women, especially from families aspiring to be middle class, to be seen running the streets with young men. ʿAbir recounted to me how "sometimes, people would tell my father that his daughters had been seen in a demonstration or march . . . so then my father would start yelling at us." Another activist from Jerusalem, a woman who had served in a wide range of elected positions within Fatah, echoed ʿAbir's experience:

> Some neighbors would keep an eye out for what we were doing and say to me, "Muna, you're hanging around those *shabāb* [young unmarried

> 'guys'] . . . they're shabāb, don't you know?! Have some shame! Don't do this!" Because of these kinds of remarks, my father forbade me at first from going and coming freely from the house; but my fellow shabāb ["activists," in this sense] in the movement and my brothers in prison and my sisters helped me, and the Intifada helped me. I could argue back that many shabāb had fallen and it was our duty to take their place.[7]

Other than the appearance of impropriety, families feared that their daughters might end up in prison or become injured—both liabilities when it came to marriage. As other female activists related to me, it was very difficult for a woman to find a husband if she had been imprisoned. Suspicion hovered over former female prisoners: were they ever raped during detention? The mere possibility stigmatized these women in a society in which attitudes about virginity as a marker of moral purity and social uprightness in an unmarried female persisted.[8] One former Fatah activist, a Christian from Ramallah, a city just north of Jerusalem, who had served a long prison sentence for attempting to carry out a bombing, told me that when her husband, a man with a speech impediment, also a liability for marriage, proposed to her, she felt this sudden prospect of matrimony and a family to be nothing short of miraculous. She was in her late thirties at the time and was despairing of ever getting married. Women who sought out or who found themselves pursuing alternative life courses through their activism thus potentially paid a high social price. Yet some women, including Sabr and ʿAbir, did take the risk, drawing both on the faction structures and the credibility that their activism bestowed on them to counter patriarchal norms.

The factions facilitated status changes not only along the axis of gender but also across the boundaries of social class. Husayn represented the experiences of former peasants turned proletarianized refugees. Born in 1970, he grew up, like Sabr, in a Bethlehem-area refugee camp. Husayn was sixteen when I first became acquainted with him in 1986. Unlike

[7] A female Intifada activist from Nablus, Siham Abdullah, expresses similar feelings in Sahar Khalifeh, "Comments by Five Women Activists: Siham Abdullah, Amal Kharisha Barghouthi, Rita Giacaman, May Mistakmel Nassar, Amal Wahdan," trans. Nagla El-Bassiouni, in *Palestinian Women of Gaza and the West Bank*, ed. Suha Sabbagh (Bloomington and Indianapolis, IN: Indiana University Press, 1998), 192–196.

[8] The literature on this issue is extensive. See, inter alia, Judith E. Tucker, "The Arab Family in History: 'Otherness' and the Study of the Family," in *Arab Women: Old Boundaries, New Frontiers*, ed. Judith E. Tucker (Bloomington and Indianapolis, IN: Indiana University Press, 1993), 195–207; Khalifeh, "Comments by Five Women Activists," 192–196; Fatima Mernisi, *Beyond the Veil: Male-Female Dynamics in Modern Muslim Society, Revised Edition* (Bloomington and Indianapolis, IN: Indiana University Press, 1975, 1987), 58–62, but see also her discussion of the conflicts created by urbanization and the breakdown of the "traditional" social order; and Leila Ahmed, *Women and Gender in Islam* (New Haven, CT: Yale University Press, 1992), 41ff.

Sabr's mother and father, his parents were the children of impoverished tenant farmers from a village west of Bethlehem. After 1948, his father joined the Jordanian army and then became an electrician, working for a time in Iraq. He eventually returned to the West Bank and settled finally in Thawra Camp near Bethlehem. Husayn attended preparatory school in the camp during the early 1980s, got involved with the Fatah youth movement at this time, and then transferred to the private Christian boarding school in which I worked from 1986 to 1989. During the Intifada, Husayn organized "the Fatah commandos," a small group of activists drawn from among his classmates at the boarding school. They carried out stone-throwing attacks on Israeli army vehicles and were arrested and imprisoned briefly for these actions. One of their members was killed. After the Intifada, Husayn went to Italy to study for a bachelor's degree on a P.L.O. scholarship and then returned to work in the late Faysal al-Husayni's office in Jerusalem.[9] He told me he had since received a P.L.O. scholarship to pursue a master's degree in International Relations at Birzeit University.

Husayn described himself as an observant Muslim. When I visited his home in 1999, he had grown a neatly trimmed beard and was dressed professionally in a crisp button-down shirt and pressed dress pants. His wife wore a white scarf (*ḥijāb*), a long-sleeved, button-down blouse, and fashionable jeans. Husayn made a point of telling me that before they were married, his wife had worn the latest miniskirts but decided on her own to adopt a more conservative style after they were engaged to indicate transition to the more "serious life" of a married woman. For his part, Husayn told me that he prayed and fasted, although his busy schedule as an aide to Faysal al-Husayni often interfered with his daily practice. In explaining his piety, he told me that he grew up in a family that "was not religiously strict [*mutashaddida*] but was conservative [*muḥāfiẓa*]." Husayn elaborated on this distinction, saying that the *mutashaddidūn* (sing. *mutashaddid*, one who is strict, zealous) attempted to subordinate all aspects of life to the literal dictates of religion. This attitude often ended up in a chauvinistic approach toward others who did not believe or practice in the same way. The *muḥāfiẓūn* (sing. *muḥāfiẓ*, one who is conservative), on the other hand, adhered to everything re-

[9] Faysal al-Husayni, son of ʿAbd al-Qadir al-Husayni, a leading resistance organizer during the 1948 war, was a high-level Fatah activist and the Palestinian National Authority official in charge of the "Jerusalem File." Having served long months in Israeli detention, he became fluent in Hebrew and forged links with Israeli political factions and social groups dedicated to achieving a two-state solution to the conflict with the Palestinians. As a Jerusalemite and head of Orient House, the unofficial P.L.O. headquarters in East Jerusalem, he symbolized Palestinian steadfastness in the city. He died suddenly of heart failure on May 31, 2001.

quired of them by religion but avoided demanding that others conform. Echoing classic Fathawi multiconfessionalism, he explained that Palestinian society was made up of many different religions and had secular people, too. The idea was to let everyone follow his or her own conscience and tradition—"*kull insān ʿalā dīnihi wa ʿalā ʿaynihi*" (roughly, "Every human being is subject to his religion and his obligations").

After our meeting, Husayn offered to drive me into town. We climbed into his Audi sedan. He turned the ignition, put on a pair of sleek Italian designer sunglasses, popped a tape of Céline Dion into the cassette player, and began conducting the vehicle through the narrow camp alleyways, one hand on top of the steering wheel. As we drove out of the camp, he shouted greetings to people in the street, who waved back at him. In between each hailing, his fingers frenetically punched the call button of his small walkie-talkie as he exchanged information with colleagues in Jerusalem about the location of "the old man" (*al-ikhtiyār*), his boss Faysal al-Husayni, whom he would be escorting to Gaza later that afternoon. Once these plans were nailed down, he began telling me about a love affair he had with an Italian woman during his studies. He wanted to marry her but his family was against the idea. They wanted him to return and settle down in the camp with a "hometown girl." He acquiesced but not without his sunglasses and Céline Dion. Like Sabr, Husayn was a typical Fathawi boundary-straddler, one hand on the inherited norms of camp society, the other gripping the trappings of the up-to-date professional.

In Husayn's case, integration into Fatah facilitated a transition in status from peasant refugee to university-educated movement bureaucrat. This transition brought Husayn's experience as an Intifada insider in parallel with the experiences of the older outsiders who had undergone a similar transition. Fatah and the P.L.O.'s quintessential historical function had been to mediate these transition experiences as they played out in succeeding generations, in the process integrating older and newer activists across diverging geographical and historical locations. Abu Qays, a forty-six-year-old former P.L.O. guerrilla who fought in Lebanon, illustrated this phenomenon. Born to a family of sharecroppers made refugees in 1948, he grew up in a massive refugee camp just northwest of Gaza City. Following the 1967 war, at the age of thirteen, he climbed into a taxi headed for the West Bank without telling his family and crossed the bridge into Jordan to join "the revolution"—that is, the Fatah militias that were forming in the aftermath of the traumatic Arab defeat.[10] Fatah sent Abu Qays to Lebanon to help establish the armed resistance there in

[10] Sayigh, *Armed Struggle and the Search for State*, 157–158, for more on the formation of Fatah's new guerrilla units in the wake of the 1967 war.

1969. He returned in 1970–71 to fight in the Jordanian Civil War and was imprisoned and tortured. Following his release, he went back to Lebanon and served as a guerrilla commander and fought against the Israeli army during the 1982 siege of Beirut. After six years in Israel's infamous Ansar prison camp, he was expelled and went to Algeria and then Tunis to rejoin his Palestinian Liberation Army unit. An insider who became an outsider, Abu Qays returned finally to Gaza in 1994 to serve as an officer in the new Palestinian National Authority police.

I first came to know Abu Qays in 1996 and saw him several times in 1999–2000. During these visits, he would often get up in the middle of our conversations to pray either on his own or with any other men who happened to be in the room with him. On one occasion, he joined with his sons and nephews to perform the dusk prayer behind a cousin who was a Hamas sympathizer. Echoing Husayn, Abu Qays told me that he had chosen to join Fatah and not the leftist factions because "we are a conservative people [*shaʿb muḥāfiẓ*]." The leftist ideologies were against the "customs and traditions [*al-ʿādāt wa al-taqālīd*] as each of us carries them," he said. Abu Qays liked to talk about religion. He owned a copy of the Bible and a Greek Orthodox prayer manual that he had picked up during his years in Lebanon. On one of the walls in his living room, there was a framed poster of a large tree. At the root was the name of Adam. In the lower branches were biblical prophets such as Noah and Moses. Jesus' name appeared still farther up on one of the offshoots. Finally, in bold highlight at the top of the tree was the name of the Prophet Muhammad. Abu Qays explained that the tree and its branches showed the interconnections between all of Allah's emissaries and their messages. "We are all related," he told me. The idea was an expansive, religious one that reflected the deeply rooted sense in Islam of Muhammad and the Qur'an superseding all previous prophets and divine dispensations; but this very same attitude also coincided with a certain kind of pluralist nationalism. Abu Qays was against an Islamic state as the Islamists conceived it because the nation included non-Muslims. Whereas the early Muslim empires, run by wise and faithful caliphs, had dealt evenhandedly with Muslims and non-Muslims alike, the ideology of the current Islamist movements threatened to polarize the nation along sectarian lines. Fatah and the P.L.O. were not perfect, but they had at least forged a sense of national unity among a very diverse Palestinian populace. Such unity was the basic requirement for any successful liberation struggle.

Abu Qays had completed only a junior high school education, serving not as one of the new breed of professional bureaucrats but rather as a foot soldier, a fidāʾī, in the national movement's guerrilla forces. Still, he had progressed through the ranks, becoming a militia commander and then an officer in the Palestinian National Authority's police forces. In so doing, he not only absorbed the basic Fathawi pluralist nationalism but also took on elements of the modern bureaucrat. He wore his police captain's uniform proudly, with a shiny pen—the quintessential symbol of an administrator who sits behind a desk—prominently displayed in his front breast pocket. Thus, in crossing the Jordan River to join "the revolution" in 1969, Abu Qays had also transited from being a peasant refugee to a professional soldier. In this respect, there was continuity between the older Abu Qays and his younger compatriots Sabr and Husayn. Despite their different temporal-spatial locations, they had undergone roughly similar journeys from one class-status milieu to another and had done so through the same faction structures.

Fatah also mediated status shifts among individuals from the lower-middle class—members of the trades, small crafts, small businesses, and the like. These activists by and large grew up in the towns and villages of the West Bank. They did not experience the dislocation of the refugees, and they began seriously to enter the P.L.O. ranks only after the 1982 Lebanon War and the first Intifada five years later. Like the refugee proletarians, however, they, too, experienced changes in social status. Abu ʿAdnan, a Greek-Catholic (Melkite) Christian who operated a nongovernmental social service organization and served as a Fatah representative in Bethlehem, illustrated this type of background. A former Intifada leader and Bethlehem University graduate, he coordinated the annual Shabiba (Fatah's youth wing) campaigns for Student Senate elections at Bethlehem University.

Abu ʿAdnan was barrel-chested, bespectacled, and in his midthirties. He lived with his wife and children in a small apartment that sat on the second floor of a three-story building. He and his brothers grew up in the original structure and inherited it from their father, who had inherited it from his grandfather. The building with its additions stood on the edge of Bethlehem's Old City. Abu ʿAdnan described his neighborhood as *shaʿbī*, by which he meant "popular," "more grassroots," and "not so much middle class." His father "worked at different things"—as "a grocer and traveling businessman." He went to Latin America for a while to work with some uncles, then returned to Bethlehem in 1969 and died that same year. Abu ʿAdnan's mother was a seamstress who did piecework. She was frugal, keeping a garden and doing her chores without the aid of appliances. Her savings helped pay for Abu ʿAdnan's education and enabled the family to build the additions to the home.

In explaining his choice of political faction, Abu ʿAdnan said he perceived Fatah to be more connected to the grass roots, to the kinds of people he had grown up around. The Marxist/pan-Arabist movements, which had attracted many Christians in the Bethlehem area, failed to appeal to him because of their "elite character." He felt that Fatah was more "shaʿbī"; it was more in tune with the true Palestinian character. "Marxism is good," he told me, "but it is not for here." Echoing Husayn and Abu Qays, he asserted that "our society is conservative [*muḥāfiẓ*] . . . people, whether you like it or not, identify with either the Muslim or Christian faith." Fatah did not require one to renounce religion like the leftists did. It allowed one to be conservative and nationalist, simultaneously.

What Abu ʿAdnan meant by "conservative" and "nationalist" emerged in his description of the role of the church in his political socialization. Abu ʿAdnan grew up attending the Greek Catholic church in Bethlehem's Old City. He got involved in the Boy Scout troop and the church youth group and regularly attended liturgies. "I was a Christian guy who went to church every Sunday," he told me. "I didn't miss one service." During junior high school he began to learn about priests who had become Fatah activists. Archbishop Hilarion Cappucci, a Syrian who headed the Greek Catholic Patriarchate of Jerusalem, was a particularly influential symbol and model for Abu ʿAdnan. The Israeli military arrested and imprisoned the bishop in mid-August 1974 for allegedly using his diplomatic status to smuggle guns and money for Fatah into the West Bank in the trunk of his car.[11] The archbishop had been a very public figure. He gave talks at the local schools and universities, and he preached on the political situation of the Palestinians. "If you read his sermons," Abu ʿAdnan told me, "you'd find a contextualized message. . . . He doesn't talk about loving your neighbor in general but about what this means in this place."

In 1984, ten years after the Cappucci arrest, there was an attempt by some Christian students during Abu ʿAdnan's third year at Bethlehem University to start a "Christian Democratic Party" in response to the emergence of the Islamic Bloc that same year. Abu ʿAdnan fought this attempt by founding a countergroup, the Shabibat Cappucci (Cappucci Youth). The group campaigned for the Fatah list in the Student Senate election by distributing postcards and leaflets about the bishop and his contributions to the national movement. In their manifestos, Abu ʿAdnan told me, he and his allies argued that the P.L.O. included all segments of Palestinian society and that Christians could live their faith and be nationalistic like the rest. Archbishop Cappucci and other prelates like him provided clear examples of this. The efforts of Shabibat Cappucci paid off, according to Abu ʿAdnan: "We moved the people supporting the idea of a separate party to join the P.L.O. ranks," he told me.

The integration of religion and nationalism at church dovetailed with a third important influence in Abu ʿAdnan's upbringing: the pan-Arabist

[11] Sayigh, *Armed Struggle and the Search for State*, 349. Cappucci was eventually released after negotiations with the Vatican.

(i.e., associated with the Movement of Arab Nationalists) orientations of his older brothers. One brother studied in Iraq and was influenced by Baʿthist ideas.[12] When he came home during breaks, he would talk about being detained and interrogated for his activism by the Israelis. Another brother who attended Bethlehem University in the mid-1970s also became politically active in groups such as the Popular Front for the Liberation of Palestine that espoused pan-Arab solidarity. "There was this atmosphere at home," commented Abu ʿAdnan, "with all the trends from the Arab world and locally." While he found the pan-Arabist ideas of his brothers compelling, he was more convinced by Fatah's pragmatic emphasis on Palestinian liberation above all other considerations. He was also looking for ways to distinguish himself from his brothers. "Maybe I wanted to be different," he concluded.

The preceding survey of the three types of background that typified my interlocutors reveals a confluence of middle- to lower-middle- and working-class status positions, "conservative" (muḥāfiẓ) social and religious outlooks, and "modern" (*ʿaṣrī*) orientations stressing individual expression and professional identity. This mix of classes and tendencies was particularly distinctive of Fathawis. Fatah's faction structures mediated between social spheres of all types. They provided different social groups, especially women, with a "higher" nationalist justification for breaking with received norms, but they also maintained a link with the inherited "customs and traditions" by construing traditional norms as an element of the pluralist collective. Thus, one could be muḥāfiẓ (conservative) as opposed to mutashaddid (strict, zealous), Muslim or Christian, and still be a nationalist. In this way, Fatah and the P.L.O. integrated diversely situated groups within a nationalist framework, thereby creating a sense of continuity across space (inside and outside), class (village and camp and city), religion (Muslim and Christian), and time (1948, 1967, 1987, and so on). Integration, however, was not the only story. Important cleavages existed within the Fathawi sociopolitical milieu. One of the main sources of division was spatial: insiders and outsiders underwent different mobilization experiences.

FACTORS OF MOBILIZATION

Political mobilization occurred through the coincidence of several factors: (a) traumatic personal experiences—a sister killed throwing stones at soldiers, an arbitrary beating at a checkpoint, witnessing mass protests

[12] The Baʿth Party was founded during the 1950s as a vehicle for pan-Arab nationalism. It provided the ideological framework for Saddam Hussein's regime in Iraq and continues to be the official philosophy of the ruling party in Syria. For more on Baʿthism, see Albert Hourani, *A History of the Arab Peoples* (Cambridge, MA: Harvard University Press, 1991), 404–405.

and riots; (b) absorption of handed-down political narratives and affiliations within families and neighborhoods; (c) interaction with faction activists in schools and universities; and (d) active participation in collective actions (marches and sit-ins, e.g.). For older activists, especially outsiders, the 1967 and 1982 wars and the ascendancy of Fatah after its 1968 takeover of the P.L.O. were most influential. As the P.L.O. institutionalized itself in Jordan and Lebanon, it came to dominate Palestinian life in the refugee camps through its schools, social service institutions, popular committees, and militias. This phenomenon featured prominently in Abu Qays's recollections. Abu Qays joined Fatah soon after the 1967 war ended. He was thirteen:

> **AQ:** I took a taxi to the West Bank and from there to Jordan. . . . I joined Fatah, since from the beginning I had friends who had joined the movement.
>
> *You were very young to do this.*
>
> **AQ:** Yes, but it was the consequence of the loss of our land and rights in 1948. . . . After the [1967] war, [the Israelis] opened fire with live ammunition on everyone who joined the demonstrations. There was a curfew on us in the camp. I looked over a wall and saw soldiers coming toward our house. They grabbed me and wanted to shoot me. . . .
>
> *For no reason?*
>
> **AQ:** For no reason . . . just because I was looking over the wall. . . . They started beating me and demanding to know if I had any weapons. . . . As a result of these kinds of things, the majority of the shabāb [young men] became oriented toward the Palestinian revolution, the Palestinian organizations, such as Fatah, the Popular Front, the Democratic Front, the factions. . . .

In Abu Qays's account, there was a convergence of personal experiences of violence and suffering in the 1967 war and its aftermath with the phoenix-like appearance of Fatah and the P.L.O. Significantly, Abu Qays linked the events of 1967, which he had personally witnessed, to those of 1948, which he did not. He attributed his early nationalist orientations to the stories of 1948 that he had heard growing up from his father and uncles. But it was his many years as a guerrilla fighter and military commander in Jordan, Lebanon, and North Africa that were most definitive in the formation of his consciousness. A particularly critical event was the Jordanian Civil War of 1970–71. Arrested in the midst of withdrawing to Jarash with other Fatah forces, Abu Qays underwent torture and prolonged detention in Jaʿfar Prison and then was expelled to Lebanon. He returned to the P.L.O. militias, got married, and settled in the al-ʿAyn al-Hulwa refugee camp. Lebanon was "a life of testing," Abu

Qays told me, one violent struggle after another. First there was the 1975 Lebanese Civil War, in which the P.L.O. sided with the Arab Nationalists (Sunni Muslims and Druze, for the most part) against the Maronite Phalangists, a fight that ended badly for the P.L.O. after Syria intervened on behalf of the Phalangists. Then there was the Israeli invasion of 1982, six years of imprisonment in the Ansar detention center, and finally expulsion to Tunisia, where the P.L.O. had found refuge. This cycle of defeat and repression, a chain of events that had literally scarred his body, led Abu Qays to extract meaning from mere survival. He remained fiercely loyal to Yasir ʿArafat and Fatah. In his eyes, without the movement, there would have been no Intifada, no Oslo, and no Palestinian National Authority. "The Intifada appeared among an already awakened people," he told me. It was the result not only of the frustration and determination to resist born of the repression of the occupation inside but also of the efforts on the outside. After all, Abu Qays recounted, it was Abu Jihad (Khalil al-Wazir), one of the founders of the Fatah movement, who had organized the United National Leadership of the Uprising, and it was he who had directed its course.[13]

A similar sentiment emerged in the statements of the twenty-two-year-old son of a lower-level P.L.O. bureaucrat who had returned to the Bethlehem area from Tunis in 1994. Hasan was a Bethlehem University student in his final year when I interviewed him. Hasan's recollections centered on growing up in Fatah schools and suffering the loss of his father to imprisonment in the Israeli-run Ansar detention center in southern Lebanon following Israel's 1982 siege of Beirut. Released in a prisoner exchange two years later, his father rejoined the family in Syria and then took them to Tunis. In Tunis, Hasan attended the Fatah-run "Jerusalem School." One of his teachers was a particularly strict female commander in the Dalal al-Mughrabi unit.[14] His description of the experience shows how P.L.O. institutions had become the primary mobilization mechanisms for the generation of outsiders born after 1967.

> In 1984, the first question I was asked in class was, "What anniversary is January 1?" I was just six years old and didn't know anything. This was the

[13] Sayigh, *Armed Struggle and the Search for State*, 618, for more on the perception within the P.L.O. of Abu Jihad as the architect of the Intifada.

[14] Mughrabi was a nineteen-year-old female participant in a guerrilla operation masterminded by Fatah cofounder Khalil al-Wazir ("Abu Jihad"). The operation, meant to show the P.L.O.'s ability to hit Israel at will, occurred on March 11, 1978. The action ended in the death of thirty-six Israelis (thirty-four civilians and two security personnel) and nine of the ten commandos after the attackers hijacked a bus and then engaged police in a gun battle at a blockade near Herzliya, just outside Tel Aviv. The event provided the justification for the launching three days later of Israel's "Operation Litani," an invasion of southern Lebanon that was aimed at wiping out P.L.O. bases. Ibid., 426.

> first question, and I didn't know. So, my teacher began beating me on my back until I learned to say that January 1 was Fatah's anniversary. And, thus, my military education [*tarbiyatī al-ʿaskariyya*] began. We didn't just learn to use weapons and to shoot. We also learned the history of the movement and the nation. We learned all the important dates like January 1 and Black September. We also learned about the South African struggle, Islamic history, World War II . . . our operations, our heroes . . . the camps, the cities, everything about Palestine I knew . . . not like today . . . nobody today knows these things.

Hasan cited this educational experience as the key factor in the formation of his consciousness. He criticized the Palestinian National Authority and the national movement, generally, for failing to instill this same deep revolutionary orientation in the new generations coming out of the Intifada on the inside.

The problems began, in Hasan's view, with the collapse of the movement in Lebanon in 1982. The military option disappeared, and treason set in as top leaders began collaborating with the Arab regimes and Israel. Hasan stated:

> After 1982, every attempt by Force 17 [ʿArafat's special unit] to carry out an operation failed. Betrayal [*khiyāna*] had reached the leadership. Look, Abu Jihad would train people and send them on missions only to find the Israelis waiting for them. . . . So he began thinking about starting the revolution from inside. The way into the Zionist fortress was from inside. . . . For your information, the decision to start the Intifada was taken on January 1, 1982.

But the revolution was already in its final throes. "From 1982 until my induction into Fatah," Hasan remarked, "the revolution came to an end." "The Intifada," he said, "was like a strong horse that had been slaughtered but was still kicking even though it was dead."

In contrast to the prominence in outsider recollections of the 1967 and 1982 wars and the consequent struggles of the P.L.O. for survival, insiders stressed their everyday experiences of the occupation and especially the mass societal mobilization of the first Intifada as the key factors in their political socialization. The experiences of occupation and uprising forged among insiders a strong sense of a distinct destiny—one that shared a general continuity with the events that had created the P.L.O. on the outside but nevertheless had cut its own special path. The first months of the Intifada were a heady, exhilarating time, a moment of collective upheaval that seemed to be giving birth to something new. Neighborhood groups and organizations appeared across the Gaza Strip and the West Bank as communities pulled together to experiment in the independent control of their lives. The shabāb (youth) went to the barricades in demonstrations of courage, hurling stones at heavily armed soldiers. The factions formed united fronts. Islamists declared a new militancy. The secular-nationalist activists who emerged from this period would stake their claim to authority within the old P.L.O. structures by harking back to their sacrifices during the Uprising. While for outsiders the Intifada may have appeared to have been the outgrowth of their long years of work and suffering, insiders viewed it as a courageous renewal of the nationalist spirit in a context of unrelenting foreign occupation, general disarray after the 1982 disaster in Lebanon, and a seemingly long quiescence in the Occupied Palestinian Territories post-1967.

The distinct sense of right and destiny that insiders claimed often found negative expression in a bitter criticism of the "outsiders" who dominated the Palestinian National Authority and the Oslo Peace Process. The views of ʿAbir, the activist who had joined Fatah during the Intifada after a brief flirtation with the Marxist Popular Front, were typical:

> Those who came from outside support the peace process because it has given them something. These are the people who have taken over the centers and dominate the higher positions in the Palestinian National Authority. After years of fighting on the outside, they have finally been able to return home. But, we on the inside, what have we gained that might be of any value? Absolutely nothing. We don't want any spoils, but we do want to feel that in the end we have achieved something, that we have arrived. We want to be recognized for our contribution. It is not the case that just those who have come back are the ones who did all the fighting, alone. No. We also contributed. . . . Now, we youth are beginning to develop a large, new rebellion. We feel that our fight still is not finished, that we are still in the beginning of our struggle. . . . The older generations have been fighting for thirty or forty years and haven't achieved anything. They argue that we need to give the peace process a chance. Maybe they are right. They have more experience and have suffered more. They went through 1948 and 1967, while we [in the West Bank] had a comparatively better life until the Intifada broke out. It was only in the Intifada that we began to think as a generation of changing things. We had great ambition and great courage to go out and demonstrate. It started with the youth and then spread to the factions and the wider population. . . . Today, though, the newest generation goes in for insignificant and superficial things . . . traveling, going on trips, their careers. They have regressed, become apolitical. This is connected to the times we are living in. The factions need to be aware of this and to work to bring them back to the nationalist ranks.

ʿAbir identified two axes of spatial-temporal divergence in this segment of her interview. The first fell between the outsiders, the P.L.O. founders, and her own generation, the insider youth of the Intifada, who overcame the defeatism that had set in to reinvigorate the "revolution" within the West Bank and Gaza Strip. While she deferred to the experience of the outsiders, ʿAbir tellingly described her fellow Intifada veterans as unsatisfied, alienated, and unrecognized by the returnees. She and her generation would ride out the peace process, biding their time until conditions changed and a new uprising began that would finally achieve the goals of the first Intifada.[15]

ʿAbir's second axis separated the Intifada generation from the new crop of youth that had come of age in the Oslo period. In her eyes, this group had gone in for the promises of stabilization and normalization that Oslo's supporters had held out as the eventual peace dividend. There was a need for the factions to politicize these individuals, to plant within them a nationalist consciousness. Implicitly, this need was also a reason for a new uprising that would mobilize the new generations. ʿAbir's comments, it should be pointed out, reflect feelings that cut across the secular-Islamist divide within the Intifada generation. Hamas activists also criticized the new Oslo generation. One Hamas stalwart, an Intifada veteran and Islamic Bloc leader at Bethlehem University, told me that he preferred speaking even to leftists of his generation than to the new youth because "at least the leftists have a political consciousness and you can debate real issues with them." But the leftists, like Hamas, also opposed Oslo in its entirety, and thus this meeting of minds followed the rule "The enemy of my enemy. . . ." The critique of the new generation by Hamas and the left was also part of a more generalized dissatisfaction with Fatah and the direction it had taken in pursuing the peace process. As members of Fatah, the new guard (the Intifada activists) found themselves tarred by this same brush of anti-Oslo sentiment. They desired to separate themselves from Oslo while also maintaining their connection to a movement that had been their vehicle to power and prestige in the face of challengers like Hamas or the Popular Front. As ʿAbir expressed it: "We Palestinian youth, the young Fatah activists, are stumbling around in the dark. We don't yet know where things stand. . . . Of all the factions, we have the most difficult position because it is not clear what we are for and against."

As ʿAbir's comments show, integration within faction structures was a

[15] The al-Aqsa Intifada, which broke out in September 2000, has been driven and directed within the secular-nationalist milieu by the younger, lower-level leaders in Fatah, partly in revolt against the older returnees who have hitched their fortunes to the currently defunct peace process. Graham Usher, "The Intifada This Time," *Al-Ahram Weekly On-Line* (October 31, 2000) at http://weekly.ahram.org.eg/2000/506/re1.htm; Khalil Shikaki, "Old Guard, Young Guard: The Palestinian Authority and the Peace Process at a Crossroads," Ramallah, Palestine: Palestinian Center for Policy and Survey Research (November 1, 2001).

critical element in the mobilization of insiders; factions were not her sole locus of identity, however, as was the case with outsiders Abu Qays and Hasan. Events such as the first Intifada that led to mass mobilization were also important. And, once an insider was mobilized, diverse mediating institutions—universities, families, local voluntary associations, neighborhood committees, church and mosque youth groups, Boy Scout troops, and so forth—could redirect or reshape an individual's interpretation of the meaning of her or his mobilization. Interfactional encounters at universities, or familial pressures, for example, could problematize certain dimensions of a person's chosen political orientation. Intisar exemplified this phenomenon in recalling her encounters with female Hamas supporters during her days at Bethlehem University. A Fatah loyalist who, like ʿAbir, had become active in the first Intifada, Intisar told me she admired the female activists in Hamas because their adherence to religious strictures, as the Islamists defined them, did not seem to interfere with their taking on public roles and responsibilities. Like ʿAbir, she dressed in a miniskirt and did not wear a scarf over her head. She felt conflicted about this, however, saying she was contemplating putting on the ḥijāb (scarf) but was not sure what such a change would mean for her life:

> I pray and fast. Perhaps many people wouldn't believe me if I said this to them. I don't wear Islamic dress. . . . But, I have a lot of respect for people who conform to all aspects of religion because they are genuinely convinced of the principles set down in the Qur'an and *sunna*. I admired the Hamas and Jihad girls at the university. They were well organized and together. There was no contradiction between their political work and religious principles. There were limits. Women and men had separate roles, they organized themselves in separate units, but they worked toward the same end. Girls in Fatah and the other blocs, on the other hand, were still taking refuge in the traditional ideas about what women's roles were. These ideas blocked them in their political work. But, the Hamas girls were free of these blocks. Anyway. . . . My fiancé is more or less religious and would prefer that I put on Islamic clothes but he has left the decision up to me. I hate the *jilbāb* [the long overcoat]. It's the ugliest piece of clothing ever made. I might wear the *mandīl* [scarf]. . . . But, this doesn't mean I will leave everything and just stay home.

Intisar's struggle with whether to put on the scarf had evolved partly from her encounter with the practices of female Islamist activists at her university. This encounter had the effect of causing her to reflect on the underlying value-orientations that her mobilization as a Fathawi activist had instilled within her. The Hamas women she came to know on campus seemed to her to have resolved the conflict in gender expectations for women that arose from their political activism: they worked as full-fledged movement cadres but did so within the confines of an "Islamic" propriety. No one, thus, could have accused them of abandoning the ʿādāt wa taqālīd (customs and traditions). They separated themselves from men and covered their *ʿawra* (adornment, i.e., any part of the body that might sexually arouse another, cf. Qur'an 24:31), thus preserving modesty in the midst of their activism on behalf of the nation. They faced no contradictions, either within themselves or from others. To be Fatah, by contrast, was to straddle the secular-religion/tradition divide and thus to be conflicted.

Intisar's inner struggles had deepened still further through interactions occurring in a second mediating institution: the family. After she was engaged to be married, her husband-to-be, also a Fathawi, applied suasion, asking her to wear the scarf and long coat. Islamist cultural politics had, in this case, transcended factional boundaries to shape the sphere of Intisar's most intimate relationships. The Islamist-like reorientation of her social circles—at school and in the family—had created a moral dilemma for Intisar, one that was increasingly causing her to rethink the direction of her mobilization. The result was a profound sense of division, an unbearable personal and sociomoral divide, and a yearning for resolution and unity. She reached for some sort of compromise:

> If there is an Islamic state one day, I will support it as long as it is based on the correct principles of *sharīʿa* [Islamic law]. It is the one thing that can unite us. Marxism can't do it because it denies belief in god. The religion of Hamas is chauvinistic. Fatah says there has to be a separation of religion and state. There is a lot of confusion and disunity among the people when it comes to nationalist and religious theory. If we were to implement the sharīʿa through a common consensus based in religion, I am sure that we would be much stronger in the face of the Israelis.

In these comments, Intisar demonstrated how the mobilization experience of insiders had become subject to diverse pressures that transcended the faction. Islamization, as it confronted her on campus and in the home, was forcing her to reflect critically on her activism and even selectively to adopt elements of Islamist ideology—for example, the need for a sharīʿa-grounded state—to resolve the tensions within her and her society.

CONCEPTIONS OF THE COLLECTIVE: RETRIEVALS AND ALTERATIONS

The split that formed between secular nationalists and Islamists during and after the first Intifada generated, as Intisar's story shows, ancillary effects within these two milieus. Both secular nationalists and Islamists had to negotiate the conflicting moral-political demands of the two generational units, or tendencies (secularist and Islamist), as they confronted one another across the spectrum of various mediating spheres (universities, families, clubs, neighborhood associations, labor unions, professional guilds, and the like). From this interaction, there emerged a range of subtendencies within the two competing cultural-political milieus. Intisar's response represented one possible direction, but there were others. I have labeled the Fathawi subtendencies "neo-Fathawism," "Islam without Islamism," and "neo-pan-Arabism." These categories represent ideal-typical formulations of the diverging responses among Fathawis to the Islamist challenge and the deepening political fragmentation of the Oslo period. Each one offers a distinct path back to a reunified collective. The differences between them reflect varying sociohistorical location (insiders versus outsiders) and the degree to which either religious orientations or traditional P.L.O. multiconfessionalism has prevailed in a respondent's outlook. As ideal types, these emergent identities mark out general tendencies among different constituencies within the Fathawi milieu. Continuities between the responses reflect the persisting influence of the overall Fathawi ethos. Individuals voicing each of the responses share the assumption that Fatah is the normative framework for Palestinian identity. How that framework is to be constructed, however, is very much at play among them.

The views of a P.L.O. ambassador—an "old-guard" Fatah bureaucrat who had spent his life in the national movement in exile, shuttling between European capitals—reflected the first type of response, neo-Fathawism. This response asserted the primacy of Fathawi movement identity, a distinguishing characteristic of the discourse of the former exiles I encountered. The conversation I had with this ambassador occurred serendipitously. As I was walking toward the front gate of my apartment in Bethlehem one evening, my late landlord, "Abu Roni," called out and invited me to come sit and drink coffee with him and another man who was sitting next to him. The following account is an excerpt taken from my later reconstruction of that encounter in my field notes.

Abu Roni was sitting in his usual spot with the garage door open and the garage light casting a pool of yellow on the sidewalk. After inviting me over, he introduced me to his friend, telling me that the man had been the P.L.O.'s representative to various European countries. The ambassador was dark, thickset, mid- to late fifties, with a gut the size of a small rum barrel. He was wearing blue jeans, a loose button-down shirt with short sleeves, and wire-framed glasses that rested above a bushy salt and pepper mustache. Leaning back in a white plastic chair, legs spread apart, he held a tin of Copenhagen chewing tobacco and a pack of Marlboro cigarettes in his right hand, tapping these against his knee. Abu Roni mentioned I was doing a project on the Intifada. "The Intifada," he said derisively in a mix of Arabic and English, "was one of the worst periods in our history. It produced an ignorant generation of fools." Pointing to Abu Roni, he went on, saying:

> We Palestinians were known for our education. . . . It was the only way for us. We had nothing, but at least we could educate our children. We exported our knowledge. Abu Roni here, we exported him to Iraq in 1962 and he came back, built this building, and put his boys through the best schools. But, then the Intifada came along, and suddenly some stupid twelve-year-old can stand up and say, "We're not going to go to classes today because we're commemorating ʿIzz al-Din al-Qassam's martyrdom."[16] All of a sudden these fools can wrap *kūfiyya*s [thick, checkered cotton scarves] around their faces and close streets down. . . . The loss of respect for authority was a disaster for our society. The first year and a half of the Intifada was positive, still under control, but after that, after the leadership was all in prison, the *ʿarṣ* [pimp] and the *jāsūs* [spy] took over."

The ambassador jumped to international realpolitik. "What was the Intifada? It was nothing," he exclaimed. Explaining, he said that after the collapse of the Soviet Union, America had a free hand to impose a solution for the sake of regional strategic and economic domination. The Intifada mattered not at all in this calculus. He said that it was the P.L.O., alone, not the "fools" and "idiots" who claimed the prestige of

[16] Qassam was an itinerant Muslim preacher (*imām*) from present-day Syria who studied under Rashid Rida and other modernist Muslim reformers in Cairo's al-Azhar University. In 1921, after being sentenced to hang by the French for his part in Amir Faysal's rebellion of the previous year, Qassam left his home village and became head of the new Independence Mosque in the northern Palestinian city of Haifa. There, he continued preaching a message of religious reform, pan-Islamic unity, and anticolonial resistance. He attracted a following among migrant workers living in Haifa's shantytowns and surrounding villages. From these groups, Qassam organized clandestine armed cells dedicated to fighting the British and Zionists. He was killed by a British patrol on November 20, 1935, and it was this event that sparked the 1936–39 revolt. Hamas named its armed wing the ʿIzz al-Din al-Qassam Brigade—a reference that links the movement to the earliest periods of organized Palestinian nationalist resistance. For more information on Qassam, see Abdullah Schleifer, "Izz al-Din al-Qassam: Preacher and *Mujahid*," in *Struggle and Survival in the Modern Middle East*, ed. Edmund Burke, III (Berkeley, CA: University of California Press, 1993); Shai Lachman, "Arab Rebellion and Terrorism in Palestine, 1929–39: The Case of Sheikh Izz al-Din al-Qassam and His Movement," in *Zionism and Arabism in Palestine and Israel*, ed. Elie Kedourie and Sylvia G. Haim (London: Frank Cass, 1982), 59–60; and Ted Swedenburg, *Memories of Revolt: The 1936–1939 Rebellion and the Palestinian National Past* (Minncapolis: University of Minnesota Press, 1995), 1–5 and passim for a discussion of Qassam in Palestinian popular memory.

the Intifada, that had understood the rules of the new game and that it, alone, under ʿArafat's leadership, had been able to realize the minimal gains that were finally achieved through Oslo. "What choice did we have?" he asked. "In the end ʿArafat had to go along [with the Americans]. But, rather than go through the Arab states, who are all American stool pigeons, he decided to go straight to the Americans and in that way keep the commission the Arab states would have gotten."[17] He laughed hard at this bit of sarcasm, and repeated it to Abu Roni in Arabic. He went on to complain about how Palestinian workers had built the settlements: "Where is their nationalism? They sell it for five hundred shekels [about US $125]."

A number of elements in the ambassador's discourse reflected an outsider/old-guard orientation. Most striking was the searing disdain for the Intifada youth activists, especially Islamist ones, and the class-based contempt for the day laborers. The ambassador described these groups as fools, traitors, and spies who had undermined the national movement and society through their utter disregard for discipline and self-sacrifice.[18] They would rather shut down schools, build settlements, and mouth pious slogans of Islamic revolution than scrimp and save and build and educate and just plain muddle through for the larger cause of the nation. The ambassador pointed to Abu Roni as an example of what Palestinians on "the inside" should really have been about. My landlord had shown a willingness to sacrifice by going to work in distant Iraq, coming back to Palestine, and investing in his society. He had used his resources, acquired through hard work, to build a multistory home and educate his sons, despite the conditions of the Israeli occupation. Abu Roni, an upstanding middle-class citizen, epitomized the proper role of the insider, a type of patriotism rooted in the value of *ṣumūd*, of steadfastness. From 1970 on it had been understood that the P.L.O. in Lebanon would carry out the

[17] In the Madrid negotiations, which preceded Oslo, no independent Palestinian delegation was allowed, and the P.L.O. was frozen out. Instead, there was a joint Jordanian-Palestinian delegation composed of leaders from the Occupied Territories. After Yitzhak Rabin became Israel's prime minister in the June 1992 elections, the Israelis opened up a direct connection with the P.L.O., and it was from this development that the Oslo memorandum came into being. For more on these issues, Camille Mansour, "The Palestinian-Israeli Peace Negotiations: An Overview and Assessment," *Journal of Palestine Studies* 22, no. 3 (Spring 1993): 5–31, and Avi Shlaim, "Prelude to the Accord: Likud, Labor, and the Palestinians," *Journal of Palestine Studies* 23, no. 2 (Winter 1994): 5–19.

[18] It should be noted that a shift did occur in the Uprising as a consequence of the mass imprisonment of Intifada leaders. After the Gulf War, in particular, the Intifada began to implode as leadership and discipline became ever more fragmented. Armed gangs with connections to the political factions began to run protection rackets and carried out retributions for one side or another in clan disputes, all the while justifying these actions in the name of disciplining collaborators and protecting the Uprising. Sayigh, *Armed Struggle and the Search for State*, 636–637.

armed and diplomatic struggle on behalf of the nation to liberate the homeland. Those who had remained in the West Bank and Gaza Strip were to contribute to the struggle by holding on to their properties, educating their kids, and raising their standard of living. A former teaching colleague of mine who was in his late fifties in 2000 had expressed this very same attitude to me just seven months before the first Intifada began. "The most important thing," I recall him saying, "is to be here, to work our fields and live in our houses as long as we can."[19]

The ambassador's outlook was hard-nosed and authoritarian. He had little time for ideology, religious or otherwise. In his view, the P.L.O. outside, not the Intifada, was the primary, effective actor since it alone, and ʿArafat in particular, understood the new rules of international politics in the wake of the first Gulf War. The credit for whatever gains the national movement had achieved belonged solely to the P.L.O. on the outside. The Intifada amounted to nothing without this leadership. ʿArafat knew the rules and played the game shrewdly, cutting out the other Arab leaders and getting the direct payoff from the United States. And it was the connections to the West that continued to keep the Palestinians afloat. Further on in our conversation, the ambassador bragged that he had been single-handedly responsible for getting two aircraft from a European government for the fledgling Palestine Airlines fleet. He also mentioned the donor aid that the Palestinian National Authority had generated to pay for Bethlehem's face-lift as part of the preparations for the millennium celebrations, a project called "Bethlehem 2000." His point was clear: Idealism, and especially religious idealism, was dangerous and ultimately self-defeating in a world in which Palestinian options were severely circumscribed. Palestinians needed to deal with the real world of American and Israeli power. They would only undermine their national aspirations by entertaining totalistic fantasies of religious revolt and "river to the sea" redemption.[20] The Intifada had actually endangered the nation by giving rise to such illusions. Fatah, under ʿArafat's leadership, had safeguarded the nation's interests even if part, or most, of that nation failed to understand this fact. Such an attitude was a quintessential expression of the outsider/old-guard orientation.

A similar attitude, but with a self-critical edge, manifested itself in the

[19] Ibid., 464–470 and 612 and 635, for a discussion of ṣumūd and its connection to how the P.L.O.'s outside leadership viewed the various constituencies in the West Bank, Gaza Strip, Lebanon, and elsewhere. Essentially, the leadership saw the Palestinian populace in the Occupied Territories and elsewhere as individuals and groups to be co-opted through patronage rather than as a society to be integrated and empowered from the bottom up through the formation of viable, autonomous mass organizations.

[20] "River to the sea"—i.e., the idea of recovering all of pre-1948 British Mandate Palestine from the Jordan River to the Mediterranean Sea.

discourse of Hasan, the Bethlehem University student who had grown up in Fatah-run schools in Tunisia and then returned with his family after the signing of the Oslo Accords. Hasan criticized the Palestinian National Authority and the P.L.O. factions, generally, for failing to instill "revolutionary ideology" (*fikr thawrī*) in the new generations coming out of the Intifada. The failure had resulted from a long, deep erosion of principles and educative processes within Fatah. The Intifada was doomed to failure because movement structures had become incapable of sustaining it. The weakness registered in a lack of training to inculcate the values of the "revolution."

> People would go out [during the Intifada] and throw stones without really understanding what they were doing. . . . They needed training in what to do in prison, how to behave in interrogation. . . . There are many things that go into making a revolutionary. Only after the basic foundation is laid do you then hand a person a weapon and tell him to go fight.

Real Palestinian identity, for Hasan, was the movement identity. One came into this identity only through strict training, not through mass mobilization experiences such as the Intifada. The failure to educate the mobilized masses had proven disastrous for national cohesiveness precisely because the movement had lost its centrality in the collective consciousness and, alongside this, its ability to impose discipline and direction on the society. It was this dislocation that lay at the root of the malaise into which the national movement had fallen.

The situation continued without remedy in the post-Intifada period. In its bid to counter Hamas, mainly, Fatah had willy-nilly recruited and absorbed former Intifada activists without providing proper training. People were joining for opportunistic reasons—to get a job or special treatment, for example—and not because they were committed ideologically to the movement. "The concern is to win elections in the different institutions without spending the time to educate supporters about the national movement," Hasan remarked. What was needed was a renewal of the liberation struggle by building a "social infrastructure so that after Abu ʿAmmar [Yasir ʿArafat's nom de guerre] there will be another strong generation ready to fight Israel . . . a new generation with a clear sense of purpose and ideology [*fikr*], a clear understanding of what nationalism means."

What was this "clear understanding of nationalism," exactly? For Hasan, the nation was the movement. Fatah encompassed all of society's fragments; it stood to reason that if Fatah imploded and disappeared, so too would the nation:

> Fatah based itself on national unity, armed action as the only path of struggle, and complete freedom from any outside intervention, Arab or otherwise. Now, Fatah has collapsed as a revolutionary movement. Is there an armed

struggle? Is there national unity? Is there freedom from Arab intervention and control? . . . The death of the Sulta [the Palestinian National Authority, i.e.] is not a problem or threat, but it is far more devastating to lose the Organization [*al-tanẓīm*, i.e., Fatah]. The Organization has to continue to exist. As long as it does, the revolution continues, the people continue. . . . The point is to have the Organization ready to step in should the Sulta collapse. . . . It has to be stronger than Hamas and the Popular Front . . . [it has to have] firm institutional control throughout the society. . . .

In these remarks, Hasan revealed the centrality of the Fatah movement to his sense of identity. Fatah was the nation, for Hasan, because it encompassed every dimension, every group, in Palestinian society. As long as the movement existed, the people existed. Without the movement, the people would fragment and the independence struggle would end. The Islam that existed in the contemporary world could never replace Fathawi nationalism, because it was fundamentally corrupt and divided:

When I see Islam torn up between Shiʿi, Sunni, and Druze and all the different movements—the problems between Hamas, Jihad, and Tahrir[21]—when I see all this, how can I allow [the Islamists] to run a state? This is not what the Prophet had in mind. . . . If the Prophet were alive I'd follow him because he would show us that Islam is built on mutual love, forgiveness, and forbearance. We need the Prophet, or some other Muslim of exceptional character, not Shaykh Yasin [the late paraplegic cofounder and spiritual leader of Hamas] or some other "shaykh" whom god only knows where he came from, to build an Islamic state. . . . We saw what happened in the West during the Middle Ages when the pope ceased being a man of god and became a corrupt and repressive ruler in the name of god. The same thing will happen with any Islamic state should it come into existence [i.e., under the Islamists]. I want to be 100 percent certain that a proposed Islamic state would be Islamic in the full meaning of this word. We Muslims do believe that one day powerful, faithful Muslims will arise and lead us all back to Islam and refound the Islamic state; but when that happens, those people will be different people, and that time will be a different time.

For Hasan, thus, the "Islamic solution" was essentially eschatological—an abstract possibility that would materialize only at the end-time with

[21] The Hizb al-Tahrir, or Liberation Party, began as a Muslim Brotherhood splinter under the leadership of Shaykh Taqi al-Din al-Nabhani, a Palestinian graduate of al-Azhar University in Cairo, Egypt. Nabhani broke with the incremental, one-soul-at-a-time approach of the Brotherhood. He stressed instead an activist philosophy centered on the resurrection of the caliphate through the support of sympathetic military and political leaders capable of overthrowing the existing nation-state system. The party has had a small following based in the intellectual and professional classes. For more details see Beverley Milton-Edwards, *Islamic Politics in Palestine* (London: Tauris Academic Studies, 1996), 64–71.

the appearance of very special, divinely appointed people free of the corruptions of mortal political ambitions. Until those "different people" and that "different time" arrived, other, more pragmatic solutions that steered a course between extremes were necessary. Fathawi secularism provided such a course for all Palestinians—Muslims, Christians, Jews, atheists, secularists, everyone:

> I support a secular ideology even though I am a Muslim and I practice my religion. The secularist is not an infidel [*al-ʿalmānī mish kāfir*]. Secularism is simply the separation of religion [*al-dīn*] from the state [*al-dawla*]. . . . One can say, "Religion is for god and the homeland is for everyone" [*al-dīn lil-lāh wa al-waṭan lil-jamīʿ*]. I am a Palestinian. I fight to liberate Palestine and build a Palestinian state in which Muslims and Christians and Jews can live together. I can't impose Islamic ideology on people who have not been brought up Muslim. According to the Qurʾan, Palestine is a land for the three religions—Islam, Christianity, and Judaism. It is the Holy Land. Okay, perhaps the majority of the people will be Muslims, but the minority religions have an equal right to live here. . . . For this reason, I support a state that is separated from religion and that allows all the communities [*al-ṭawāʾif*] to exist in peace. [Moreover], if there is an Islamic state, what will happen to me? I'm a Muslim Fatah activist, and there are other guys who are secular and support the Popular Front. How would such a state deal with us? There are directions in the sharīʿa about Christians and Jews as *ahl al-dhimma* [protected subordinate peoples], but what about us Muslims? I pray but the other guy doesn't. This guy is *mutadayyin* [observant] but the other guy is not. This guy is secular and the other guy is Marxist. How should we deal with this? What will bring us all together? There will be a lot of problems [if the Islamists are followed]. Now, if we built a people with a social infrastructure and consciousness that are purely Islamic, then on that basis we could rise up, fight for, and build an Islamic state. You don't do this by gathering together ten jerks with long beards, with Israel behind them,[22] and then build a movement that carries out four or five operations in the name of an Islamic state. How many individuals among the Palestinian

[22] Hasan was echoing the charge prevalent among secular nationalists that Israel aided the emergence of the Muslim Brotherhood and its successor organization, Hamas, in a bid to divide the national movement. The charge has historical basis: From the late 1970s onward, the Israeli military, seeking to undermine the P.L.O.'s political hegemony, gave Islamists breathing room to organize and allowed a flow of funds from Saudi Arabia and other Gulf states into the Occupied Palestinian Territories. The Islamists took full advantage of the space afforded them. Avoiding Israeli repression by eschewing participation in the P.L.O.-led nationalist resistance, they made secular nationalism and the spread of "foreign" cultural influences (European styles of attire, mixed-gender activities, pop music, etc.) their primary target. During this period, the Islamists gained control of mosques, set up an extensive social service network, and engaged in missionary activity within Palestinian

people actually pray? Very few. So, how can they build an Islamic state on this basis?

Fatah was the nation, for Hasan, because it alone reflected and protected the actual multisectarian character of Palestinian society. Hamas and Jihad, by contrast, could never embody the national collective precisely because they fragmented it along religious lines. For Hasan, the solution was the reassertion of classic Fathawi pragmatism: a political secularism that separated religion from the state while allowing religious practices and institutions to persist at the individual or communal levels. It was possible to be a secularist in this sense and remain a good Muslim; secularism was perhaps the most religiously authentic option, one implicitly sanctioned by the Qur'an's recognition that the Holy Land was the home of three religions. Hamas's vision of an Islamic state, by contrast, would necessarily end in a farce that not only undermined the nation but also made a mockery of Islam. Fathawi secularism alone enabled Palestinians to preserve religion for god while keeping the nation open to everyone.

Several parallels existed, as we will see, between Hasan's critique of the Islamists and the perspectives of insider Fathawis. Insider perspectives, however, subtly reordered the hierarchy of solidarity to view Fathawi factional identity as an element of a broader, multisectarian society that had become mobilized as a whole in the struggle for liberation. While, for insiders, Fatah still most fully reflected the nation's character and values, the nation nevertheless was seen to exceed the movement. For outsiders like Hasan, by contrast, the nation *was* Fatah, and vice versa. This key difference between insider and outsider orientations derived from the specific nature of insider historical experience. Insiders had come into their identities through the mass mobilization of the first

communities, especially in Gaza. Only in the 1980s, with the emergence of Islamic Jihad, and then, during the first Intifada, Hamas, did Islamists turn definitively against Israel, biting the proverbial hand that had fed them. In noting Israel's role in these developments, however, one must be careful not to reduce Islamism merely to an effect of Israeli manipulation. Islamists operated with their own agenda, made their own strategic decisions, and ultimately proved capable of powerfully asserting independence not only against Israel but also against the P.L.O. For more on these issues, see Milton-Edwards, *Islamic Politics in Palestine*, 151–152; Ziad Abu-Amr, *Islamic Fundamentalism in the West Bank and Gaza: Muslim Brotherhood and Islamic Jihad* (Bloomington and Indianapolis, IN: Indiana University Press, 1994), 42; Khaled Hroub, *Hamas: Political Thought and Practice* (Washington, DC: Institute for Palestine Studies, 2000), 29–41, 91–94. See also Shaul Mishal and Avraham Sela, *The Palestinian Hamas: Vision, Violence, and Coexistence* (New York: Columbia University Press, 2000), 1–26, and Ze'ev Schiff and Ehud Ya'ari, *Intifada: The Palestinian Uprising—Israel's Third Front*, ed. and trans. Ina Friedman (New York: Simon and Schuster, 1989, 1990), 220ff.

Intifada. They remembered the Intifada not as the last gasp of the revolution—the "dying horse" in Hasan's metaphor—but as a drama of paradise gained and paradise lost. The "paradise gained" was the Uprising's smashing of the barriers separating social classes, regions and clans, political factions, and religious communities from one another. Insiders, whether secular nationalists or Islamists, wistfully recalled this time as a period in which warm patriotic love of one's neighbor had suffused one's relations with others regardless of their backgrounds. New institutions transcending social divides had appeared, and individuals across the spectrum had carried out spontaneous acts of solidarity: Christians and Muslims attending each other's funerals, warring families setting aside their grievances, and so on. Suddenly, however, as the story went, this paradise of national unity evaporated in the heat of intense faction conflicts. The Hamas-Fatah divide was the most bitter and intractable of the divisions.

In the wake of the secularist-Islamist split, the overriding concern for insiders was to regain the lost paradise of broad societal unity. This unity did not necessarily entail the dominance of a single faction like Fatah. Insider approaches to achieving this end varied. The Fathawi insiders whom I interviewed divided into two main subgroups on this question. The first group attempted to bridge the religious-secular divide by incorporating religious practices and ideals into individual and collective identity while at the same time insisting, much like Hasan, on the necessity of a secular state. Proponents of this position—a stance that I call "Islam without Islamism"—incorporated a number of Islamist themes, for example, the necessity of females wearing scarves, daily prayer, fasting, and the institution of the sharīʿa (the Islamic customary code) as the basis of the Palestinian legal system. Some also adopted the Islamist theodicy that explained Israel's ascendancy and Palestinian national failure as the consequence of the neglect of individual and collective religious duties.[23] At the same time, however, these Fathawis viewed the Islamists politically with suspicion. They argued that while the ideal of an Islamic state was salutatory, Hamas's goals and tactics were not. Like any other faction, Hamas focused narrowly on selfish political ends and

[23] Theodicies arise in monotheistic religious and cultural settings. They explain how suffering and evil can exist when the one god is presumed to be wholly good, omniscient, and omnipotent. In the Palestinian context, the Islamist theodicy has particular appeal in the face of the apparent failure of the secular-nationalist movements to achieve the aims of liberation and statehood. The assertion is not only that Palestinian Muslims have failed to be faithful and thus have earned god's displeasure but also that Jews have been faithful and therefore have received god's favor. A similar logic operates among certain Jewish groups in Israeli society. Religious settlers in the Occupied Palestinian Territories, for instance, argue that secular Israel is on the brink of ruin and can save itself only by regaining god's favor. Such favor will return only if Israel fights to regain the entire land of Israel that god bestowed

employed manipulative methods to advance them at the expense of the national interest.

Husayn, the Céline Dion fan, exemplified this first type of insider response, which incorporated a much more consciously Islamic identity while rejecting Islamism. The excerpt below from his tape-recorded life-history interview followed a question about positions commonly taken by Hamas, particularly the need for an Islamic state based on Islamic law (the sharīʿa). The first distinction Husayn made was between being "conservative" (muḥāfiẓ) and being "chauvinistic" (mutashaddid).

> The mutashaddid deals with all aspects of daily life, individual and social, solely in religious terms [*bi khiṭṭat al-dīn wa min khilāl al-dīn faqaṭ*]. The muḥāfiẓ, by contrast, does everything within the prescribed limits [*fī niqāṭ al-ḥudūd*]. He guards and maintains [*yuḥāfiẓ ʿalā*] his duties and beliefs [*ʿaqīdatihi*] and his Islam. He performs his prayers, pays the tithe [*al-zakāt*], undertakes the fast, observes the religiously prescribed limits [*al-ḥudūd al-dīniyya*], but always respects freedom of opinion in religious matters. . . . I pray and fast and try to carry out all the duties required of me by religion with an attitude of devotion, not chauvinism. I still go to the sea, for instance, and go swimming. I go to the disco and other hangouts where young people get together, but I do this within limits, of course. I have friendships with my female colleagues but at the same time I respect the limits of my religion. There is no fornication or adultery and no alcohol.

The distinction between muḥāfiẓ (conservative) and mutashaddid or *mutaʿaṣṣib* (fanatical or chauvinistic) created a space within which Husayn could be both a practicing Muslim and a participant in social settings that potentially diverged from the moral limits of Islam and the inherited ʿādāt wa taqālīd of Palestinian society. Being a Muslim in this sense meant developing an internal moral compass that allowed an individual believer to remain oriented toward these limits while still engaging in a society characterized by diverse sociomoral spheres. One could be a good Muslim and also go to nightspots and have friendships with female colleagues at work. Just because there was alcohol at a bar or the possibility of extra-

---

on Jews in the biblical period. Sephardic Jews in the Shas movement also condemn secular Israeli society. They argue that Israel, in embracing the secular West, fails to live up to the religious precepts that, to their mind, define what it means to be Jewish. Shas desires to transform Israel into a state based on the *halakha*, or Jewish religious law. Ironically, some Shas leaders have expressed a greater sense of common purpose with Islamic Movement activists among the Israeli Arab population than with fellow Jews who support the secular Labor and Likud parties. Religious revitalization in Israeli and Palestinian societies thus appears to be linked in a reinforcing dialectic that shares a common set of assumptions about the place of religion in society and the consequences of ignoring duties toward god while simultaneously expressing competing nationalist claims to the land of Palestine/Israel.

marital affairs in the workplace did not mean that an individual was less of a Muslim for participating in these settings. Islam's true measure lay in the internal discipline of the believer, not in the strict conformity of every institutional sphere with the law of Islam. Husayn spelled this out further in relation to Christians and the idea of an Islamic state:

> **H:** I pray but I also respect the freedom of others. Jews and Christians have the right to practice their religion. As the saying goes, "To each individual his religion and his conscience."
>
> *What is your perspective on an Islamic state?*
>
> **H:** The Islamic method is among the most scrupulous and honest in the world. I am not against religious governance within the state, even if there is a difference between religion and state. The sharīʿa must have a role. The religious courts, Muslim and Christian, will of course base themselves on religious law. Religion and state must be kept separate, but in some things they are inseparable.
>
> *What are the limits?*
>
> **H:** Take the example of elections. There is no place for religion in the elections. In elections, there must be freedom of choice, and religion may not allow this. . . . Islam allows freedom of expression. It is accommodating, expressive, democratic, and conservative [*muḥāfiẓ*]. I support a system of governance based on these religious principles. But, there are people who implement religion in a chauvinistic way, and this is the problem.

Husayn's "conservative" vision of Islam was congruent with the multiconfessional disposition of Fathawi nationalism as reflected in the perspectives of outsiders like Hasan; but it was the multiconfessional society, not the political movement, per se, that was Husayn's primary vehicle of solidarity. Even though he worked for one of Fatah's main leaders in Jerusalem, his conception of the ideal collective was not the faction but rather a society made up of Muslims, Christians, and Jews who would coexist within a democratically run society. This society would allow these groups a significant degree of autonomy in running their internal affairs as religious communities. The arrangement envisioned by Husayn echoed the Ottoman *millet* system and the medieval Islamic ahl al-dhimma (protected peoples) concept. But instead of an empire based on kingship legitimized by divine commission in which one group (Muslims) was privileged, Palestine's citizens would be equal before a common law, at least at the national level, and choose their leaders according to the democratic principle of one person, one vote. In Husayn's view, Islam was compatible with such a structure because it was a religion that valued individual conscience and collective deliberation above all other considerations.

Like Husayn, Intisar's sense of identity stressed the central role of society as opposed to the faction. Her solution to the post-Oslo fragmentation described above echoed Husayn's but highlighted the specific dilemmas for women. Islamists had made women's bodies a main site of their cultural struggle, seeking to impose the head scarf and long coat as the standard form of female attire in public. Recall that Intisar's fiancé, a Fatah activist, wanted her to start wearing "Islamic clothing" (the Islamist scarf and coat). She was considering wearing a scarf but worried about what such an act would signify to others about the role she was agreeing to as a woman. She was proud of her Intifada activism and the position she had attained in the Fatah movement. She wore fashionable short skirts as an expression of her up-to-date professional identity as a social worker in a Fatah-associated service organization. Yet, at the same time, she saw herself as an observant Muslim. She said she fasted and prayed even though others would conclude otherwise from her appearance. Intisar admired the female Hamas and Jihad activists at Bethlehem University because they seemed to have achieved consistency between the demands of Islam and the "liberated" public role that she prized so much as a member of Fatah. Intisar said she approved of the sharīʿa because she was "convinced" of her religion and was trying hard to adhere to it, yet she had doubts: "There are things that I have a hard time accepting . . . especially the passages in the Qurʾan that are against the rights of women. I know god's wisdom goes beyond ours, but I also know he does not make women less than men."

Intisar's internal conflict was quintessentially an insider's one. It derived in large part from the social polarization that the cultural politics of Hamas and its allies had created. Confronting this polarization at multiple levels, Intisar sought some kind of third way that could bridge the divide and achieve a new social unity. The contradictions animating her struggle played out internally as a yearning for consistency between her inner sense of religiosity and her outer practice of dressing in clothing that other Muslims (and Intisar herself) deemed to be un-Islamic. The contradictions manifested themselves externally in the analogous confusion she perceived around her. She resisted Hamas because of its alleged chauvinism. It used religion for its own purposes and distorted the basic equality that was, for her, the heart of Islam. At the same time, she implicitly accepted the Islamist theodicy that explained Palestinian suffering as the outcome of Muslim unfaithfulness. Muslims needed to return to Islam since Islam alone could truly unite the Palestinian people. Fatah and the leftists confused people about their identities by offering atheistic or secular options that did not fit the society; but Hamas was also not much of an option, since it behaved as divisively and self-interestedly as any other political group. In the end she reached for middle ground. She wanted Islam, but with a difference. She might acquiesce in her fiancé's wishes and begin wearing a head scarf, but she would never put on the hated *jilbāb* coat that the Islamists required of their female followers, and she would never give up her career ambitions. Politically, she supported the idea of an Islamic state, but insisted that such a state "must be based on justice and democracy." She declared: "My whole life has been dedicated to democracy. There are many ways to practice it. The basic thing is to respect and protect the rights of others."

In contrast to this Islamizing (but not "Hamas-izing") tendency, other insiders revived a much more consciously secularist identity in response to the Islamist challenge. Like those who wanted Islam without the Islamists, they shared in the general orientation toward the wider society, as opposed to strict faction identity, as the primary basis of solidarity. They also often expressed a commitment to Islam at the level of individual piety. Unlike the first group, however, they placed far greater stress on pan-Arab ethnicity as the framework of collective identity.

An example of this second tendency was Sabr. Like Hasan and Intisar, Sabr described herself as a devout Muslim. She claimed to fast and pray. Like Hasan and Intisar, she was critical of the Islamists. While applauding their military operations because they contributed to the national struggle, Sabr argued that groups like Hamas and Jihad "exploit religion to accomplish political, financial, or economic interests." She was much more sharply critical than Intisar of their ideas about the role of women in society and much more explicit in rejecting their implications for her autonomy:

S: . . . they might impose the ḥijāb [scarf] on me like they do in Iran. I can't live under something like that. . . .

Hamas would counter that they are not against women working and studying. Islam is not against women, they would say.

S: But, it is a question of a woman's free will. A woman alone should decide what she wears. There is something negating your own individual, personal will and ideas here. . . .

What do you think should be the relation between the sharīʿa and the state?

S: Religion is a personal issue. It is something between you and your god. Look, there is something called *ijtihād* [individual intellectual exertion to expand and advance the interpretation of sharīʿa in new situations]. It is one of the sources on which the religious law is based. It has not been used in a long time and the neglect is killing Islam. *Ḥarām* [It is shameful] that they are doing this! At one point people were allowed to think, but

> now they aren't? Why did they stop ijtihād? There are still scholars who can think and develop ideas suitable to our times. We say the Qur'an is *ṣāliḥ li kull al-zamān wa kull al-makān* ["true and right for all time and place"], but this applies to the soul of religion. What worked for people 1,400 years ago will not work for us today. We should be able to use ijtihād to make religion more appropriate for our times.

In contrast to Husayn's recognition of the sharīʿa's legal and public dimension, and Intisar's implicit, albeit ambivalent, agreement with Islamist conceptions of female virtue, Sabr explicitly secularized religion, viewing it fundamentally as "a personal issue," one open to new interpretations. Each individual had the right to determine the scope and style of her practice. Scarf wearing and all other matters of piety, work, and thought should be left to personal decision, not collective imposition. Sabr equated an Islamic state with the Iranian example and viewed this possibility as fundamentally antidemocratic and opposed to full rights and equality for women. It also, in her view, ignored how women participated as equals during the Intifada. This legacy alone should have demonstrated the capacity and right of women to full and equal membership in society. Instead, the Islamists sought to impose the ḥijāb, restrict women's ability to travel freely (a point mentioned elsewhere in her interview), and constrict women's "free will," generally. Sabr, by contrast, demanded an Islam "appropriate for our times." Islam was immutable only in its essential core, which in Sabr's view accorded with values of equality and basic ritual observances (prayer, fasting, pilgrimage, tithing, and so on). It was thoroughly open to change, however, in all its other dimensions. These latter aspects could and had to change to be more congruent with modern principles of individual self-determination.[24]

[24] It is also possible that Sabr's attitude reflects the long-established emphasis among Muslims on individual responsibility for interpreting and implementing the sharīʿa dictates. For Sunnis, especially, Islam is a matter of decentralized practice within families as opposed to a state-imposed legal regulation of individual conduct (although modern states have increasingly concerned themselves with delimiting the sphere of sharīʿa and the forms of individual conduct that it governs). Yet, as Saba Mahmood has argued in her analysis of female *dāʿiyāt* in Egypt (predominantly self-taught female experts on sharīʿa who lead public lectures on matters of piety as part of the women's mosque movement), the practice of individual interpretation occurs within the handed-down normative framework and accepted methods of disputation that comprise the religio-legal tradition and its elaboration. The objective of such practices is the formation of a particular kind of subjectivity, one rooted in and expressive of sharīʿa prescriptions. These prescriptions, of course, take on a range of inflections and embodiments as they are adapted by dāʿiyāt embedded within different class and status milieus. But, again, this process of interpretation and adaptation presumes the normative frame of the sharīʿa and its elaborative procedures and the necessity of the individual to conform to this frame, however understood, to achieve piety. My claim that Sabr, by contrast, is voicing a secularizing sensibility flows from the stress she

At the societal level, Sabr further secularized religious identity by reviving an older pan-Arabism (*al-qawmiyya*) that located the Palestinian cause in the broader anticolonial struggle of the Arab masses. By stressing Arabness, qawm-ism enabled secular nationalists to contest and displace the Islamist stress on the *umma* (the notion of a worldwide Muslim community). Qawm-ism shaped Sabr's outlook quite directly. She told me that she had participated as a Fatah representative in the regional qawmī conferences that were revived in the late 1980s. She said these meetings had reawakened within her a transcendent sense of ethnic unity:

> Pan-Arab unity is still a dream despite what happened in the Iraq-Kuwait war. The Arabs are my nation. [In our meetings] I have suggested that we organize country-specific activities in order to spread the idea of pan-Arabism. Very few people know about what we are doing. If we start working within each country, then in the long run we will achieve unity. Otherwise, our efforts will be limited to the few who take part in the meetings. . . . We are having an impact. We went to the border after South Lebanon was liberated [a reference to Israel's unilateral pullout from its self-declared "security zone" at the beginning of 2000]. And, some of our counterparts came from Lebanon and Syria to meet us there. It is a small hope but it is important in the midst of all of our frustration.

Sabr's third way toward renewed Palestinian unity lay not in Hamas's vision of an Islamic state, or in an Islamic-democratic amalgam as Husayn and Intisar envisioned, but in a rejuvenation of Arab ethnic solidarity. "The Arabs" were her "nation."

Perhaps not surprisingly, this kind of ethnic transcendence also appealed strongly to Christians. Historically, Arab Christians had been pioneers of qawmī ideas and organizations. A Christian native of Damascus, Michel ʿAflaq (1919–89), for example, founded the Baʿth Party. ʿAflaq argued for a "single Arab nation" that "had the right to live in a single united state."[25] This nation had emerged under the Prophet Muhammad and the Islamic empires and societies that followed him. The resulting historical deposit was the possession not only of Muslims but of all groups that shared the Arabic language and contributed to the ongoing life of Arab societies. On this basis, this nation deserved independence and a state. It could achieve this through a "double transfor-

---

places not on forming an Islamic self but on the priority of individual will and the need to reinterpret sharīʿa, accordingly. The sharīʿa becomes individualized ("privatized") rather than the individual being "sharīʿa-ized," in her case. See Saba Mahmood, *Politics of Piety: The Islamic Revival and the Feminist Subject* (Princeton, NJ: Princeton University Press, 2005), 83–99.

[25] Hourani, *A History of the Arab Peoples*, 404–405.

mation" in which individuals absorbed "the idea of the Arab nation through understanding and love" and then reoriented state and society in congruence with their new inner disposition.[26] Such ideas attracted the rising Arab Christian bourgeoisie in the early decades of the twentieth century. They did so by shifting the basis for collective identity and political inclusion away from religion. No longer would prestige and power rest on whether or not one was a Muslim; rather, what mattered now was one's Arabness. Such ideas held out the promise of a fuller inclusion and equality for religious minorities.[27] Pan-Arabism remained a particularly strong current among Palestinian Christian supporters of Fatah. For these individuals, the memories of life under the Israeli occupation and common participation in the Intifada simply reinforced the idea that Christians and Muslims shared a single fate as Arabs and Palestinians.

Abu ʿAdnan, the Greek Catholic admirer of Archbishop Cappucci, illustrated how Christian Fathawis drew on pan-Arab themes in response to the secularist-Islamist split. Although he chose to join Fatah rather than the more explicitly pan-Arabist movements—the leftist Popular Front, for instance—he nevertheless articulated a sense of identity that integrated Fathawi emphases on Palestinian liberation with broader themes of inter-Arab unity:

> **AA:** If you are more aware of your *waṭaniyya* [national identity] you become more qawmī [pan-Arabist] in orientation.

> *What's the distinction here?*

> **AA:** Qawmī means you are aware of the Arab world and you see your struggle to liberate Palestine as part of the larger effort to bring justice, socialism, equality, and so on to the entire Arab nation. But at that time [the period in the mid- to late 1980s when he was developing his sense of identity], we were thinking of ourselves more as Palestinian nationalists [than as pan-Arabists].

For Abu ʿAdnan, the distinction between Arab and Palestinian nationalism was a matter of emphasis and priority. In explaining why he leaned toward Fatah, he pointed to the example of the Egyptian leader Jamal ʿAbd al-Nasir, the preeminent symbol of pan-Arab unity. Nasir, according to Abu ʿAdnan, "didn't differentiate between Christians and Muslims and had three enemies—the Zionists, the Jehovah's Witnesses, and

[26] Ibid.

[27] For an elaboration of this argument, see Robert M. Haddad, *Syrian Christians in Muslim Society: An Interpretation* (Princeton, NJ: Princeton University Press, 1970), and Hourani, *A History of the Arab Peoples*, 404–405.

the Islamists."[28] He also invoked the memory of the Greek Catholic archbishop Cappucci, saying Cappucci "wasn't Palestinian—he was from Syria, but he was a pan-Arabist." Ultimately, Abu ʿAdnan supported the P.L.O. and pan-Arabism because, to his mind, they were the sole options for Palestinian Christians. Twice during the Intifada he had worked to thwart attempts to establish separatist Christian parties in response to Islamism. "The Christians here are a very small group," he recounted. "The Maronite Phalangists failed in Lebanon. What would happen if we tried this here? [Rather than pursuing a separatist option] we should be like leaven in a loaf of bread [that is, by remaining active participants in the national movement as a whole]." Separation not only undermined national unity; it also provoked Islamist reaction. This in turn potentially endangered the Christian community. However, under the P.L.O., "we Christians can live our faith and be nationalistic like the rest." The antidote for Hamas, in his view, was renewed commitment to a pan-Arabist identity framed within a multiconfessional P.L.O. nationalist orientation.

CONCLUSION

The continuities and tensions that defined Fathawi nationalism in the post-Oslo period reflected the continuing relevance of Fatah's factional framework as an integrating force as well as the deep, differentiating impact of diverging geographic and generational locations. Fatah and the P.L.O., generally, had historically succeeded in mobilizing and shaping the identities of diverse constituencies: displaced peasants and sharecroppers, present and former landowners, the new urban professionals, Muslims and Christians of all types. Most critically, they provided a structural and ideological bridge for activists traversing the gaps between various class and status milieus. They extended scholarships and employment opportunities to the new generations of peasant refugees who were entering the universities and making the leap into the professional

[28] The mention of the Jehovah's Witnesses had a local resonance: the group had a strong missionary presence in the Bethlehem area. Their proselytizing activities worry Palestinian church leaders. In the adjoining town of Bayt Sahur, the Greek Orthodox priest refuses to allow parish members who join the Witnesses to be buried in the church's cemetery. Abu ʿAdnan also refers to Nasir's antipathy toward the Islamists. Initially supportive of the Free Officers, the Muslim Brotherhood soon fell out of favor with Nasir after one of its members allegedly attempted to assassinate him. Nasir then carried out a wide-ranging crackdown on the movement that continued in intermittent waves into the mid-1960s. The repression culminated in 1966 with the execution of Sayyid Qutb, one of the Brotherhood's most important and influential intellectuals.

classes. In doing so, Fatah and the P.L.O. provided an ethos that integrated the value orientations of the diverging social segments. Its pluralist nationalism utilized the discourse of the "customs and traditions," valorizing the peasant-turned-revolutionary; drew on religious concepts and symbols (ʿArafat, for example, often would be photographed praying in mosques or attending important church ceremonies); and apotheosized the image of the movement bureaucrat and intellectual. The nation, as a whole, was the sum total of these elements, drawing its character from them even as it remained above them. What mattered in the end for Fathawis was that one was committed, beyond all other considerations, to the liberation of the homeland and to the P.L.O. as the expression and vehicle of that liberationist project.

At the same time, the geographic and generational divisions among insiders and outsiders produced diverging perceptions of authority and identity. Seen through these lenses, Fathawism appeared to be developing two main fault lines. First, there was the diachronic divide between the old and new guard. This division reflected the different spatial and historical contexts of outsider and insider identity formation. The 1967 and 1982 wars were decisive for the articulation of outsider/old-guard identity, while the first Intifada was the main crucible that produced insider/new-guard orientations. The Oslo negotiations in the early 1990s collapsed this geographical-historical separation, bringing, for the first time, outsiders and insiders into proximity—a closeness that produced tensions centering on the control and direction of Fatah, the Palestinian National Authority, and the negotiations with Israel. In a nutshell, the new guard resented its marginalization under the Oslo order and sought to advance its claim to authority and power within the movement while the old guard refused to relinquish control, invoking its historical right to leadership.

In addition to the diachronic divide, there was a synchronic split that further shaped insider identity. This tension originated in the fracture between secular nationalists and Islamists, a fracture that crystallized during the first Intifada and took the form of an intense Fatah-Hamas rivalry. Because Fatah and Hamas anchored broader, overlapping sociopolitical milieus in the Occupied Palestinian Territories, the competition between the two formations occurred at a wider generational level as young activists across the sociopolitical spectrum came to share Fathawi or Islamist orientations, or various amalgams of the two, regardless of whether or not they were core members of either of the competing factions.

In responding to the Islamist challenge, the Fathawis I interacted with had developed three different responses—neo-Fathawism, Islam without Islamism, and neo-pan-Arabism. These emerging orientations reflected both the persisting relevance of outsider-insider distinctions as well as the continuing tensions among the various value orientations that, up to this point, Fathawism had more or less successfully bridged. Neo-Fathawism reasserted the faction as the primary framework of national identity. Among my interviewees, it typified the outlook of outsiders, although insiders, too, shared in this orientation to varying degrees. The P.L.O. factions played a far more central role in the organization of Palestinian life for the exile; hence, it was not surprising that outsiders would elide the boundaries between faction and nation. Insiders, by contrast, came into their identities through the experience of mass societal mobilization against the occupation. The factions were central to this mobilization but never transcended it: especially in the West Bank, other important structures—such as neighborhood groups, church and mosque-based associations, university campuses, and the like—played equally important roles in shaping insider identities. Secular nationalists and Islamists negotiated their conflicting orientations within these settings, in the process often adjusting or adapting their value orientations. Islam without Islamism and neo-pan-Arabism were two ideal-typical directions in which the insider Fathawis with whom I interacted appeared to have moved in response to the Islamist cultural-political challenge. Islam without the Islamists reshaped Fathawism as a type of multiconfessional religious nationalism, a "muḥāfiẓ" nationalism, which moved in the direction of Islamization without necessarily embracing the Islamist factions, themselves. Neo-pan-Arabism, by contrast, was much more explicitly secularist, insisting on the privatizing of religious identity, or at least its resubordination under the category of Arab ethnic solidarity.

Not surprisingly, female activists felt the strain of the struggle between Islamism and secular nationalism most acutely. Islamism had made women's bodies a field of cultural-political contestation, adopting and indeed, in some cases, forcibly imposing the ḥijāb and long coat as signifiers of the religiously framed neopatriarchalism it sought to promote. The spread of these ideals within diverse mediating institutions (families, schools, universities, workplaces, etc.) reinforced a general sense of moral polarization that affected other political-ideological spheres. The admiration and partial adoption of Islamist values by Fathawis such as Intisar, on one hand, and their near total rejection by activists such as Sabr, on the other, indicated the extension of this polarization to the Fathawi milieu itself. Under the pressure of the Islamist challenge, Fathawis were reinterpreting their core narratives, in the process producing new types of orientation that emphasized one or another of the ideological strands that comprised old-time Fathawi multiconfessionalism. The question at the end of 2000 was whether Fatah would remain a coherent, unified entity or whether it would divide, with the resulting fragments forming into new movements or melding into preexisting ones. Hamas and Islamic

Jihad stood ready to assume leadership of the national community in such an event. Since the outbreak of the al-Aqsa Intifada, this possibility has become even more acute with the near implosion of the Palestinian National Authority, a concomitant weakening of internal discipline in Fatah after ʿArafat's death on November 11, 2004, the strong showing by Hamas-associated candidates in elections for town and city councils in the Gaza Strip and West Bank in 2004 and 2005, and Hamas's victory in the elections for the Palestinian Legislative Council in January 2006. The ascendancy of the Islamists has worried Fatah supporters, other secular nationalists, and outside observers concerned about a renewal of an uncompromising Palestinian demand for Israel's annihilation. But it is a mistake to view the Islamists as an undifferentiated and unchanging monolith bent uniformly on a single objective. A closer look reveals the Islamist milieu to be as diverse and multivectored as the secular-nationalist one.

CHAPTER THREE

The Islamist Milieu

ISLAMIST ORGANIZATIONS pose the primary challenge to Fatah and the secular nationalists, generally.[1] Their growing strength lies in their alternative cultural-political milieu, which includes independent financial, social, political, and paramilitary structures. In a manner analogous to the secular-nationalist sphere, these structures integrate diverse constituencies, serving especially as bridges for individuals who grow up in village, *fallāḥī*-refugee, or lower-middle-class settings (taxi drivers, small-shop owners, etc.) but who then traverse into the professions after completing university studies. Like the Fathawi milieu, the Islamist sphere achieves this integration by harnessing the symbols and narratives of religion (*al-dīn*, i.e., Islam) and the fallāḥī "customs and traditions" (*al-ʿādāt wa al-taqālīd*) to the image of the up-to-date revolutionary. But whereas Fathawism tends to secularize the religions (Islam and Christianity) and traditions by integrating them into a multiconfessional conception of a territorially bounded nation-state, the Islamists draw on Islamic religious discourse and symbols to reframe the national purpose as a religious effort and duty (*jihād*) to achieve a "Muslim Palestine"—an entity grounded in the traditions of the past and, most critically, the customary practices stipulated in the *sharīʿa* (Islamic customary law). This counterthematizing of collective Palestinian identity has increasingly resonated beyond the Islamist sphere, attracting support among activists who have become, for one reason or another, oriented away from secular nationalism.

[1] The terms "Islamist," "Islamism," and "Islamic Movement," as I employ them, denote the entire range of groups committed to the social and political revivification of Islam as a framework for Palestinian national aspirations. Views described as "Islamist" are understood to apply across the different organizations that are generally oriented in this direction. Islamist factions share not only a general ideological outlook that draws from the same intellectual and historical sources but also often coordinate with one another as a single political bloc against secularist parties during elections for university student councils, for instance. Although comprising an identifiable milieu, especially, in contrast with the secular-nationalist sphere, critical differences nevertheless obtain between the smaller, sectarian Islamic Jihad and the larger, inclusive Hamas. Also, individual activists within these two groups will articulate varying interpretations of key concepts and symbols. This chapter explores these differences.

One should not overstate Islamist popularity, however. As summarized by Khaled Hroub, the regular polling data of the Palestinian Center for Policy and Survey Research indicate that support for Hamas between 1993 and 1997 hovered around a mean of 18 percent compared with a 40 percent mean during the same period for Fatah. Hroub's own estimate, which factors in Hamas's contention that it commanded between 40 to 50 percent support during this period, strikes the balance, putting the popularity of the Islamists at 30 percent. Gil Friedman's work, significantly, indicates a severe decline in trust for all factions, including Fatah and Hamas, in the moments just preceding the collapse of the Camp David negotiations and the start of the al-Aqsa Intifada in September 2000.[2] The situation has changed yet again since the outbreak of the al-Aqsa Intifada. With the near collapse of the Palestinian National Authority, Hamas's level of support in the West Bank and Gaza Strip has achieved parity with, and even exceeded, Fatah's in some places. According to a June 2004 survey by the Palestinian Center for Policy and Survey Research (P.C.P.S.R.), approval of Fatah had stayed even since March 2003 at 28 percent, "but that of Hamas has increased from 20% to 24%" during the same period. When backing for Islamic Jihad and Islamist-leaning independents was added, Islamist popularity rose to a combined 35 percent, up from 29 percent in March of the previous year. In Gaza, Hamas received 29 percent support compared with Fatah's 27 percent. With the inclusion of Islamic Jihad, Islamist popularity in Gaza shot up to 38 percent.[3] The results of municipal elections in the West Bank and Gaza in December 2004 and January 2005 confirmed Hamas's growing level of support: Hamas candidates won 76 of the 118 seats up for election in Gaza, nearly two-thirds of the vote tally. In another round of voting in May 2005, a poll that included the Gaza Strip, Hamas secured 33 percent of the vote and won majority control of the councils and mayoral positions in three of the largest cities: Rafah, Bayt Lahiya, and Qalqilya. In January 2006, Hamas won an overwhelming majority in the Palestinian Legislative Council, thereby ending the Fatah movement's forty-year dominance of Palestinian politics.[4]

[2] Khaled Hroub, *Hamas: Political Thought and Practice* (Washington, DC: Institute for Palestine Studies, 2000), 229–233. See also Gil Friedman, "Popular Trust and Distrust in Palestinian Politicians and Factions" (Jerusalem: Jerusalem Media and Communications Center, August 2000), http://www.jmcc.org/research/reports/study1.htm#intro.

[3] Palestinian Center for Policy and Survey Research, "Poll Number 12" (June 24–27, 2004): 4–5, http://www.pcpsr.org/survey/polls/2004/p12epdf.pdf.

[4] John Ward Anderson, "Hamas Dominates Local Vote in Gaza," *Washington Post* (January 29, 2005), A22, http://www.washingtonpost.com/wp-dyn/articles/A44058–2005Jan28.html; "Fatah Prevails but Hamas Gains in Palestinian Polls," *Daily Star* (May 7, 2005), http://www.dailystar.com.lb/article.asp?edition_id=10&categ_id=2&article_id=14886; and Arnon Regular, "Unofficial Results: Hamas Strong in Local W. Bank Elections," *Haaretz* (December 24, 2004), http://www.haaretzdaily.com/hasen/pages/ShArt.jhtml?itemNo=518353&contrassID=1.

The P.C.P.S.R.'s research ("Poll Number 13") suggests that these polling and election results reflected dissatisfaction with Fatah and the Palestinian National Authority (P.N.A.). Just weeks before the December 2004 elections, perception of corruption within the Fatah-controlled Palestinian National Authority was high, according to P.C.P.S.R.'s data, at 88 percent of the population in the West Bank and Gaza Strip. An overwhelming majority, 93 percent, desired "fundamental political reforms in the PA." Yet, negative feelings toward the Fatah-controlled P.N.A. alone are insufficient to account for the persisting appeal of the Islamist movements. Islamist formations have become deeply rooted within Palestinian society and politics during the past two decades and as a result command large and important constituencies in their own right. To comprehend why this is the case, we must explore a series of questions that probe beyond the survey data: What kinds of individuals became integrated within the Islamist structures? What institutions and experiences mobilized these individuals in an Islamist direction as opposed to a secular-nationalist one? What were the effects of this mobilization process on their political identities? How have these identities evolved in response to the structural and political changes that accompanied the shift from uprising to installation of the P.N.A. and to a crisis-ridden negotiating process? The discussion that follows approaches these questions by first reviewing the historical evolution of Islamist structures and ethos. Islamism, in the Palestinian context, represents a well-developed parallel sociopolitical milieu whose symbols, narratives, and institutions provide a countermodel of the nation.

THE STRUCTURES AND ETHOS OF THE ISLAMIST MILIEU

Historically, Palestinian Islamism has its roots in the Muslim Brotherhood as it took form in Egypt and then spread to the wider Arab and Muslim world from the late 1920s onward. Founded by Hasan al-Banna, a schoolteacher and onetime Sufi, the Brotherhood got its start in Isma'iliyya, a city situated along the Suez Canal. It began as a reform movement that offered an "up-to-date," nationalistic Islam for newly emerging proletariat and lower-middle-class groups—such as dock workers, teachers, and lower-level bureaucrats whose roots, like Banna's, lay in rural settings. The Brotherhood offered these groups a bridge between the village cultures of their upbringing and the politically and socially turbulent urban milieus to which they had migrated; it did so by reformulating the patriarchal and religious values of small-town life into a powerful critique of British colonialism, the established religious scholars (the *'ulamā'*), and the secularized mores of the new ruling urban elites. From an original core of seven men, the movement expanded rapidly, comprising by 1944 as many as half a million members organized in more than one thousand branches from Sudan to Syria.[5]

Although the Muslim Brotherhood was brutally repressed by the Egyptian government in 1949, activists reconstituted the movement in the early 1950s after the Free Officer's Revolution brought down the last vestiges of British rule.[6] The reprieve was fleeting. In 1954, the Brotherhood once again became the target of a severe government crackdown following an unsuccessful attempt on Egyptian president Jamal ʿAbd al-Nasir's life. There was another rehabilitation following the succession of Anwar al-Sadat, "the Believer President," in 1970. Originally intended to counter the influence of the Socialists and Nasirists, Sadat's support for Islamist groups led to an unintended proliferation of movements, some of which began organizing clandestinely to take power. A new round of repression resulted, culminating ultimately in Sadat's assassination in October 1981.[7]

The alternating dynamics of repression and rehabilitation in the Brotherhood's relations with the Egyptian state produced competing conceptions of authority within the movement. These conceptions reflected the contrasting leadership styles of the Brotherhood's founder, Hasan al-Banna. Banna projected the charisma of the pious saint who had become a living manifestation of the spirit of the sharīʿa. Simultaneously, he was a symbol of militant jihād, becoming the first Islamist martyr to fall at the hands of a repressive, seemingly apostate Muslim government.[8] After his death, Brotherhood leaders appropriated one or the other of the founder's

[5] Brynjar Lia, *The Society of the Muslim Brothers in Egypt: The Rise of an Islamic Mass Movement, 1928–1942*, foreword by Jamal al-Banna (Reading, UK: Ithaca Press, 1998), 152–154.

[6] For details on the Brotherhood's institutional evolution, see Lia, *The Society of the Muslim Brothers in Egypt*; Richard P. Mitchell, *The Society of the Muslim Brothers*, foreword by John O. Voll (Oxford: Oxford University Press, 1969, 1993); and Banna's autobiography, *Mudhakkirat al-daʿwa wa al-daʿiya* [Remembrances of the Summons and of the One Who Issues It] (Beirut: al-Maktab al-Islami, 1947, 1966, 1974, 1979).

[7] An army lieutenant who was also a secret member of the Organization for Divine Struggle (*jamāʿat al-jihād*) carried out the killing. On Sadat's support for Islamist groups and his eventual assassination, see John L. Esposito, *The Islamic Threat: Myth or Reality?* 3rd edition (New York: Oxford University Press, 1999), 93–96, 139, and 146. For an excellent study of the Islamization of Egyptian society during and after Sadat, see Patrick D. Gaffney, *The Prophet's Pulpit: Islamic Preaching in Contemporary Egypt* (Berkeley, CA: University of California Press, 1994), passim, but especially 80–112; see also James Toth, "Islamism in Southern Egypt: A Case Study of a Radical Religious Movement," *International Journal of Middle East Studies* 4, no. 35 (November 2003): 547–572.

[8] Agents of the Egyptian "political police" assassinated Banna on February 12, 1949. The attack was in retaliation for the killing of Prime Minister Muhammad Fahmi al-Nuqrashi by a Brotherhood activist on December 28, 1948. This act had itself been a response to the government's banning of the Brotherhood and mass imprisoning of its activists. Mitchell, *The Society of the Muslim Brothers*, 67–71.

personas as a model for legitimacy and action. The "gradualists" stressed a missionary approach, arguing for the necessity of cultivating Muslim virtues in the hearts of believers as a first step in the long-range formation of an Islamic society. Once such a society was in place on the cultural and social levels, it would then be possible to acquire political power by mobilizing mass opinion against anti-Islamic policies and practices. Prior to this, any attempt to take the state would be premature, causing a violent crackdown that would endanger the movement's future. The militants, by contrast, argued for going underground, reorganizing into small guerrilla groups, and carrying out immediate armed action against the state. An Islamic polity, it was argued, could emerge only from the top down, through the imposition of Islamic governance by an enlightened vanguard.

Both tendencies drew from a second seminal Brotherhood figure, Sayyid Qutb, who also attained martyr status when Nasir sent him to the gallows in 1966. Qutb was born the same year as Hasan al-Banna and followed the same trajectory that Banna traced from village Qur'an school to the new Dar al-ʿUlum Teacher's College in Cairo. Like Banna, he also got a job as a schoolteacher and then became a bureaucrat in the government's Ministry of Education. He found his way into the Brotherhood in the late 1940s after a trip to the United States confirmed his deepening sense that an aggressive and morally vacuous West threatened Egyptian religion and traditions. Qutb proposed in the course of his extensive writings that contemporary Egyptian society, by embracing Westernization and secularization, had regressed to the pre-Islamic condition of *jāhiliyya*—that is to say, a state of polytheistic chaos and permissiveness marked by a willful "ignorance" of the one god and his ethical commandments for social organization and life conduct. The only viable option for the believer in this situation was to renounce such a god-forsaking society. He was to withdraw into separated communities of the faithful, purify his consciousness of foreign values, and then reengage society through missionary outreach and, when the moment was right, join in outright revolution. This concept of purification and struggle inspired both radicals and gradualists. It seemed to vindicate the importance that some placed on the transformation of souls prior to any political action. Conversely, it was taken as a clarion call to violent revolution against an apostate regime and society.[9]

Banna and Qutb's thought, along with the writings of the Pakistani intellectual Abu al-ʿAla al-Mawdudi, have provided the core themes of Sunni Islamist ideology and practice. In the Palestinian setting, Banna's example

[9] On Qutb, see ʿAbd al-Baqi Muhammad Husayn, *Sayyid Qutb: hayatuhu wa adabu* [Sayyid Qutb: His Life and Literature] (Al-Mansura, Egypt: Dar al-Wafa', 1986); Ahmed S. Moussalli, *Radical Islamic Fundamentalism: The Ideological and Political Discourse of Sayyid Qutb* (Beirut: American University of Beirut Press, 1992); Giles Kepel, *Muslim*

has remained a vibrant one for Hamas and Islamic Jihad activists. His continuing iconic importance became vividly clear to me during an exhibition hosted by the Islamic Bloc student organization in a large gymnasium at Bethlehem University in 1999. The exhibit commemorated the September 1996 clashes on the Haram al-Sharif (the "Noble Sanctuary," i.e., the Temple Mount) and elsewhere. The violence, touched off by the Netanyahu government's decision to open up a tunnel under the Haram, had left 14 Israelis and 65 Palestinians dead and approximately 1,100 other Palestinians wounded.[10]

The exhibit featured photos of those who had fallen during the fighting. The emotional crescendo occurred as I walked toward the "martyrs's tent" through a reconstructed "Intifada street" replete with burnt tires, rocks, and soiled Israeli and American flags underfoot. Inside the incense-filled *khaymat al-shuhadā'* was a mock cadaver wrapped in a green Hamas flag. Photographs of dead activists who were similarly shrouded tiled the interior walls of the tent. Then, as I exited, a large, framed portrait of Hasan al-Banna, dressed in a Western-style suit, appeared. In an instant, the exhibition established a direct line of continuity from the "first martyr," Banna, to the martyrs of the Palestinian Islamist resistance and the "living martyr," Shaykh Ahmad Yasin—eventually assassinated in an Israeli missile strike in Gaza on March 22, 2004—whose portrait I had encountered at the exhibit's entrance. This metonymic link between Yasin and Banna, a link tethered by the Intifada street and the martyrs's tent, transformed Palestinian suffering and sacrifice—specifically, that of Islamic Movement activists—into a symbol of the transnational and trans-

---

Extremism in Egypt: The Prophet and the Pharaoh, trans. Jon Rothschild (Berkeley, CA: University of California Press, 1985); Ibrahim M. Abu-Rabiʿ, *Intellectual Origins of Islamic Resurgence in the Modern Arab World* (Albany, NY: SUNY Press, 1996); Yvonne Y. Haddad, "Sayyid Qutb: Ideologue of Islamic Revival," in *Voices of Resurgent Islam*, ed. John L. Esposito (New York: Oxford University Press, 1983), 67–98; Sayyid Qutb, *Al-ʿadala al-ijtimaʿiyya fi al-islam* [Social Justice in Islam] (Beirut and Cairo: Dar al-Shuruq, 1975); Qutb, *Hadha al-din* [This Religion](Beirut and Cairo: Dar al-Shuruq, 1986); Qutb, *Maʿalim fi al-tariq* [Signposts along the Path] (Beirut and Cairo: Dar al-Shawq, n.d.), 20–54. See also Roxanne Euben, *Enemy in the Mirror: Islamic Fundamentalism and the Limits of Modern Rationalism, a Work of Comparative Political Theory* (Princeton, NJ: Princeton University Press, 1999). William E. Shepard, "Sayyid Qutb's Doctrine of *jāhiliyya*," *International Journal of Middle East Studies* 4, no. 35 (November 2003): 521–545, points out that among the groups that emerged after Qutb's execution only the *takfīr wa hijra* movement attempted to implement Qutb's notion of radical self-segregation from society.

[10] On these events, see Jerusalem Media and Communications Center, "Report on Today's Incidents" (September 28, 1996); the Online Newshour's "Middle East Background Reports" for September 26–30, 1996, http://www.pbs.org/newshour/bb/middle_east/middle_east-pre2001.html; and United Nations Security Council, *UNSCR Resolution 1073* (1996), http://www.palestine-UN.org/news/oct96_r1073.html.

Figure 5. Jerusalem in danger. This two-story mural was hung by Islamic Bloc activists from the main administration building at Bethlehem University in 1999. Just above the mural to the left is a statue of the boy Jesus. The mural itself depicts what had become a central theme of Islamist propaganda in the Oslo era: the endangerment of Jerusalem under Israeli domination. The rivers of blood flowing from the Dome of the Rock shrine refer to the various clashes between worshippers and Israeli police and military during the 1990s. The blood congeals at the bottom into the words of the Islamic testimony, to which the lives of the "martyrs" bear witness: "There is no god but God and Muhammad is God's messenger." The immediate cause of the clashes included the archaeological tunnels opened up by the Israeli government beneath the Haram compound. The portrait suspended in the sky to the left is a rendering of the visage of Yahya ʿAyyash, the Hamas guerrilla commander responsible for organizing human bombing operations within Israel. Israel, it is widely assumed, assassinated ʿAyyash by planting an explosive device in his cell phone. The words at the top declare, "We sell [our] life for al-Aqsa; they [the leaders] have sold [their] consciences." Author's photograph.

generational struggle against foreign domination and despotic secularist regimes, regionally. At the same time, it revalued the symbols of this broader struggle as an expression of *Palestinian* resistance.

Qutb's ghost was also felt. At the end of the exhibit, after passing a section with racks of *ḥijāb* scarves and *jilbāb* coats for women, I came upon rows of tables with books by the leading intellectual figures of Sunni Islamism. The texts covered such topics as Islamic banking, jurisprudence (*fiqh*), basic ritual practices, jihād, Israel and the Jews, the distortions of Orientalist scholarship, and the threat of Western Christian missionary activity. Prominent among the books were Sayyid Qutb's Qur'anic commentaries and political tracts. Qutb's ideas suffuse Palestinian Islamist orientations. Especially critical have been his concepts of jāhiliyya, tactical withdrawal, and jihād. These ideas have had varying valences at different points in time, providing an orienting framework for the cultural and political struggle aimed primarily at P.L.O. nationalism and secularism, generally.

Banna and Qutb have not been the only influences on Palestinian Islamism. Equally critical has been the impact of the 1979 Iranian Revolution and the successful Hizbullah guerrilla struggle against Israel's occupation of southern Lebanon. Both events have provided examples of the efficacy of militant Islamist action. The Islamic Jihad movement, in particular, has drawn inspiration from these examples. One of my interlocutors, a longtime Islamic Jihad activist who was expelled to southern Lebanon in December 1992 along with some 408 other Islamist leaders, drew direct inspiration from Hizbullah and the Iranians to reimagine a revived Palestinian armed struggle. This individual illustrated a central dimension of contemporary Palestinian Islamism: the nationalist reorientation of Islamist ideology. Both Islamic Jihad and Hamas prioritize the liberation of the nation. Banna, but especially Qutb (drawing on Mawdudi), argued, by contrast, that national independence struggles were not to end in the reinforcement of the nation-state but rather in the revitalization of global Muslim solidarity. Palestinian Islamists have reversed this order, placing the global solidarity of the *umma* at the service of overcoming the occupation and establishing an independent Palestine, one based, to be sure, on the sharīʿa but nevertheless bounded by the borders of the former British Mandate. This nationalist turn in Palestinian Islamism is new and occurred in opposition to the culturalist tendencies of the 1970s.

Prior to the first Intifada, Palestinian Islamists made a strategic and ideological decision to focus on long-term institution building through cultural action, for example, charity work, missionary outreach, and network development. This culturalist approach contained within it a rejection of the ascendant pan-Arabism and its Palestinian variant, the multiconfessional secular nationalism of Fatah and the P.L.O. Palestinian Muslim Brotherhood activists during this period by and large viewed these conceptions of collective identity as contradicting the idea of a transnational Islamic umma; consequently, they construed their primary problem as one of combating the spread of secular-nationalist ideals. Only when Palestinians had turned their backs on such notions and embraced Islam as their primary identity, they argued, would it be possible to overcome Israel. This antinationalism created a conundrum for those Palestinian youth post-1967 who, on one hand, had absorbed religious values at home, and thus were predisposed to gravitate toward the Muslim Brotherhood's message of Islamic revival, and yet, at the same time, had grown up "with the nationalist feeling," as some of my interviewees put it. Fathawi nationalism had so thoroughly molded Palestinian consciousness by the 1970s and 1980s that it was virtually impossible to define oneself as a Palestinian separate from the P.L.O.'s ideals of secular, multiconfessional unity and liberation of the homeland through self-reliant armed struggle. Hence, any social or political movement, if it was to have any mass appeal, had to espouse these ideals in one form or another.

The Muslim Brotherhood's refusal to support the P.L.O. and engage in nationalist resistance against the Israeli occupation post-1967 prevented the movement from attaining support beyond its specific cultural-political milieu; nevertheless, its drive to develop social service institutions, control the mosques, and take over university student councils, labor unions, and professional associations created the basis for the future transformation of the movement into the P.L.O.'s primary competitor. Shaykh Ahmad Yasin was instrumental in this institutionalization process. He along with other Islamists of his post-1967 generation created the Islamic Collective (*al-mujammaʿ al-islāmī*) in 1973 as an umbrella organization for the various Muslim Brotherhood–affiliated organizations and activities. By the 1980s, the Collective had developed an extensive social service network in the Gaza Strip based around the mosques and at Gaza Islamic University. Collective activists saw their struggle as a cultural-political one to stem the spread of secularization and secular nationalism among Palestinians. They sought to transform Palestinian practices and ideals in accordance with Islam through missionary outreach and sometimes physical coercion. Their propaganda cast supporters of the secular-nationalist factions as "traitors to the Muslim faith."[11]

In 1978, the Israeli military allowed the Islamic Collective to register

[11] See Beverley Milton-Edwards, *Islamic Politics in Palestine* (London: Tauris Academic Studies, 1996), 84–93, 97–105, and Graham Usher, "What Kind of Nation? The Rise of Hamas in the Occupied Territories," chap. in *Dispatches from Palestine: The Rise and Fall of the Oslo Peace Process* (London: Pluto Press, 1999), 18–33. Milton-Edwards notes that Mujammaʿ activists would disrupt social life in Gaza, breaking up wedding celebrations

as an official charitable organization. This preferential treatment—P.L.O. social service organizations were banned—enabled the Collective to institutionalize itself even more powerfully as money from Jordan, Saudi Arabia, and other Gulf countries flowed in. With this infusion of funds, the Collective greatly expanded its network of clinics, orphanages, study centers, and charitable societies. The Israeli tactics only strengthened the suspicions of many Palestinians that the Islamic Collective was a tool of the occupation. For their part, Islamic Collective leaders viewed any advantage over the secular nationalists, however attained, as justifiable since it advanced the cause of Islam. As the 1970s ended and the 1980s progressed, tensions heated up with the secular nationalists and Fatah in particular. In one instance, a major violent clash broke out during the 1979 elections for officers of the P.L.O.-controlled Red Crescent Society. During 1981–85, Islamic Collective activists became a major presence at Gaza Islamic University. They undertook campaigns to encourage women to wear the scarf and ankle-length coat and clashed with the secular nationalists who dominated the student council. In the early months of 1986, Collective activists managed to gain control of the university, clashing severely with secular nationalists, particularly supporters of the Marxist Popular Front and Fatah, in doing so.[12] Meanwhile, as the Collective pursued its cultural-political initiatives against the P.L.O., Shaykh Yasin and other leaders began planning for an underground paramilitary apparatus that would be capable of contending with the armed secular-nationalist groups in the struggle against Israel. The Intifada preempted these plans, but already in the early 1980s Yasin and others were beginning to develop an armed option. Yasin, for example, had been sentenced by Israel in 1984 to thirteen years of imprisonment for hoarding sixty rifles. Released one year later as part of the Ahmad Jabril prisoner exchange, he encouraged his followers to continue

---

and attacking other practices deemed un-Islamic. Milton-Edwards, *Islamic Politics in Palestine*, 111–116. Special emphasis was placed on getting middle-class women in Gaza City to wear the scarf (ḥijāb). This campaign became violent during the first Intifada as Hamas activists in Gaza pelted women without scarves with rocks or even, on a few occasions, threw acid at them. On this latter point, Rema Hammami, "Women, the Hijab, and the Intifada," *MERIP* 164/165 (May–August 1990): 24–31.

[12] Between 1982 and 1986 several clashes occurred between respective supporters of the P.L.O. and the Muslim Brotherhood, the precursor to Hamas, at Gaza's Islamic University and at al-Najah University in Nablus, an important economic center in the northern West Bank. The conflicts had to do with determining the results of student council elections. See Ziad Abu-Amr, *Islamic Fundamentalism in the West Bank and Gaza: Muslim Brotherhood and Islamic Jihad* (Bloomington and Indianapolis: Indiana University Press, 1994), 43–46. On the clashes that took place in the early 1990s, see Beverley Milton-Edwards, *Islamic Politics in Palestine*, 153–157.

Figure 6. Shaykh Ahmad Yasin. These campaign posters, which appeared during the 1999 elections for Bethlehem University's student council, convey key symbols of the Islamic Resistance Movement (Hamas). The center poster shows the Dome of the Rock with a fist clutching a rod that is simultaneously a pen, spear, and staff to which is attached a banner bearing the words of the *shahāda*, or testimony, that "there is no god but God and Muhammad is the messenger of God." Beneath the dome are an open Qur'an and the words "Love and Fraternity, Sacrifice and Offering, Knowledge and Action." The two posters flanking the central one feature the late Shaykh Ahmad Yasin, cofounder and spiritual leader of Hamas, in the upper right-hand corner. Author's photograph.

focusing on propaganda and institution-building work.[13] The emergence of the Islamic Jihad during this same period, however, would soon push the Islamic Collective activists in a much more militant direction.

The Jihad made its initial appearance in 1981 under the leadership of Dr. Fathi Shikaki, among others. The movement integrated four different factions that broke away from the Muslim Brotherhood/Islamic Collective and also the Fatah movement. It styled itself an elite band of highly educated activists committed to liberating Palestine as the first step in igniting the broader pan-Islamic revolution. Taking its cues from the Iranian

[13] For more on these issues, see Ze'ev Schiff and Ehud Ya'ari, *Intifada: The Palestinian Uprising—Israel's Third Front*, trans. and ed. Ina Friedman (New York: Simon and Schuster, 1989, 1990), 220–221.

Revolution, which had powerfully revalidated armed struggle as a mode of Islamist activism, the Jihad argued that Marxism and other Western revolutionary concepts would inevitably fail in societies such as the Palestinian one in which Islam was the dominant cultural frame. It was therefore necessary to translate the concepts of revolution into Islamic ideals of just struggle. The Jihad also criticized the gradualism of the Muslim Brotherhood/Islamic Collective. It argued that pan-Islamic unity would emerge on a mass level only through direct action to liberate the holy land, site of the third-holiest Muslim shrine, the Dome of the Rock, and al-Aqsa Mosque. By prioritizing Palestine, the Jihad effectively created an Islamist analogue of Fathawi nationalism and in so doing gave proto-Islamists in Fatah's ranks a viable Islamist-nationalist alternative. The Jihad dramatically enacted its slogans with spectacular actions such as the assassination, in broad daylight, of Israeli captain Ron Tal in August 1987 as he walked along a Gaza City street. It also carried out a series of grenade attacks on Israeli military checkpoints and patrols throughout August and September of that year. Such actions transformed the movement into a highly prominent element within the national resistance. The Jihad never attempted to position itself as a replacement for the P.L.O.; on the contrary, it saw itself as working in tandem with secular forces that sought to end the occupation and liberate historical Palestine through armed revolution.[14]

The Islamic Jihad's militancy radicalized a new generation of Islamists. These activists began pushing the Muslim Brotherhood leadership to take a more aggressive political stand against the occupation. This push for a more overtly nationalist orientation received its greatest impetus from the outbreak of the Intifada, however. The mass demonstrations created a societywide ethos of activism and resistance that reinforced the nationalist orientations of the new generation of Islamists. The quick response of the secular nationalists in asserting leadership over the Uprising through their new body, the United National Leadership of the Uprising, moreover, threatened to relegate the Islamists to irrelevancy. To align with the pervasive mood and ensure that the they maintained a stake in the emerging political situation, Islamic Collective leaders decided to allow the formation of a proxy front, the Islamic Resistance Movement, known commonly by its acronym Hamas. This new formation would project a much more militant, antioccupation stance in a bid to assert the Islamist presence against the secular-nationalist forces. As a separate entity, it would protect the Islamic Collective parent structure by absorbing the inevitable Israeli repressive response.

[14] On the Islamic Jihad, see Milton-Edwards, *Islamic Politics in Palestine*, 116–123, 139–142; Abu-Amr, *Islamic Fundamentalism in the West Bank and Gaza*, 90–127; Schiff and Ya'ari, *Intifada*, 72–78.

Hamas continued the earlier policy of the Collective of separation from the P.L.O. It issued its own leaflets, organized its own strikes, and carried out its own actions against the Israeli military. The earlier suspicion directed at the Islamists by secular nationalists carried over to Hamas; however, the new organizational face of the Collective soon succeeded, on its own terms, in attracting an increasingly large following. Younger proto-Islamists were especially attracted to the integration of Islam and nationalism that Hamas embodied. In its charter, Hamas, echoing the ideological themes of the Islamic Jihad movement that had preceded it, defined its goal as the retrieval of "Muslin Palestine" through the overthrow of the Israeli state and the establishment of an Islamic one. While it refused to join the P.L.O., it affirmed "brotherhood" with the other Palestinian organizations that were fighting Israel. It called for solidarity on the shared aim of ending Israel's presence in historic Mandate Palestine while simultaneously issuing, in *daʿwa* fashion, an invitation to the P.L.O.-associated groups to embrace the ideals of Islam. With this essentially nationalist reorientation of the Islamist milieu, the new generation of Intifada activists had a viable and authentic Islamic alternative to the standard P.L.O./Fathawi multiconfessional secular nationalism. Gradually, across the political-factional spectrum, though not without tension and violence, the Islamists received grudging recognition of the space they had carved out in the mass uprising against the Israeli occupation.[15] Hamas signaled the final arrival of a radicalized Islamist-nationalist orientation in the Palestinian setting.

SOCIAL BACKGROUNDS

The tension that Hamas's emergence generated flowed not only from its refusal to take direction from the secular-nationalist Intifada leadership but also from the large degree of overlap in the social backgrounds and personal trajectories of Islamist and secularist activists. The Islamist and secular-nationalist factions drew from, and competed for, the same kinds of constituencies. The question thus arises as to why major segments of these constituencies opted for the Islamists against the historically dominant P.L.O. An exploration of Islamist social backgrounds provides part of the answer.

Mujahida, an unmarried Islamic Jihad activist, exemplified the first type of background that typified both my Islamist and my secular-nationalist interviewees. This group comprised the professionalized

[15] Milton-Edwards, *Islamic Politics in Palestine*, 103–116, 124–139; Abu-Amr, *Islamic Fundamentalism in the West Bank and Gaza*, 1–52; Usher, "What Kind of Nation?" 18–20; Schiff and Ya'ari, *Intifada*, 220–223.

descendants of rural landowning families. During our interviews, Mujahida wore a head scarf pinned tightly beneath her chin, an ankle-length coat, and a mask called *niqāb*, which revealed only her eyes. We met in the small charitable society she had founded soon after her release from an extended period of administrative detention—a renewable six-month arrest order that requires no formal charges or trial—in an Israeli prison. Her initial incarceration had occurred just prior to the first Intifada and commenced after her arrest for membership in a cell that had been planning to bomb the Israeli Knesset (Parliament). When I made her acquaintance, Mujahida had attained a professional certificate in social work and was finishing a B.A. in education at Bethlehem University.

Born in the early 1960s in Thawra Camp on the outskirts of Bethlehem, Mujahida came from a large landowning clan that was expelled from a village in the southern portion of the former al-Ramla District during the 1948 war: "My grandfather had bought a lot of land in different areas. [In the war] we actually took refuge on some of that land near Bethlehem [the Wadi Fukin area, due west of Bethlehem]. So, we were a little better off than other families that had absolutely nothing." During the war, her father joined the resistance and was imprisoned for a year. Her uncle was shot and killed in the fighting, as well. Afterward, the family moved into a U.N. tent in Thawra Camp and eventually built more permanent shelter. They would later move into a house in Bethlehem, where Mujahida attended school. Following the 1948 war, Mujahida's parents worked the land that they still possessed in Wadi Fukin and also opened a small dry goods store. Mujahida told me that her father would stay in the store while her mother trekked to their fields to do the planting and harvesting. Her mother still dressed in a style typical of older village women. She came into the room during our second interview wearing a colorfully embroidered *thawb*, an ankle-length dress cinched at the waist with a belt. Over her head she wore a long, loose, gauzy white scarf called *shāsha* (literally, "screen").

In Mujahida two key dimensions coincided: a basic nationalist outlook and a reconfigured Islam. Both orientations had their basis in the discourses and practices that had structured her upbringing. Mujahida's father was the source of her nationalism. A veteran of the failed 1948 resistance, he would spend long hours after school telling her about the war and what it meant, along the way instilling "a revolutionary consciousness within me from an early age." Alongside the nationalist narrative, Mujahida also inherited a deep connection to religious values. Like most of my Islamist interlocutors, she described her parents as "traditional Muslims." They fasted and prayed and kept the other religious observances, she told me, because these practices had been handed down to them. They were what one did if one was a Muslim. This "traditional" environment provided the ground for a religious conversion experience at the age of thirteen or fourteen. The catalyst was her brother's death from a severe beating at an Israeli checkpoint on the border between Bethlehem and Jerusalem. After the death, Mujahida withdrew into deep mourning. Her illiterate mother urged her to seek solace in the recitation of the Qur'an. After further coaxing, Mujahida, in an Augustinian-like moment, "took [the Qur'an] and began reading." The daily practice of recitation calmed her. It also began slowly to reshape her political orientation. Slowly, she said, "my entire view on life began to change." She felt she had more "faith force" (*quwwa īmāniyya*) within herself, and she began to reinterpret her life in Qur'anic terms as a struggle [jihād] for "Muslim Palestine" (*filasṭīn al-muslima*), a struggle to achieve "right" (*al-ḥaqq*) and "justice" (*al-ʿadl*).

There was, in this moment of death and reorientation, a confluence of the political violence that had become the pervasive reality of Palestinian life under occupation after 1967 with the basic nationalist and religious proclivities embedded within the family. Mujahida's mother—a "believer" (*muʾmina*), albeit a "traditional" (*taqlīdiyya*) one, in Mujahida's terms—served as the midwife of this integration. In taking up her mother's suggestion to turn to the Qur'an for comfort, Mujahida forged a transgenerational link with the "customs and traditions" (al-ʿādāt wa al-taqālīd) of the fallāḥī past that complemented and made further sense of the narrative of dispossession she had received from her father and experienced directly through her brother's death. This integration of custom and tradition was not an uncritical repetition of the same, however. Rather it reflected a creative reinterpretation that was part of a broader shift afoot within her generation. Mujahida was a member of a cohort of activists who had grown up under the occupation, graduated from the recently established universities, and become mobilized during the 1980s into the clandestine P.L.O. factions. All this diverged from the circumstances that had shaped her mother's life. Unlike her daughter, Mujahida's mother had married early, had never learned to read, had never joined any factions, had never learned how to use bombs and rifles, had never gone to university, and had never founded any institutions. Her religious orientation was magical: she had referred her daughter to the Qur'an because it was a talisman, a source of extrahuman power that would bring Mujahida comfort. Dressed in the thawb, she remained symbolically and psychologically rooted in her vanished village.

Mujahida, by contrast, had developed, through her access to education and politicization, a "rationalist" sensibility. The Qur'an was a source of power, to be sure, but that power lay primarily in its moral condemnation of oppression, not in its magical qualities. It made sense of her brother's death by linking it to the dramatic tensions contained within the Qur'an's fundamental thematic opposition of *shukr* (thankfulness toward god) and *kufr* (ingratitude and rebellion toward the divine order). Mujahida's struggle now became the Qur'anic struggle for a just society, one founded on divine principles and law. She signaled her alignment with this struggle by adopting an extreme form of Islamized outerwear that contrasted sharply with fallāḥī garb: her garments were a stripped-down, sober, and radicalized version of her mother's colorfully embroidered thawb and white shāsha. A reappropriated and reconfigured, "Islamized" tradition that included but transcended the ethos of the village thus became a vehicle for a revalued nationalism. Rather than being a constituent element of the nation, a reformed tradition became the quintessential expression of it. Significantly, Mujahida admitted no fundamental difference between her retooled Islamist orientation and her mother's "traditional" one. Perhaps if pressed, she might have agreed that her approach was more "rational" and less "talismanic" than her mother's. But the overriding sense present in her discourse was one of continuity with the past, and this continuity grounded her claim to authenticity and difference vis-à-vis the secular nationalists.

Other Islamists whom I interviewed, by contrast, defined themselves precisely by a perceived fundamental discontinuity with the generation of their parents. Like Mujahida, they described their parents as "traditional Muslims"—people who did their prayers and fasting because that was what Muslims had always done. They diverged from Mujahida, however, in explicitly rejecting this traditionalism. They claimed to have studied the sources and assented to Islam, rationally. Moreover, these individuals told me that they had embraced activism in opposition to the defeatism of their parents. In this experience of intergenerational difference, they identified a parallel with the secular nationalists. Even if they differed on basic social and political questions, at least, I was told, secular nationalists shared a common commitment to politics and struggle on behalf of the nation—unlike their elders and unlike the "materialist," cappuccino-drinking generation that was coming of age on university campuses during the Oslo period.

Hakim, a veteran of the first Intifada and leading Hamas activist at Bethlehem University, expressed these kinds of sentiments. He represented the second type of social background that typified both my Fathawi and my Islamist informants: descendants of former sharecroppers who, after 1948, had formed large pools of unskilled and semikilled workers in the new massive refugee camps. The new U.N. schools, technical institutes, and universities established after 1967 had enabled individuals from this background to attain a high school education and advanced training in the trades and professions.

Hakim was a Bethlehem University senior in his late twenties when

I first met him in October 1999. Born in 1970 in the Husayn Refugee Camp just outside ʿAmman, Jordan, he had moved back to the West Bank with his siblings and parents during the 1982 Israeli invasion of Lebanon to settle with family in a refugee camp just outside Bethlehem. He spent five years in various Israeli prisons during and after the Intifada. He returned to his studies following his release in the wake of the arrival of the Palestinian National Authority in 1994 and quickly emerged as an Islamic Bloc leader on Bethlehem University's campus. At the time I got to know him, Hakim was majoring in mathematics and undergoing additional training in computer programming at a center in Ramallah, a city just north of Jerusalem, under license from the Microsoft computer firm. To support himself and contribute to the family, he worked nights at a stonecutting factory. Hakim talked of wanting eventually to go to Seattle, Washington, to live with his brother and work for Microsoft. He was uncertain however that he would ever be allowed to leave, because he remained in Israeli and Palestinian National Authority computer databases that tracked Islamist activists. During 1999–2000, Israeli authorities prevented him from crossing the bridge into Jordan to meet with a prospective marriage partner—a first cousin whom his family had picked out for him.

Hakim's grandparents had been tenant farmers. They fled with their children from their village, al-Walaja, following the Dayr Yasin massacre.[16] Hakim's father was nine years old at the time. He eventually became a construction worker in Iraq during the 1960s. He returned to be with his family in Jordan in 1970 at the start of the violent conflict between King Husayn and the P.L.O. The main lesson his father drew from his experiences in 1948 and 1970 was "never to trust the Arab leaders." This negativism of Hakim's father seemed to have developed into a general pessimism toward politics of any sort. When the first Intifada broke out, Hakim recounted, his father challenged him, saying, "What can a stone do against the gun?" Hakim explained that his father's generation was "much more afraid of the Jews." His father had never been an activist and apparently had no defined political position. "He was," Hakim said, "like the regular people, just trying to get by."

Hakim's perception of his parent's generation as afraid to rise up was a common one among Intifada activists. Yet even as Hakim criticized this supposed fear, he also expressed agreement with his father's critique of the Arab political leadership, extending it to the P.L.O. The P.L.O., he said, had initially been on the right track in calling for self-reliant

[16] On Dayr Yasin, Baruch Kimmerling and Joel S. Migdal, *Palestinians: The Making of a People* (Cambridge, MA: Harvard University Press, 1993, 1994), 151–152, and Walid Khalidi, *Dayr Yasin: al-jumʿa, 9 nisan/abril 1948* [Dayr Yasin: Friday, 9 April 1948] (Beirut: Mu'assasat al-Dirasat al-Filastiniyya, 1999).

armed struggle. With the Oslo Accords, however, ʿArafat had gone the way of all the other treacherous Arab dictators. ʿArafat feared Hamas, Hakim told me, because the Islamist movement disputed the P.L.O.'s claim to represent the Palestinians, especially after the signing of the Oslo Accords.

Hakim's embrace of an Islamist political identity constituted both a rejection and a reappropriation of tradition. Hakim described a family atmosphere in which his parents, especially his father, prayed and fasted only occasionally. The religious attitudes that his parents did possess, he told me, tended to reflect "traditional thinking" (*tafkīr taqlīdī*), not "Islamic thinking." His parents, he said, lacked a true "Islamic consciousness" (*thaqāfa islāmiyya*).[17] Explaining what he meant, Hakim related that his mother fasted and prayed and his father occasionally did so, but if one asked them why they bothered to perform these duties, they would reply, "Because god ordered it." In contrast to this unthinking, "traditional" mind-set, those with Islamic thinking understood that "god helps only those who help themselves first." Islam was a complete, rational way of life. Every aspect of existence—politics, economics, personal piety—had consciously to be brought into conformity with the core principles of Islamic law. Hakim had learned to see Islam in these more rational terms through his encounter with Muslim Brotherhood mentors in the local mosque that he attended as a teenager just before and during the first Intifada. When pressed on what led him to begin going to mosque, he was vague, stating: "I have always prayed since I was ten, at least. . . . No one really influenced me. I went to mosque as a kid by myself. I liked going there, by myself."

Hakim's Islamist turn was facilitated by institutions (the mosque, principally) that lay outside the family. Yet the family provided an important source and foil for this evolution of his identity. The family may have lacked a rational, "Islamic" consciousness, but it also presented no open renunciation, or absence, of religion; on the contrary, it preserved religious practices as part of the family ethos, even if the dad seemed less than assiduous in his prayers and fasting. It was against this background that Hakim then fashioned his own distinct rational appropriation of the religious tradition. Hakim, a computer science and mathematics major, and the first in his family to go to university, bridged the "traditional thinking" of his peasant-refugee family with the value orientations of the professional middle classes by retrieving and reconfiguring religion as

[17] The term "thaqāfa" can mean "education," "culture," "cultivated refinement," or "sophistication." I translate the word as "consciousness" here to convey the sense of a total outlook that one comes to possess through educative processes in the broadest sense. Hakim's parents do possess a consciousness that could be called "Muslim" or "Islamic" but not in the sense that Hakim has in mind.

the epitome of an overarching, integrating, and alternative rationality. It reappropriated religion as a holistic and rational outlook that reoriented science and education, the professional lifestyle, and the collective national struggle toward divinely established legal-moral principles. The result was a new unity, a new sense of wholeness that replaced his father's pessimism and traditionalism with a seemingly more authentic alternative: Islamic nationalism.

The conscious break with the "ʿādāt wa taqālīd" (the customs and traditions) of the fallāḥī (peasant) past that appears in Hakim's account parallels Mujahida's experience. Even if Mujahida may have claimed continuity with the fallāḥī past, her interpretation of the Qur'an as a blueprint for nationalist struggle, her style of dress, her status as a professional, and her history as a political activist indicated the emergence of a very different kind of consciousness. In what sense, then, could Mujahida have seen her evolution not as a disjunction but rather a continuation of the orientations that typified the 1948 generation? How exactly was Hakim's development not so much a radical departure from the "traditional thinking" of his parents as an adaptation and restructuring of their "traditional" attitudes and practices?

Answers to these questions emerge in the life history of Shaykh Taqi al-Din, a Hamas leader and mosque preacher born in 1970 in a village just south of Bethlehem. Taqi al-Din was from the third type of social background that typified my interlocutors: the middle to lower-middle classes of the West Bank towns and villages occupied in 1967. This group primarily encompassed the skilled trades and lower-level bureaucratic and professional positions (clerks, teachers). Taqi al-Din described his father as a pious man who spent his life working as a blacksmith and construction worker in Israel. While his older brothers inherited the blacksmithing business, Taqi al-Din attended to his academics. He enrolled in the "scientific stream" in high school, receiving 82 percent on the exit examination in the final year. He could have gone on to study science in any university of his choosing but instead decided to pursue religious studies in college. He eventually became the *imām* (a term that refers both to any person who leads the prayer and to the head preacher/administrator of a mosque) and religion instructor in his village. During the Intifada, he joined Hamas and was in and out of Israeli and Palestinian National Authority prisons.

Taqi al-Din's autobiographical account clarified how Islamist discourse established continuity with the fallāḥī ethos. In his narrative, the peasant past represented an ideal period in which daily life was itself an expression of basic Islamic values. Those values had been lost in the contemporary urbanizing society. Returning to essential Islam, then, entailed a return to the elders and their orientations. Taqi al-Din expressed this sentiment in his description of his father. The father had never gone to school; he was a "simple man." But, according to Taqi al-Din, he gained knowledge through his daily practice. Religion was more than *ʿaql* (intellectual thought, rationality); it was also *rūḥāniyyāt* (spiritual principles and practices). Islam demanded application of its moral principles in daily life. His father understood and had taught Taqi al-Din these principles of "right from wrong . . . not to steal, to be honest in all my dealings, and so on."

The example his father set was, for Taqi al-Din, the quintessential model of the good society. Such a society relied on the inculcation of basic Islamic morality. Taqi al-Din claimed that in his village perhaps only five or six people drank alcohol. People did not steal. You could still leave your house or car open and unattended. This was true, he said, despite the fact that the villagers lived in a very unstable situation. They could not rely on the police. It had been this way for decades. But still they supposedly did not have the major social problems that plagued Bethlehem and Jerusalem and other towns and cities. This was so, according to Taqi al-Din, because the villagers had absorbed and practiced basic Islamic morality. There was, to be sure, a need for guidance and education. Islam gave a complete program for life. It gave instructions on details as minute as what percentage of inheritance men and women were entitled to, how divorce and marriage should proceed, and even what one should do about technological inventions like the Internet. Islam thus guided and reinforced the inherited values of the family and extended them to every aspect of life. Hakim, the aspiring Microsoft programmer, might have added that Islam corrected fallāḥī traditionalism, transforming its supposedly unreflective repetition of prayers and feasts into a much more conscious, orthoprax enactment of sharīʿa prescriptions. Yet even in Hakim's case, the fallāḥī past was not so much rejected and erased as reformed and reoriented toward what he felt to be the authentic religious foundation of the ʿādāt wa taqālīd.

MOBILIZATION: EVENTS AND STRUCTURES

In addition to the influence of family environments, Islamist activists came into their identities as a result of historical events and forces that shaped their consciousnesses in specifically Islamist ways. Four factors were most salient for my respondents: (a) the humiliations of the occupation and the mass mobilization of the Intifada; (b) the predominance of secular-nationalist groups such as the Fatah movement, the Popular Front, and the Communists—all my Islamist informants started out as P.L.O. supporters and activists of one sort or another; (c) the emergence of Hamas and Islamic Jihad as religio-nationalist alternatives; and (d) the consequent disciplinary crackdown on religiously oriented activists within the secularist ranks.

Ismaʿil, an independent Islamist and religion lecturer at a Jerusalem university, illustrated the interweaving of these various factors. The occupation and incipient acts of resistance figured centrally in his account. He recalled that he began to develop a nationalist consciousness through his friendships with the residents of a refugee camp across from the house his family rented in Bethlehem. Initially, Ismaʿil had a neutral, even favorable view of the Israeli soldiers who guarded the Rachel's Tomb pilgrimage site (important to both Muslims and Jews). They sent him to buy cigarettes and tea and gave him tips in return. But after he began attending school in the refugee camp across from his home, he developed a very different perspective. His refugee peers organized demonstrations, engaging the same soldiers who tipped Ismaʿil in rock-throwing encounters. Ismaʿil joined these protest actions.

Ismaʿil's experiences with his refugee friends sowed a basic nationalism within him. This orientation not only changed whatever positive predispositions he might have had toward the soldiers who sent him on errands; it also led him, ironically, to be highly critical of the Muslim Brotherhood, the organization that provided the institutional basis for Hamas and Islamic Jihad. "I always hated religious people," he commented. "I would see the shaykhs and imāms praying on TV for the King of Jordan [the late King Husayn, father of the current King ʿAbdullah II] and I had this impression from early on in my life that the king was the source of all our problems and to pray for him therefore was to betray my rights and identity as a Palestinian."[18]

Later, at the age of eighteen, Ismaʿil would undergo a shift and begin praying and attending mosque; but this change did not immediately lead to alignment with the Islamists. Ismaʿil described how he approached the Muslim Brotherhood but became quickly dissatisfied with their seeming obliviousness toward politics. Fatah, he found, far better expressed what he felt to be most important. He recalled Brotherhood cadres openly refusing to participate in nationalist actions, instead "playing soccer" while shooting was occurring around them. The Israelis, consequently, "didn't bother with them." Later, during the Intifada, Brotherhood leaders would claim they had been preparing to be active, but Ismaʿil rejected this claim, saying: "The majority of the Hamas activists who went to jail

[18] The Muslim Brotherhood has long recognized the Hashimite rulers of Jordan as legitimate patrilineal descendants of the Prophet Muhammad. Despite periodic crackdowns, King Husayn and his successor, King ʿAbdullah, have worked to co-opt the Brotherhood by allowing it to register as a political party and run for seats in the parliamentary council. For further details, Abu-Amr, *Islamic Fundamentalism in the West Bank and Gaza*, 4–6, and Milton-Edwards, *Islamic Politics in Palestine*, 57–59.

were new recruits from other parties, especially Fatah." Every one of my Islamist interlocutors described a similar trajectory: the development of an early nationalist orientation and then an initial sympathy with or connection to the Fatah movement—a result due both to the lack of an Islamist alternative that was engaged in resistance and to Fatah's basic ideological pragmatism that subordinated specific ideologies to a broad, common-denominator nationalism.

A similar pattern emerged in the account that Hakim, the Bethlehem University Hamas leader, gave of his politicization. In 1982, when he was twelve years old, he and his family moved from Jordan to the West Bank. He tied his memory of the war in Beirut during that year to the dawning of an understanding that he was a Palestinian: "I remember hearing the news on the radio of the Israeli invasion of Lebanon and the Sabra and Shatila massacres as we crossed the bridge," he told me. Later, in high school, he started joining demonstrations, and then during the Intifada his best friend was shot dead next to him during a stone-throwing confrontation with soldiers. Hakim and others hid his friend's body from the military and then buried it clandestinely in the cemetery behind Rachel's Tomb. Hakim joined Hamas during the Intifada, but initially he supported the groups associated with the P.L.O. even though he never officially aligned with them. His initial positive inclination toward the P.L.O., he said, came from hearing the legends as a kid of larger-than-life heroes like ʿArafat and Abu Jihad and the fidāʾiyyīn guerrilla fighters who, against all odds, started the national resistance and took on the mighty Israeli army. He learned to admire these figures. They embodied the "nationalist feeling," as he put it, which had become deeply rooted within him.

A Bethlehem University senior who headed the campus's Liberation Party (*ḥizb al-taḥrīr*[19]) contingent described a similar early orientation toward the P.L.O. In his account, P.L.O. structures and propaganda and the daily humiliations of the occupation served as key mobilizing forces in his early politicization.

> I wasn't exactly Fatah. Let's just say that I had a "nationalist inclination" [*mayl waṭanī*]. The [P.L.O.] propaganda had a strong effect on us. We'd see pictures of the guerrillas [fidāʾiyyīn] in Lebanon during the Israeli invasions in the 1980s. . . . And the Jews—we hated them naturally because of the martyrs and the beatings and the suffering.

Only later, after the signing of the Oslo Accords, would he reject the P.L.O. and embrace the Liberation Party in reaction against what he saw as the erosion of principle in the leading secular-nationalist forces:

[19] The *ḥizb al-taḥrīr* is a small, elitist Muslim Brotherhood splinter that formed in the 1960s. It advocates top-down military coups among army officers with sympathies for Islamist aims. See Milton-Edwards, *Islamic Politics in Palestine*, 64–72.

> I was an ordinary Muslim [*muslim ʿādī*] who fasted and prayed and that was it. I didn't carry Islam as a complete system of thought, a system of economic and social thought. . . . In 1994 [the year after the Oslo Accords were signed and also the year the Palestinian National Authority was established in Gaza], I began to read the Liberation Party materials. . . . I began to internalize the movement's ideas in the weekly lecture and discussion circles [*al-ḥalaqāt*—a term used specifically to denote study groups in a mosque].

This Liberation Party activist followed the typical path of Islamist mobilization: an orientation toward religious values and practices, the parallel development of a general "nationalist feeling," initial positive regard for the P.L.O., and finally integration into the Islamist milieu through mosque-based movement structures, especially the ḥalaqāt (study circles). The timing of the Islamist turn was important: it occurred at the very moment that the P.L.O. moved toward a negotiated two-state settlement with Israel.

A similar trajectory, one that played out a decade earlier, marked the life course of Ibn Fadlallah. His account showed in more precise detail how the Fathawi structures increasingly proved incapable of integrating religiously oriented activists as the 1980s progressed. The son of a taxicab driver, Ibn Fadlallah joined the Fatah movement in the early 1980s. He received weapons training and then was jailed after the Israeli military discovered his cell.

In explaining why he joined Fatah, Ibn Fadlallah remarked that despite growing up with a pious orientation, resistance to the occupation became an ever more important value for him. Fatah was well known as a secular movement, but it nevertheless allowed him to continue practicing his religion while enabling him to get involved in the collective struggle to overthrow the occupation. During his time in prison, however, he began to see that "in the end the people in Fatah were not fully committed to Islam. I felt they actually sought to push Islam to the side." He remained in prison more or less continuously for fifteen years. During this period, he was recruited into the emerging Islamist wing within Fatah. This group eventually broke away to help form the Islamic Jihad with militant Muslim Brotherhood contingents in the mid-1980s. In December 1992, Ibn Fadlallah was exiled to Israel's self-declared "security zone" in southern Lebanon as part of the Israeli military's mass deportation of Islamist leaders. He came into contact with Iranian advisers and Hizbullah leaders during this sojourn. He was impressed by their example and began giving much thought to overcoming the Shiʿi-Sunni split as a necessary step in initiating a pan-Islamic revolution with Palestine at its center. When I went to interview him, I found posters and photographs of Ayatullah Khomeini plastered across his doors and walls. I also found books by the Hizbullah intellectual and spiritual leader Al-Sayyid Muhammad Husayn Fadlallah on his desk in his Bethlehem office.

A final example—that of Mujahida, the female Islamic Jihad leader—illustrated yet again the centrality of the conditions of occupation and the institutions of the secular nationalist movements in the formation of incipient Palestinian Islamist consciousness. Mujahida recalled the humiliations that she personally experienced growing up in a refugee camp during the occupation. She recounted, in particular, the way soldiers would check identities during surprise raids, "forc[ing] people to dance and sing for them." One of her relatives apparently died of a heart attack from being made to stand all night in the rain during one of these raids. These autobiographical experiences of humiliation melded with the memories of 1948 that she had received from her father to create a deeply personal narrative of dispossession; they became a reservoir of anger and resentment that would find expression in her adolescence in a full-blown nationalist orientation.

The existence of nationalist political parties at school was an especially crucial factor in Mujahida's mobilization. She first aligned with, of all groups, the Communist Party.[20] She explained that what was foremost in her mind was not the Communist ideology but the desire to "do something in the path of liberating the nation."[21] The Communists had good propaganda; their "slogans coincided with what you felt inside." The course of Mujahida's early politicization reflected the dominance of the pre-Intifada secular-nationalist milieu. This dominance was both structural and ideological. Like all my Islamist informants, Mujahida was a nationalist at heart. She came into this nationalism not only as a consequence of direct experiences of oppression under the Israeli boot but also through the absorption of the basic P.L.O. interpretation of what these experiences signified. The interpretation was mediated by the faction structures that mobilized activists. Ironic in retrospect, the early integration of these proto-Islamists into secularist movements reflected the lack of any comparable Islamist option. The Muslim Brotherhood had effectively ceded the political field, focusing instead on daʿwa (missionary work) and the construction of a network of charitable societies. This situation would soon change, however, with the appearance of Islamic Jihad and Hamas.

[20] See Joost R. Hiltermann, *Behind the Intifada: Labor and Women's Movements in the Occupied Territories* (Princeton, NJ: Princeton University Press, 1991), 38–55, for a discussion of the political organizing role of the Jordanian Communist Party, which would later become the Palestinian Communist Party, in the West Bank following the 1967 war. The Communists were well represented in the Bethlehem area. Their stress on a negotiated, two-state solution stood at odds with Fatah's more militant line. The position would cost the movement the ability to attract wider support.

[21] Mujahida used the expression "*fī sabīl taḥrīr al-waṭan*" (in the path of liberating the homeland). The phrase echoes the Qur'anic language of *al-jihād fī sabīl illāh*, or "struggle in the path of god."

Hamas and Jihad drew support away from secular-nationalist groups because they finally provided a religio-nationalist option that resonated with proto-Islamist orientations. The already existing Muslim Brotherhood structures in the mosques and charitable networks provided the vehicle for conceiving, conveying, and inculcating this new religio-nationalist outlook. In recounting their path to the Islamist movements, my interlocutors described becoming involved with mosque-based institutions. The Liberation Party activist who joined a study circle that also doubled as a political cell in his neighborhood mosque exemplified this phenomenon as did Hakim, the Bethlehem University Hamas leader, who participated in Qur'an study groups and other educational activities for boys led by Muslim Brotherhood activists in the mosque he attended. In one such activity in the Bayt Jala mosque, Hakim and other youths put on a play that dealt with the "flight" (*khurūj*) of the Muslims from al-Andalus (Spain) in the fifteenth century. This event was a crucial moment: It marked, in Hakim's mind, the point at which the Muslim empires began to weaken and recede. He told me that he and his friends dramatized the expulsion from al-Andalus to help others better understand the reasons for the current sorry state of Muslim societies, particularly the Palestinian one, and how they might begin to reverse the situation.

The mosque also served as a key catalyst of the transformation that Mujahida underwent following her brother's death. Soon after the tragedy, she began attending a neighborhood *masjid* where she met the woman who would become her spiritual and moral mentor. This woman—a teacher in a government secondary school for girls—took a keen interest in Mujahida, giving her books to read and inviting her home for further discussion. In describing her mentor, Mujahida recounted an incident in which the teacher entered into a struggle at her school with a headmistress with "leftist political sympathies" who demanded that she not wear her head scarf while in the classroom. The headmistress tried to have her mentor fired when she refused to remove the scarf. Mujahida's mentor eventually prevailed but apparently lost her eyesight from the stress she experienced. "This is the extent to which people must struggle and suffer just to be able to follow their religion in the current time," commented Mujahida. This example of principled resistance profoundly impressed Mujahida. It was "a model, a model that taught me that the deed or action is what speaks." The meaning of such action found its fullest expression in *al-jihād fī sabīl illāh* (struggle in the path of god). Through jihād, she began to integrate her "religious learning" with her "other deep commitment that I had developed since I was a very young girl," that is to say, her fundamental nationalism.

Mujahida's turn toward jihād highlighted yet another critical factor in the mobilization of proto-Islamists into the ranks of Hamas and Islamic

Jihad: profound disillusionment with secular-nationalist moral and political "corruption" and a concomitant desire for renewed authenticity. Actions taken on behalf of others in the cause of justice, in a word, al-jihād fī sabīl illāh, could flow authentically, in Mujahida's view, only from a solid inner conviction grounded in a love for one's nation and god. For Mujahida, this kind of inner commitment was fundamentally lacking in Palestinian society, especially among the secular nationalists. In the post-Intifada Oslo period, the secularists had either followed Fatah in the delusion that an agreement with Israel would deliver liberation or had simply contented themselves with making grand statements about continuing the fight while providing no concrete action to back up the rhetoric.

The disgust and disillusionment with the secular-nationalist factions that Mujahida expressed echoed in almost every explanation that Islamists gave of their transition to Islamist formations during and after the Intifada. Hakim, the Hamas leader at Bethlehem University, recounted hearing "disturbing things" about the P.L.O. leadership even before the Uprising began. Most troubling for him was learning that the P.L.O. leaders were secular (*ʿalmāniyyīn*), that Islam did not really mean anything to them. Then, during the Intifada he began listening to the new Sawt al-Quds (the Voice of Jerusalem) radio station that broadcasted from Lebanon and was leftist (connected to the Popular Front for the Liberation of Palestine–General Command, a Syrian-controlled P.F.L.P. splinter). Although Hakim suspected that the Syrian regime had some hand in the station's propaganda, he nevertheless took heed of what it revealed about corruption within the P.L.O. and the organization's plans to negotiate with Israel. So gradually he lost trust in the older secular-nationalist leaders, seeing them as similar to other autocratic and repressive Arab heads of state. Around 1990, he finally joined Hamas. The leftists were not an option, he said. They were completely against religion.

Corruption, disregard for Islam, and the move toward negotiations with Israel in the P.L.O. also were central concerns for Ibn Fadlallah, the Islamic Jihad leader who was expelled to Lebanon in 1992. Ibn Fadlallah started out in Fatah but left the movement in the mid-1980s. His transformation coincided with an internal reassessment among Maoist-oriented leaders in Fatah's "Student Brigades" in the wake of the 1979 Iranian Revolution and the expulsion of the P.L.O. from Beirut three years later. These activists, led by a Christian, Munir Shafiq, argued that the attempt to import leftist concepts as a mode for organizing the Palestinian struggle now appeared to have been an utter failure, especially when seen against the backdrop of the spectacular success of the cleric-led Iranian revolt. These Maoists argued, in a manner similar to that of leading Iranian Islamist-Marxist thinkers such as Ali Shariati, that it was necessary to translate secular concepts of revolution into terms that the tradition-oriented masses would understand. Islam could provide the requisite symbols and language for reigniting the Palestinian struggle on a much wider level.[22] As this fundamental reassessment of strategy and ideology began to attract supporters from the rank and file, it sparked a coercive reaction among Fatah activists loyal to the old-guard leadership outside the Occupied Palestinian Territories. The resulting acrimony and tension pushed Ibn Fadlallah even more toward the incipient Islamist nationalism:

> The people who headed up Fatah [in prison] began targeting Islam. It got to the point that when a new prisoner would arrive they would prevent him from speaking with you about prayer. You would feel eyes watching you, as if there were some police unit keeping tabs. We tried to deal with this issue democratically by referring this internal dispute to the leadership outside. We did this as a united front, as an Islamic bloc within the movement. We weren't asking to transform the movement into an Islamic one. We argued that the Arab and Islamic context of the struggle necessitated a special concern for Islam, generally. The head of the movement's leadership in the prisons, however, was completely hostile toward religion. He rejected our overtures and refused to convey our grievances to the leadership outside. Of all the opinions that were solicited on this issue ours was utterly neglected. This is what, in the end, caused us to feel that Fatah could never embody our aspirations.

The conflict between Fatah loyalists and Islamists intensified in the late 1980s with the appearance of Hamas and the Islamic Jihad. But, as Ibn Fadlallah indicated, the tensions had already reached into Fatah itself and were polarizing the movement from the inside out. The subsequent internal crackdown caused gaps to appear for Ibn Fadlallah and others like him between Fatah's stated tolerance of diverse ideologies and its actual responses to religiously oriented activists. The plausibility of Fatah as a vehicle for political identity and action began to collapse for these activists as the repression progressively forced them to decide between the emerging but still inchoate Islamist-nationalist option and an increasingly rigid secular-nationalist movement whose leadership viewed the new religious tendency as a threat to its control and Fatah's

[22] This line of thought is reminiscent of Antonio Gramsci's reflections on the problem of the separation of the revolutionary intellectual and the tradition-oriented masses. Antonio Gramsci, *The Antonio Gramsci Reader: Selected Writings, 1916–1935*, ed. David Forgacs (London: Lawrence and Wishart, 1986 and 1999), 300–362, especially 340–343. For a discussion of the Maoist-Islamist faction in Fatah, see Yezid Sayigh, *Armed Struggle and the Search for State: The Palestinian National Movement, 1949–1993* (Oxford: Oxford University Press, 1997), 630, and also Hroub, *Hamas*, note 71, 32–33.

ideological integrity. The conflict rapidly became intolerable for Ibn Fadlallah, pushing him toward a definitive break with Fatah:

> The atmosphere was intimidating [*al-jaww kān irhābī*—i.e., in prison]. They began saying we were people who didn't recognize and support the P.L.O.[23] . . . The word went around that this Islam we were advocating was dangerous and insidious [*mutawaḥḥish*]. They would say, "Israel does not recognize the P.L.O., so why is it that you all do not recognize the P.L.O.?" It got to the point where they started carrying knives in the prisons. They exchanged dialogue for violence. . . . Fatah was not prepared to allow any other faction to develop that would be capable of challenging it. . . . The vast majority of the [Fathawi] activists were regular Muslims susceptible to a religious-nationalist ideology and this is what made the movement block anything that might raise their Islamic consciousness. . . . So, I got out of prison and left the movement. . . . Islamic Jihad had emerged by that time, and we coordinated with them.

Ibn Fadlallah's account indicated the extent to which Fathawi/P.L.O. structures were proving incapable of integrating the new Islamist-nationalist tendencies. Ironically, Fatah's harsh internal crackdown, as Ibn Fadlallah remembered it, exacerbated the very tensions it was trying to overcome. In Ibn Fadlallah's case, it closed off options within the movement, causing him finally to leave to become one of the founding members of the Islamic Jihad.

ISLAMIST CONCEPTIONS OF THE COLLECTIVE

The melding of nationalist and religious values in the new Islamist movements produced a diversity of orientations with the potential for further subdifferentiation. Ideological differences among Islamists became particularly pronounced during the 1990s following the signing of the Oslo Accords and the establishment of the Fatah-dominated Palestinian National Authority. The Islamic Jihad and Hamas, along with the leftist Democratic and Popular Fronts for the Liberation of Palestine, rejected Oslo but stopped short of open rebellion despite the P.N.A.'s periodic suppression campaigns against them. In response to the constriction of their operating space, a constriction that resulted from the P.N.A.'s tac-

[23] This was a damning criticism. From the moment Fatah took over the P.L.O. in the late 1960s, its primary goal was to gain universal recognition for itself and the P.L.O. as "the sole legitimate representative of the Palestinian people," as the phrase went. It was a measure of the P.L.O.'s ascendancy among Palestinians that any attempt to put forward alternatives to itself was widely seen as traitorous.

tics of direct coercion[24] and bureaucratic regulation, both Jihad and Hamas made tactical decisions to deflect the crackdown by refraining, with the notable and bloody exceptions of the bombings in Israeli urban centers in 1995 and 1996, from violent actions that would undermine the Palestinian National Authority's position vis-à-vis its Oslo commitments and Israel. During this time, some elements began exploring options for a party-political transition that would position Islamists to participate in and shape whatever structures and collective political direction might emerge from the Oslo Process. The elections for the presidency and Palestinian National Council in 1996—a poll in which 75–80 percent of the population in the West Bank and Gaza Strip participated—provided the main impetus for this developmental direction. As with overt coercion and regulatory intervention, the elections functioned to limit Islamist operational space by shifting public opinion away from militancy and toward support for negotiations.

The decisions to refrain from military actions and explore electoral options produced tensions. Hamas and Jihad had won their popular legitimacy through a radical return to armed revolt just as the P.L.O. was openly advocating a two-state deal with Israel. Many of the activists who joined the Islamists at that time were attracted by an alternative that revived the original, maximal objectives of national liberation. Whereas the P.L.O. was willing to revise long-held principles, Hamas and Jihad had called for rededication to the armed struggle to win back the entire usurped Palestinian-Islamic patrimony. To now engage in the politics of the Oslo Peace Process was, for many Islamist activists, to undermine the purity of the Islamist message and to flirt with the very hypocrisy and treason that Fatah and the Palestinian National Authority stood accused of. The tensions produced by these shifts generated a number of diverging conceptions of solidarity. Three main ideal-typical perspectives emerged among the Islamists I interviewed.

Al-jihād fī sabīl al-nafs: The Struggle for the Soul

The first orientation, a*l-jihād fī sabīl al-nafs* (the struggle for the soul),[25] sought to preserve ideological and organizational integrity through

[24] On the P.N.A.'s use of armed force against Hamas and Jihad, see Graham Usher's account in "The Debut of the Palestinian Authority," chap. in *Palestine in Crisis: The Struggle for Peace and Political Independence after Oslo* (London: Pluto Press, 1995), 68–72.

[25] The titles I have given to each category reflect the themes that my informants articulated. None of my interlocutors used these exact terms to describe their positions; rather, the terms capture the distinctions that I saw emerging as I contrasted their discourses with one another.

withdrawal. Mujahida represented this reflex. For someone like Mujahida, for whom al-jihād fī sabīl illāh (the struggle in the path of god) became a total life-orientation, the new environment of Oslo raised the problem of how to remain true to self. The present period, marked in her mind by the naked pursuit of self-interest, called for a moment of inward retreat. The struggle now was for the Palestinian soul. On one side were former Intifada activists who had become caught up in a self-deluding "politics" (*al-siyāsa*) that made fair seem foul and foul, fair. On the other were those who remained faithful to god's path, to al-jihād fī sabīl illāh:

> I have no faith in anything that comes under the label of "politics" [al-siyāsa] . . . I hate this word. In the name of politics, all of our rights and possessions and land have been sacrificed. So that [America and Europe] will see that I am reasonable [*mutafahhima*] and democratic and god knows what, I have to do the opposite of what I know to be true and right. [But], I refuse to follow the law [of self-interest]. I derive my law from my religion [*min khilāl dīnī*] so that I might be faithful and true to the people.

Against the "siyāsa" (politics) of the Oslo period, which involved "deception and betrayal," Mujahida called for a return to sharīʿa politics, a politics marked by "jihād," the pole of authenticity. Mujahida's concept of sharīʿa politics quite possibly derived from Ibn Taymiyya (d. 1328), an important intellectual reference point for contemporary Sunni Islamists throughout the Middle East. Along with Hasan al-Banna and Sayyid Qutb, the writings of Ibn Taymiyya are widely available across the Middle East in bookstores that cater to Islamist sensibilities. In an important tract titled *Al-Siyasa al-shar'iyya* (Administration [according to] the Religious Law), Taymiyya argued that the caliphate had no utility and, indeed, no real Islamic legitimacy beyond the first four leaders after Muhammad, the "Rightly Guided Caliphs"—Abu Bakr, ʿUmar, ʿUthman, and ʿAli. With the disappearance of this first generation of Muslims, the umma, the Islamic "community," became the repository of authority. This authority was symbolized in the sharīʿa. On the basis of the sharīʿa, the umma contracted leadership with rulers, with the understanding that the primary responsibility of political authorities was to implement the provisions of the divine law. The ʿulamāʾ, or scholars and guardians of the sharīʿa, served as mediators between the faithful and their ruler. The ruler needed to support and facilitate the activities of the ʿulamāʾ as part of his duties of enforcing divine law. The umma and their scholarly representatives, moreover, retained the right to dissolve their contract with the ruler if he failed to fulfill these duties. All that was needed was the formation of a consensus among the faithful on the necessity of change. By echoing Ibn Taymiyya's insistence on placing authority within the umma and relegating governance to its needs and dictates, Mujahida drew on a deeply embedded notion of legitimate political authority within Sunni Muslim culture to advance an alternative communal conception of politics, one that contrasted starkly with the authoritarian-patrimonial style of ʿArafat and his Palestinian National Authority. Against ʿArafatism, Mujahida asserted the primacy of the umma and its tradition of consultation, consensus, and contract.[26]

Implicit within this distinction was the right to withdraw *bayʿa* (the oath of allegiance traditionally given to the caliph by the ʿulamāʾ on behalf of the umma) in the case of a corrupt ruler. Whereas the ʿulamāʾ during the medieval period generally counseled against rebellion, viewing it as leading to the grave sin of *fitna* (civil war, chaos), modern Islamist intellectuals such as Sayyid Qutb retrieved and developed the activist implications contained within the contractualist tradition for the umma's right to dissent and rebel. This retrieval represented a significant departure from the settled tradition of the medieval scholars, a tradition that viewed politics skeptically and sought to preserve Muslim unity by counseling obedience even in periods of political repression and corruption. Contemporary Islamists have openly rejected this tradition of quiescence and have done so by invoking the Qurʾanic notion of al-jihād fī sabīl illāh (struggle in the path of god). This concept of jihād, however, is susceptible to multiple interpretations. It can validate not only armed struggle but also a nonviolent, cultural one or even a highly personal, internal effort to lead a pious life. "Modern" Islamists move along this continuum in response to shifts in the objective conditions of power and opportunity. Mujahida is a case in point. In locating jihād within the inner self and associating it with the act of seeking after truth, Mujahida slid along the semantic range in an effort to reconfigure the meaning of "struggle in the path of god" during a period in which continued militancy was becoming increasingly difficult to sustain. Some Qurʾanic interpreters have distinguished between the "lesser jihād" and the "greater jihād." The distinction derived from an address attributed to the Prophet in which he told his followers after the conquest of Mecca in 630 that the physical struggle to establish Islam, the lesser jihād, was completed and that they should now focus on the inner effort, or greater jihād, to create moral selves and societies.[27]

[26] I draw my summary of Ibn Taymiyya's concept of "sharīʿa politics" from Frederick Mathewson Denny, *An Introduction to Islam*, 3rd edition (Upper Saddle River, NJ: Pearson Prentice Hall, 1994, 2006), 204–205. On the quietism of the medieval tradition and the novelty represented by contemporary Islamist approaches to politics, see L. Carl Brown, *Religion and State: The Muslim Approach to Politics* (New York: Columbia University Press, 2000).

[27] On these issues see Ahmad ibn al-Husayn al-Bayhaqi, *Kitab al-sunan al-kubra* [Book of the Major Traditions], as cited in Martin Lings, *Muhammad: His Life Based on the Earliest Sources* (London: Unwin Hyman, 1983, 1986, 1988), 330. On classical juridical and Sufi

In moving from the extrinsic "lesser" to the intrinsic "greater" pole, Mujahida revised the meaning of jihād in a way that enabled a morally consistent response to the challenges of the post-Oslo period. While armed jihād against Israel was becoming impracticable in the present context, the inner jihād to transform hearts and minds was still possible and indeed incumbent upon all believers in a time when the pursuit of self-interest reigned supreme. Mujahida drew a direct parallel between the current period of backsliding and the Prophet Muhammad's early struggles against unbelief in Mecca. Unable to impose the new order, he sought instead to purify himself and his followers of polytheistic practices and to remain personally committed to the larger principles of a god-centered umma. Drawing the parallel, Mujahida commented:

> The most important thing for me right now is not only how much I am concerned to remain true to my faith but also that I am not simply thinking of myself, only. This is an extremely difficult form of jihād. . . . It is hard not to lose one's principles, to lose one's soul [*akhsar al-nafs*].

The social-spiritual fraying in post-Oslo Palestine manifested itself in very specific ways for Mujahida and other Islamists. The signs of deterioration included the bars, nightclubs, loud restaurants that served alcohol, big and boisterous weddings, satellite TV that beamed in North American sitcoms and steamy Latin American soap operas, and the new casino in Jericho that the Palestinian National Authority had established to generate tax income and employment.[28] Shaykh Taqi al-Din, the Hamas leader and village mosque preacher, linked these developments to Palestinian National Authority policies that supposedly aimed to sup-

---

conceptions of jihād, see Rudolph Peters, trans. and ed., *Jihad in Mediaeval and Modern Islam: The Chapter on Jihad from Averroes' Legal Handbook 'Bidāyat al-mudjtahid' and the Treatise 'Koran and Fighting' by the Late Shaykh-al-Azhar, Mahmūd Shaltūt* (Leiden: E. J. Brill, 1977); John Kelsay, *Islam and War: A Study in Comparative Ethics* (Louisville, KY: Westminster/John Knox Press, 1993); Majid Khadduri, *War and Peace in the Law of Islam* (Baltimore: The Johns Hopkins University Press, 1955); Mustansir Mir, "*Jihad* in Islam," in *The Jihad and Its Times*, eds. Jadia Dajani-Shakeel and Ronald A. Messeir (Ann Arbor, MI: University of Michigan, Center for Near Eastern and North African Studies, 1991); Rudolph Peters, *Islam and Colonialism: The Doctrine of Jihad in Modern History* (The Hague: Mouton Publishers, 1979); Abdulaziz A. Sachedina, "The Development of Jihad in Islamic Revelation and History," in *Cross, Crescent, and Sword: The Justification and Limitation of War in Western and Islamic Traditions*, ed. James Turner Johnson and John Kelsay (New York: Greenwood Press, 1990); Annemarie Schimmel, *Mystical Dimensions of Islam* (Chapel Hill, NC: University of North Carolina Press, 1975), 112. See also David Cook, *Understanding Jihad* (Berkeley, CA: University of California Press, 2005).

[28] The Palestinian National Authority restricted the casino to Jewish and Western tourist clientele. Anticipating criticism, it strictly forbade Palestinians from going there to gamble and drink. These polices were described to me on separate occasions by two unrelated Palestinian men who worked at the casino.

press the Intifada resistance activities by providing opiate-like diversions. During the Intifada, the Palestinian populace would listen to the radio and watch TV only to get news about the Uprising and learn about planned actions. Today, these media peddled mind-numbing sitcoms. The new work and leisure opportunities were like a drug that stopped people from thinking about their anger and dissatisfaction. The Intifada had been a time of struggle and suffering. There was a unity of purpose and seriousness about life. Oslo had undermined all this, according to the shaykh.

The rising materialism and concomitant loss of principles and social unity were, in the view of my Islamist interlocutors, directly threatening to the very foundations of society and its most central pillar, the family. This linkage emerged prominently in the criticism that Mujahida directed at the secular women's movement. The women's movement was her primary competitor in the field into which she had shifted her activism. Mujahida had established a center that provided child care, domestic income-generation projects, and health services for women, especially wives of prisoners and widows of men who had been killed in guerrilla operations. Her center also sought to cultivate Islamic virtues within its clients through weekly lessons (*durūs*, sing. *dars*) on Qur'an and *aḥādīth* (sing. *ḥadīth*: sayings attributed to the Prophet Muhammad).

In Mujahida's view, through the self-serving logic of self-realization and personal "liberation," the secular women's movement had eroded the complementary nature of male and female roles that had been the basis of social unity since the rise of Islam. The consequence was a loss of security for women and a weakening of the general social structure, as children ceased to receive the nurturing and moral education that women traditionally provided:

> Palestinian women, in particular, and Muslim women, in general, have always been known for their ability to sacrifice [for] their children, their husband, their family, their society, and their people. But, the movements that seek to liberate women tell them, "You have to be independent, to rely on yourself! You have to go out and get a job!" Of course, it is not wrong to go out and work; but don't leave your children behind. I know many women who smoke cigarettes and cross their legs like men and talk to you about the liberation of women. But, you find their houses uncared for and crisis ridden.

For Mujahida, the crisis of corruption and disorder in Palestinian society was the result of a loss of fundamental social values at multiple levels. Secularist demands for liberation were false and destructive of social unity. They resulted in selfishness, abandonment of families, and crisis-ridden homes. To end the chaos, women needed to return to their natural and Qur'anically established functions as childbearers, home keepers, and educators of the next generation.

The dangers of secularism extended, in Mujahida's view, to the legal structures of society as they were emerging in the Oslo period. The push for secularized personal-status laws was leading to state intervention in the once sacrosanct affairs of the family. The Model Women's Parliament of 1998 exemplified the threat.[29] Participants in the Parliament, she recounted, "tried to pass laws for us that said, 'I have the right to travel on my own without my husband's permission'; and, 'if my husband hits me, then I have to be able to take him to court.' " Mujahida agreed there was a need to hold men accountable for domestic abuse but argued that state mechanisms created more problems than they solved. She proposed the "traditional" patriarchal model of marital arbitration set forth in the Qur'an:

> In Islam, it is written, "And if you fear a breach between them twain (the man and the wife), appoint an arbiter from his folk and an arbiter from her folk. If they desire amendment, Allah will make them of one mind. Lo! Allah is ever Knower, Aware."[30] The family will always be more sensitive in dealing with problems between a man and a wife. The police, however, will be more bureaucratic [*mihniyya*—literally, "professional"]. They will focus on the fact that there is a complaint, and they will record it in their files and that will be that. When I go to the police, I have introduced a foreign element into my life.

Family mediators, Mujahida presumed, would act justly because they had the best interests of the aggrieved parties at heart. The state would intervene without this knowledge and concern and impose solutions in line with an external and impersonal legal logic and political interest that would end in fracturing the family. Contrary to the view of advocates of women's liberation, as Mujahida portrayed them, it was the family as underwritten by sharīʿa custom, and not the individual as such, that was sacrosanct and required protection.

Despite her emphasis on the autonomy of the family, Mujahida did see the need for an overarching state structure. She conceptualized this structure, however, in personal-patriarchal terms. The state was the family writ large. Its authority was grounded in the sharīʿa, and its leaders, ideally, possessed a god-fearing piety (*taqwā*) that ensured the same kind of wisdom that families exercised in arbitrating disputes. The sharīʿa pro-

[29] A consortium of secular women's groups organized the Parliament in response to what they perceived as a lack of progress in the Palestinian Legislative Council in codifying personal-status laws that enshrined civil and democratic rights. See Rema Hammami and Penny Johnson, "Equality with a Difference: Gender and Citizenship in Transitional Palestine," *Social Politics* (Fall 1999): 327–329.

[30] This verse is from Q 4:35. Unless otherwise indicated, English renderings of quoted Qur'anic passages come from Mohammed Marmaduke Pickthall, *The Meaning of the Glorious Koran* (New York: Penguin Books, n.d). For the Arabic original, I have consulted *Al-qur'an al-karim* [The Glorious Qur'an] (Saudi Arabia: Majmaʿ al-Malik Fahd li-Tabʿat al-Mushaf al-Sharif, n.d.).

vided the baseline standard from which women could argue their rights. Women, however, were generally ignorant of the sharīʿa, and men applied it selectively to suit their interests. The problem of women's oppression was one of cultivating a correct understanding of sharīʿa along with a deeply rooted taqwā that would ensure correct application of the law:

> If someone said to me, "You should give up your right to your father's inheritance and let me control your affairs," I would say, "What do you mean? God, *subḥāna wa taʿālā* [glorious and supreme], wrote in the Qurʾan that I have a right to this. How can you subvert my rights? I will not allow you to do so! I will only give you my rights if I want to." So, in this respect it is not wrong for a woman to defend her rights. But, the problem comes when she no longer knows what she wants. We talk about the Western model or the Chinese model. . . . We are like a patchwork dress [*badla imraqqaʿa*] made of fragments from here and there. We have left behind our ʿādāt wa taqālīd [customs and traditions] and our *dīn* [religion] and become muddled.

From Mujahida's perspective, the revitalization of the sharīʿa would actually empower women. It would secure women's place in the home by holding men accountable for their conduct according to authentic religious stipulations and long-established customs. Contrary to secularist assertions, these customs (the sharīʿa and the ʿādāt wa taqālīd, for example) would not stifle women's ability to pursue careers outside the home. They would allow women to work if they first fulfilled their domestic duties or if they faced dire circumstances such as poverty or war. The sharīʿa was practical and flexible, responding to the contingencies and needs of individuals while always upholding the ideal of a family-rooted society. Mujahida's own life course bore this out:

> I'm the director of this place. My husband is in prison, and he has twelve more years before he gets out. I don't have any kids, but I am the guide [*murshida*—a term that Sufis use to refer to a spiritual master] for the nursery school here [at her center]. What I can't give to my own kids I can give to others in the [nursery]. I am a person who has the ability to produce so why not do so? You see Islam is not against women working. But, Islam considers my work as a woman a type of hardship or toil. We find this brought up in the stories of Adam and his wife. [Because they listened to Satan] god imposed work on the two of them, but the toilsome, difficult labor [*shiqqa*, pl. *shiqāq*] was placed on the man's shoulders.

Work outside the home, in Mujahida's gloss of the Qurʾan, was a hardship imposed primarily on men; it was, however, sometimes necessary for women to take up this burden, especially in times of war:

> The Prophet, on him be prayers and peace, once said that if an enemy invades and occupies the lands of Islam, then the wife must rise up against the

attacker in the place of her husband and the servant must resist in the absence of his master. Everyone must fight occupation for the sake of preserving freedom and existence. When they come to take my boy from my house, or my brother, it is as if they have attacked us all. They have violated the boundaries of the home and entered.

Under the circumstances of Oslo, however, the situation had changed. Even though the occupation continued, fellow Muslims and citizens were now partially in control, and so to resist violently was potentially to initiate a civil war.[31] Individuals like Mujahida therefore had to adjust their notions of struggle. Mujahida turned inward. She set aside her role as guerrilla fighter and embraced the persona of social reformer and surrogate mother through the work of her organization, The Islamic Women's Purity Society. Mujahida's center was a space within which the corruptions of the secularizing post-Oslo society were kept at bay. Within its confines, women learned the ethic of self-abnegating care for others, especially children and husbands. In doing so, they "guarded their souls" against the corrosive impact of individualism, feminist and otherwise. The center's services—day care, marketing needlework and home-baked goods, and so forth—were attempts to make more viable the family-based, patriarchal social order it recommended to its clientele. The nation, for Mujahida, was figured in the center. It was a model of the just and good society, one based on an authentic, religiously mandated ethic of self-help. In returning to this ethic, Palestinians would regain the moral unity and purpose they required if they were ever to achieve the liberation they so intensely desired.

Al-jihād fī sabīl al-siyāsa: The Struggle for Politics

In sharp contrast to the inner-looking orientation that Mujahida advocated, my informants manifested two other types of response to the constriction of the Islamists's political operating space. These responses were oriented more toward an external political overcoming of the threats to the society and Islam than toward an internal cultural reordering and reinforcement of the Islamist milieu (as figured in Mujahida's perspective). I have labeled these orientations *al-jihād fī sabīl al-siyāsa* (the struggle for politics) and *al-jihād fī sabīl al-thawra* (the struggle for the revolution). Two events featured particularly prominently in the discourse of

[31] The Arabic term *fitna* [civil dissension] carries connotations of treason and treachery. In addition to the historically strong Palestinian insistence on preserving national unity, Islamic religio-political thought has universally condemned civil conflict ever since the bloody internecine wars that accompanied the early succession struggles during and after the period of the first four caliphs.

the individuals who represented these approaches: (a) the Palestinian Legislative Council elections of 1996, and (b) the skyrocketing stature of Hizbullah following the withdrawal of Israeli forces from southern Lebanon in June 2000. The Hizbullah victory yielded dual implications: On one hand, it seemed to justify entry into parliamentary politics. Hizbullah held seats in Lebanon's legislative assembly and declined to set up an independent sphere of control in the south following Israel's withdrawal. On the other, Hizbullah proved the efficacy of armed struggle as a means to forcing Israel out of the zones it had occupied militarily and establishing Islamic governance in a freed Palestine.

The Legislative Council election, for its part, presented Islamists with the dilemma of whether to join in the Oslo Process as political parties or refuse participation on principle. Opting for participation risked undermining Islamist credibility, especially if the peace process failed. It also risked alienating the armed elements that supported a more militant line. Opting out of the election, however, carried an equally great risk because public opinion overwhelmingly backed the idea of an election. In the end, Hamas and Jihad fudged their positions. They refused to participate as formal parties but allowed individual members to stand for election as independents. The tactic failed in the short term. Fatah solidified its legitimacy, and the legitimacy of the peace process, by winning a landslide victory, while the Islamists lost ground in public opinion polls. In opting out, the Islamists were attempting to position themselves should Oslo collapse. But, because this eventuality was not certain at the time, they tried to find a way to avoid lending support to the peace process through participation, while at the same time keeping their options open for a future political role should the peace process somehow succeed in achieving the baseline national aims—that is, full Israeli withdrawal from the territories occupied in the 1967 war, Palestinian statehood, and the return of the refugees. One significant outcome of this equivocating was the launching of Hizb al-Khalas (the Salvation Party) by advocates within Hamas of an electoral transition. Although the Hamas leadership prevented the party from formally contesting the elections, the formation of the party signaled the movement's potential future readiness to operate within the emerging democratic structures of Palestinian politics.[32]

[32] On these issues, see Jamil Hilal, "The Effect of the Oslo Agreement on the Palestinian Political System," in *After Oslo: New Realities, Old Problems*, ed. George Giacaman and Dag Jørund Lønning (London: Pluto Press, 1998), 121–145, and Hroub, *Hamas*, 220–229. See also Glenn E. Robinson, "Hamas and the Islamist Mobilization," chap. in *Building a Palestinian State: The Incomplete Revolution* (Bloomington and Indianapolis, IN: Indiana University Press, 1997), 169–173, for a cogent analysis of Hamas's attempts to hedge its bets in the post-Oslo period, and Shaul Mishal and Avraham Sela, *The Palestinian Hamas: Vision, Violence, and Coexistence* (New York: Columbia University Press, 2000), 138–146.

Abu Hasan, an Islamic Jihad activist in his late thirties who spent twelve years in Israeli prisons for Intifada activities, illustrated the tendency advocating party-political transition. He argued that in the wake of the 1996 Palestinian Legislative Council elections the Islamist movements had, of necessity, to develop constructive platforms from which to contest the plebiscitary legitimacy that Fatah had gained. The Islamists needed to engage in an "issues-based politics" that would generate mass participation at the civil and political levels. Up until now, Palestinian politics had been based on loyalty to the faction and its dictates and its leaders. One was either with ʿArafat or Shaykh Ahmad Yasin, or one was against them, for example; and if you were against them, then you faced a struggle for power and authority. It was clear to Abu Hasan that Fatah would never be able to defeat Hamas and Jihad; conversely, Hamas and Jihad were not powerful enough to displace Fatah as the central force in Palestinian politics. A faction war would be too debilitating and discrediting for both sides.

In contrast to the old factions-based politics, Abu Hasan wanted Islamists to reach beyond their social-political milieu to engage the broad range of organizations active on refugee and labor issues. He himself served on the board of a leftist organization in the Bethlehem area that advocated for refugee rights and opposed a number of Palestinian National Authority policies. By cooperating with such groups, the Islamists could begin to create cross-faction alliances around the common concerns of specific populations—the refugees, textile workers, teachers, and so on. A good model for this was Hizbullah in Lebanon. Hizbullah forged alliances with other political and nationalist forces around the common goal of ending the Israeli occupation. It contested elections and controlled seats in the Lebanese Parliament. After its victory against the Israelis and the South Lebanese Army, it declined to set up an autonomous area under its control and instead deferred to the Lebanese government and its army in working out truce arrangements with the United Nation along the still disputed border.[33] Hizbullah showed no sign of wanting to establish an Islamic state through force of arms. On the contrary, it was actually a model for overcoming secular-nationalist/Islamist divisions. In contrast to the Taliban in Afghanistan, Hizbullah provided a progressive, open concept of society in which all groups, including women, could realize their potential.

Such sophistication gave the Islamists an ability to interact with groups across the social spectrum. They utilized dialogue, not brute force, to

[33] It should be noted that even as Hizbullah declined to set up an autonomous zone in the south, the Lebanese national government is by and large absent, institutionally, in the Shiʿi areas. Hizbullah is thus the de facto, if not de jure, authority in the south.

Figure 7. Beyond religion: the right of return. This photograph shows murals and graffiti in a Bethlehem-area refugee camp during 1999–2000. The key symbolizes the door keys that refugees carried with them as they fled their homes in 1948. These keys have been passed down through the generations as a reminder of the fundamental desire to reverse the dispossession that made the refugees homeless in the first place. The number "194" is a reference to the U.N. resolution that calls for the repatriation and compensation of the refugees. Author's photograph.

advance their concerns. Abu Hasan pointed to himself as an example. As a board member of a leftist refugee advocacy group, he frequently engaged his secularist colleagues on religion. There was an atmosphere of tolerance. His colleagues never harassed him about his commitment to keeping the prayers, and he reciprocated by displaying tolerance, especially toward female employees who dressed in attire he did not approve of.[34] This had been Hizbullah's model, too:

> When Hizbullah established itself in Lebanon in Baʿlabakk (Baalbek) and the south, the girls would wear short skirts and nothing on their heads. The movement didn't confront them and force them to cover up. They educated them about what was *ḥarām* [forbidden] and *ḥalāl* [permitted] in Islam; they never imposed anything on them through violence.

[34] It would be easy to dismiss Abu Hasan's description of his openness toward his leftist-secularist colleagues as generous self-justification. How open was he, really? There were

Abu Hasan wished to see the Islamic movement develop this essentially progressive, open outlook to become more fully integrated into and thus more capable of shaping wider Palestinian politics. But for this to happen, fundamental changes needed to occur in how this politics was currently organized. As with other Arab regimes, Fatah and the Palestinian National Authority acted arbitrarily and violently against opposition forces. Islam provided a radically different alternative. The Islamic state, as he conceived it, would base its laws on the sharīʿa while also making space for non-Muslim minorities within a democratic constitutional framework:

> The Islamic state will be a modern state, a state of laws. It will have a constitution that establishes and guarantees these laws, and these laws must be in accord with the spirit of the Qurʾanic injunctions. What about non-Muslims? Islam addresses this from the beginning. It is true that the official religion of the state will be Islam. But, there can be exceptions in the law [as in allowing Jews, Christians, and atheists to buy and sell alcohol in restricted areas and run their own schools]. These exceptions can provide safeguards for the daily lives of non-Muslims. There is a basic injunction in the Qurʾan that all Muslims must obey: *lā ikrāha fī al-dīn* [Q2:256: There is no coercion in religion]. [We must remember that] god created us within *shuʿūban wa qabāʾil* [nations and tribes, cf. Q49:13].

Abu Hasan expanded on this ideal by linking it directly to democratic practice. The Islamic state he envisioned would come about through plebiscitary measures, not force:

> First, we need a parliament. No basic law can be put into place without a parliament. So, first of all, the parliament, a real parliament that truly represents the Palestinian people from below through a pure and free election. Moreover, a parliament requires a constitution, one that guarantees representation of all the various political forces among us through free elections. Now, if the Islamists should enter and win the majority, then they should be allowed to alter various provisions in the constitution just as the secularists over the last four years have been able to alter various provisions

---

indeed limits on Abu Hasan's willingness to accommodate divergent positions. At one point, he commented, disapprovingly, on a female colleague who came to work in the center dressed in short skirts. He did not like her choice of attire but was quick to say that he would never openly express these feelings to her. He chose to lead by example, performing his prayers quietly in a corner and answering questions about religion when asked. The secularists on staff at the refugee rights center, including the woman whose style of dress Abu Hasan disliked, all spoke of Abu Hasan in admiring tones, saying he was an Islamist who listened to them and who conveyed a comparatively open and progressive vision.

> through the majority that they control. If real democracy were to be practiced not one Islamist would resist it. Now, there are aspects of mistaken thinking in Islamist ideology in Palestine, the main one being the idea of personal rule by a single individual. Perhaps an Islamic state will come into existence, but if it does I want it to have a constitution and to be based on the rule of law.

Abu Hasan's democratic perspectives reflect a fundamental refashioning of Islamist ideology in the direction of a secular multiconfessional nationalism. First, he reads the Qur'an as constituting a multisectarian order as a fundamental dimension of the creation. God created *shuʿūban wa qabā'il* (nations and tribes). Second, Abu Hasan's embrace of the democratic process entailed a sharp criticism of Islamist conceptualizations of authority that placed trust and power in a single individual, a caliph. Supposedly, this would be no better than what now existed under ʿArafat. Finally, in accepting the logic of a *Palestinian* democracy, Abu Hasan reduced the universal horizon of Islam to the confines of the territorially bounded nation-state and the play of competing political interests within that entity. Islam thus became simply one more political program on offer within Palestinian electoral politics. This move shifted the basis of Islamist political legitimacy. Not divine fiat but "the people" would now decide if Islam was indeed the solution.

Al-jihād fī sabīl al-thawra: The Struggle for the Revolution

In contrast to Abu Hasan's democratic Islamism, a third response among my Islamist interlocutors to the constraints of the post-Oslo context sought to reconstitute the Palestinian "revolution" by reigniting the global campaign for the *khilāfa* (caliphate). The main stress of this orientation was on reviving the armed struggle against Israel. Among my respondents, Ibn Fadlallah made the most impassioned case for a revolutionary turn. A tall, imposing, and yet jovial figure, he had broad shoulders, powerful arms and hands, a bit of a paunch, a bushy beard (with streaks of gray) reaching down to his collarbone, and closely cropped, graying hair. When I visited him in his home, he smiled widely, revealing lost molars and crooked lower incisors. He reached out his hand, welcomed me in a strong bass voice, and led me into a sitting room that featured pictures of Ayatullah Khomeini and other Iranian leaders. In one of the photographs, Khomeini was leading a group of men in prayer in a wooded area. A small, wallet-size photograph of Ibn Fadlallah was wedged into the corner of the frame that held this picture.

On another wall, I noticed a small brass plate with a laminated depiction of the Dome of the Rock in its center.[35] The room itself was painted yellow. There were worn armchairs and couches pushed against all four walls. Carefully folded prayer rugs rested on the seats of the chairs.

Ibn Fadlallah was a committed pan-Islamist, but with an unorthodox twist. At one point in our discussion, he brought up the age-old contentious issue in ḥadīth scholarship of whether all the *ṣaḥāba* [the Companions of the Prophet] were on an equal level, arguing strenuously against the notion of equivalent status. Tradition had made into ṣaḥāba, he stressed, people who may have seen the Prophet only once or from a distance while on a pilgrimage to Mecca, say. But these people, obviously, should not be viewed as having the same authority as those who were closest to the Prophet, among them the Prophet's family, since it was these latter individuals who associated directly with him, observed and noted his ways, and were most intimately involved in the struggles of the early community.

Yet to privilege the Prophet's family was implicitly to affirm the Shiʿi idea of the descent of Muhammad's charismatic authority through ʿAli to his descendants, the Imams. This idea undercut the Sunni principle of consensus as the basis for the caliphal succession.[36] Aware of how his remarks might be taken, Ibn Fadlallah carefully went on to say that he considered himself to be neither Sunni nor Shiʿi. Rather, he stressed that he was a Muslim, which he defined as one in search of truth. He respected ʿAli as among the most loyal, moral, and intelligent of the first Muslims; and he looked to ʿAli's son, Husayn, who was killed at Karbala in 680 C.E. as he led an ill-fated uprising against the Umayyad ruler Yazid, as the model of true Islam. "Husayn internalized the revolution [*thawra*—a term that came from the P.L.O.'s secular-nationalist lexicon of the 1970s], he lived it completely, was totally committed to it until death," he said. As we were talking, automatic rifles burst out in a firecracker staccato. I ducked, instinctively. "It's the wedding over there," he said. A deep laugh rumbled from his chest, his bearded face widening into a bemused grin.

Ibn Fadlallah's positive regard for Imam Husayn, the central symbol of uncompromising commitment and self-sacrifice for Shiʿa Muslims, revealed how his Islamist turn had come to reshape his core nationalist com-

[35] Depictions of the Dome of the Rock were common in Palestinian Muslim homes. Such displays reinforced connections to Jerusalem and expressed a shared national consciousness that transcended the divisions of Gaza Strip and West Bank, city dwellers and villagers, rich and poor, and so on. Christians, too, projected attachment to Jerusalem: they often displayed photographs of the city that featured not only the Dome but also Christianity's holiest shrine, the Holy Sepulcher Church.

[36] The vast majority of Palestinian Muslims are Sunnis.

mitments. Husayn—and contemporary revolutionary Shiʿsm, generally—were, for Ibn Fadlallah, primarily a lens through which to analyze the failures of the P.L.O.-led struggle for Palestinian liberation. Ibn Fadlallah's first direct encounter with Hizbullah and its revolutionary reinterpretation of Shiʿa symbols such as Husayn occurred during his period of exile to southern Lebanon with 408 other Palestinian Islamist leaders in 1992–93. The high degree of personal and collective discipline among Hizbullah activists impressed him. He noted how through this discipline they had won the hearts and minds of the wider population. The Lebanese Shiʿa as a whole, he told me, were prepared for a decades-long guerrilla war against Israel, one in which heavy losses had already been incurred.

This Shiʿi preparedness brought the Palestinian situation into painful contrast. The Palestinian failure to sustain the first Intifada had been due in large part, he said, to the lack of a "revolutionary consciousness." This lack reflected a failure of leadership. Intifada activists, like himself, had imposed the Uprising by force on the petty bourgeoisie and proletariat. It would have been better, he argued, to have found ways to meet the needs of these key groups while instilling within them a deep internal commitment to prolonged struggle. The Hizbullah leadership interacted with its constituencies with respect and a very high degree of fairness and morality, by contrast. They did not abuse the farmers and shop owners. They did not come in armed gangs and demand protection money, which happened during the first Intifada as it began to implode.

Moreover, the contrast between Hizbullah and the Palestinian National Authority, the institutional successor to the Intifada, could not have been starker, he remarked. The P.N.A. had sold out. It was corrupt. It had given up the armed struggle and effectively ceded the 1948 territories. Only Hamas leader ʿAbd al-ʿAziz al-Rantisi—whom the Israeli military would eventually assassinate on April 17, 2004—had stood up and openly criticized the negotiations with Israel. For speaking the truth, the Palestinian National Authority had jailed him. The rot among the Palestinian leadership had set in long before the Oslo period, however. Already in the early 1980s, P.L.O. leaders were "riding around in chauffeur-driven limousines and living in expensive high-rises." Meanwhile, the Shiʿa activists built water pipelines, social centers, clinics, hospitals, and housing for their constituents.

The consequences of the Palestinian implosion were quite apparent in Lebanon. Everywhere he went, Ibn Fadlallah found misery and resignation:

> I traveled to Beirut and the camps there. Everywhere the Palestinians were completely defeated and depressed. Imagine that a commander in the Popular Front for the Liberation of Palestine, a twenty-eight-year veteran, a lieutenant

> trained in the U.S.S.R., told me, "Go home and feed your children!" I replied to this guy, "*In shā' allāh* we will meet in al-Aqsa [on al-Haram al-Sharif, the Noble Sanctuary, known also as the Temple Mount]." The guy said, "Go! We will never see each other again."

The sense of crisis deepened for Ibn Fadlallah the more he learned of the Palestinian despair. At one point, he addressed a group of Palestinian students at American University in Beirut. He emphasized the necessity of continuing to fight for the 78 percent of historic Palestine that had become Israel after the 1948 war. As he talked, he said his audience began to weep: "By god, they began to shudder with tears . . . you could have heard a pin drop," he told me. The root of all the misery, Ibn Fadlallah concluded, was the P.L.O.'s abandonment of its historic mission to liberate the homeland through revolutionary action. Since the 1974 Palestinian National Council meeting, the P.L.O. had been talking about accepting a national authority on any piece of historic Palestine. Palestinians rejected this idea at the time, but it became the basis for the P.L.O.'s eventual acquiescence in the autonomy idea, first set out in the Camp David Accords of 1978 and then the Oslo Declaration of Principles. Ibn Fadlallah desired a different future:

> Seeing the conditions in the camps planted within me the determination to speak out and to do whatever it took to lift the people up. . . . How does the ḥadīth [saying attributed to the Prophet] go? . . . correcting the wrong with one's tongue is the weakest form [of resistance] . . . no, [the weakest is] correcting it in one's heart. . . . Let's aim for the middle! Let's say somewhere between the hand and the tongue. I was going to do what was possible for me at that point, and that was to speak out. To do more, to seek to change things with my hands, would have meant military action and this option was beyond my possibilities at the time.

Ibn Fadlallah's rededication to the struggle was not simply a return to the old P.L.O. maximal objective of the complete overthrow of Israel. The P.L.O. had long ago lost any credibility it might have had in his eyes. His revolutionary return passed instead through the militancy of Iran and Hizbullah and the core symbols of that militancy. Iran and Hizbullah's successes had lent legitimacy to these symbols. Ibn Fadlallah adapted them to reanimate and redefine the objectives and methods of the Palestinian cause. We have seen, for example, how he recast the memory of Husayn, ʿAli's son and the Prophet's grandson, as a model of the true revolutionary.

Like the Palestinians, Ibn Fadlallah told me, Husayn and his band of followers faced overwhelming odds in their effort to reverse a historical injustice: the Umayyad usurpation of the succession to the Prophet, a succession that, in Shiʿa eyes, rightfully belonged to the Prophet's closest kinsman, ʿAli ibn Abi Talib, and his descendants. The revolt failed miserably when the Umayyad forces encircled the rebels, beheading Husayn and massacring his small band of soldiers on the plains of Karbala in southern Iraq in 680 C.E. During the Iranian revolution the annual commemoration of this event became reinterpreted as an allegory for the repressiveness of the Shah and the imperative to remove him from power by force if necessary. This activist recasting of the Karbala memory represented a fundamental revision of quiescent meanings that the Shiʿa had previously attributed to the event.[37] Drawing from this more militant reinterpretation of Shiʿi memory, Ibn Fadlallah saw Husayn as a principled revolutionary who, because he had absorbed the core dictates and spirit of the Qur'an, fought for justice in the face of impossible odds. Even in the midst of certain defeat, he resisted through speaking out or, if this was impractical, then by refusing within his heart to consent to defeat. He was, in short, a model of militancy perfectly suited to the late-Oslo conditions of betrayal and repression of "the Palestinian revolution."[38]

Ibn Fadlallah's regard for Hizbullah and the Iranians had caused him to rethink the historical divide between the Ahl al-Sunna wa al-Jamaʿa (the People of the Prophet's Way and Community, i.e., the Sunnis) and the Shiʿat ʿAli (Partisans of ʿAli, i.e., the Shiʿa) that went back to the bitter conflicts of nascent Islam:

> I am accused of becoming a Shiʿa! [But], look, I am not content with blindly calling myself a Muslim who follows only the sunna. Millions within the

[37] This quiescent interpretation derived from the concept of the occulted imām. Shiʿa scholars argued that only the imām, in his capacity as the direct political-spiritual and genetic descendent of ʿAli, Muhammad's divinely blessed, handpicked successor and closest kinsman, had the authority and capacity to rule, justly. In the absence of the imām, the Shiʿa, and especially the scholars, were to shun the potentially corrupting consequences of political power. Ayatullah Khomeini inverted this interpretation. He argued that the scholars, as the preservers of the teachings of the imām and as his earthly representatives, had a duty to exercise political guardianship on behalf of the imām. Khomeini expressed this idea in his famous dictum of *wilāyat al-faqīh* (the guardianship of the jurist). Moojan Momen, *An Introduction to Shiʿi Islam: The History and Doctrines of Twelver Shiʿism* (New Haven, CT: Yale University Press, 1985), 147–171, 184–207, 246–299, and Ruhollah Khomeini, *Islam and Revolution: Writings and Declarations of Imam Khomeini*, trans. and ed. Hamid Algar (Berkeley, CA: Mizan Press, 1980).

[38] The logic of the example that Husayn set for Ibn Fadlallah was similar to the one that underlay Max Weber's concept of "an ethic of ultimate ends." Such an ethic subordinated consideration of the consequences of action to the desired ends of that action. The moral value of the ends, however construed, outweighed whatever damage might result from the means chosen to achieve the ends. Thus, while Husayn may have known that his revolt was potentially suicidal for him and his entourage, what mattered more—at least in Ibn Fadlallah's reading of the event—was unwavering fidelity, regardless of consequences, to universal principles of right and justice. Max Weber, "Politics as a Vocation," chap. in *From Max Weber: Essays in Sociology* (New York: Free Press, 1946), 118–121.

> Muslim umma call themselves Shiʿa. Who are they? Why do they exist? The point isn't that I want to align with a particular school of thought. Rather if the truth appears for you, say, in Christianity, then you must honor your conscience and become a Christian. If in Marxism, then be a Marxist. God is the source of conscience and conviction.

For Ibn Fadlallah, conscience, via the symbols of militant Shiʿism and the concrete example of Hizbullah and the Iranians in Lebanon, had directed him back to the foundational struggles of early Islam. Palestine needed selfless, principled leaders like the Prophet, his beloved cousin and son-in-law ʿAli, and, above all, his grandson Husayn. It needed the generosity of spirit that the Iranians and Hizbullah leaders had shown him and his fellow Sunni deportees:

> Their actions spoke louder than any words. They brought us . . . better tents and wood to build beds. The [Iranian] Revolutionary Guards brought these things to us over a distance of eight kilometers over steep mountains and under cover of darkness to avoid detection by the Israelis. They also brought us an electrical generator, TVs with satellite reception, special videos about the resistance. . . . They also gave each of us five hundred dollars for our personal expenses. If anyone needed medical care, they took us to Iman Hospital in Baʿlabakk (Baalbek) or to the American University's Beirut Hospital. The Iranians were completely selfless.

Describing an incident in which he got lost, Ibn Fadlallah recounted that Hizbullah commanders had welcomed him, served him tea, and then personally escorted him back to the deportees' camp:

> They were very hospitable and spoke to me respectfully and then took me back to the area just above the camp. There they handed me over to the commander responsible for security in that area. He did not leave me until he saw me headed directly for the camp. He didn't just give me a bunch of directions but personally made sure I made it back, safely. This level of care only increased my respect for them. I felt that these were very sincere people who could actually accomplish something on this earth.

A return to this kind of solidarity and leadership would overcome history, healing the deep division in Islam and, by extension, the rips in the national fabrics of Muslim societies, especially the Palestinian one. The encounter with Palestinian despair and Shiʿa empowerment in Lebanon had led Ibn Fadlallah to a new transnational conception of Muslim identity that linked his people's struggle to a worldwide effort to revive the umma and its caliphate. For it to succeed, the Palestinian *thawra*—"revolution"—needed to become a liberationist jihād on behalf of all Islam. While Ibn Fadlallah's adoption of Shiʿa symbols and discourse was a highly idiosyncratic one within his heavily Sunni Palestinian milieu, his admiration for what Iran and Hizbullah had accomplished reflected a wider, shared sentiment. Since the outbreak of the al-Aqsa Intifada, Hizbullah flags have appeared in Palestinian demonstrations; and Hizbullah has openly praised the Uprising and sought to associate itself with it through its propaganda.

CONCLUSION

The emergence of Islamism in Palestinian society represented a generational shift in the political identities of activists who, in earlier eras, would have aligned with one of the P.L.O. factions. The basis of this shift lay in events that radicalized the Islamist milieu, particularly the 1979 Iranian Revolution, Israel's 1982 invasion of Lebanon, and the first Intifada of 1987–93; it also lay in the parallel Islamist networks that, like the P.L.O. factions, provided integrating structures for groups crossing into the professional and middle classes. The subsequent fracturing of P.L.O. hegemony produced intense competition between the secular-nationalist and Islamist milieus; it also led to ideological subdifferentiation as activists crossed over faction boundaries, bringing with them orientations forged elsewhere. The incorporation of proto-Islamist activists from the secular-nationalist milieu reinforced the nationalist reorientation of the Islamist milieu. In Simmelian fashion, these activists carried their nationalism into Islamist circles, integrating it into their new religio-political orientations.[39]

At the individual level, P.L.O. nationalists became Islamists for a variety of reasons: disillusionment with what they saw as corruption in the factions after 1982 and most especially following the signing of the Oslo Accords and the establishing of the Palestinian National Authority; dissatisfaction with the turn toward negotiations and acceptance of a two-state solution that accompanied these events; a closer link to the traditional ideals and practices that had structured their family life during childhood; a perception that Palestinian society was rapidly trading in these ideals and their supporting structures for the empty promises of "women's liberation," self-fulfillment, and the naked pursuit of individual greed; and the appearance of viable Islamist-nationalist options. Taken together, these factors pointed to a pervasive sense of crisis. Secularism was seen as a corrupting force that undermined the unity of the

[39] Georg Simmel, "The Web of Group-Affiliation," chap. in *Conflict and the Web of Group-Affiliations*, trans. Reinhard Bendix (New York: Free Press, 1955), 125–195, describes the formation of diverse social milieus and their crosscutting interaction and influence on one another through the multiple, overlapping affiliations that any given individual will possess.

nation and its liberation cause by attacking the key foundational institutions, especially the patriarchal family. In making their Islamist turns, the activists who joined Hamas and Islamic Jihad sought to stem the corrosion by performing a double return: a re-turning of society toward a sharīʿa-governed, neopatriarchal order and a reorientation of Islamist identity as a preeminently nationalist one. A key part of this twofold revision was the redefinition of the fight against Israel as a cosmic struggle to overcome the enemies of god without and the forces of corruption within.

In the new, more militant Islamist perspective, the liberation of Palestine was the necessary first step in the effort to revitalize the umma, the transnational Muslim community. The priority placed on Palestine's liberation was a significant departure from established Islamist orthodoxy. As Andrea Nüsse has observed:

> On the question of nationalism, *Ḥamās* makes an even more innovative and unorthodox move away from Islamic thought of the past. The Palestinian fundamentalists discarded the old incompatibility between Islam based on ideological grounds and the Western idea of the nation-state which is based on territorial claims: "Fatherland (*waṭan*) and nationalism (*waṭaniyya*) are (. . .) part of the Islamic creed." . . . As Palestinian nationalism is considered part of the Islamic creed, to give up any inch of Palestine would mean abandoning a part of the creed. . . . [The] forefathers of the Islamist movement, Hasan al-Banna and Sayyid Qutb, never developed any theoretical basis for this. Mawdudi explicitly condemns any "national or racial vanity."[40]

Nüsse notes further that Banna, Qutb, and Mawdudi viewed the end of struggles for independence to be not the nation-state but rather the transnational umma. The ideological statements of Islamic Jihad and Hamas, however, de-emphasize "this 'rhetoric.' . . . [N]ationalism and the defence of a territorial homeland seem to have become more acceptable with time." She comments further that, for these groups, not only has nationalism become more acceptable, but also "the question of Palestine is . . . preeminent in shaping the future of the Islamic *Umma*." Palestine, within its boundaries as conceived under the British Mandate, is the essential core of the umma. Without its liberation and establishment as an independent nation, there would be no revival of the transnational Islamic community: "the control over Palestine announces control over the world."[41]

Yet Islamism in the Palestinian setting faced unique sociohistorical circumstances that set in motion a process of internal ideological and struc-

[40] Andrea Nüsse, *Muslim Palestine: The Ideology of Hamas* (Amsterdam: Harwood Academic Publishers, 1998; reprint, London: Routledge Curzon, 2002), 49–50. Nüsse quotes from Hamas's covenant and Abu al-ʿAla al-Mawdudi, *Tafhim al-Qur'an*.

[41] Nüsse, *Muslim Palestine*, 50.

tural differentiation. By 1999–2000, Islamists had begun to diverge on what "the control over Palestine" implied and how to achieve that control, however understood. A key catalyst of this internal differentiation was the persisting vibrancy of the secular-nationalist milieu. Far from disappearing, the secular nationalists remained strong, indeed dominant as the Oslo Process instituted itself and Fatah consolidated its grip on power through the Palestinian National Authority. The Oslo Process thus resulted, for the opponents of Oslo (the Islamists, primarily), in the narrowing of what sociologists term the "political opportunity structure." Miltant jihād on behalf of national liberation became increasingly untenable as the new P.N.A. security services and regulatory apparatuses began tightening the noose around dissenters, principally the Islamist groups. The elections of 1996 further isolated Islamic Jihad and Hamas. Under these conditions, activists at all levels within the Islamist milieu began revising their orientations to explain the shifts that had occurred and to mark out new paths of action. The process generated multiple responses among my informants. Mujahida illustrated one type of response—a shift from an expansive, militant outlook to an inward-looking orientation. She diagnosed the Palestinian condition as a spiritual one that required the re-forming of inner dispositions. Ibn Fadlallah, by contrast, called for a revitalization of pan-Islamic militancy. Unlike Mujahida, he remained very much rooted in his primary identity as an activist-fighter. The problem for Palestinians in the Oslo period, in his view, was a lack of selfless, dedicated leadership and absence of revolutionary consciousness. Husayn at Karbala and Hizbullah provided his countermodels for the way forward. Abu Hasan advocated party-political transformation. The primary problem, for him, lay not in a lack of religious or revolutionary consciousness in the society but rather in the absence of a credible opposition that could effectively contest Fatah's political hegemony within the emerging state structures. Islamism could become this kind of opposition only if it presented itself as inclusive of multiple interests and open to debate and dialogue. Significantly, such a move implied a willingness to base Islamist legitimacy on electoral tallies and not on the stigmata of heroic suffering, or on inherited patrimonial right, as with the caliphs after Muʿawiya, or on the intrinsic justice of the Qur'anic call. This shift toward a disenchanted criterion of authority implied a secularizing reconfiguration of the Islamist outlook.

In the post-Oslo period, thus, Islamist identity, like the secular-nationalist one, was very much in flux. Generational processes, the differential impact of the Oslo Process on the political opportunity structures of the competing milieus, and the creative adaptations of key symbols and discourses by activists across the political-cultural spectrum had shaped contrasting and contesting tendencies and subtendencies that continued to evolve as the tensions between Islamists and secularists remained unresolved and indeed intensified under the conditions of state formation. At stake within and between the two milieus were the core issues of identity and domination. To what extent would Palestinian society and a Palestinian state be based on the sharīʿa and the personal-patriarchal ideal of caliphal rule? To what extent would they be revolutionary or democratic and pluralist in nature? The debate played out within and between the milieus, but it became especially sharp among yet a third critical constituency, the refugees—the group that stood to gain or lose the most in any final peace settlement.

CHAPTER FOUR

Thawra Camp: A Case Study of Shifting Identities

THIS CHAPTER, and the one that follows it, explore in detail how the process of rearticulation and reformulation of milieus and identities has worked among Palestinians living in two refugee camps, one pseudonymously called Thawra in the Bethlehem area in the West Bank and the other, Karama, in the heart of the Gaza Strip. Focusing on refugee camps yields two analytical advantages. First, as a group, refugees have historically comprised the core constituency of the Palestinian national movement. It has been their experience of dispossession and expulsion in 1948 that Fatah and the P.L.O. appropriated and thematized in defining the content and goals of Palestinian nationalism from the mid-1960s onward. And it has been from the refugee camps that the national movement has drawn many of its leaders and fighters. The camps, especially those in Gaza, also provided the seed and soil for the Islamist movements. It has been in the camps that the most bitter of battles between the secularist and Islamist forces have occurred. The analysis of camp settings thus focuses attention on a key constituency and how secularists and Islamists have "crossed circles" within this group as part of the process through which individuals articulate and rearticulate their identities.

Second, an emphasis on refugees highlights the generational aspect by eliminating economic and social class as a determining factor. Refugee families, by and large, share the same type of social background. They have also undergone a shared process of proletarianization as they became integrated into day wage labor in Israel post-1967; and they have experienced, equally, the status transitions, however truncated, that resulted from access to specialized training and university education during the past three decades. The issues separating individuals within these settings, thus, have less to do with class-based interests and more to do with competing value orientations. The differences among these orientations reflect the presence of diverse, overlapping milieus, the development of generational distinctions in response to the conditions of persistent political upheaval, and the creative acts of symbolic/discursive reinterpretation by individuals located within and across these generational and milieu settings.

The contrast between Thawra and Karama is important. Refugees in the Bethlehem area inhabit a highly urbanized and cosmopolitan zone with relatively easy access to Jerusalem and Tel Aviv—at least, that is, until the recent al-Aqsa Intifada and the construction of the barrier wall.[1] Gazans, by contrast, have been much more cut off from the rest of the world because of the accident of their geographic location and the far more stringent enclosure that resulted from the construction by Israel of walls and fences along Gaza's entire perimeter. These sociophysical differences between the West Bank and the Gaza Strip have correlated, as the case studies will show, with contrasting cultural and political dynamics. The refugees in Gaza who are featured in the next chapter, for example, tended to define their differences by deploying the symbols and discourse of the "customs and tradition" (*al-ʿādāt wa al-taqālīd*). In the West Bank camp, the lines appeared to get drawn much more in terms of a perceived conflict, as leftists put it, between a "progressive" secular outlook and a "regressive" religious one, or, as the Islamists preferred to

[1] In response to the sharp spike in Palestinian-initiated "human bombings" against Israeli civilian and military targets, the Sharon administration implemented the policy of building a "separation/antiterrorism fence," in Israeli parlance, or an "apartheid/annexation wall," in Palestinian terms. (The "barrier" is both a massive concrete wall with gun turrets in some place and an electrified fence in other areas.) The sections of the barrier that exist have been built within the West Bank, encircling cities like Qalqilya, Tulkaram, and Bethlehem, cutting through Palestinian communities in Jerusalem, and dipping deep into other Palestinian areas to ensure incorporation of Israeli settlements on the de facto Israeli side of the boundary. While Israelis argue that the barrier is a temporary measure that aims to prevent "human bombers," Palestinians charge that it is a tool unilaterally to annex land in the West Bank and to impose a permanent border. The Israeli human rights monitoring organization, Btselem, estimates that the wall will result in the appropriation of approximately 16.1 percent of the West Bank and will affect the lives of some 490,000 Palestinian individuals. The legal status of the wall has been brought into question, recently, as well. The International Court of Justice (I.C.J.) issued an Advisory Opinion on July 9, 2004, that declared the wall to be in contravention of Israel's responsibilities as an occupying power as determined by a host of international treaties, including Article 2, Paragraph 4, of the U.N. Charter and U.N.G.A. Resolution 2625 (XXV) on the inadmissibility of the acquisition of territory through force as well as the Hague Convention and the Fourth Geneva Convention concerning the protection of civilians in times of war. Just prior to the I.C.J. ruling, on June 30, 2004, Israel's High Court of Justice determined that the proposed route of the wall violated the principle of proportionality and ordered the rerouting of the fence to ease the impact on Palestinians. The current proposed route follows the "Green Line" (the 1948 armistice line) more closely but nevertheless will continue to be built within the West Bank. Meanwhile, the barrier's impact remains immense. In the cities and towns that lie along its route, farmers are cut off from their fields, and children and parents must cross through long, slow-moving lines at checkpoints to get to schools and jobs and hospitals. According to the U.N. Development Program, poverty rates have increased dramatically in these communities. Alongside the barrier, Israel has continued to build and expand settlements and construct Israeli only roads to connect these colonies with the major Israeli urban centers. The combined effect of these policies has been to create what

say, an artificial Western orientation and an authentic Islamic one; yet even in this setting, during the late-Oslo period, milieu boundaries were shifting as activists selectively adapted the symbols and narratives of the competing orientations to produce new identities that creatively integrated religious and secular-nationalist themes. Ten years after the first Intifada, what it meant to be secularist or Islamist appeared not to track evenly with milieu location or faction membership.

SETTING, INSTITUTIONS, AND ETHOS OF THAWRA CAMP

Thawra sits on a dusty hillside that turns to mud in the winter rains. Established in 1949 as a U.N. aid distribution point, the site, approximately four hundred acres, slowly became a built-up tenement of small concrete and corrugated fiberglass-roofed houses haphazardly stacked on top of one another. The buildup occurred organically as expanding families transformed tents into one-room hovels and then into the present-day multistoried structures. In 1997, Palestinian Central Bureau of Statistics (P.C.B.S.) reports put the community's population at approximately four thousand residents.[2] As in other camps, a web of narrow

---

Israeli anthropologist Jeff Halper has called a "matrix of control," the purpose of which is to dominate as much territory as possible in the West Bank while isolating the main Palestinian population centers. Btselem, "Separation Barrier," http://www.btselem.org/english/Separation_Barrier/Index.asp; International Court of Justice, "Advisory Opinion: Legal Consequences of the Construction of a Wall in the Occupied Palestinian Territory," http://www.icj-cij.org/icjwww/ipresscom/ipress2004/ipresscom2004-28_mwp_20040709.htm; "Israeli Supreme Court Judgment Regarding the Security Fence" (HCJ 2056/04) http://www.jewishvirtuallibrary.org/jsource/Peace/fencesct.html and http://www.israelemb.org/articles/2004/June/2004063002.htm; Jeff Halper, "The Key to Peace: Dismantling the Matrix of Control," http://www.icahd.org/eng/articles.asp?menu=6&submenu=3; Ray Dolphin, *The West Bank Wall: Unmaking Palestine* (London: Pluto Press, 2006); United Nations Development Program, "UNDP Calls for Immediate Action to Address Emergency Needs of Palestinian Communities Affected by Israeli Separation Wall," http://www.papp.undp.org/undp_papp/pr/wall.htm. On my use in this note of the term "human bombers," as opposed to "suicide bombers" or "homicidal bombers," see Ivan Strenski, "Sacrifice, Gift and the Social Logic of Muslim 'Human Bombers,'" *Terrorism and Political Violence* 15, no. 3 (Autumn 2003): 1–34.

[2] The official figure has been altered somewhat to protect Thawra's anonymity. The P.C.B.S. estimate accounts for residents of ten years and older who, at the time of the survey, were living within the camp's confines. By contrast, the tally of the U.N. Refugee Works Agency (U.N.R.W.A.) doubles the P.C.B.S. number. The U.N.R.W.A. statistics include all actual residents of the camp as well as individuals who have moved out of the camp to surrounding communities or who are now living abroad. Palestinian Central Bureau of Statistics, *Population, Housing, and Establishment Census—1997, Final Results, Population Report, Bethlehem Governorate, First Part* (Ramallah, Palestine: PCBS, May 1999).

roads and alleyways connected the different sections of the community. During the winter, the rains washed garbage and sewage down the crumbling asphalt. In the summer, the muddy alleys turned to baked dust.

At the camp's main entrance, two roads split instantly from each other. One branch forked north and then east while the other spurred to the south and then also east. In both directions, the roads climbed immediately up the steep incline to which the camp clung. The road to the north passed the central mosque. Farther on, as it turned east up the incline, a second mosque built during the first Intifada by Islamist activists nestled amidst a tightly packed collection of homes. This second mosque operated a summer day camp, child care, and a preschool and provided religious instruction and school tutoring for children. In the opposite direction, down the hill from the mosque, lay a cultural center that was established by former activists of the Marxist faction, the Popular Front for the Liberation of Palestine. This center sponsored a "*dabka*" dance troupe that had performed in Europe and the United States.[3] It also supported an Internet computing center, a library, a day care, a range of after-school programs for youth, and a new hostel for international volunteers. One of its projects utilized the electronic World Wide Web to link the community's children with their peers in other refugee camps in Lebanon as well as with non-Palestinian youth in other countries, including Israel. The Islamist-oriented preacher at the mosque up the hill criticized the center for allowing boys and girls to mix together in its activities and for undermining camp institutions, particularly the family, by exposing youth to "immoral" foreign influences.

Thawra's other main institutions included two primary-through-preparatory United Nations schools, one for boys and the other for girls, a U.N. clinic and social center, two additional mosques, the elected camp committee that coordinated with the Palestinian National Authority, and the various political factions, particularly the Popular Front, the Communists, Fatah, and Hamas. The leftists were the dominant force. They controlled key social and political committees and organizations in the camp and had done so consistently since the 1950s. A mural at the camp's entrance depicted the figure of Ghassan al-Kanafani, a writer of short stories and a leading figure of the Popular Front for the Liberation of Palestine up until his assassination in Beirut, apparently by undercover Israeli commandos, on July 8, 1972. With the arrival of the Palestinian National

[3] *Dabka* is a line dance that was performed in villages during festive occasions, especially weddings. Political factions, through their "cultural" work, have revived the dance as an expression of authentic Palestinian life rooted in the pre-1948 past. This revival has led to the further elaboration and stylization of dabka. Nationalist symbols (e.g., the checkered scarf, or *kūfiyya*, and the long embroidered dress called *thawb*, also artifacts of the peasant past) and patriotic music have become integrated into these performances.

Authority, however, Fatah had become an increasingly influential force. The Islamists established a small presence in the camp in the early to mid-1980s, the same period in which, in Gaza, the Islamic Jihad emerged and the Islamic Collective was becoming more politically assertive.

As a refugee community, Thawra defined itself principally in opposition to the middle and upper classes of Bethlehem City to the north. By shared taxi or bus, it was a fifteen- to twenty-minute trip from just below Manger Square in the city's center to the camp's main entrance. The route passed under the ostentatious Italianate villas that had recently sprung up on overlooking hillsides. The white marble mansions with their terra-cotta roofs contrasted starkly with the crowded tenements of Thawra and the other two refugee camps in the Bethlehem area. Such sharp visual distinctions reflected the dichotomies that shaped the terms that town and camp residents used to describe one other. If one was from the camps, one was *fallāḥī*, of "peasant" origin. My late landlord, an electrical engineer and a Christian, once used this term to explain to me why he never drank tea or coffee or ate with the refugees from the camp across the street from our building. Despite exchanging greetings with them every morning, the refugees remained for him "fallāḥīn" (peasants, sing. fallāḥ), a categorically incommensurate social class. A member of the landowning and professional middle class, he simply did not mix socially with the *lāji'yyīn* (refugees).[4]

Thawra Camp residents inverted these distinctions in their own conception of the refugee/town-dweller dichotomy. They saw themselves both as the victims of social discrimination and inequity, a source of resentment, and also as the vanguard of the Palestinian national revolution, a point of pride. The resentment often came out during my taxi rides from Bethlehem to Thawra. On one such occasion during the fasting month of Ramadan, a time among pious Muslims for taking stock of wayward ways and renewing commitment to Islam's moral requirements, my driver commented: "These days, no one cares about heaven . . . there's so much cheating and corruption." I responded that it was understandable if people resorted to less than ethical means in times such as these in which money and jobs were scarce. "But there's plenty of money

[4] That the refugees were Muslims was of less significance. Muslims came to the lunch held after my landlord's untimely death and funeral in spring 2000. These Muslims, however, were of an equivalent urban, middle-class background. Moreover, being displaced was equally of no import. My landlord's widow was herself a refugee. Her parents and aunts and uncles were once wealthy landowners in the Jaffa district prior to 1948. They lost everything in the war when they fled their homes to seek shelter with family in Bethlehem. What mattered in the refugee/town-dweller distinction, hence, was not so much whether one had been displaced but rather whether or not one's family came from a sharecropper or small, subsistence-farming background as opposed to a landowning or educated professional one.

around," he shot back. "Just look at all those houses up there!" He pointed out the big, gleaming villas on the sunlit hillside to the left. "Just look at the palaces and the Mercedes limos," he went on. "Those people who control the Sulta (the Palestinian National Authority) are making out like bandits." One of the passengers in back cautioned the driver to be more circumspect. You had to be careful with your opinions in these times, he said; you never could know who was listening and what might get passed on to someone else. The driver protested that he was "a straight talker," simply telling it like it was. Bitter soliloquies on social perfidies peppered my conversations with people across the social spectrum in 1999–2000. In a taxi headed for Thawra, these discussions took on the added dimension of local class and status-group tensions. To be a refugee in Bethlehem was to remain a landless social outsider still condemned fifty odd years after the *nakba*, or "disaster"—the term Palestinians use to refer to the events of the 1948 war—to life in a crowded camp. The sense of deprivation and displacement that pervaded camp identity reconstituted itself in the daily encounters of camp residents with a sociophysical topography that featured an increasingly sharp contrast between opulent villas and cramped tenements.

At the same time, however, being a refugee was also to claim special honor: the refugee, not the "bourgeois" town dweller or the newly arrived, limousine-driven P.N.A. official, was the pulsating heart of the Palestinian national cause. For refugees, the Palestinian narrative was fundamentally the story of expulsion and the dream of return and restitution. Moreover, it was the camps that had provided the bulk of the battlegrounds and fighters of the liberation struggle. The litany of massacres in Lebanon rang with the names of Tal al-Zaʿtar and Sabra and Shatilla. The first Intifada and now the second one, the al-Aqsa Uprising, had seared the collective Palestinian consciousness with the names of other camps—Jabalya, Rafah, Balata, Jenin, and "Thawra."

The themes of resistance and suffering that coursed through refugee narratives were symbolically enshrined at the main entrance to Thawra. There, two memorials recalled the community's heroism and losses during the first Intifada. The first monument was a tall, metal turnstile gate with a Palestinian flag draped over it. The gate was the sole remnant of the massive chain-link and barbed wire fence that once spanned the entire length of the camp. Constructed by the Israeli army in 1985, its ostensible aim was to prevent the stoning of Israeli settlers, who, prior to the construction of separate Israeli-only bypass roads in the 1990s, raced their cars up and down the Jerusalem-al-Khalil (Hebron) highway to and from Jewish colonies in the southern West Bank. Situated as it was on a hillside, Thawra overlooked the road. Activists easily rained rocks down on the yellow-plated settler cars bolting by at breakneck speeds.[5] For this reason, the Israeli army built its fence several meters high, giving Thawra the look of a prison camp. The turnstile at the front of the camp became the sole pedestrian entry and exit for residents and a useful choke point for the army whenever it imposed curfews on the community. In 1995, following the installation of the Palestinian National Authority in the Bethlehem area, residents tore the fence down, leaving only the turnstile in place. Once a symbol of humiliation and repression, the gate now stood, for camp residents, as a testament to the community's heroic perseverance during the occupation.

The second memorial was a huge stone rendering of the entire territory of historical Palestine, including what is considered today Israel proper, as it was demarcated under the pre-1948 British Mandate. The sculpture went up soon after the arrival of the Palestinian National Authority, with funds from both the Authority and the camp community. The monument rested on a raised concrete platform at the mouth of the main road that led into the camp. A commemorative plaque at the base explained that the structure was a memorial to all camp residents who had been killed during the first Uprising. In such depictions, memorials, and monuments, the message was clear: Thawra, and all refugees, were the heart of the national movement. It was their suffering, their narrative of displacement, and their demand for return that gave the nation its purpose and unity despite any divisions.

Yet divisions did exist, splitting refugee identity in multiple ways. Despite its reputation as a leftist stronghold, one of the sharpest divides in Thawra lay between secularists and Islamists. The divide formed in the mid-1980s just as the Islamist movement was beginning to expand its network and move toward greater militancy in the Gaza Strip and, increasingly, in the West Bank. The event that marked the definitive emer-

[5] Israeli vehicles carry yellow license plates. Up until the arrival of the Palestinian National Authority in 1994, Palestinian cars from the West Bank bore blue plates with differently colored tags and Hebrew lettering that indicated the specific region in which a vehicle had been registered. Gaza cars had white or silver plates with similar regional indicators. The color coding aided the Israeli military in segregating the Israeli and Palestinian populations, especially at checkpoints. Ironically, the system also helped Intifada activists in targeting settler vehicles. But sometimes the distinctions were not so clear, since Palestinian residents of East Jerusalem, which Israel had unilaterally annexed immediately after the 1967 war, also drove cars with yellow plates. In the instance of East Jerusalemites, during the Intifada, Palestinian identity was signaled by placing a checkered *kūfiyya* head scarf on the dashboard while driving in the West Bank. At Israeli checkpoints, this identity could be concealed by quickly removing the scarf, thereby increasing the chance, it was hoped, of not being stopped and asked for identification. After 1994, the color of Palestinian license plates in those areas controlled by the new Palestinian National Authority changed to green.

gence of Islamist-secularist animosity in Thawra was a 1985 riot between Popular Front and Muslim Brotherhood partisans. The confrontation featured knifings, rock throwing, and Molotov cocktails. Several people were seriously injured, and one family at the center of the conflagration was forced to leave the camp. The Muslim Brotherhood meeting center was burned to the ground, as well. The Popular Front, by most accounts, won the fight, reestablishing its prestige as the main force in the camp.

The reasons for the violence were highly contested and varied. A Popular Front activist who took direct part in the violence—a man I will call Abu Tha'ir—blamed the Islamists. He claimed that activists from the Islamic Association, the Muslim Brotherhood front organization in the camp, got hold of a picture of Che Guevara and drew donkey ears on it. They also apparently disfigured images of Lenin, making the Bolshevik leader look like a cow. The pictures were distributed at the Islamic Association's meeting center. Word spread quickly, and Popular Front activists raided the center to confiscate the offending pictures. During the raid, the trespassers "accidentally" caused a copy of the Qur'an to fall from a shelf. The raiders, according to Abu Tha'ir, failed to notice what they had done and left the building without returning the book to its original location. The next day, Muslim Brotherhood activists publicly accused the Popular Front of desecrating the holy book and produced more caricatured pictures of Guevara and Lenin that were then torn, trampled, and strewn in the camp alleys. "They purposefully exploited the Qur'an thing to provoke a fight," Abu Tha'ir argued.

Events intensified quickly. According to Abu Tha'ir, knife-wielding Brotherhood henchmen attacked a Popular Front leader. Popular Front toughs retaliated by chasing down the assailants and returning the favor. This counterattack led to an all-out riot. The fighting also spread to the Bethlehem University campus. By this point, Abu Tha'ir told me, the secular-nationalist leadership of the camp had decided that the Islamic Association needed to be put out of business. The organization, he explained, had violated the sacrosanct rule against undermining camp unity (and, by implication, challenging secular-nationalist dominance). The center was burned down because "they were to blame," Abu Tha'ir concluded, adding, "I am sure Shaykh Abu Banna [the *imām* of the mosque just up the hill from the leftist cultural center] was behind it. . . . There is a good chance that he was working for the Israeli intelligence services."

Shaykh Abu Banna had a quite different perspective on the events. He placed the shoe of treason on the leftist foot and portrayed Islamist motives in a much more positive light:

> *Al-jam'iyya al-islāmiyya* [the Islamic Association] . . . tried to tell the camp leaders that we were not putting forward a political position. But they im-

> mediately assumed that any social action or social expression in the camp had to reflect the agenda of a party or faction. . . . Of course, maybe the Israeli *mukhābarāt* [intelligence services] encouraged them, or sent their spies to tell them that one of the members of our association had threatened some of the members of the Al-Azraq family [an alias for one of the well-known clans in the camp that supported the left]. We tried to distance ourselves from the tension and bring an end to the issue. [After the violence] we rebuilt our association from the bottom up. We tried to learn from the mistakes and what went wrong. We have continued to try to help people gain a religious-nationalist understanding [*fahm dīnī waṭanī*] of Islam, not a religious-chauvinistic or fanatic understanding [*mish fahm dīnī taʿaṣṣubī*]. Of course, religion does not create intolerance and fanaticism; social conditions do. Muslims live under siege here from every side.

Two basic themes defining the Islamist-secularist dynamic emerged in this account. First, the shaykh portrayed the initial Islamist activism as social and cultural, not political. This interpretation coincided with the dominant antinationalist and cultural-activist orientation of the Muslim Brotherhood prior to the first Uprising. Yet while the defacing of Lenin's portrait may have been, for the Islamists, an attack on the cultural values of *secularism*, such an action could not have been taken as other than a political challenge by the leftist movements. In attempting to reshape the basis on which authority was made legitimate in Thawra at the cultural-symbolic level, the Islamic Association was engaging in a long-term project that aimed at gradually undermining secularist authority in the camp. Second, the shaykh described the Islamists as pure in motive and under siege. It was the left, by contrast, that may have been collaborating with Israel to defeat a challenge to its entrenched leadership. The shaykh was at pains to cast Islamists as patriots. After the 1985 disaster, the Islamic Association worked to inculcate a "religious-nationalist orientation" among its members. Such an emphasis reflected both the radicalized, nationalist shift that Hamas's emergence during the first Intifada forged within the Islamist milieu and the need to take account of, and counter, the persisting accusations of treason.

There was yet another important perspective on the 1985 conflagration, and it came from a grandmother who was legendary in Thawra for her Intifada activism and longtime membership in the Fatah faction. She interpreted the 1985 clash as a feud between individuals that escalated into a clan conflict pitting an outside Bedouin community against camp families and factions:

> It wasn't a factional thing at first. It was an issue between individuals. One of them, it turned out, was working with the Israeli intelligence. The other side included X, Y, and Z. They were all friends at first but then they began

> to have differences, god only knows about what. Each side began rallying their allies and the problem got bigger. The problem really became huge when people started bringing in others from outside the camp. Some of them brought people from Taʿamara [settled Bedouin renowned prejudicially for being clannish and aggressive]. The leadership in the camp could not allow interference from outside like this. Fatah's *shabāb* ["guys," young male activists] got involved and said they would not allow the Taʿamara people to interfere by writing on the camp walls, harassing our young women, and generally stirring people up. They surrounded X's house and ended up throwing a Molotov at it. But, the main point was that this was a feud between individuals, not a factional thing, at first. "The organization" [*al-tanẓīm*, i.e., Fatah] only got involved to stop the conflict from spiraling out of control. It stopped the violence and investigated things. X and his family were expelled from the camp.

Imm ʿAli's narrative was distinctive in two respects. First, it emphasized the individual and clan-based nature of the conflict over and against the factional and religious element. In Thawra, and not just in Thawra, political identity was inherited: one was Popular Front or Fatah or Hamas because one's siblings or parents had aligned with these groups and had passed these affiliations down—hence, individual and family disputes could quickly draw in the factions either as partisan supporters or third-party mediators. The narrative also stressed Fatah's role as reconciler. Fatah alone intervened, investigated, and worked out a solution accepted by everyone. Here, in dramatic form, was the classic Fathawi claim: only Fatah could represent and reconcile the nation to itself.

The variegated and contradictory accounts of the 1985 clashes reveal the importance of the secularist-Islamist divide to the definition of identity in the camp, but they also show how this tension had become interwoven with other types of division, especially familial ones. Identity in Thawra could thus take on multiple variations as individuals negotiated the demands of competing social circles. A closer look at the backgrounds, mobilization experiences, and conceptions of solidarity among Thawra's residents will show how individuals forged a range of contrasting identities by reformulating the received narratives embedded within different mediating institutions, especially families, as well as within the competing secular-nationalist and Islamist milieus.

SOCIAL BACKGROUNDS OF THE INTERLOCUTORS

Thawraites, regardless of their religious and political orientations, shared a common history of externally imposed and violent transition from subsistence agricultural life to proletarianized wage labor in the wake of the 1948 and 1967 wars. Beginning in the 1970s, with the development of the universities, Thawraites, as a group, also underwent a degree of professionalization. Yet the capital accumulation necessary for refugee families to climb out of the camp confines and into the middle classes was still lacking. While some families had achieved this transition, the vast majority of camp residents who had attained postsecondary education of one sort or another consistently confronted structural obstacles to employment in their professional fields.[6] The primary block came from the Israeli military occupation policies that had prevented the emergence of a strong and independent Palestinian economy. The policies had actually resulted in the structural "de-development" of Palestinian economic life.[7] Consequently, Palestinians in the refugee camps faced two choices for work: day wage labor in the Israeli construction, agricultural, and service sectors, or emigration to Gulf countries such as Saudi Arabia and Kuwait. With the collapse of oil prices in the 1980s and early 1990s and the choking off of work opportunities in Israel beginning with the first Intifada, Palestinians suffered severe economic decline as unemployment rates skyrocketed. Structural underemployment shot up, as well.

For each of my interlocutors, the peasant past was actually quite recent. The parents or grandparents of my interviewees were, prior to 1948, farmers and sharecroppers who, in the wake of the war, sought shelter either with extended family or in U.N. refugee camps in the Bethlehem-Jerusalem-Ramallah corridor. Born near to or after 1967, most of my respondents among the Intifada generation entered the day wage labor market in Israel or became professionals—teachers, social workers, nurses—in local schools, hospitals, and U.N. institutions. Those who entered the professions were able to do so because other, usually older, siblings and parents had devoted their incomes to the education of a younger child. This younger child was then expected upon graduation and employment to help provide for the rest of the family. Maya Rosenfeld has labeled this process a "work chain."[8]

[6] Maya Rosenfeld, "Power Structure, Agency, and Family in a Palestinian Refugee Camp," *International Journal of Middle East Studies* 34, no. 3 (August 2002): 523. In the camp that she studied, Rosenfeld estimates that among twenty-five to forty-year-olds approximately 35 percent of all males and 25 percent of all females had achieved postsecondary education. She comments that nevertheless "only a relatively small part of the educated and professionally qualified were absorbed in suitable jobs in the local labor market, predominantly in the teaching and nursing professions."

[7] "De-development" is Sara Roy's term. Sara Roy, *The Gaza Strip: The Political Economy of De-development* (Washington, DC: Institute for Palestine Studies, 1995).

[8] Rosenfeld, "Power Structure, Agency, and Family in a Palestinian Refugee Camp," 521.

Work chain strategies had two main effects. First, they often resulted in the postponement of marriage of older siblings. For women, this delay sometimes led to a degree of independence and empowerment even though daughters who worked by and large remained socially and materially dependent on their families. The freedom from family that work bestowed was constrained by the expectation that sibling workers would contribute their incomes to the general family budget. Secondly, work chains, in combination with the unrelenting and immiserating conditions of occupation—conditions that undermined the development of state and civil society structures that might have mitigated the family's centrality—enabled inherited patriarchal authority patterns within families to persist despite proletarianizing and professionalizing trends.[9] Even in younger two-income families, basic patriarchal arrangements remained intact. This phenomenon cut across both the secularist and Islamist milieus. Against this background, the tensions between secularists and Islamists appeared to have more to do with the quality, or form, of the resilient and evolving patriarchal structure of social relations in the camp rather than with the patriarchal structure per se. The question for camp residents was whether Thawra should self-consciously model itself according

[9] Ibid., 521, 538. By "patriarchal," I mean a structure of social authority within which men, usually older men, monopolize public prestige and power, and women's social honor and life opportunities derive from child rearing and maintenance of the domestic sphere. During the occupation, the emergence of political factions and the revaluing of social honor according to one's record of resistance—measured, for example, in time spent in prison or becoming wounded in an action—tended to undermine age-based factors in the patriarchal arrangement. Younger male activists increasingly found themselves being thrust into positions of authority as community arbiters and leaders after being released from prison. Moreover, during the initial period of the Intifada, popular committees, headed by younger nationalist leaders, increasingly supplanted family and clan-based authority structures. The mass imprisoning of male heads of families contributed to the undermining of patriarchal arrangements by forcing women suddenly into the role of breadwinner and family head. Yet these changes proved temporary. Patriarchal norms were resilient, especially as Islamist forces gained greater legitimacy in the wider society and the Palestinian National Authority, in a bid to counter Islamist influence by currying the favor of *ḥumūla* (clan, pl. *ḥamāʾil*) groupings, increasingly deferred to traditional authority figures in the regulation of community disputes. On the impact of the Intifada on patriarchal structures, see Julie Peteet, "Male Gender and Rituals of Resistance in the Palestinian *Intifada*: A Cultural Politics of Violence," *American Ethnologist* 21, no. 1 (1994): 31–49. For analyses of how secular-nationalist forces failed to develop a progressive, antipatriarchal social alternative, see Rema Hammami, "Women, the Hijab, and the Intifada," *MERIP* 164/165 (May–August 1990): 24–28, and Salim Tamari, "Left in Limbo: Leninist Heritage and Islamist Challenge," *MERIP* (November–December 1992): 16–21. On the complex relationship between the Palestinian National Authority and ḥumūla groups, see Joshua Hammer's account of how, in 1998, the prosecution and punishment of a so-called honor killing among the Taʿamara, a settled Bedouin community on the eastern edge of Bethlehem, was handled, in *A Season in Bethlehem: Unholy War in a Sacred Place* (New York: Free Press, 2003), 47–52.

to a religious patriarchalism that resituated and reinterpreted the ʿādāt wa taqālīd (customs and traditions) within a revitalized Islamic framework or whether it should adopt a "liberal" orientation that accommodated a plurality of lifestyles within the limits of the patriarchal "customs and traditions" (understood, in this instance, to be the handed-down conventions of the peasant past whose content and form were more "cultural" than "religious"). How one answered this question did not always track with the faction or milieu to which one belonged.

The complex and varying overlap of patriarchal and liberal orientations in the Islamist and secularist milieus became apparent in the life histories of activists situated in two separate generational groups. One group became politicized in the 1970s and early 1980s; the other, during the first Intifada. Their stories revealed not only the impact of different events—an artifact of contrasting temporal locations—but also the effects of several other interacting factors, including gender, access to education, integration into day wage labor, and diverging experiences of integration into either the secular-nationalist or Islamist milieu. Khadija, a longtime local Popular Front leader, illustrated the impact of these factors on women during the decade immediately following the end of the 1967 war. The structural shifts that shaped Khadija's life produced a basic tension between the new social roles afforded by work in the Israeli market, membership in the emerging P.L.O. factions and faction-based labor unions, and the continuing force of patriarchal norms at home. Born in 1957, Khadija was a single woman who served as a social worker for the U.N.-sponsored women's centers in the southern half of the West Bank. In 1999–2000, at the age of forty-three, she continued to live with her family of origin—a grouping that comprised her elderly mother and two sisters.[10] Her two brothers, both of them married with children, lived next door and directly across from her. During the workweek, Khadija dressed in trim nylon slacks, short, practical pumps, a matching dress jacket, and a white button-down collared blouse. Sometimes she wore a vest that she had decorated with a traditional red and black needlework pattern. She wore no scarf on her head and kept her hair cut short. A black leather briefcase completed her professional look. By contrast, her mother wore a *thawb*, a black or white ankle-length dress with stitched needlework patterns on the breast and along the

[10] Rosenfeld argues that "the family has appropriated the period of spinsterhood (and bachelorhood) from its working daughters (and sons), in the sense that the latter were prevented from converting economic resources into social independence, and to the extent that the status of being unmarried, of being single or on one's own, was denied value. Therefore, although far-reaching changes have occurred in the realm of education and employment of women in Dheisheh, these changes have not been accompanied by similar changes in the domain of social relations within the family of origin." Rosenfeld cites the

sides. Older women of fallāḥī (peasant) background most often wore this garb. Her mother also wore the *shāsha* ("screen"), a long, gauzy white scarf that fallāḥī women used to cover their heads.

Khadija came close to marriage in the 1980s. At the time, she was collaborating closely with a fellow Marxist Popular Front activist who was from a town within the 1948 armistice lines—the area that had become Israel, de facto. Khadija broke off their engagement when it became clear that her husband-to-be would insist on her quitting her job and taking up the role of a housewife: "At first he agreed that I would continue working and we would share the house responsibilities," she told me, "but then after a week he began insisting on certain restrictions, like leaving my job and staying at home."

Khadija was the oldest of four girls and two boys. After becoming a refugee in 1948, her now-deceased father started work as a day laborer in the local agricultural economy. After 1967, he found a low-paying job with the Israeli-controlled Bethlehem Municipality. He continued to travel to Jordan during this period to work in the annual harvest there as a temporary hired hand. His income was meager, and so the family was forced to subsist for several years in a one-room shack that the United Nations had helped them build. Khadija's mother performed occasional domestic labor but largely stayed at home. The family's tight economic circumstances forced Khadija into the Israeli labor market just as she was completing the third preparatory level (roughly, the ninth grade)—the maximum limit of the available U.N. schooling in the camp. In 1970, at the age of thirteen or fourteen, she enrolled in a U.N.-run textiles training program and then went to work in an Israeli sewing factory. The eldest brother also quit school early to work in a factory in Israel. The combined incomes of the two older siblings enabled the family to build additions to their single room and to educate the younger brothers and sisters beyond the secondary level. Khadija's sisters became nurses and found work in hospitals in Bethlehem and East Jerusalem. The youngest brother—the pride of the family—completed a bachelor's degree at Bethlehem University and worked as a U.N. program officer. The first Intifada dealt a severe blow to the family's income-earning capacities as travel to and from Israel and Jerusalem became increasingly difficult and unpredictable. Khadija had to leave her sewing job. She found new work for much lower pay at an Arab-owned factory. She quickly left this job for work in a pharmaceutical workshop. By this point, how-

---

lack of professional employment opportunities, largely the consequence of the continuing occupation, and the corresponding continuing need to rely on families of origin for economic support, as the primary factors in perpetuating patriarchal modes of social control. See Rosenfeld, "Power Structure, Agency, and Family in a Palestinian Refugee Camp," 536, 538.

ever, the youngest brother was working as a U.N. employee, and his steady salary kept the family afloat.

Khadija's current employment as a U.N. program officer for women's projects evolved from her long work in the women's movement, union organizing, and activism in the Popular Front. It was through the faction—as opposed to formal education—that she underwent professionalization. She became mobilized into these structures at her workplaces. Her status as eldest child and primary income earner gave her a certain amount of leverage against the patriarchal gender norms within her family and refugee community, but it was the work for her faction that opened up new life-course possibilities:

> **K:** My only goal [in starting work in the Israeli sewing factory in 1972] was to bring in money so that we could build some additional rooms for the family. But, I got to know a lot of people and started getting politically involved. I began to travel to Nablus and Gaza to help with the organizing.
>
> *Did you face any difficulties from your family at the time?*
>
> **K:** Since I was the oldest child, my father would give me a lot of responsibilities. I would do all the errands and began to bear all the responsibility for the home. So my parents came to trust me a lot. They didn't put obstacles in front of me. Yes, there were things that I hid from them. The work I was involved in was secret. I told no one about it. I would hide my leaflets and literature in a thousand ways. . . . I did tell my father, finally, that I visited prisoners. Only he knew. At times, I would face obstacles from the society around me. People would question my parents and confront me on why I was traveling around so much. There were people from the camp who would visit their children in the prisons. So, they would question me on my reasons for visiting the prisoners. I would lie and say the prisoner I was visiting was my fiancé or my maternal first cousin [*ibn khālī*]. You had to justify to people why you were doing what you were doing. You couldn't tell them it was nationalist or political work. . . . You had to hide the real motives . . . not tell them the truth. The *mukhābarāt* [intelligence agencies] had eyes and ears and you had to be careful.

There was, in Khadija's account, a tense in-betweenness. In addition to the inherent dangers of antioccupation political work, her activism and labor outside the home represented new possibilities for social prestige and authority that undermined the regnant patriarchal conceptions of women's roles. At the same time, the received norms continued to exert pressure on her, as camp residents who saw her at the prisons suspected her reasons for being there. What was she doing there unchaperoned? Did she have a romantic relationship with an activist? Did her family know what she was doing? And, despite forging an independent career path, she never broke with her family of origin to set up a household of her own as a single woman. Patriarchal values dictated that a woman remain at home until she was married into another family. Khadija conformed to these expectations. Doing so was perhaps a financial necessity and also may have helped to deflect censure of her other unconventional activities; in either case, her accommodation served to reinforce the basic patriarchal arrangements that powerfully undergirded the camp's collective life. Khadija recognized the continuing force of patriarchal patterns, noting elsewhere in our interview how difficult it was to mobilize women into the faction-based women's groups. "We have a very conservative society here," she told me. "We had a lot of work to do to convince women to leave their homes and attend meetings. It took a lot of effort and coordination."

Whereas, for Khadija, integration into day wage labor and eventual professionalization through the secular-nationalist faction structures created tension and contradiction with, and partial undermining of, the patriarchal norms, the story of the Islamist leader Shaykh Abu Banna, Khadija's exact contemporary, demonstrated how similar processes could lead instead to a reappropriation of these same norms as part of the articulation of a revitalized religious identity. Like Khadija, Shaykh Abu Banna's parents and grandparents had been agricultural workers when they were forced out of their village in 1948. After 1967, his father spent his life as a day laborer in the Israeli construction industry. His intermittent income was insufficient to fund the education of all his children. In an inversion of the typical work chain dynamic, it was Shaykh Abu Banna's eldest sister who was the first to complete all twelve years of school and then a bachelor's degree at the new national university in ʿAmman, Jordan. She initially studied nursing but later switched to education, returning to Thawra to become a teacher. Her income supported the studies of the rest of her siblings.

Educating the eldest daughter meant that the family, comprising twelve children and two parents, had to make severe initial sacrifices. They lived for a prolonged period in only three rooms built with U.N. aid from the 1950s through the 1970s. At times, younger siblings temporarily halted their education to find work and contribute to the family income. The youngest sister, for instance, left high school early to work as a nurse's aide in a local Bethlehem hospital after the Israeli military arrested the eldest sister for membership in the Popular Front for the Liberation of Palestine. She was able to return to her studies some months later, eventually earning a college degree and becoming a fully certified nurse. Her income enabled her younger brothers, in turn, to complete their postsecondary studies.

Shaykh Abu Banna (born 1958), the eldest son in the family, studied in the scientific track during high school and went to Jordan in 1976 in hopes of pursuing a medical degree. By this time, his eldest sister had married and moved to Jordan and, having long since distanced herself from the Popular Front, was now studying Islamic jurisprudence (*fiqh*) at the University of Jordan. After failing to get into the medical program—his scores on the Tawjihi high school exit exam apparently were insufficiently high—Shaykh Abu Banna followed his sister's advice and enrolled in the university's religious studies major. He took courses in the Islamic sciences and graduated with the necessary credentials to serve as a mosque functionary. Upon his return to the West Bank, he landed a position in the *awqāf* (Islamic endowments) administration as a preacher at the al-Aqsa Mosque on al-Haram al-Sharif (Temple Mount) compound in Jerusalem's Old City. Following a series of arrests during and after the first Intifada, Shaykh Abu Banna limited his activities to Bethlehem-area mosques. During the first Intifada, he founded a mosque in his neighborhood in Thawra Camp as part of an effort to expand *daʿwa* (missionary activity) and thereby shore up the Islamist presence in the community.[11]

The professionalization that Shaykh Abu Banna underwent succeeded largely because he was able to find employment in the field in which he was trained. It remained an open question, however, whether or not his children would be able to replicate this feat. The incomes of the shaykh and his wife, who also possessed postsecondary certification in the Islamic sciences and served as a religion teacher in a local school, while steady, were nevertheless relatively meager. Moreover, they were supporting the shaykh's elderly parents. Their home, the second floor of the expanded original U.N. dwelling, was a modestly furnished apartment situated in the heart of the camp just thirty meters from the mosque that Shaykh Abu Banna had founded.

In the examples of Shaykh Abu Banna and Khadija we see how patriarchal values constrained and contributed to identity formation among those activists who emerged in the decade and a half preceding the first Uprising of 1987–93. Patriarchal patterns and structures proved resilient in responding to the proletarianizing effects of the post-1967 Israeli occupation and its policies of encouraging Palestinians to serve as cheap labor in various sectors of the Israeli economy. Even as it contested certain aspects of patriarchalism, secular nationalism, even in its most leftist forms, also implicitly accommodated, as Khadija's life course shows, the inherited structures of familial and gender authority. Islamists, by

[11] He described his work in Thawra as similar to that of the Prophet Muhammad during his early preaching in Mecca. In both instances, he implied, the message of Islam confronted a polytheistic society with an entrenched and corrupt political culture.

contrast, explicitly validated the received patriarchal arrangements; but they, too, made accommodations of their own to the secularizing impact of wage labor and modern state-sponsored education. An examination of the life paths of Intifada-era activists illustrates further how these dynamics manifested themselves and mutated under the conditions of a mass uprising and the subsequent peace process.

The persisting impact of patriarchalism on leftist secularists of the Intifada generation was detectable in the lives of three Popular Front activists. Each of these three men—all in their early thirties in 1999–2000—completed only the third preparatory level. Their desire for further education fell victim to the more pressing demands of the Uprising, extended and repeated prison time, the total, two-year closure of all educational institutions (roughly 1988–90), marriage post-Intifada, and the need to support their families. The men worked as skilled day laborers or low-paid staff in the Palestinian National Authority. One of them, for example, was an electrician who, during my research year, managed to land a better-paying job as a security guard at the new Palestinian National Authority casino in Jericho. The other two were painters who were subcontracting with Israeli bosses when I got to know them. The wives of two of these men, by contrast, held salaried professional positions in the teaching and nursing fields. One of them had a bachelor's degree from Bethlehem University.

The men took great pride in the "progressive" character of their marriages. Their wives, they pointed out to me, were free to go and come as they pleased "within limits." Shunning convention, they wore short skirts and went about unveiled. It was a point of honor for these men that their wives did not cover up like the Islamist women and that they, as families, did not observe the daily prayers and various minutiae of sharīʿa regulation. Ramadan was a secularized practice of family gathering, nothing more, just as Christmas was for the Christians. One of the men even put up a plastic evergreen tree and bought inflatable Santa Claus balloons for his three-year-old daughter during the Christmas season. Secular liberals embraced all of Palestine's customs, it seemed. They also drank whiskey and beer. Doing so was the definitive test of their break with received mores. Getting drunk for the first time coincided in the men's narratives with their first steps into the Popular Front faction as teenagers.

For married men, however, drinking was also a sign that one still maintained one's *kalima* (colloquial, *kilma*—literally, word, weight, or authority) within marriage. The men often teased me when I would demur on their invitations to go to a Bethlehem bar until after I had called my wife. They told me that I was henpecked and that I should follow their example by simply doing what I wanted to do rather than "asking permission." To be a man was to remain unfettered and in control: women were to be told what to do while men were simply to act of their own accord and whim. The example I was told to follow, however, was far less straightforward than was presented to me. At one level, it did seem that my friends had preserved their kalima in the home: when I would visit them, it would be their wives who made the coffee, produced the dinners, and made sure the children were being looked after. At the same time, however, my friends had to perform far more domestic work than they admitted to simply because their wives' work schedules demanded a more equitable distribution of home labor. Moreover, their assertions of machismo contrasted sharply with the actual inverse status relations of their marriages: in two of the cases the wives had postsecondary certifications and held jobs as professionals while the men had not progressed beyond the preparatory level at school and worked as day wage laborers in Israel. So, as in Khadija's case, patriarchal mores constrained secularist "progressive" orientations. In this instance of my three friends, patriarchalism (preserving one's kalima) actually served as a resource for reasserting male privilege in the face of challenges to that privilege that resulted from the enhanced social status of their wives.

By contrast, I encountered far less overt machismo from another male friend in his early thirties, a former Fatah activist who became an Islamist sympathizer. Majdi and his wife Amal, who was also very sympathetic to the Islamist movements, were both teachers. They did not yet have children. Both individuals expressed a desire to pursue graduate education at some point. They claimed to share the domestic labor even though during my visits it was Amal who carried out the tasks of preparing the coffee and food.[12] Majdi also explained to me that while Amal did all the cooking, he washed the clothes. Still, regardless of these elements of a less traditional arrangement, patriarchal values were very much consciously at the core of the life of this young couple. When I first met her, Amal, who wore a scarf and long coat, made a point of shaking my hand only once. She explained that she was making an exception for me as a foreigner. From that point onward we would not be able to shake hands, she told me, because "in our religion it is not permitted." It was a complex act. On one hand, the handshake itself demonstrated the flexibility and liberalness that she and Majdi claimed was typical of Islam, and of their life together as a couple; on the other, the proviso that followed the handshake was a very conscious and cre-

[12] Majdi told me that he would make the coffee when Amal's friends came for visits. I never personally witnessed such behavior; however, his assertion bears out the normative stress that this couple placed on equitable distribution of domestic labor as a sign of a more "modern" lifestyle.

ative extension of the social and religious practice of gender segregation.[13] The Islam that Majdi and Amal had implemented in their lives seemed to be a hybrid, or a bridge, between sharīʿa-based patriarchal mores and liberal-progressive ideals.

The status transformations brought on by proletarianization, education, and professionalization, as well as the continuing normative relevance of the patriarchal family structure, shaped the lives, thus, of individuals in both the Islamist and secularist milieus in Thawra. The resulting dynamics could have "liberalizing" and "patriarchalizing" effects in both settings. Majdi and Amal, who shared equivalent status as university-educated professionals, appeared relatively "progressive" by secularist standards in the structure of their domestic arrangements, while the machismo of my three left-leaning secular-nationalist friends indicated a persisting patriarchal orientation seemingly at odds with their self-professed progressivism. While socioeconomic factors help explain the emergence of these liberalizing and patriarchalizing tendencies within and across the two cultural-political milieus, they do not account for how or why individuals came to associate themselves with one milieu or another in the first place. They also leave unexplained what impact these milieu associations had on the identities of activists and how these attachments and their effects on identity could change. For this level of analysis, one must examine the events and structures that forged the particular political orientations of Thawra's residents.

MOBILIZATION: EVENTS AND STRUCTURES

The formation of political-cultural orientations among Thawraites reflected the interaction of a range of structures, processes, and events. First, by the late 1980s, the camp's sociopolitical topography had become sharply divided. The secular nationalists remained dominant, but the Islamists had become an increasingly more vital presence. At the core of these competing formations were the faction structures of groups such as the Popular Front for the Liberation of Palestine, the Communist Party, and the Muslim Brotherhood—and, subsequently, Hamas. In addition to the factions, families and neighborhood and peer groups/cliques (*shallāt*, sing. *shalla*) served as key modes of politicization. Activists formed their political orientations through interactions with their

[13] This practice manifests itself among Muslims and Christians alike in the segregation of men and women in mosques and churches as well as during social occasions (visiting at homes, wedding celebrations, and so on).

parents, uncles and aunts, older siblings, and friends. Finally, the occupation and the uprising against it, along with the subsequent peace process, reinforced, undermined, and transformed the orientations of activists in various ways.

Identity Formation in the Secular-Nationalist Milieu

The secular-nationalist ethos of Thawra Camp had its roots in the institutions that took form through the post-1948 mobilization efforts of the Movement of Arab Nationalists (M.A.N.), or *ḥarakat al-qawmiyyīn al-ʿarab*. The *qawmiyyīn* began with a group of students that formed at the American University of Beirut in 1951.[14] One of the movement's earliest steps was to institute the Committee for Resistance to Peace with Israel (*hay'at muqāwamat al-ṣulḥ ma' isrā'īl*)—a body that promoted rejection of the resettlement proposals that the United Nations Refugee Works Agency (U.N.R.W.A.) and the United States had put forward in the immediate aftermath of the war. The committee's agitation drew in new recruits and led to cell formation within the refugee camps located in the West Bank, Syria, and Lebanon. One of the main constituent groups brought into the movement comprised U.N.R.W.A. schoolteachers in these camps.[15] The movement also worked at forming youth programs and scout troops among refugees. This strategy resulted in a significant influx of student membership from the mid-1950s onward.[16] Strategically, the M.A.N. sought to institutionalize "revolutionary" Arab nationalist governments as the first step toward the liberation of the Palestinian homeland. The rise of Jamal ʿAbd al-Nasir in Egypt in 1952 and the integration of Egypt and Syria into a single entity—the United Arab Republic—six years later seemed to vindicate this approach; however, the subsequent humiliating defeat of Egypt in the 1967 war dealt a crushing blow to pan-Arabism. In the aftermath, Fatah's brand of nationalism began to grab the imagination of Palestinians, everywhere. Responding to these events,

[14] For more details on the founding of the M.A.N., see Yezid Sayigh, *Armed Struggle and the Search for State: The Palestinian National Movement, 1949–1993* (Oxford: Oxford University Press, 1997), 71–80, and Walid W. Kazziha, *Revolutionary Transformation in the Arab World: Habash and His Comrades from Nationalism to Marxism* (New York: St. Martin's Press, 1975).

[15] The rate of teacher recruitment in the camps was steep and impressive: the number of teachers in the movement's branch in the ʿAyn al-Hulwa camp in Lebanon, for instance, went from two in 1955 to forty in 1957. Yezid Sayigh, *Armed Struggle and the Search for State*, 74.

[16] Ibid.

the M.A.N. took on a much stronger "Palestine first" orientation and changed its name to the Popular Front for the Liberation of Palestine. A string of armed raids on Israeli targets at the close of 1967 heralded the group's emergence in its new guise.[17]

Two other institutionalized political forces have shaped the secular-nationalist milieu of Thawra Camp: the Communists and Fatah. The Communists, who were divided between the Jordanian Communist Party and Communist Party Organization in Gaza, had one of the better-established organizational networks in the 1950s and 1960s. Their fortunes in the West Bank suffered a major setback following the Jordanian crackdown on the left in 1966. A year after the 1967 war, they sought, like the Muslim Brotherhood, to reconstitute their networks by generally eschewing military action and focusing primarily on cultural and social activism. West Bank Communists officially broke with the Jordanian party in 1982 and joined the Communist Party Organization in Gaza—a move that resulted in the creation of the Palestinian Communist Party. The main block of its membership has tended to come from the Ramallah-Jerusalem-Bethlehem urban corridor. The party has been particularly strong in the Bethlehem area and has had a significant following in Thawra Camp.[18]

For its part, the Fatah movement began to make inroads into Thawra and other West Bank camps in the mid-1970s and 1980s—but especially after the P.L.O.'s forced evacuation from Beirut in 1982. Following its installation in 1994, the Fatah-controlled Palestinian National Authority enabled the Fatah movement to monopolize patronage and coercive power, thereby facilitating extension of Fathawi influence into areas that had once been the preserve of other P.L.O. factions. In Thawra, Fatah had, by 1999–2000, achieved near parity with the Popular Front in elections for various camp institutions.[19]

M.A.N. and Communist faction structures were the primary agents of mobilization for the generation of secular-nationalist activists that emerged in Thawra in the 1950s and 1960s. These structures and the ideological orientations associated with them often dovetailed with the political traditions of extended families. Khadija illustrated this phenom-

[17] Ibid., 75–80, 164–167, and 227–232, on how, within a little more than a year, the "leftist" wing of the movement broke away to create the Democratic Front for the Liberation of Palestine under the leadership of thirty-two-year-old Nayif Hawatma.

[18] Ibid., 167–168, 476–477.

[19] Former Popular Front leaders cited the results of the 2000 elections for Thawra's "athletic committee," in which the Popular Front managed to hold onto the majority but Fatah came in a close second. Leftists tended to downplay Fatah's rise, preferring to contrast secularists as a group with Hamas. One informant pointed to the elections for the camp's central coordinating committee, noting that the Popular Front and Fatah came through with a combined two to one advantage over Hamas among the votes cast. It should be noted that a Fatah leader headed the coordinating committee at that time.

enon in recounting the role her uncles played in her early politicization in the mid-1960s:

> All of the young men in my mother's family at the time were very involved with the Arab Nationalists [*al-qawmiyyīn*] and the Communist Party. I remember the Jordanians arrested one of my mother's brothers because of his party membership [in 1966]. I would listen to my uncles' discussions, but I didn't fully understand them. When they listened to the news, they would close the doors and windows. I didn't know what all that meant, but my uncles would give me things to do like carrying leaflets from home to home and store to store. As a girl, I would have attracted less suspicion. Maybe this was a kind of training. Maybe these kinds of things caused me to think of other possibilities in life.

Khadija's account revealed the extent to which family and faction had begun to overlap one another. Khadija became a secular nationalist partly because she was a member of a family that had become intimately interconnected with the networks and sociopolitical milieu that supported secular-nationalist traditions. She carried her uncles' leaflets, sat in on their secret deliberations, and, through this "training," absorbed their ideology of pan-Arab unity and national liberation. At the same time, however, emerging events shaped her politicization in very specific and unforeseen ways. The key occurrences, coinciding with her entry into young adulthood, included the installation of the Israeli occupation after the 1967 war and the subsequent transmutation of the Movement of Arab Nationalists into the explicitly "Palestine first" Popular Front faction.

The occupation opened up new opportunities for personal mobility and political mobilization beyond the confines of the family. In Khadija's case, integration into the Israeli labor market ironically facilitated contact and alignment with emerging Popular Front networks. Khadija entered the market as a seventeen-year-old textile worker in 1974. She recounted meeting Popular Front activists at her work site. These individuals recruited her into the early attempts at mobilizing Palestinian women through a campaign to extend health services and health education to the villages and camps. This secret work took her the length and breadth of the West Bank and Gaza Strip. In 1979, she helped found the first Women's Work Committees. She also began at this time to be a liaison to political prisoners in Israeli detention centers. During the Intifada, she helped set up a camp medical committee and worked to provide services to the elderly during the prolonged curfews and sieges. After the signing of the Oslo Accords in 1993, she began work for the United Nations as a program officer for the different women's centers in the camps of the southern West Bank. She remained active during this time as a

Popular Front leader and attended the meetings of the camp's Central Coordinating Committee—one of the few women to do so.

Family-faction networks were also crucial in the mobilization of Intifada-generation secularists, the generation that immediately followed Khadija's. The Uprising augmented the mobilizing force of these preexisting institutions by creating a new mass ethos that apotheosized political activism. For men, the entrance into manhood now occurred through stone throwing, arrest, and injury. The stories of male Intifada street fighters featured extended recollections of serial detention, torture, imprisonment, and wounding. Activists of Khadija's generation also told such stories, but they described their era as generally much more quiescent and fearful of political action. One Popular Front veteran who was severely tortured and spent several years in prison during the 1970s told me of how friends and neighbors, fearing Israeli surveillance and reprisal, shunned him after his release. In the Intifada, the collective attitude was completely otherwise: arrest and imprisonment became widely accepted badges of honor and prestige.

The stories of the three men mentioned earlier in the discussion of machismo among secularists shed light on the unique interaction of family, faction, neighborhood, and mass mobilization during the Uprising. Born in the same year, 1969, the men were childhood friends who grew up as next-door neighbors, school pals, and Popular Front comrades. Abu Fida' described becoming politically conscious during visits with his mother at the age of ten to different prisons to see his older brother—a Popular Front activist serving a six-month sentence at the time. At twelve, Abu Fida' himself went to prison for the first time. He was picked up in a sweep and held for ten days at the Bethlehem military headquarters following a stone-throwing demonstration to protest the killing of an activist in Thawra. A year later he was back in prison. There had been a demonstration in his neighborhood, and he was rounded up along with other individuals whose names appeared on a list of previously arrested individuals. After ten days of interrogation, he was sentenced to two months. Thus began a long chain of arrest, short-term detention, release, and rearrest.

Narratives of imprisonment and suffering featured centrally in the accounts of a second man in the triumvirate. At the height of the Uprising in 1988, Abu Tha'ir was beaten and dragged behind a jeep by a patrol that was looking for the perpetrator of a Molotov cocktail attack. The bludgeoning left him unconscious for several hours; in 1999–2000, he still suffered from severe back pain incurred from the abuse. While he recounted his story partly to impress on me the depravity of the occupation and the moral necessity of resistance, it was also clear that his narrative had an apotheosizing effect—it transformed humiliation into heroism, thus rendering the storyteller deserving of respect and authority.

Alongside the camp's ethos of resistance and the premium placed by young males on daring actions, one of the main forces that shaped the politicization of the three friends as Popular Front activists was the family. Abu Fida' told me that all his older brothers were members of the Popular Front. There was also a maternal uncle who took a special interest in him: "I looked up to my uncle. . . . He was a Marxist and a Popular Front leader. I saw how people really loved and respected him. His thinking was advanced and progressive. He spoke about Marxism and science." His uncle had also spent a number of years in prison, thus adding to his credibility in the eyes of his Intifada activist nephew. Abu Samir, the third member of the triumvirate, explained his mobilization in similar terms. He, too, was from a well-known Popular Front family. He told me: "My brother was the one who gave me instructions [*taʿlīmāt*] . . . he was the one who guided me." Similarly, older brothers played a key role in Abu Tha'ir's mobilization into the Popular Front. Eight of his ten siblings, all males, either leaned toward the Front or were card-carrying members. Abu Tha'ir walked a well-worn path when he, too, joined the faction in the late 1980s.

But family tradition alone did not lead Abu Tha'ir to the Popular Front. Rather, he felt a deep resonance between the faction's stated ideological positions and the mass ethos of resistance that became so powerfully instituted in the first Uprising. The Front also seemed to exude a certain sophistication that set it off from other "run-of-the-mill" movements like Fatah. To be Popular Front was to be a part of the vanguard, the intelligentsia. Despite being a housepainter and handyman, Abu Tha'ir, whose wife was a graduate of Bethlehem University and a schoolteacher, saw himself as a member of a new educated and professional generation that had advanced beyond the supposedly tradition-bound (*taqlīdī*) consciousness of its fallāḥī (peasant) predecessors.[20] For Abu Tha'ir, the Popular Front was both militant and "modern":

> Fatah did a lot of talking but I didn't see them taking action. It was different with the Popular Front. I heard about Layla Khalid [one of the first airplane hijackers] and all the other fighters . . . and they were all Popular Front people. In my eyes, to be Fatah was to say you smoked [i.e., something all Palestinians, especially men, did]. To say you were Popular Front, however,

[20] The couple had only one child, a four-year-old son. Abu Tha'ir and his wife were committed to having a small family despite the pressure from parents and neighbors to have many more children. While he saw the economic benefits of a smaller family, Abu Tha'ir also described the decision he and his wife had made as a sign of their break from the "traditional" ways of their parents.

> was to say you carried a weapon, that you were ready for action and sacrifice. When I asked a Fatah supporter to tell me what Fatah stood for as opposed to the Popular Front, he told me the Popular Front people were all Communists and didn't believe in god, that they drank beer and chased girls. Fatah, on the other hand, were Muslims, respectful people, people who didn't drink alcohol. He didn't tell me about what Fatah had done for the nation. I could have been talking to an ignorant child. Now, when I met with the Popular Front people, I spent five hours straight asking questions and talking intensely. Five hours! I came away from this interaction convinced of their position. I wanted to join a movement with principles. I didn't want to just join something for the hell of it. There was a real seriousness with the Popular Front. You had to go through a six-month secret trial period before you could become a member. They didn't just sign you up to inflate their numbers [i.e., like Fatah]. You see the difference? Even today, if you were to get together with two Fatah people and one Popular Front person, the two Fatah people would never be able to tell you exactly where they were coming from. But the Popular Front person, even if he were young, could lay out for you from A to Z what it meant to be Popular Front. I also noticed how most of the collaborators were, at one time, tied to Fatah. If this were the case, wouldn't you be careful about dealing with them? But you might ask me why today most people say they are Fatah. Most of these people lack consciousness. Of course, religion plays a big role. Religion is sacred to us. The people continue to be conservative [*muḥāfiẓīn*]. They can't understand Marxism. Not everyone is progressive and sophisticated.

Popular Front supporters put themselves forward as the intellectual and political vanguard of Thawra. They had scientific consciousness, ideology, and action, while the others had "traditional" (taqlīdī) consciousness, religion, and inaction. At the same time, Popular Front supporters like Abu Tha'ir had come to feel insecure and embittered. In the late-Oslo period, they found themselves politically marginalized by a dominant Fatah movement and confronted with an ever more assertive Islamism. Under such circumstances, reassertions of a vanguard identity served a defensive, self-justificatory purpose: the Popular Front may have become relatively less important in late-Oslo politics and society, but at least it once was the clearest, most uncompromising expression of Palestinian aspirations.

Identity Formation in the Islamist Milieu

The forces that mobilized secularists also were responsible for shaping the identities of Islamists. As with secularists, family, faction, neighborhood, and school networks converged with the culture of mass resistance during the Intifada to give form to Islamist identity. At the same time, however, Islamism represented a protest against the dominant secularist milieu. This element of protest, which animated and marked off Islamism as an alternative orientation within the Palestinian political field, became especially clear among Muslim Brotherhood and Hamas supporters in Thawra. Like Islamists elsewhere, many of these supporters started out as Popular Front and Fatah activists but then switched loyalties to the Islamist factions during or after the Uprising. The stories of mobilization and realignment among these individuals shed light on how disenchantment with secular nationalism combined with persisting, and reviving, Islamist orientations and networks to reshape their political consciousness from the late 1980s onward.

Family networks and Muslim Brotherhood mobilizing efforts were particularly evident in Shaykh Abu Banna's account. In his case, an older sister played a particularly important mentoring role. Originally a Popular Front activist, this sister, as mentioned earlier, turned away from her leftist political orientations and began studying Islamic Jurisprudence (fiqh) at the University of Jordan in the late 1970s. Shaykh Abu Banna arrived in ʿAmman during this period and, following his sister's advice, began taking classes in Islamic religion. During this period, the Muslim Brotherhood was gaining greater political and social influence in Jordan, especially in the universities.[21] Although he did not indicate any direct connection with the Brotherhood during his student days, he clearly had formed a strong Islamist orientation by the time he returned to Thawra in 1981. He helped found Thawra's Islamic Society (al-jamʿiyya al-islāmiyya) soon after his return, and within four years he was locked in a violent conflict with the dominant secular-left leadership in the camp.

The shaykh quickly became a leader of the Islamist cause in the camp.[22] Although he denied having any formal connection to Hamas or Islamic

[21] By the mid-1970s, King Husayn had effectively shut down the secular-nationalist opposition in Jordan. Cultivating the Muslim Brotherhood as a counterbalance, he brought the movement's members into the Jordanian Parliament and governing bureaucracies. While marked by occasional tension and repression, the relationship between the Crown and the Brotherhood was mutually useful. In exchange for recognizing the ruling family's legitimacy as descendants of the Prophet and guardians of the holy places in Jerusalem, the Brotherhood gained a foothold within a range of Jordanian institutions, especially the high schools and universities. They also benefited from the government's support for its social and religious activities in the West Bank. Ziad Abu-Amer, *Islamic Fundamentalism in the West Bank and Gaza: Muslim Brotherhood and Islamic Jihad* (Bloomington and Indianapolis, IN: Indiana University Press, 1994), 4–6, and Beverley Milton-Edwards, *Islamic Politics In Palestine* (London: Tauris Academic Studies, 1996), 57–59.

[22] His influence has since spread to the general Bethlehem area. In 1999–2000, he hosted his own TV program, in which he issued opinions (*fatāwā*, sing. *fatwā*) on questions of religious practice that viewers would pose to him. He also invited guests to discuss various

Jihad, he nevertheless recounted at length his numerous arrests and detentions. In these stories, he portrayed himself as simply conveying the moral precepts of Islam. For this, and not for any organizational affiliations, he said, he was arrested.

> [The Israelis] are afraid of Islam. . . . For this reason, you will find many religious people [*ikthīr min al-mutadayyinīn*] among the Palestinian prisoners in Israeli jails. . . . These people are not necessarily in prison because they have resisted the occupation by throwing stones in the Intifada. I never threw stones or joined any demonstrations or any Intifada actions. I wasn't involved in obtaining weapons or producing leaflets. They told me that the words I spoke from the pulpit were even more dangerous than leaflets, weapons, explosives, or any other type of weapon.

There was an element of heroism—the solitary prophet standing against the unjust ruler—in this description. The account performed the same kind of rhetorical labor as other prison narratives: it established the protagonist as willingly embracing suffering and self-sacrifice on behalf of higher principles—be they religious, national, or religio-national—and, therefore, deserving of trust and respect. The particular religious casting of the shaykh's story reflected his specifically Islamist conception of collective identity in Thawra and in Palestinian society, as a whole; it also was congruent with his professional identity as a preacher, an identity that was viewed culturally as filling the central functions of teaching and prophetic truth-telling that the Prophet Muhammad had embodied.[23] Like the Prophet Muhammad railing against his enemies among the powerful Quraysh tribe, the shaykh stood up to Israel's occupation, confronting it with the words of the Qur'an. And, also like the Prophet, he was a forerunner and catalyst of a larger shift in collective consciousness. He explicitly referred to this parallel in describing his work in the camp as similar to the Prophet's early efforts to advance Islam in an unbelieving Meccan society. He stood out as idiosyncratic in aligning with the antinationalist Muslim Brotherhood in a camp society dominated by the Popular Front, the Communists, and Fatah. Two decades later, however, Islamist ideology and structures had entered the mainstream of

---

problems confronting Palestinian society. I appeared on the show once to talk about "Islam and the West." The television station was owned by a Christian who had been a P.L.O. official in Jordan and Lebanon and possessed high-level connections in the Palestinian National Authority.

[23] For an insightful discussion of how preachers appropriate and project the received memory of the Prophet Muhammad's charismatic authority in various ways, see Patrick Gaffney, *The Prophet's Pulpit: Islamic Preaching in Contemporary Egypt* (Berkeley, CA: University of California Press, 1994).

Palestinian politics. The shaykh's pathbreaking presence was crucial to the local manifestation of this shift within Thawra.

The definitive emergence of a new generation of Islamists in the camp occurred with the nationalist-activist reorientation of the older Muslim Brotherhood just prior to and during the first Intifada. The structures of the new Hamas and Islamic Jihad movements provided the channels through which individuals who might otherwise have aligned with Fatah, or even the left, became oriented toward Islamism as an authentic—in their eyes, the most authentic—expression of Palestinian identity. Four main factors were crucial in the Islamist reorientation of Intifada-generation activists in the camp: the general, collective mobilization that occurred during the Uprising; initial integration into the secularist milieu followed by disillusionment with it; exposure to, and integration within, Islamist structures such as Shaykh Abu Banna's mosque (built during the Uprising) or the Islamic Bloc at Bethlehem University; and, finally, the influence of friends, coworkers, and family.

The narratives of Majdi and Amal shed light on the complex interrelation of these four factors. I got to know Majdi through Shaykh Abu Banna. In May 2000, I sat in the back of the shaykh's mosque during the evening prayer, *ṣalāt al-ʿishāʾ*. Afterward, Shaykh Abu Banna invited the worshippers to meet with me. Majdi, who had majored in English at Bethlehem University, was particularly interested in getting to know me, and, following the discussion in the mosque, accompanied us back to the shaykh's house for tea. I met with Majdi at his home on multiple occasions afterward and got to know his wife, Amal, as well.

Majdi and Amal were born in 1969 and 1971, respectively. The primary factors that shaped their sociopolitical proclivities included the influence of parents, older siblings, and friends who were religiously observant, and, in Amal's case, a fiancé (Majdi) who had begun to adopt an Islamist orientation. Several other factors played a critical role, such as the arbitrary killing of friends and neighbors in the Intifada (an experience that led Majdi, for instance, to question his previous behavior and values and to turn to religion in preparation for his own possible death); alienating encounters with secular-nationalist, particularly Fathawi faction politics at Bethlehem University; negative or alienating experiences related to the general secular ethos of Bethlehem and Thawra; and a consequent crisis of values that resolved itself through positive interactions with Islamists and Islamism. It is critical to appreciate the particular historical moment of the couple's politicization: Majdi and Amal finished high school just as the Uprising began. Between 1988 and 1994, they attended Bethlehem University in the midst of prolonged closures, multiple curfews, constant protests and strikes, and unrelenting repressive violence. It was during this period, as well, that Fatah and Hamas entered into an intense and often bitter competition for power and influence in the major Palestinian institutions. This competition was very much in play at Bethlehem University when Majdi and Amal were students there.

One of the main sources of the couple's predisposition to Islamism was their upbringing in what they described as "traditional" (taqlīdī) families. Majdi described his parents as Muslims but not *multazimīn* (committed adherents). He saw them as adhering to Islam by force of custom and not by an act of will that led to study and a rational assent to precepts. Majdi rejected his parents' traditionalism, and yet he was keen to retrieve and preserve elements of tradition in response to the erosion of moral values that he saw occurring in present-day Thawra. In Amal's case, the influence of family was much more direct and positive. Amal described herself as being religious from very early on in her life. She grew up in a family that observed the prayers and kept the fast. She also had a father who took an active role in eliciting and cultivating a religious orientation within her:

> I prayed and fasted and loved to talk about religious topics. We studied religion in school, but there you basically had to memorize a bunch of stuff. At home, my father took a completely different approach. He tried to convey the idea that we needed to love god and fulfill his requirements for this love. He knew that if we didn't love god, if we weren't internally convinced and committed, then one day we might reject religion. In the wintertime, he would sit and tell us the stories of the prophets (*qiṣaṣ al-anbiyā'*).

While Thawra's political ethos may have been predominantly secular, Amal grew up in a family where religious orientations remained rooted and actively integrated within the formation and articulation of familial bonds. Religion provided the language and metaphors through which Amal's relationship with her father developed. The warmth that suffused this relationship not only positively predisposed Amal toward religion but also made her potentially more resonant, as she entered into late adolescence and early adulthood, with Islamist assertions about a crisis in morality within late-Oslo society. Amal experienced this crisis as a type of alienation. Islamism offered a resolution that returned her to the warmth she once experienced in her family of origin.

A second factor in Majdi and Amal's Islamist turn was early mobilization into the secular-nationalist Fatah movement followed by a process of disenchantment, then realignment with the Islamic Bloc during the first year of studies at Bethlehem University. In both cases, Fatah initially appeared to be the least objectionable option, since one did not necessarily have to renounce religion to be a supporter or member of the movement. To have grown up in Thawra was to have inherited strong prejudices against the Islamists; this bias became even more pronounced in the wake of the 1985 Popular Front–Muslim Brotherhood clashes. The appearance of Hamas three years later only amplified suspicions in Thawra that "reactionary" religious forces sought to undermine the P.L.O. and perhaps were also collaborating directly with Israel. Hence, to align with the Islamists in the camp was to risk ridicule and isolation. By the early 1990s, however, the Islamists had become firmly entrenched and were successfully contesting the dominance of secular-nationalist forces at Bethlehem University and elsewhere. It was in this unsettled period that Majdi and Amal broke from the secular-nationalist ranks.

Majdi's initial alignment with Fatah occurred while he was attending the U.N.R.W.A. preparatory school between 1981 and 1983. He had been one of the founding members of the camp's local Shabiba chapter (the Fatah youth wing). The group's activities included field trips, classes in dabka line dance, and general recreation like table tennis. His association with Shabiba was particularly critical to gaining acceptance into Bethlehem University. The major P.L.O. factions had special arrangements with the administrations of various Palestinian universities whereby they could "recommend" a certain number of party loyalists for studies. This quota system enabled activists with low test scores or no high school diploma, owing to imprisonment or other considerations, to pursue university degrees. The activist students, in turn, became the main pillars of the political blocs that were associated with the different factions on the campuses. Majdi, whose scores on the Tawjihi exam were mediocre, gained entry to Bethlehem University as an up-and-coming Fatah youth leader. He was expected to reciprocate the assistance by advancing Fatah's interests at the university. Within his first year, however, he withdrew from Fatah and declared himself an independent.

For her part, Amal also initially supported Fatah but only after beginning her university studies. Previously, while a preparatory- and secondary-level student, she avoided faction politics, preferring instead to stay abreast of the news and contribute to general Intifada activities such as providing help and shelter to shabāb (young men, street fighters) as they threw stones at, and then ran from, Israeli soldiers. Her initial alignment with Fatah was actually involuntary, as she described it. As an incoming student at the university she faced heavy recruitment by the different faction blocs. She increasingly found it impossible to maintain political independence. Her father advised her to vote with Fatah. Fatah seemed the most flexible option: "I had the idea," she told me, "that if you thought of yourself as nonaligned, then the closest expression of this was probably Fatah."

Both Majdi and Amal, however, became disillusioned with Fatah during their first year at Bethlehem University. It seemed to them both that

Fatah's leaders had little concern for the interests and well-being of its members and supporters. On the contrary, the movement appeared to view its rank and file as mere numbers or bodies with which to win elections. Power, not the needs of individuals, was uppermost. Amal put it this way:

> [Fatah] just wanted your vote to increase their control in the Student Council. In the election during my second year they suspected that I was not going to vote for them. They started to really pay attention to me, warning others against letting the left woo me away. I began to hate politics. Really! You go through the Intifada and develop many different ideas and then you come to the university and see these games going on. No longer sisters and brothers but just seats. That's what it amounted to, winning seats on the Student Council. So, I decided not to vote for anyone . . . no one! . . . That same year, I joined the Islamic Bloc.

In Amal's experience, politics, or *al-siyāsa*, became an alienating practice devoid of the warm brotherly and sisterly solidarity that she remembered from the days of the Intifada. Fatah was concerned with winning elections, nothing more. People were pawns, and principles counted for nothing. Support was rewarded with perks—a job in a movement-affiliated institution or, later, the Palestinian National Authority, or help with university admission. Conversely, withdrawal of support was punished with ostracism. After Majdi declared his resignation from Fatah, his friends in the movement ceased interacting with him. He bore up under the pressure because, as he put it, he desired to keep his "dignity and self-respect." Inverting the ostracism, he anathematized his former colleagues, declaring most of the "Fatah people" to be "failures" who had given up their autonomy and become reliant on movement patronage. His former friends now worked in the Palestinian National Authority security services, he told me, implying that in doing so they had squandered their integrity. Majdi, although less financially secure as a low-paid teacher, claimed to be at peace with himself since, unlike his onetime friends, he was beholden to no one party or faction. He was not a "sheep."

The alienation that Majdi and Amal experienced in their encounters with Fatah's party-political practices at Bethlehem University was part of their more general disenchantment with secularity as it manifested itself in the main P.L.O. factions. Particularly problematic was the "mixing" or "commingling" (*ikhtilāṭ*) among the sexes that secularist groups in the camp and at the university promoted. Majdi spoke of feeling ashamed of his behavior during his sojourn among the secularists. He had ceased praying, had begun entertaining ideas of "dialectical materialism," and went to parties where there were girls and dancing and singing. (This rebellious period apparently started with a brief dalliance as a Popular

Front supporter during junior high school.) However, during the Intifada, with neighbors and friends dying around him, he began reconsidering the direction in which he was headed:

> **M:** I began thinking that if I died, if I were shot, god would not be satisfied with me. I did not pray regularly. I felt something was wrong inside. I felt guilty about things like spending a lot of time with girls and boys partying, singing, dancing dabka. . . . Before joining Shabiba, when I was ten or eleven, my friends were mostly from *al-jabha al-shaʿbiyya* (the Popular Front). . . . The older guys would always talk about how there was no god. I thought a lot about this. I listened to this talk. They spoke about dialectics and other complicated things. They would say, "There is no god and nature developed by itself." You know, in Thawra, the Shaʿbiyya (Popular Front) was . . . the majority, the strongest, ahead of Fatah and everyone else. Thawra was the center of the leftists. Anyway, at that time, I didn't pray or fast. My Popular Front friends talked about girls in a very bad way, and I didn't oppose it. I feel ashamed when I remember this. I went along with [this behavior] because all my friends were like this, but I felt there was something wrong. . . . At that time, there was what we called the "*ikhwānjiyya*" [Islamic types—i.e., the Muslim Brotherhood]. . . . We used to sing: *yā ikhwānjī bikafī kharāb al-qiṭāʿ wa al-ḍiffa / wa li-naʿmilnā zaffa ʿalā al-khiṭṭa al-mārksiyya* [O Muslim Brother! Enough with ruining the (Gaza) Strip and the (West) Bank! / Let us march down the Marxist path!] You see what I mean? We used to sing these songs without realizing what we were singing. We used to attack anyone who was religious at that time. No one accepts you if you are religious. I don't know why. If you are religious, you are a black sheep. No one speaks with you. You are alone, deserted. No one deals with you. This can be very scary when you are a child. I began to think that religious people were bad people and that we should not be religious or think about religion. I told myself, "Leave religion in the mosque! Don't think about it! " You should only think of yourself and your friends, that you are happy now, enjoying your time, not caring about others. Those who go to the mosque . . . they were. . . .
>
> *Backward. . . .*
>
> **M:**. . . backward . . . yes, backward. . . . I began to hate those [religious] people. I managed to convince myself even though I wasn't really convinced. I tried to convince myself they were bad. But, I began to see that my friends . . . we were very bad, also. We weren't moral.
>
> *Did they drink alcohol?*
>
> **M:** No, no! They didn't have enough money!

So how were they not moral?

M: You know, the way they dealt with the girls and each other. They used bad language, bad words. I may not have been religious, but I couldn't accept this.

The encounter with secularity in Thawra—a secularity that openly scorned religion—left Majdi deeply conflicted, internally. The ethos of the nationalist-leftist milieu actively undermined the values that he had grown up with. Particularly problematic was the "mixing" that went on with girls and the attitudes that his friends had toward females. Majdi went along with his friends because he wanted to fit in. During his university studies, in the midst of the Intifada, the inner conflict intensified. In response, he started to pray again. As he did so, "the gap inside began to fill." He began to read the Qur'an along with the accompanying medieval commentaries (*tafāsīr*) and handed-down accounts (*aḥādīth*) of the life of the Prophet Muhammad. Gradually, the clash he felt between his inherited values and those of his secularist friends gave way to a resolution grounded in a reappropriation of religion. He would enact this retrieval by dissociating himself from secularism.

A similar dynamic was at work in Amal's rejection of secularism and the factions linked to it. This rejection coalesced in a yearlong process of wrestling with the idea of putting on the scarf (*ḥijāb*) and long coat (*jilbāb*), the style of dress that the Islamist movements had imposed and spread as part of their wider cultural struggle. Three main forces appeared to have been at work in Amal's decision to adopt these visible signs of Islamist identity. First, it was at this time that Majdi, after a long crush, finally declared his love to her. The couple decided they would get married. Majdi, however, conditioned his proposal of matrimony on Amal wearing the scarf. Second, also at this time, Amal had, independently of Majdi, withdrawn her support from Fatah and joined the Islamic Bloc. She went for a relatively long period as an Islamic Bloc member without wearing the scarf. Her fellow activists regularly pointed out this anomaly to her, arguing that it contradicted her professed beliefs in the Islamist program. Taking the criticism to heart, she began to become increasingly convinced of the Islamic Bloc's positions and practices. In stark contrast to Fatah, she found the Islamic Bloc people to be very principled in their nationalism and very solicitous of others. They cared about people, extending material and spiritual aid where needed, and their word was their word. They manifested their honesty interpersonally and politically. They took a strong stand against compromising with Israel on such key issues as the refugees' right of return to lands lost in the 1948 war, unlike Fatah, which appeared ready to forfeit these rights for a deal with Israel. They also unambiguously expressed their feelings about the moral conduct of fellow activists. "I remember very clearly," she told me, "how one of their *shabāb* [male activists] came up to me and said, 'Amal, we truly and sincerely hope that as a sign of commitment to your religion you will change your clothing.' " She interpreted the request not as pressure but as a heartfelt expression of concern for her moral well-being and as a desire for her fuller identification with Islam:

> I really confronted a big contradiction at the university: I had aligned myself with religion but my outward appearance communicated to others that I had absolutely no connection to religion. The Islamic Bloc people, however, told me that my inner convictions and outward behavior had to be the same. When I thought about this, I realized that I really did have "two faces" [said in English]. I read the Qur'an and prayed. I realized that my Lord was telling me that my body belonged to me and not to anyone else. If I wore the ḥijāb [scarf], it didn't mean I was backward. I used to wear the latest fashions, whatever caught my fancy, even if it upset my parents and the entire world! Short skirts, whatever! So I asked myself, "Why are you afraid of wearing the ḥijāb?" Slowly, as I prayed, I sensed something inside me that knew this [wearing ḥijāb] was what I had to do. In November, my sister came for a visit [an older sister in ʿAmman, Jordan, who had begun wearing the scarf]. I had written a letter to her telling her to buy me some nice-looking scarves and long clothing. She asked me who it was for and I told her it was for me. She replied, "Really! Have you finally decided?" I told her I had. She told me, "If you decide to do this, you have to be absolutely sure. You can't go back on it. Think it through." I told her I had been thinking about it for a long time and I was ready. She brought me the things and I put them in the closet. Every day I would look at them and ask myself, "Why don't you wear them? What's holding you back? Is it because if you wear them now people will talk about you and say Majdi influenced you to do this? Are you convinced or not convinced?" Finally, I made the decision. I had to do it . . . especially before I married Majdi . . . at least a year before. It is my personality that I do not follow anyone. I make my own decisions. I started wearing the clothes on January 1, 1995. I went to class in them. I didn't look around at all. Everyone was shocked! Oh god were they shocked! They stared, especially the shabāb [guys] . . . they were afraid to talk to me. I asked them, "Why don't you talk to me!" They said, "Oh hi, Amal, how are you? Congratulations on the ḥijāb. . . ." With time, things went back to normal. The guys started telling me, "If only the other girls would do what you have done . . . it would be much better." I felt that the ḥijāb brought me a greater degree of respect. . . . [But], I really struggled with the question of what the role of the woman was in the social problem of clothing. We have this theory that one's legs can cause desire in members of the opposite sex. Women have feelings, men have feelings. . . . So, yes, we

> can cause desire in each other. . . . I believe this. . . . But why did the responsibility for preventing this desire fall on the woman's shoulders? I guess after thinking it through and talking with people more, I began to feel that in truth we women really did carry a greater degree of responsibility for these things. . . . In our so-called secular society women have no rights at all. But, [guys] are free to look at women from their cars while they are walking in the street. . . . Nothing stops them from looking at you and saying things.

As with Majdi, the turn to religion resolved a sharp inner conflict in values for Amal. Her biggest hurdle was to reconcile the perception of backwardness that wearing the scarf signified within Thawra and Bethlehem University's predominantly secular-nationalist milieu with the demands of religion as the Islamic Bloc construed them. She straddled both sides. As an educated, professionalizing woman, she had taken on the liberal values of equality between men and women. Yet she had rejected the impersonal and manipulative character of secularist practices as she had experienced them at the university and in Bethlehem's streets. Despite secularist rhetoric about individual freedom, patriarchal attitudes remained entrenched; secularism seemed merely to deprive women of protections against these attitudes. To wear the ḥijāb and jilbāb, thus, was to protest the vulnerability and anomie she felt within the secularist milieu. It also was an attempt to bridge the divide. Putting on the scarf and long coat did not signal a simple reversion to patriarchal arrangements. Rather, it indexed a critical and selective reconstitution of these arrangements. This revision integrated certain liberal orientations even as it rejected others; and, in so doing, it achieved a consistency that had been lacking for Amal between her professed inner religious orientation and her outward practices.

HIERARCHIES OF SOLIDARITY

As the stories of Amal and Majdi show, sociopolitical identities in Thawra during the late-Oslo period could take multiple forms. While refugee status united all residents of the camp, the competition among political factions and the destabilizing effects of occupation, uprising, and a crisis-ridden peace process combined to create the conditions for a multidirectional reevaluation and reinterpretation of collective identity among the generation of activists born near to, or after, 1967. Embedded in, and crossing among, multiple, overlapping social and political spheres, these activists reworked the inherited symbols and discourses of secular nationalism and Islamism to produce new conceptions of solidarity. Four ideal types were most prominent among my informants: sheer secularism (liberalism, *al-lībrāliyya*); Islamic secularism (a secular-religious hybrid that originated in the leftist milieu); liberal Islam (a transposition of certain Fathawi orientations into an Islamist frame); and sheer Islamism (Hamas-oriented Islamic nationalism).[24] These types represented interactive reinterpretations of collective orientations. Each one responded to the others in articulating its themes.

Sheer Secularism: Al-Lībrāliyyīn

Proponents of sheer secularism in Thawra made a key distinction between two inversely related categories: *al-lībrāliyyīn* (the liberals) and *al-mutadayyinīn* (the pious or the religious). To the "liberal" pole, they attached the values of individuality, tolerance, political pluralism, and democratic process. To the "pious" pole, they ascribed religious and political intolerance, inflexible political strategies, and an insistence on uniformity—qualities they associated with the Islamist movements. This polarity was not only ideological but also existential in character. Liberals saw an Islamist victory as necessitating the elimination or exclusion of the values and practices that defined "liberalism." By contrast, because it advocated tolerance and individual expression, liberalism, its proponents argued, was able to accommodate religion as individual philosophy or practice. One could be a pious Muslim in a liberal social order as long as one's religious beliefs remained within the bounds of individual preference.

These themes emerged in an interview with Abu Samir, one of the three Popular Front street activists mentioned earlier, and Maryam, a politically independent Palestinian-American journalist who met and married one of Thawra's principal Communist Party and Intifada leaders at the height of the Uprising in 1988–89. The following segment of tape-recorded conversation was prompted by a question eliciting reaction to Islamist notions of a sharīʿa-based state:

> **Abu Samir:** Hamas is composed of people who draw their theory from the Qur'an, from the religious perspective. . . . The struggle against the Jews is, they say, a part of the Prophet [Muhammad's] path [*sabīl al-rasūl*]. . . . I disagree with this. I think it is possible to build alliances with the Jews, with certain groups, say, like Peace Now [the main umbrella for Israel's peace movements that took form during Israel's unilateral invasion of Lebanon in 1982]. But, Hamas would not be ready to do this. They

[24] These labels are my own. They reflect the main themes underlying the orientations to which they refer. None of my informants referred to their identities in these specific terms, however.

would say, "They [the peace camp] are Jews and so it is necessary to fight them."

Maryam: Pardon me, but there is an important point to be made here about people's acceptance of the idea of an Islamic state. There is a large group in the camp who, though they've been born Muslims, are secular in their orientation, neither pray nor fast. . . . We feel that if Hamas succeeds in the future, and imposes something called an Islamic state, this state will be perhaps something of a danger to Israel but an even greater one to Muslims like us who do not share the Islamist perspective. Someone who supports Hamas is totally against something like Communism. [Hamas] will not be prepared to allow party-political pluralism [*al-taʿaddudiyya al-ḥizbiyya*] . . . and then they won't accept the idea of women leaving their houses without dressing according to code [i.e., in "Islamic dress," meaning a scarf and long coat]. . . .

Abu Samir: We can look at the example of Algeria. We see that even though the Islamic Movement won the elections there [in 1990 and 1991] they were unable to live in the contemporary social reality of the country.[25] Most of the people in Algeria are very "Frenchified." Their thinking and ways are French, so they are not suddenly going to be prepared to accept the *mandīl* [scarf] and long overcoats [*malābis sharʿiyya*]. . . .

As in Iran. . . .

Maryam:. . . Yes. . . . Here, in Palestine, it will be difficult to follow the Iranian example.

Abu Samir: Yes, in our society, one person is committed to definite religious ideas and is ready to defend them while another carries ideas other than Islam, other than religion. . . . So, therefore, an Islamic state cannot coexist with the reality that we live in. . . .

Maryam: Look, many people in Thawra are "liberal" (lībrāliyyīn) in their ideas, right? And they have always been this way. It is really difficult for people in their midtwenties and thirties to go back and change. . . . At the same time, and correct me if I am wrong, these same liberals are able to accept the religious people. We liberals don't have a problem if someone wants to be religious, but the religious have a problem accepting the liberals.

[25] The Algerian Islamic Salvation Front (F.I.S.) was a coalition of Islamist movements that successfully contested the 1990 municipal and regional elections and the 1991 multiparty parliamentary ballot. On the eve of parliamentary runoff elections in January 1992, the Algerian government, with the backing of the military and, tacitly, France and the United States, canceled the pending poll and outlawed the Salvation Front. An extremely violent and prolonged civil war then ensued. For more details, see John L. Esposito, *The Islamic Threat: Myth or Reality?* 3rd edition (New York: Oxford University Press, 1999), 171–191.

Two seemingly antithetical visions of the future were at play in the conversation above. Against the monochromatic and authoritarian notion of an Islamic state, as Abu Samir and Maryam presented it, the liberal perspective posed a single, secular-democratic society that encompassed Muslims, Christians, and Jews of all types. This secular-pluralist social vision had been at the center of P.L.O. nationalism since the late 1960s. The core argument that liberals leveled against Islamists, and in favor of the P.L.O., was that the Palestinian nation was multivocal in character and, therefore, fundamentally at odds with ideals of religious and cultural uniformity. Only democratic secularism was capable of accommodating the diversity of contemporary Palestinian society by allowing for individual expression and beliefs at private, personal levels.

Yet, for many secularists in Thawra and elsewhere in Palestinian society, the organizational vehicles of the left—the Popular Front for the Liberation of Palestine, the Democratic Front for the Liberation of Palestine, and the Communist Party—had become ineffectual. In their view, the higher leadership, situated in the diaspora, had abdicated its responsibility and betrayed the core principles of national resistance by agreeing to support the Oslo Accords, or by failing to come up with viable alternatives to it. For individuals like Abu Tha'ir, Abu Fida', and Abu Samir—the three friends who were also erstwhile Intifada street fighters linked to the Popular Front—a general disillusionment had set in. Both Abu Tha'ir and Abu Fida' had withdrawn in disgust from active participation in their faction even though they still displayed symbols of their loyalty, such as portraits of the Popular Front founder, George Habash, in their homes. For his part, Abu Samir still remained active but was bitterly critical of the compromises that his faction had made with the Palestinian National Authority. These men bided the day of Oslo's collapse, anticipating the moment when their services as fighters would be needed again. Other, older Popular Front activists in the same neighborhood in Thawra had withdrawn their memberships, too, redirecting their energies toward building the community center mentioned earlier.

This turning away from formal political activism toward social or cultural work within the nongovernmental sector was prevalent beyond the camp. A longtime friend who had been a staunch Democratic Front activist in Jerusalem formally renounced her membership in the faction after it split on the question of whether to support the Oslo Process. She felt the faction had forsaken every shred of democratic practice, becoming like Fatah, an authoritarian movement that relied on patronage. Social work replaced faction work. She became the director of a women's advocacy organization in the Old City of Jerusalem, arguing that the primary struggle was now the cultural one to combat the spread of Islamist ideals, especially as they applied to women, within the larger society. Still other friends who had been active in the Popular Front in Ramallah had turned away from faction politics and were focusing instead on their careers as schoolteachers. A Popular Front friend in Gaza also withdrew, reflecting bitterly on the repressive character of the Palestinian National Authority. He was scratching out a living in a small sewing factory that made jeans for the Israeli market.

The Palestinian National Authority's repression of dissenters, leftist and Islamist, partly motivated the shift away from faction activism among Popular Front, Democratic Front, and Communist supporters. Abu Samir, Abu Tha'ir, and Abu Fida' had all been dragged into the interrogation rooms—rooms formerly used by the Israeli military—of the Palestinian National Authority's security services in the immediate aftermath of the P.N.A.'s installation in the Bethlehem area. The P.N.A. also effectively absorbed leftist activists, many of them trained professionals, into its new ministries. Alternatively, as the Oslo Process increasingly made Intifada-like resistance activities untenable, leftists began to reorient themselves toward "cultural struggle," focusing on the reinforcement of their social service networks. These networks had evolved into full-blown nongovernmental organizations funded by European and American donors during the 1980s and 1990s. In Thawra, the left now concerned itself with advocating "progressive" (*taqaddumī*) social change through cultural centers like the one described earlier, in which youth took part in mixed-gender activities and could use the Internet to communicate with peers around the world. The directors of the center were most concerned with combating Islamizing trends as well as the antidemocratic and authoritarian tendencies of the Palestinian National Authority. For them, and other leftists in Thawra, the Oslo period was a time of political and social constriction that required activists to retrench, reorganize, and reconceptualize their work. Like Mujahida, the Islamic Jihad activist who had reoriented herself away from the armed struggle and toward efforts to reinforce Islamist institutions and values, the leftists in Thawra had also turned inward, reinterpreting their struggle as a long-term campaign to combat Islamist inroads by cultivating progressive (taqaddumī) social orientations within camp society from the bottom up.

Islamic Secularism

Withdrawal and retrenchment, however, was not the only response within the secularist milieu to the polarizations of late-Oslo society. In contrast to "liberalism," which required religion to remain a strictly individual practice, Islamic secularism—a hybrid orientation originating within the secularist sphere—attempted to overcome the secularist-Islamist split by reinterpreting leftist values as Islamic ones. Hamdi, a former Communist Party member and the youngest brother of Khadija, the Popular Front activist who became involved in organizing women before and during the first Uprising, exemplified this tendency. The only sibling in his family to have gone to university, Hamdi graduated with a bachelor's degree in social work from Bethlehem University just prior to the start of the Intifada in 1987 and went immediately to work in Israeli factories in the Talpiot area of southern Jerusalem (a zone that, before the construction of the checkpoints and wall, was less than ten minutes by car to the north of Bethlehem). Within a year, however, he was able to land a job as a refugee affairs assistant with the United Nations Refugee Works Agency (U.N.R.W.A.). When I interviewed him in 2000, he was still working for U.N.R.W.A. as a program officer. Hamdi's perspective may have been idiosyncratic, but his shift toward a more religious outlook reflected a trend that many staunch leftists, such as Khadija, identified as an increasingly prevalent one within their ranks.

Politically, Hamdi told me, "from the moment I first opened my eyes to the world I have been with the Communists." Hamdi's family had been a pillar of the secular-left milieu in Thawra since the 1950s. His maternal uncles were all members in either the Movement of Arab Nationalists or the Communist Party. One cousin—Maryam's husband, a major Communist Party figure in Thawra and a onetime member of the United National Leadership of the Uprising—had a particularly powerful impact on him. "He was a fighter who knew how to speak and convince others," he said. He became very attached to this older cousin and "kind of automatically" found himself "marching with the Communists." He took part in party activities in the camp, and later, at the university, he became one of the party's campus leaders. It was during this period that he, like Amal and Majdi, became disillusioned with the tactics that political factions used in elections for the Student Senate. But rather than leading him to reject the left, this dissatisfaction caused him to withdraw from activism altogether and seek out a career in social work.

> I began to undergo a political transformation in my fourth year [at the university]. I began to see that politics [al-siyāsa] was a vulgar, despicable game [*la'ba ḥaqīra*]. It was a game in which you stabbed people in the back. If you were going to be a politician then you had to leave behind your morals. At the same time, I learned through my major at the university that I was really drawn to social work and that it would be hard to serve everyone and be

> involved in politics. . . . I could not be a political activist. . . . I don't want to say I stopped being concerned about politics, but my involvement in it was over.

Like Amal and Majdi, Hamdi reacted against what he saw as the unprincipled pragmatism of the factions—all of them. Yet Hamdi professed to remain very much predisposed to the Communist left even as he turned away from on the backstabbing that "politics" seemed to require. Despite the seeming immorality of al-siyāsa (politics), he remembered the Communists, in particular, as the most "ethical" of people:

> [The Communists] focused on the poor, whereas the other factions never really addressed this [issue]. The Communists demonstrated their readiness for sacrifice. [They] were sentenced to long years in prison for actions that were very threatening to Israel. They underwent severe torture and never broke. This demonstrated the strength of their ideals, and this is what encouraged me to support them. They were principled, honest with the community, and morally upstanding . . . they didn't go after women to have sex.

Contrary to the typical Islamist critique of secularist "politics," Hamdi actually construed the left, and the Communists in particular, as the *most* moral of Thawra's residents. They were serious people, thinkers who had a very sophisticated grasp of the Palestinian situation. They shunned silly, frivolous pursuits. They displayed courage and conviction, bearing up under far greater pressure than any other group. Most importantly, for Hamdi, they upheld the best of the ʿādāt wa taqālīd (the customs and traditions) of the camp. They were honest in their dealings and especially solicitous of the received attitudes about limiting the interaction of the sexes. Hamdi said his leftist family never allowed him "to do anything with girls." Communists did not "go after women for sex."[26]

[26] Hamdi's point about how the Communists were the most solicitous of the inherited mores echoed the comments of other observers. A foreign journalist with long experience in Palestinian society and several female activists pointed out to me that the left in Thawra and elsewhere had often ironically been more traditional than the most traditional elements of society. They explained this phenomenon as a type of self-justificatory response to the charges of atheism and immorality that had hounded the left, especially in recent years with the revitalization of the Islamic Movement. The left sought to deflect such criticism by becoming hypervigilant about the customs and traditions. A longtime leftist friend of mine in Gaza employed this logic in once explaining to me why Marxists affirmed the customs and traditions: it was necessary, my friend said, to "contextualize" the left in a still very "traditional" society. One had to make compromises with the social environment to gain any kind of audience. Other analysts and activist contacts made similar observations about Fatah. Recall the remarks of one of my Fatah interviewees earlier about how, although her movement claimed to be secular, in reality it upheld traditional and religious values. For a critique of the left's failure to articulate a stronger countercultural, secular social vision, see Tamari, "Left in Limbo," 16–21.

In Hamdi's view, then, the left was moral but politics was not. Why then did he turn to religion? And what did this turn consist of? In other conversion stories, such as Majdi's and Amal's, a deeply felt conflict of values was the driving force. While Majdi and Amal were, like Hamdi, put off by "politics," especially the impersonal and manipulative practices of the Fatah faction with which they initially associated, they were still more alienated by the pressure to drink, talk lewdly, wear revealing clothes, and mix and flirt with members of the opposite sex. They described an almost visceral repulsion, a deep sense of misgiving and guilt that rose up within them, as they engaged in or confronted these activities. In aligning with the Islamists, they overcame the conflict of values and the disturbing feelings this conflict generated by embracing the religious reframing of both tradition and secularity proffered by Hamas. Hamdi, too, underwent a severe crisis of values—one produced by a totalizing "either/or" logic that confronted him as he interacted with an increasingly observant and pious environment both at home and at work. Unlike Majdi and Amal, however, his path of resolution did not lead to an alignment with the Islamists. Instead, Hamdi produced a unique synthesis, one that preserved his loyalty to the left, and thereby to his family, while simultaneously embracing an Islam that was, to his mind, thoroughly compatible with Thawra's secular-left milieu.

Like most of my other interlocutors, Hamdi grew up in a household that adhered to received religious values and practices. His parents kept the five daily prayers and fasted during Ramadan. Although he stopped praying, Hamdi continued to participate in the fast and held on to a belief in god as he grew into adulthood. His older sister, Khadija, an avowed atheist, was very much an exception; her orientation reflected the secularizing impact of the pan-Arabism and leftist ideals ascendant in the 1970s. Hamdi bridged the gap between the secularizing tendency of Khadija's generation and the retraditionalizing trend in the generation that emerged with the rise of the Islamist movements in the late 1980s and early 1990s. He claimed to adhere to Communist and secularist political values; yet, at the same time, he spoke about how the attitudes and practices embedded within his childhood family had predisposed him to seek religious reasons for the traumatic political events that had shaped his adulthood.

Hamdi's definitive return to religion occurred between 1994 and 1997. The first Intifada had come to a close, and the Palestinian National Authority was consolidating its control in the Bethlehem area. Hamdi, still working for U.N.R.W.A., had married a distant paternal cousin who had been born and raised in Saudi Arabia. She was very observant in her religious practice and had been gently cajoling her husband to become more regular in his prayers. The main catalyst of his shift, however, was a young, knowledgeable, and unobtrusive U.N.W.R.A. colleague who was also a local Hamas leader in Thawra Camp. Hamdi described him as a "shaykh," an unusual one. Hamdi had believed that *rijāl al-dīn* (men of religion) "were not trustworthy, were not honest with themselves, played games with religion, and just grew their beards long to make a show in front of people." His colleague, however, did not exhibit these characteristics. On the contrary, he was clean shaven, dressed professionally, and displayed tolerance and acceptance toward others, especially younger women, who did not conform to the religious norms: "He didn't tell them that they needed to cover up and begin praying or else they would face hellfire," Hamdi recounted. Such self-restraint and courtesy sparked the curiosity of the office staff. The women would tease him: "You're a shaykh, but you don't say anything about how we dress." Hamdi recalled that the shaykh would reply respectfully, saying that he was simply their colleague and did not want to create obstacles or problems in their work environment. Moreover, he felt that the best advocate of religion was a faithful example of right practice. Islam, the shaykh said, spread through exemplary behavior, not coercion. If his practice elicited questions and discussion, then he would be happy to engage others about religious topics; but he was not out to proselytize. The women, according to Hamdi, became intrigued and began drawing the shaykh into conversation on basic points of doctrine and practice—how to pray, reasons for the fast, why men and women should avoid contact if they were not *maḥram* (i.e., individuals forbidden to marry because they are within the Qur'anically proscribed degrees of consanguinity).

Hamdi, too, became curious and listened quietly without commenting. After a few weeks, he began more actively to seek out the shaykh. He accompanied him on his rounds and, during their car rides together, began asking him questions about religion. Hamdi stressed repeatedly that the shaykh never once asked him to pray or overtly attempted to proselytize. "Had he tried to get me to pray," he told me, "I probably would never have listened to him. . . . I was the one asking the questions." He had a lot of questions, and a growing sense of crisis.

H: I had begun to feel as if I were facing a big decision in my life . . . a change in my life. I fasted but didn't pray regularly. I knew that prayer was a basic part of religion . . . the basic duty and work of religion. On the Day of Resurrection our Lord will ask us about our prayer. If you were praying in life, then this was evidence of your faith. If not, then that was that. It was either A or B. I was convinced of the need for prayer, but I knew it was a major commitment. If I started to pray five times a day then I couldn't go back on the decision. If I went back on my decision then it would mean I was not really a believer. My indecision told me that I either lacked faith or there was something wrong with the religion itself. If I chose not to pray, then it would mean that I had found the religion to be entirely false. I read many, many books on prayer and the war within me raged on. Then came Ramadan in 1997, and I finally made the decision that I needed to begin praying. So, I began. For fifteen days I was doing this and I told no one. No one knew except my wife. I made her promise to tell no one. But then one day my brother came into my home while I was praying and saw me. . . . He had been praying for a long time. When he saw me praying, he started to weep. I lost my place in my prayer when I saw him. I was still very conscious of every movement, of everything I needed to do in the prayer. It was all still very new for me. After that, people started to know I was praying.

Why were you afraid to tell people?

H: I was afraid that I would not stay with it . . . that I would quit. I was so unsure for so long. Sounds strange, no? . . . So, I came to religion as something that was a tradition, as something that was just a part of my environment, but then I began to study it methodically and became convinced of it in a scientific way. Many shaykhs come to our mosques and say things that are nonsense and have nothing to do with religion. But, I don't consider these people to be examples to follow. The man I told you about who worked with me is the only person I consider to be a real model of faith. He is the main reason I began to pray. When I told him this, he was surprised and said, "I never talked to you about this decision!"

The role of Hamdi's colleague in his reorientation illustrated the effects of interaction among individuals embedded within the competing secularist and Islamist milieus. These interactions occurred at points of overlap within mediating structures such as workplaces. In such spaces, a convergence of style and orientation could occur. Islamists adopted "up-to-date," professional personae; secularists might rethink their secularism and integrate Islam, if not Islamism, into their sense of identity. The shaykh, for example, was an educated professional and comported himself accordingly. He was not bombastic or overbearing. He eschewed the long beard, the ankle-length tunic, and other overt displays of piety. He was at ease in a heterogeneous environment, adhering to Islam in his daily routines while tolerating those who did not conform to the same strictures, especially women who flouted convention by wearing European dress styles. The shaykh, in short, was an "up-to-date" model of the integration of religion with the demands of the contemporary world. For Hamdi, the shaykh's example was important because it undermined the secular-religious dichotomy upon which secularism rested and from which secularism drew its emotional force. Islam was not backward; it was "up-to-date."

The shaykh played an additional role: he triggered a moral crisis. While Hamdi may have been content to continue avoiding prayer and other questions of faith and practice, he nevertheless felt the pressure of religio-moral imperatives both at home and in the workplace. Unlike his older sister, he never made a definitive break with religion; rather, as Hamdi presented it, religious orientations subsisted below the surface, bubbling up later in his life under the heat of a moral catalyst, in this case his work colleague. This catalyst generated a dramatic moral polarity that forced Hamdi into a transforming decision. A dichotomous "A or B," all or nothing, logic began to operate. Having withdrawn from formal Communist Party structures, Hamdi may have been particularly susceptible to strong moral claims from other quarters. In such polarized settings as Thawra and Palestinian society, generally, in 1999–2000, Hamdi may have found it difficult to continue straddling the divides that defined camp and work. So he declared himself for Islam, but it was not the Islam of the Islamists. Rather, it was an Islam that, at least for Hamdi, was quite compatible with Thawra's secularist ethos. For instance, he interpreted the strictures against shaking hands with women outside the given lines of consanguinity in a way that allowed him nevertheless to have this kind of social interaction so long as he was careful to stifle any sexual desire that might surge forth.[27] He recognized that many, if not most, devout Muslims would take issue with his liberal approach to handshaking; for Hamdi, however, religion was a matter of inner motives, above all else. For this reason, he said, many of the people with whom he had grown up and whom he respected greatly—secularists and atheists and the like—would go to heaven: "Even though they are not believers, god works through them; and on the Resurrection Day, god will elevate them."[28]

[27] Amal Amireh points out that inner control is viewed as a critical dimension of mature masculinity in Arab societies. Amal Amireh, "Between Complicity and Subversion: Body Politics in Palestinian National Narrative," *South Atlantic Quarterly* 102, no. 4 (Fall 2003): 747–772.

[28] Hamdi appeared to contradict himself, here. He stated earlier that his turn toward a more pious orientation was driven by an "A or B" logic. On Resurrection Day, he said, one's fate would rest not only on good works but also on whether one had kept the stipulated ritual duties such as prayer. Hamdi clearly desired to downplay any perceived break with the leftist milieu in which he had grown up and still lived. The values he had inherited from this milieu continued to operate, indeed were more perfectly expressed, in the religious dimension, he argued. At the same time, prayer mattered. Hamdi had made a distinct shift despite his protestations that the change was less a qualitative break than a quantitative increase in his previous understandings and commitments. Hamdi may not have seen his shift as a crossing over into a qualitatively different moral realm, but others around him, such as Khadija, certainly did.

While Hamdi saw no inherent contradiction between religion and secularity, others around him viewed his turn toward piety with distress. His religiously observant brother wept, for joy presumably, but his older sister, Khadija, became perplexed and worried. She attributed the religious transformation of both of her formerly secularist brothers to the failure of the left to realize the promise of national liberation and to a weakening of faction recruitment and education:

> The religious movement has drawn away many of these younger activists. Maybe it was because there wasn't a better choice . . . there wasn't a quick alternative or solution to the occupation. Maybe they thought the religious direction was a faster way to achieving a solution. . . . [Hamdi's] turning to religion points to the failure of the left . . . to implant the values of the movement within the people. The Islamic movements have been very active in this area . . . much more than we have.

Given the intensity of Islamist-secularist competition, especially in Thawra, it was hardly surprising that Khadija viewed her brother's religious turn as a rejection of the secular left. For Khadija, a self-styled old-time leftist who had long turned her back on religious faith, there was no middle ground. Hamdi's move was not an evolution of secular nationalism but rather a turning away from it that said more about the sorry state of the left than anything else. Hamdi viewed things quite differently. "I haven't changed at all in the way I deal with people," he told me. "My whole life I have sought to reach out to people, to help them. Before, perhaps I did this because it was in my nature, but now I have religious reasons, as well." Part of this "nature" was shaped under the tutelage of Communist uncles and cousins and in Communist Party structures at school and university. This leftist milieu in which he was raised upheld the "customs and traditions." Rather than being a rejection of the values with which he had grown up, religion was, for Hamdi, a further extension and evolution of his earliest orientations.

Liberal Islamism

A similar type of hybridizing of orientations characterized Majdi and Amal's conceptions of solidarity. Using the English term in their discourse, Majdi and Amal referred to themselves as "modern." The modernity they invoked entailed not a wholesale repudiation of a putatively fossilized past but rather a selective appropriation of the traditional and the modern that problematized both the past and the present. Majdi and Amal both had university degrees and careers as schoolteachers. They said they wanted only three or four children, rather than the eight to ten kids their parents and grandparents had raised. They also claimed to share domestic duties—cleaning, cooking, and so on. Although Amal did the cooking, Majdi told me that he washed all the couple's clothes—a task he did for a long time by hand until they finally purchased an old washing machine. Amal's work, and her ambitions for further study, necessitated a nonpatriarchal distribution of labor in the home and a nonpatriarchal, or more precisely a differently patriarchal, ideology to justify it. This revised patriarchalism recast the received interpretation of female roles by simultaneously stressing the need for women to remain responsible for the home while amplifying the right of women to personal independence. Lurking in the background of this reinterpretation was a profound ambivalence with secular "liberalism" as Majdi and Amal had experienced it in Thawra and Bethlehem.

For Majdi and Amal liberalism had created moral chaos, and the result was conflict, confusion, and abusive relationships in the camp.

Amal: . . . Those who are not religiously committed [*multazimīn bi al-dīn*] do not possess understanding of where the limits need to be in this society. Most women who are not religious today do not possess this knowledge [of limits]. I am speaking of the majority of women whom I know. They have no sure guidance and for these reasons our families suffer financial problems, divorce, marital strife, children left to run the streets. . . .

Majdi: Religion provides regulations. The rules tell you how to raise your kids and relate to your wife. Your wife has a role to play in society. She is not meant simply to stay at home. If she wants to work, then she should do so. If not, then fine. But, she must have the chance to contribute to society. Amal serves others through her work. She doesn't stay secluded at home. Religion provides her with guidelines for how to deal with the men in her workplace. The relations are not open and unguided. There are limits so that there will not be commingling and muddled relations [*ikhtilāṭ*]. In the workplace, without religion, things might happen that go against your conscience and beliefs.

And, your opinion, Majdi, is that these regulations are not fully in place.

Majdi: No, they are not. If they were, many of our problems would have solutions. For example, religion tells us to ask permission before entering a house. But, people just walk right into other people's homes here in the camp. This kind of behavior leads to problems among neighbors. I'll give you another example. Our next-door neighbors are building a multistory house. They are producing a lot of dust and noise, and the construction is encroaching on the road in front, but they won't listen to our concerns. They have no basic understanding of religion and its rules, so we have no basis on which to appeal to them. Instead, what we have is moral "ebb and flow" [*madd wa jazr*]. This is a disaster for our society. Thawra is basically a conservative [muḥāfiẓ] society. We cannot base such a society on ebb and flow: today something appeals to me and then tomorrow it doesn't? We are playing around with the limits. . . . They tell you, "Go and pray at the mosque but then go and spend your money at the casino" [a reference to the casino at Jericho established by a Palestinian-Austrian partnership]. The secular system creates contradictions. It tells you it's okay to pray in the mosque, but in the street, religion has no place. How can you get along in the street without guidelines? Perhaps this is what Amal was getting at.

Amal and Majdi described a society that lacked a basic consensus on social regulation. There were no longer any clear frameworks for adjudicating conflicts or ordering social behavior, generally. Neighbors did as they pleased in complete disregard of others living around them; men ogled and abused women with no fear of censure or punishment; and women experimented in social relations with disastrous consequences. Secularism, or "liberalism," in this view, was largely to blame for this predicament because it had undermined the religiously sanctioned social patterns that once provided basic stability. A return to Islam could correct this problem by reinstating these patterns. Thawra was a "conservative" (muḥāfiẓ) society, as Majdi put it; Islam accorded with this reality.

In arguing for a return to Islam, however, Majdi and Amal actually articulated not a simple, literal reapplication of sharīʿa stipulations but rather a reinterpretation of what it meant to be both "progressive" (*taqaddumī*) and religiously committed (*multazim*). Both secular-liberal and Islamist values, as the following excerpt shows, became revised in this creative rearticulation:

Amal: From time to time, even today, girls are married off without consulting the girl herself. Religion, however, gives girls a right to say if she wants to get married and to whom. If she is attracted to someone, and there is no other channel of communication, she also has the right to go directly to a man and say, "I have strong feelings for you and would like to marry you." In our society today, however, this is impossible. A girl who does this is seen as insane and immoral. So, you see, there are many things that religion allows you to do that completely contradict accepted traditional practices in our society. I'll give you another example. A woman, according to Islam, has the right to support from her husband and the right to work. She has the right to hire a wet nurse and servants to help her raise her kids and run the house. She has the right, that is, to lead a complete and secure life. If she is insecure for any reason, then she has the right to request a divorce. Islam also requires that a woman be educated and literate. She must work outside the home and learn what the world is like. She needs to learn about society and culture.

Majdi: She needs to be "up-to-date" [said in English].

Amal: Yes. Exactly. She shouldn't be forced to work, but she should have the right to choose to do so.

Does she have to remain responsible for the home?

Amal: Yes, of course. She must be able to balance the outside with the inside. If she can't do this, then it is better for her to remain at home. As a Muslim, I believe religion encompasses all of life: my social struggle [*niḍālī al-ijtimāʿī*], my life struggle, even my struggle with my husband and my family . . . all of this is based on my religion. My children and family will learn and respect religion through the example I set. If my children learn well from me, there will be no later social problems. I concentrate on the mother because usually she is the one who is responsible for the home and raising the children.

Islam allowed a woman the best of both the "conservative"/patriarchal and the "up-to-date"/"modern" worlds. She could choose to stay home and be supported fully by her husband, or she could have a career all her own. Given the economic realities of Thawra, the "choice" to work was also an unavoidable necessity for a family seeking to move from the precarious proletarian existence of most camp residents to a more stable middle-class, professional life.

Beyond bestowing certain rights, Islam also protected women in the workplace, as Majdi noted earlier, by clarifying boundaries. Physically and symbolically, these limits expressed themselves, for example, in Amal's scarf and long coat—garb that, through bodily adornment, revived and imposed the religio-patriarchal constructs of *ḥarīm* (a sacred, inviolable zone, but also a term that refers generally to "women") and maḥram (an individual one is forbidden to marry) on new spaces such as the public school or government office in which men and women mixed together.[29] Majdi and Amal argued that such interventions that revitalized and adapted religio-traditional practices could rectify the worst, most out-of-control aspects of Palestine's urbanizing and secularizing spaces. At the same time, the revivification and extension of Qurʾanic conventions such as ḥarīm/maḥram did not imply backwardness. On the

[29] The concept of ḥarīm refers to the segregation of women and men in the home, especially when non-maḥram individuals are present. A maḥram is someone who is "forbidden" to marry another individual because of proximate lineage ties—fathers, mothers, sisters, brothers, in-laws, grandparents, and so on. A non-maḥram, by contrast, is anyone whom one might legally be able to marry.

contrary, it facilitated the emergence of "up-to-date" Muslims. Islam promoted the education of men and women. It also counteracted certain patriarchal practices, like early marriage, that limited individual freedom, particularly the individual freedom of women. In this stress on individuality, Majdi and Amal brought Islam, as they interpreted it, into line with aspects of liberalism as earlier articulated by Maryam and Abu Samir. This liberalizing dimension not only made Islam and "muḥāfiẓ" conservatism compatible with Majdi and Amal's precarious entry into the professional classes but also effectively parried the liberals' derisive rejection of religion as retrograde.

Sheer Islamism

Alongside the liberal Islamism that Majdi and Amal articulated, more uncompromising formulations had also emerged among Thawra's Islamists. What I have labeled as "sheer Islamism" transcended Palestinian and Arab solidarity by insisting primarily on a monistic religious bonding rooted in an Islam purified of distortions. In a manner typical of the Muslim Brotherhood precursors in the Palestinian context, it sought to revitalize the spirit and practice of the first generations of Muslims who accompanied and succeeded the Prophet Muhammad.[30] Only in returning to these origins would leaders emerge who would act resolutely from Islamic motivations to found a morally cohesive society. Such people, it was said, struck fear in their enemies because true Islam refused any compromise with injustice.

Shaykh Abu Banna represented the tendency of sheer Islamism in the camp. For Abu Banna the power of Islam lay in its ability to reorient hearts and minds toward transcendent purposes. It was not a political ideology interchangeable with any other ideology. Rather, it was a total life orientation that could transform a society. Abu Banna often recounted how the Prophet Muhammad's preaching converted staunch enemies like ʿUmar ibn al-Khattab, the eventual conqueror of Jerusalem, into champions of the Qur'an. The Palestinian crisis, the shaykh told me, flowed from Islam's absence: although the mosques had been full during the Intifada, Palestinian society had failed to "absorb Islam as a complete ideology" and thus remained divided and vulnerable before its enemies. The social service program at Abu Banna's mosque sought to address this problem by providing "Islamic" alternatives to the leftist institutions. A distinguishing feature of this alternative program was the

[30] For more on the orientation of the pre-Intifada Muslim Brotherhood, see the earlier discussion and references in chapter 3.

application of ḥarīm/maḥram practices to new public spaces, as in the separation of the sexes in youth activities; education in the sharīʿa-mandated duties of males and females; and vigilance against foreign cultural influences that might undermine Islam.

The shaykh divided the world into two fields: the forces of righteousness and faith versus the battalions of waywardness and oppression.[31] This bifurcation corresponded to the religo-political tension between the god-fearing *mujāhidīn* ("strugglers" or "fighters" in god's path), on one side, and the Israeli and Palestinian National Authority security apparatuses that were targeting Islamist activists, on the other. These dualisms structured and animated Shaykh Abu Banna's self-presentation, a presentation that made use of prophetic storytelling as a discursive style. In Islamic religious tradition—and, for that matter, in Christianity and Judaism—the prophet was an individual who had received a mission from the divine to proclaim against social wrongs and the failure to uphold religious mandates.[32] The prophet suffered for his outspoken denunciations of wayward and repressive rulers and regimes. His suffering, in turn, signified and verified the authenticity of his mission and message. The effect of prophetic rhetoric was to cast collective social crises and struggles as transcendent religious dramas. These dramas turned on the conflict between divinely appointed agents and the opposing forces of evil. In such cataclysms, the true faithful became not only god's elect but also national heroes.

The prophetic structure of the shaykh's discourse emerged in his account of two arrests: one during the 1990–91 Gulf War, when Thawra was under a prolonged curfew; the other in December 1992 just prior to the expulsion of the 408 Hamas and Islamic Jihad leaders to southern Lebanon:

> [The Israelis] arrested me once for fourteen days [during the Gulf War]. When I got out, I went to the mosque. [Soldiers] stopped me. When I asked them why, they told me that I had broken the curfew. . . . The soldiers then took me away. . . . My court date came. The judge . . . brought out my file. The soldiers and their commander said I was guilty of breaking the curfew

[31] This formulation drew from and reconstructed basic moral dichotomies in the Qur'an: e.g. *īmān* (the attitude of thankfulness) versus *kufr* (the attitude of ingratitude toward god and his prophets), *mu'min* (god-fearing believer) versus *kāfir* (ungrateful rejecter of god's message and blessings), and so on. See Toshiko Izutsu, *Ethico-Religious Concepts in the Qur'ān* (Montreal: McGill University Press, 1966).

[32] The classic formulation of the prophet as a sociopolitical ideal type is found in Max Weber, *Economy and Society: An Outline of Interpretive Sociology, Volume One*, ed. Guenther Roth and Claus Wittich (Berkeley, CA: University of California Press, 1968, 1978), 439–451, and Max Weber, *Ancient Judaism*, trans. and ed. Hans H. Gerth and Don Martindale (New York: Free Press, 1952), 267–335.

> and undermining their orders. They said everyone who came to pray at this mosque [the new mosque that Shaykh Abu Banna had founded near his home in Thawra] created chaos and destroyed order. The judge could not believe it. He replied, "Since when has prayer undermined order? Do not soldiers also take time to pray?" He threw the file down and chewed out the commander and the soldiers and the lawyer who brought the case. He refused to rule. . . . The judge said that he knew I was a "man of religion" [*rajul al-dīn*, a religious specialist or member of the clergy] and that I should be able to hold the prayers and that this was not against public order. He fined me 300 shekels. I told him if it were 150 shekels I still wouldn't pay. He gave me an invoice and told me to go pay. I refused and said I would rather go to prison.

This account portrayed a dramatic encounter between a "man of religion" (rajul al-dīn) and the minions of an unjust ruler. The shaykh was arrested for attempting to give the obligatory call to prayer during a curfew. Religious practices, in this narrative, proved a deeply disruptive force that undermined an unjust regime. In adhering to Islam's prescriptions, believers found themselves in a showdown with the occupation's enforcers.

In his account of the second arrest, Shaykh Abu Banna illustrated how the very words of the Qur'an, and those who proclaimed them courageously, became the sharpest weapons against the occupation:

> Another time, one year later, I went through nine days of intense interrogation and lost sixteen kilograms of weight. There were no charges. They needed to trump something up. They took all my books from the house. They put together a file. What was in it? . . . The titles of the books along with page numbers and descriptions of what was on each page! They picked out anything that could be read as against the Jews. . . . They imprisoned me for three days here in Bethlehem. They then took me to the court. The judge had a copy of the Qur'an in front of him. He told me to open it where he had marked it. I began reciting. Apparently, I was reading something that was forbidden. The prosecutor told me, "Plead guilty and we will close the file. If you refuse, we will put you in prison for another two months and bring a truck to remove all the books from your house." I told them, "This talk is utter nonsense. I am not guilty of anything. Here is the Qur'an. It is full of things that you Jews forbid us to say and think."

In this passage, the very Qur'an brings believers into confrontation with the Israeli occupation. The *yahūd* ("Jews") are condemned by god's word and react by repressing those who hold to and proclaim it. Like a true prophet—and a courageous nationalist—Shaykh Abu Banna refuses to acquiesce in his arrest and instead demands an accounting from his captors. What has he done wrong? What has he said that is so egregious other than the direct words of god conveyed to the Prophet Muhammad by the angel Gabriel? Like the Prophet before him, the shaykh is unjustly repressed for simply speaking the Qur'an's truth. He threw no stones and fired no rifles. God's word alone was powerful. It could win over enemies to the side of truth by penetrating hearts and making plain injustice. The acceptance of suffering was a critical element in this prophetic truth-telling. It not only established the authenticity of the shaykh's motive by demonstrating selfless courage of conviction, but it also revealed injustice and mobilized forces to resist the repression. The Israelis confronted mass uprisings, in the shaykh's view, precisely because they perpetuated injustice and thereby caused a violent reaction. The suppression of the tribunes of truth, such as the shaykh, was but one manifestation of this dynamic.

Implicit throughout the shaykh's self-presentation was a hierarchy of solidarity, at the head of which stood the truly believing Muslims, the people of faith who sacrificed themselves for the sake of god's moral imperatives as laid down in the Qur'an. While all Palestinians who resisted Israel were bearing out the Qur'anic truth, it was the believers who formed the vanguard of the nation's struggle. Their overwhelming presence in the prisons gave witness to this reality, according to the shaykh. They were the greatest threat to Israel because they alone presumably possessed the depth of conviction necessary to suffer for the sake of truth. The Qur'anic word, conveyed through its spokesmen, convinced men and women of the truth, solidifying within them the willingness to lay down their lives for its sake. The lone teacher and preacher of god's divine writ, hence, stood at the forefront of the believing vanguard. It was this vanguard that would rescue the nation by leading it back to its true Islamic identity. In Thawra, such leadership entailed direct preaching against secularist attitudes and practices.[33] Like the Prophet Muhammad, who encountered stiff resistance in his early days as Allah's messenger in

[33] My leftist informants repeatedly complained to me of the shaykh's regular denunciations of them and their cultural center during his Friday sermons from the mosque pulpit. I never actually heard such sermons being preached and, thus, cannot independently confirm these charges. However, in our conversations together, Shaykh Abu Banna, while carefully applauding the nationalism of the secular left, was bitterly critical of the leftist social attitudes and practices as embodied in their center. Leftist antipathy toward the shaykh became very clear to me when, during a visit to the home of Abu Samir, one of the three friends who had been Popular Front street activists, I needed to excuse myself to go to meet with Abu Banna at his mosque for a previously scheduled appointment. Surprised that I would have been conversing with Abu Banna at all, Abu Samir said he would accompany me to the door of the mosque but would go no farther. He refused to have anything to do with the shaykh. As Abu Samir and I were approaching the mosque, Shaykh Abu Banna met us in the road from the other direction. Abu Banna invited us both in, but Abu Samir refused and said a quick and curt good-bye. Later, Abu Samir and his friends kidded me, asking whether I was converting to Islam.

Mecca, Shaykh Abu Banna sought to transform hearts and minds in Thawra as the first step toward a new nation, one rooted in the authentic soil of Islam.

CONCLUSION

The preceding discussion of Thawra revealed the central importance of three main structural factors in shaping the changes in the orientations of camp residents during the late-Oslo period: mediating institutions, principally the patriarchal family; status transformations deriving from socioeconomic changes (professionalization and proletarianization); and generational shifts linked to key historical events (the 1967 war, the outbreak of the Intifada in 1987, the 1993 Oslo Accords, etc.). The continuing centrality of the family highlighted the key variable of patriarchal values and their effects on the articulation of Islamist and secularist orientations. Amal Amireh has pointed out that Palestinian secular nationalism always construed the struggle with Israel as a drama of emasculation (the collective disaster of 1948) and violent reassertion of masculine virility (the rise of Fatah and the idea of armed revolution). The homeland—figured as a woman raped repeatedly in the various wars and defeats of the Palestinians—was to be redeemed by the heroic guerrilla or martyr who reclaimed his manhood and rightful role as protector of the family/nation by penetrating the homeland's borders, now occupied by the Zionist aggressor. This act of insertion sparked new life by inseminating the collective with the will to resist.[34] The patriarchal core of this nationalism was reproduced in the narratives of male secularists and Islamists, alike, in Thawra. Their accounts of daring defiance, near death experience, and imprisonment and torture conferred authority and legitimacy on them while also signifying a coming into manhood. Reclamation of virility as a masculine political act was a theme that cut across the Islamist-secularist divide.

At the same time, the transformations in status that accompanied the processes of proletarianization and professionalization threatened this masculinity. Forced into wage labor by economic need, women in Thawra began to experience new life possibilities. Their integration—however partial and subordinate—into the main P.L.O. factions before and during the first Intifada reinforced these shifts by legitimating their participation in spheres outside the home as part of the effort to redeem the lost patrimony. Postsecondary education added further momentum to these changes, in some instances creating status imbalance between hus-

[34] Amireh, "Between Complicity and Subversion," 747–772.

bands and wives. The insistence of the three male Popular Front activists in Thawra that men had to preserve their kalima (authority, word, in the household) indexed both the continuing normative force of patriarchal values across the social spectrum and the anxiety that accompanied the undermining of the structural bases of these values post-1967.

These structural processes combined with the formation of the camp's Islamist-secularist generational divide to create the conditions for a multidirectional reinterpretation of inherited nationalist and religious symbols and discourses. These reinterpretations occurred within a shared set of parameters that perpetuated "conservative" (muḥāfiẓ) values—as figured, for instance, in the continuing vibrancy of the discourse of the ʿādāt wa taqālīd—as the taken-for-granted ground of a common social order. At stake in the diverging reinterpretations of identity as described in this chapter was, then, not so much the patriarchal/conservative order per se but rather its form and content: Was this order to have a "liberal" or "progressive" casting? Or should it reflect a "more authentic" revitalized religious framework? The new narratives that emerged from this process, at least among my interlocutors, did not always track neatly with the politico-generational divide in the camp. The secularists in my sample subdivided into two tendencies: a liberal retrenchment that construed Islamism as a threat to the pluralist and secular ethos of Palestinian society, and an Islamic secularism that elided the difference between Islam and secularism by redefining Islam as a type of liberalism. Islamists subdivided, too. One tendency reasserted maximalizing Islamist orientations by assimilating and subordinating the nation to the cosmic religious drama of the struggle of the believing umma—the worldwide Islamic collective—against the forces of unbelief. The other integrated elements of the secular-liberal orientation to create a liberal Islamism that functioned much like the Islamic secularism originating within the secularist milieu. Taken as a whole, these diverging and overlapping orientations reflected an ongoing interactive process that conditioned both sides of the synchronic generational divide. Activists on both sides responded to the structural changes and, for anti-Oslo dissenters, the constriction of the political space brought on by the Oslo agreements by creatively drawing on and rearticulating the symbols and discourses of the competing secularist and Islamist cultural-political milieus that organized Palestinian identity. The result was the formation of new orientations that opened up the potential for alternative cross-faction, cross-milieu solidarities.

CHAPTER FIVE

Karama Camp: Islamist-Secularist Dynamics in the Gaza Strip

Pedestrians streamed by the *falāfil* stands and the U.N.R.W.A. clinic. A woman dressed head-to-toe in black with a facemask and white gloves waited on the corner. She stood out against the older *baladī* ["country"] women in their long billowing black cotton skirts [*dāʾir*] and gauzy white scarves [*shāsha*] draped loosely over their heads. Other younger women walked by in white scarves pinned tightly under their chins and the ubiquitous long coat. . . .

[Farther on] kids called out "Hello!" in heavily accented English. Little Musa saw me and announced my arrival to anyone within earshot. The *ḥājja* (grandmother) sitting hunched over in the door, pushed herself to her feet, smiled broadly and boisterously, and offered me her *shāsha*-wrapped hand. Abu Jamil appeared. Grabbing my arm, he pulled me inside and began a heartfelt greeting, kissing me on my cheeks four times while asking, *kīf ḥālak* and *shū akhbārak* and *kīf ṣiḥḥtak* [How are you? What's your news? How's your health?]. Imm Musa, Abu Jamil's wife, was in the kitchen. She threw on her headscarf as I stepped in, tossing the ends loosely over her shoulders. She came over and shook my hand. [Extract from field notes, entry no. 85, Gaza Strip, May 10, 2000: 188–190]

Palestinians and foreign expatriates commonly described Gaza as "conservative" (*muḥāfiẓ*) or "traditional" (*taqlīdī*) or "religious" (*mutadayyin*). Hamas was particularly strong here, it was said, and women covered up, especially in the camps. But what did these signs of conservatism really point to? Compared to Bethlehem, with its mix of churches and mosques and proximity to Jerusalem, Gaza certainly had a stronger "Islamic" feel to it.[1] Hamas's slogans covered walls everywhere. And

[1] Christians are a tiny minority in Gaza, concentrated primarily in Gaza City. According to the Palestinian Central Bureau of Statistics, there were 1,688 Christians in the Gaza Strip in 1997. The total population of Gaza City at that time came to 291,596. The population of the Gaza Strip as a whole was 1,001,569. Palestinian Central Bureau of Statistics, *Population, Housing, and Establishment Census—1997, Final Results, Population Report, Gaza Strip, First Part* (Ramallah, Palestine: PCBS, 1999), 45 and 112.

every woman wore some kind of scarf and long skirt or overcoat. Yet there were as many graffiti in support of Fatah as there were backing Hamas.[2] And not all women covered up in the same way. Before Hamas's campaign to impose the scarf during the first Intifada, some women—mostly university educated, middle class, and urban—used to not wear any head covering at all.[3] By 1999–2000, this had changed: almost all women, urban and camp, were conforming, to one extent or another, to Islamist dress code in public, but there was still wide variation in style and practice. Some women—virtuosi of Islamist asceticism—dressed entirely in black, complete with gloves and face masks. These women refused to shake hands with a man if he was not within the Qur'anically prescribed sphere of consanguinity. Then there were women like Imm Musa, Abu Jamil's wife in the vignette that started this chapter, who wore scarves more as a matter of conventional piety than religio-political commitment and shook hands with non-*maḥram* men who were relatives or good friends of the family. Older women also would often shake the hands of these same types of men but sometimes wrapped their own hands first in their shāsha (light gauzy head scarf) to avoid losing

[2] Some of the most intense clashes between Hamas and Fatah during and after the first Intifada took place in the Gaza Strip. Tensions increased during the Oslo period as the Fatah-dominated Palestinian National Authority attempted to consolidate power. For more on these issues, see Shaul Mishal and Avraham Sela, *The Palestinian Hamas: Vision, Violence, and Coexistence* (New York: Columbia University Press, 2000), 49–82; Andrea Nüsse, *Muslim Palestine: The Ideology of Hamas* (Amsterdam: Harwood Academic Publishers, 1998), 161–170; Graham Usher, "The Islamist Challenge" and "The Debut of the Palestinian Authority," chaps. in *Palestine in Crisis: The Struggle for Peace and Political Independence After Oslo* (London: Pluto Press, 1995, 1997), 25–34 and 61–77; Beverley Milton-Edwards, *Islamic Politics in Palestine* (London: Tauris Academic Studies, 1996), 153–180; Khaled Hroub, *Hamas: Political Thought and Practice* (Washington, DC: Institute for Palestine Studies, 2000), 113–119.

[3] Hammami notes that before 1988 "there was wide variation both in the forms of *ḥijāb* worn and in its use or non-use by women of different social classes and groupings." The different forms signaled class and regional identities as well as religion and age differences. In the 1950s, middle-class women in Gaza and throughout the Middle East dispensed with the ḥijāb and adopted Euro-American clothing styles as a signal of their social status. Camp women continued to wear the loose white or black head coverings and embroidered dresses or black skirts; the latter item was developed in response to material shortages following the 1967 war. Hammami argues that the style of dress of these women marked peasant and camp status rather than gender, primarily. In the late 1970s, however, the Islamic movements, principally al-Mujammaʿ al-Islami—the Islamic Collective, a Muslim Brotherhood derivative that preceded Hamas—attempted "to impose or, as they saw it, 'restore' the ḥijāb on women in Gaza who were not wearing any form of head covering—mainly educated, urban and petit bourgeois women." In the process, the movement made the ḥijāb a gendered marker of piety and political affiliation as well as national loyalty. The long coats (*jilbāb*) appeared at this time and were referred to as *sharʿī* dress (dress that adhered to sharīʿa regulation). The campaign became aggressive one year into the Intifada as

the ritual state of purity (*ṭahāra*) required for prayers.[4] Many university-educated women of the secular professional segment of the middle classes grudgingly wore light scarves over their heads in public but dispensed with them instantly upon entering their offices and homes.

Both the variation and the conformity in women's public comportment pointed to deeper dynamics that had implications for social identity and the struggle between Hamas and the secular-nationalist factions, generally. The ubiquitous *ḥijāb* (scarf) and *jlibāb* (coat) were tangible signs of the degree to which Islamism had succeeded in shaping the cultural terrain of Karama and the other communities in the Gaza Strip. Another sign was the extent to which Islamist sociomoral and political arguments had shifted the terms of debate about identity. The Islamist theodicy—the idea that Palestinian failures and Israeli victories were the result of Muslims not upholding the *sharīʿa*—figured in the discourse of activists across the factional spectrum. Critique of the Islamists, moreover, took the form not of a rejection of a sharīʿa-based society per se but rather of a question as to whether such a social form was feasible under present historical conditions and whether the Islamists themselves measured up to the morality they were purveying.

The retrieval and integration of patriarchal traditionalism as a more conscious element of collective identity in Karama and elsewhere in Gaza had a generational dimension to it. It occurred primarily in reaction to a relatively recent cultural re-Islamization and the rise of a corresponding politically vibrant Islamist-nationalist movement during the first Intifada. The split between Islamists and secular nationalists that resulted was principally a division within a repatriarchalizing milieu.[5]

Hamas activists attacked unveiled women violently. Ironically, the secular-nationalist factions failed to counteract this campaign. Hammami views this failure as indicating that male secular-nationalist leaders shared the patriarchal assumptions underlying the Islamist initiatives directed at women: they just did not see the veiling initiative as a threat. They became concerned only when Hamas directly contested their leadership of the Uprising. See Rema Hammami, "Women, the Hijab, and the Intifada," *MERIP* 164/165 (May–August 1990): 24–28.

[4] After offering me her shāsha-covered hand in greeting, the ḥājja mentioned in the opening vignette above told me, "My dear, excuse me; the afternoon prayer is approaching." "Ḥājja" is a term that describes a woman who has made the pilgrimage to Mecca and, generally, any older female who has reached the status of a grandmother. For a discussion of ritual purity in Islam, see Frederick Mathewson Denny, *An Introduction to Islam*, 3rd edition (Upper Saddle River, NJ: Pearson Prentice Hall, 1994, 2006), 104–108.

[5] Patriarchal metaphors and assumptions had long been a key part of secular nationalism. Repatriarchalization in the secularist milieu retrieved and reinforced these already embedded orientations. Hamammi, "Women, the Hijab, and the Intifada," 24–28, and Amal Amireh, "Between Complicity and Subversion: Body Politics in Palestinian National Narrative," *South Atlantic Quarterly* 102, no. 4 (Fall 2003): 747–772.

Although highly proletarianized and exposed to secular Israeli society (i.e., through the mass media and the day wage labor market), family-clan (*ḥumūla*) structures remained dominant in Karama and gained in strength during the Uprising in the absence of alternative modes of social organization and control. Access to advanced education and trade specialization had indeed increased with the establishment of Gaza Islamic University and al-Azhar University and U.N. vocational education centers. The arrival of the Palestinian National Authority, moreover, had amplified possibilities for employment in various security and social service bureaucracies. Still, much more so than Thawra, which was in proximity to a diverse, cosmopolitan, and urban environment, Karama had the feel of a dense, sprawling village where social life was organized primarily around clans and everyone knew everyone else's name.[6] Trips to Gaza City were limited to work, shopping, and the occasional family excursion. Day to day, life, especially for women, was lived out within the confines of one's camp neighborhood, generally organized by paternal family groupings (the ḥumūla). These constraints solidified even further as Israel progressively tightened its closure of Gaza during the first Uprising.

The various dimensions of repatriarchalization and its particular relationship to the Islamist-secularist tension in Karama manifested themselves in the lives of the Asdudis—the family featured centrally in this chapter.[7] The three brothers and one paternal first cousin who comprised the family's male core spanned the spectrum of Palestinian historical experience and political identity. They were, individually, and at different points in time, members of Fatah, the Palestinian Communist Party, the Popular Front for the Liberation of Palestine, and Hamas. Their personal experiences encompassed the war in Lebanon; the P.L.O.'s exile to

[6] Thawra, too, shared this feeling of a tightly interconnected village in which everyone knew everyone else and the primary mode of identification was the family or clan (ḥumūla). Still, its proximity to Jerusalem and Bethlehem gave the camp a more urbane character. Thawra residents prided themselves on being members of a community that was unlike more insular camp settings in the southern West Bank and Gaza Strip. It shared in the multireligious and multiethnic character of the larger metropolitan region. Despite the security barricades, many of my contacts secretly made regular trips for work across the porous West Bank border into Israel, occasionally spending a risky overnight in Tel Aviv to drink at the bars. Fluent in Hebrew, they often succeeded in passing for Israelis. They also enjoyed the company of foreigners. Since the first Intifada, Thawra had been a regular stop for Western journalists and human rights activists of all sorts who were based in Jerusalem. Karama, by comparison, was much more cut off from these kinds of encounters. The isolation increased as the Israeli closure of the Gaza Strip tightened.

[7] I made several visits to this family's home during a period of volunteer teaching in the West Bank (1986–89). Our connection developed further while I worked as an English teacher in Gaza City with a U.S.-based nongovernmental organization from 1991 to 1993.

Tunis and Algiers and eventual repatriation to Gaza and the West Bank in 1993; the 1967 war; the Black September conflict in Jordan; the first Intifada; and the Oslo period. These various experiences forged diverging social and political orientations that tracked with the generational tendencies that had shaped Palestinian identities in the Occupied Palestinian Territories as a whole. The Asdudis, in particular, demonstrated how, in Gaza, the "customs and traditions" (*al-ʿādāt wa al-taqālīd*) and religion (*al-dīn*[8]) took on multiple meanings as they interacted with the contrasting, yet overlapping, conceptions of political identity within the Intifada generation. At issue among the brothers and cousin was not so much the basic structure of society—patriarchal values remained the shared, unquestioned substratum of their lives—but rather how the common patriarchal order was to be expressed and lived out. Did the basis of this order lie in the ʿādāt wa taqālīd (custom and traditions) of the *fallāḥī* (peasant) past, a past remembered for its putative intersectarian unity founded on common patriarchal values? Or were the values that were embedded within Islamic texts and the memory of the practices of the first generation of Muslims a more authentic source for reconstituting the Palestinian nation, a nation that was, in the end, essentially a Muslim one?

The tensions that formed among the brothers and their cousin on and around this question reflected the broader cultural-political split between the secularist and Islamist generation-units that took form in the society as a whole during the first Intifada. While Karama, because of its particular historical, geographical, and social characteristics, may perhaps have amplified the repatriarchalizing dimensions of the split, the community never-

[8] The concept of "al-dīn" denotes the set of practices (prayer, pilgrimage, charitable giving, and so on) and beliefs (assent to the one god, acceptance of Muhammad as god's final prophet, etc.) that comprise the baseline requirements of Islam as set forth in the Qur'an, *aḥādīth* (sing. *ḥadīth*, handed-down sayings attributed to Muhammad and his companions), *sunna* (Muhammad's exemplary practice as derived from the aḥādīth), and the sharīʿa (the codified customary law that draws from the ḥadīth, sunna, and Qur'an). While there is broad consensus among Muslims about this baseline, we will see how individuals in this case study argue, for very different purposes, that the essence of al-dīn lies not in the performance of these ritual acts but in the spirit with which they are undertaken. This is a very old debate among Muslims. Sufi mystics, for instance, have emphasized the believer's inner attitude. Some Sufis have argued that achieving states and stations of ecstatic union with the divine should take precedence over slavish attention to the demands of external piety (i.e. the legally imposed practices of the sharīʿa). Most, however, have followed such foundational scholars as Abu Hamid Muhammad al-Ghazali (1058–1111 C.E.) in insisting that inner experience and outward piety be dialectically interrelated; to sever one is to sunder the other. For general background on Sufism, see Denny, *An Introduction to Islam*, 211–235, and Annemarie Schimmel, *Mystical Dimensions of Islam* (Chapel Hill, NC: University of North Carolina Press, 1975).

theless reflected general trends in post-Intifada identity formation already noted in more diverse settings such as Bethlehem and its surrounding communities. Even in Thawra, with its historically strong leftist-secular milieu, patriarchal structures and values remained in place despite the partial "liberalizing" transformations that had resulted from female education, access to secular liberal-arts universities, professionalization, political mobilization, and the creation of social service institutions that experimented in mixed male-female activities. Male leftist activists still insisted on their *kalima* ("word," authority) in the home; and leftist factions were, according to several reports, careful to appear to uphold the "ʿādāt wa taqālīd" in practice even as they claimed to be Communists, leftists, or "liberals" in ideology. Thawra and Karama thus represented different points on the continuum of repatriarchalization. In Karama, the Islamist-secular-nationalist cultural struggle revolved much more explicitly around the issue of what custom and tradition were and who got to define these terms. This debate coincided with the continuing centrality of the family (ḥumūla) to social organization in Gaza's camps. Factions and their associated institutions (labor unions, professional associations, mosques, etc.) shaped the orientations embedded within ḥumūla structures in various ways by relating them to nationalist or Islamist themes.

KARAMA CAMP AND POST-OSLO GAZA

The Camp

Karama Camp is situated in the heart of the Gaza Strip. It came into existence in 1948 as thousands of southern Palestinian villagers and town dwellers sought refuge from advancing Zionist militias during the war that coincided with Israel's founding. After the signing of the armistice agreements, Israeli forces continued to carry out mass expulsions, especially in al-Faluja and al-Majdal, areas that would become incorporated into the Israeli cities of Qiryat Gat and Ashkelon. The Asdudis came from a small village on the outskirts of Asdud, today's Ashdod, an Israeli city. By 1997, Karama Camp's population had reached approximately 50,000.[9] The Gaza Strip, as a whole, had one of the highest rates

[9] This figure comes from Palestinian Central Bureau of Statistics. It has been altered to preserve Karama's anonymity. Sara Roy, drawing on U.N.R.W.A. and various others sources, puts the population of the camp in 1992 at a significantly lower number. The difference possibly results from the high birthrate in Gaza, among other factors. See Sara Roy, *The Gaza Strip: The Political Economy of De-development* (Washington, DC: The Institute for Palestine Studies, 1995; reprint, 2001), 16.

of population growth, internationally, at 4 percent per annum in the early 1990s; and it was among the most demographically dense places in the world: more than 12,000 individuals for every mile squared of Arab-owned land. Population density in the camps was even higher. The largest camp, Jabalya, registered 133,400 individuals per mile squared in the early 1990s, a figure double that of the Island of Manhattan and far outstripping Israel's average density of 80 per square mile.[10] The local economy had been primarily dependent on day wage labor in Israel since the 1967 war, but with the prolonged closures of the Gaza Strip that Israel imposed during and after the first Intifada, camp residents came increasingly to rely on patronage jobs in Palestinian National Authority agencies and projects.[11] The camp had a large central market with an extensive warren of small stores, workshops, and offices. U.N.R.W.A., the United Nations institution set up to aid Palestinian refugees after 1948, operated primary and secondary schools for boys and girls as well as health clinics and development programs in all the camps. An U.N.R.W.A. vocational training center situated in Gaza City provided postsecondary certification in the trades for refugees across the Strip.

There were two ways into Karama. One route cut east from the shore road through dunes and privately owned date palm and fruit tree plantations (*bayyārāt*) toward Martyrs Square in the central market. The other

[10] Ibid., 15.

[11] After the outbreak of the "al-Aqsa Intifada" in September 2000, the Palestinian National Authority became severely weakened in the face of a massive Israeli assault on its infrastructure and financial assets. Unemployment consequently skyrocketed in Gaza and the West Bank, reaching in some areas to well above 50 percent of the workforce. Destitution rates concomitantly climbed in equal measure. The U.N. Special Coordinator in the Occupied Territories (U.N.S.C.O.) estimated that between October 1, 2000, and January 31, 2001, the Palestinian economy lost half of its Gross Domestic Product for a total decline of US$1,150.7 million. Average unemployment by the end of the first month of 2001 stood at 38 percent, or more than 250,000 able-bodied workers. The United Nations also estimated a 50 percent increase in the number of individuals living below the poverty line—a standard set by the World Bank at US$2.10/person per day. United Nations Office of the Special Coordinator in the Occupied Territories, "The Impact on the Palestinian Economy of Confrontations, Mobility Restrictions and Border Closures, 1 October 2000–31 January 2001" (New York: February 2001). This report and other related documents can be found at http://domino.un.org/unispal.nsf/0/edadfb71ec0f110085256c3a0066fd23?OpenDocument and http://www.arts.mcgill.ca/mepp/unsco/unfront.html. Also, Hugh Dellios, "Clashes Choke Palestinian Economy: Israeli Blockades Restrict Flow of Workers, Goods," *Chicago Tribune*, December 12, 2000, sec. 1, p. 3, and Dan Cork, "Information Brief, Number 79: The Palestinian Economy Post-Oslo: Unsustainable Development" (Washington, DC: Center for Policy Analysis on Palestine, July 11, 2001), http://www.palestinecenter.org/cpap/pubs/20010711ib.html.

was a wide boulevard[12] that headed due west off the main north-south artery—a highway coursing down the Strip's midsection from the northern Erez checkpoint to the Egyptian border. As one turned west off this highway onto the main camp boulevard, a long concrete wall running for several hundred meters to the left became visible. In 1999–2000, graffiti and murals commemorating the fiftieth anniversary of al-Nakba—"the Disaster," the term Palestinians use to refer to the 1948 war—still covered the length of the structure. Slogans reaffirmed the long-frustrated right of return and asked, "Until when?" Drawings depicted masked fighters throwing rocks and wielding rifles; farther on, a rendering of the Dome of the Rock in Jerusalem appeared.

Along the approach to the central market, unfinished buildings with steel reinforcement cables protruding like whiskers from the bare concrete rose up on both sides of the boulevard. The road often became choked at this point with pedestrians, donkey carts, the long Mercedes limousines used as cooperative taxis between camps and towns, and the dusty, dented Fiats, Peugeots, and Deltas that ferried riders to different points within the camp. A memorial to camp residents killed in the first Intifada stood in the central intersection of the market. Four concrete ribbons situated on the compass points swept up toward a small gold dome in an inescapable gesture toward Jerusalem's al-Haram al-Sharif (the Noble Sanctuary or Temple Mount). Photocopied "martyr" pictures, some fresh, some faded and tattered, clung to the concrete ribbons below the dome. Just past the memorial, cars in various states of repair lined up to transport riders to the southern sections of the camp. The drivers were usually unemployed or moonlighting camp residents.[13] An unspoken

[12] These wide streets were known among camp residents as "Sharon boulevards." In 1970–71, Ariel Sharon, a tank commander who, thirty years later, would be elected to the office of prime minister, led the Israeli army in sweeps to crush nascent Palestinian guerrilla resistance in the camps. During the campaign, the army widened the main roads to allow easy passage of tanks and other armored vehicles, in the process destroying hundreds of homes. After his election at the start of 2001, Sharon once again spearheaded a massive military assault to smother Palestinian militias that had initiated attacks on Israeli settlements, army outposts, and civilian targets with the outbreak of the al-Aqsa Intifada on September 28, 2000. For more on Sharon's actions in 1970–71, see Sara Roy, *The Gaza Strip*, 104–106.

[13] Once, I was riding with my friend Abu Jamil in his used yellow Delta. He had purchased the battered vehicle soon after getting a job as head of maintenance in the Gaza City headquarters of one of the many police apparatuses that ʿArafat had set up as part of the Palestinian National Authority. The job gave Abu Jamil a regular paycheck for the first time in his life. Spotting a neighbor as we pulled onto the road leading from Section B to the market center, my friend stopped and offered the man a ride. The man got into the back seat and a few seconds later passed Abu Jamil a shekel coin. Abu Jamil laughed, telling the man to keep his money. "I thought you were working the line, Abu Jamil," the neighbor responded apologetically. Abu Jamil replied, "No, thank god, I have a job these days."

rule dictated that the automobile at the head of the cue should fill first. Depending on the time of day, the vehicle either filled quickly or one waited for up to half an hour. The trip to the neighborhood in which the Asdudis lived usually lasted five to ten minutes, depending on the number of drop-offs and pickups and the amount of traffic. The dusty and potholed route passed by a mosque next to which lived one of the original founders of Hamas. Farther down, there was a U.N.W.R.A. girls' school and a rubble-strewn soccer field. The section of the camp in which the Asdudis lived abutted the southern end of the field. The roads leading off the main route were little more than packed dirt crisscrossed with open sewer channels. People were everywhere. Children ran around in the dust. Elderly individuals sat on mats in front of doorways. Women and men passed by on foot continuously as they performed errands and visits. The Asdudi home was off a narrow passage that threaded between the densely packed breeze-block structures that had replaced the tents and shacks of the first generation of refugees. Corrugated asbestos roofing provided rudimentary protection against the intense summer sun and the driving rains that slashed the eastern Mediterranean coast in wintertime. At night, mice scampered across the undulating asbestos surfaces.

The Gaza Strip

The social, economic, and political currents that shaped life in Karama during the period of my fieldwork had their headwaters in Gaza's history under the British Mandate, Egyptian military administration, and Israeli occupation. Four aspects of this history are especially pertinent to the ethnographic analysis to follow in the remainder of this chapter: (a) the persisting clan-based patriarchal structure of social life combined with the emergence of trade unions, professional associations, and the like in response to proletarianization and nationalist mobilization; (b) the progressive processes of economic underdevelopment and de-development that have typified each phase of Gaza's experience of occupation by external powers; (c) the formation of contending political movements based in Muslim Brotherhood and P.L.O. structures from the 1950s onward; and (d) the enduring dynamics of upheaval and violence that are intrinsic to the experience of occupation, resistance, and generational transformations of collective political identities. Each of these aspects is interlinked with the others.

Social life in Gaza's refugee camps bases itself, in part, on clan-based systems of social organization that place a premium on personal-patriarchal authority as embodied in such concepts as the *kalima* (word) and *qarār* (decision) of fathers, husbands, sons, and brothers and the ʿādāt wa taqālīd, the "customs and traditions" of village life. The basis for this order lies in the persisting patterns of fallāḥī (peasant) solidarity; in the corresponding absence or relative weakness of alternative state and non-state (civil society) structures that might replace various functions of the family, especially the provision of social welfare and policing services; and in the lack of a developed industrial economy that creates diverse forms of social solidarity beyond the family.

The continuance of fallāḥī solidarity among Gaza's refugees, historically, reflects the transposition of the patriarchal structures of village life to the camps in the wake of the 1948 war. Rosemary Sayigh has described this process in detail in her groundbreaking ethnography of Palestinian refugee communities in Lebanon. In her studies, she documents how refugees, in the immediate aftermath of the 1948 disaster, coped with the violent dispersion by reproducing the same patterns of family and clan-based affiliation that had existed in their former villages.[14] Sara Roy has documented a similar phenomenon in Gaza, observing:

> In response to their profound dislocation, the refugees turned inward. They clung to traditional forms of social organization and authority relations, which has given camp life in Gaza a homogeneity that it does not have in the West Bank.[15]
>
> Refugees remained with their relatives and townsmen. As a result, even today, the camps are divided into district quarters, each with its own *mukhtar*, or leader, which preserve the original village framework. Refugees in the camps, even the youngest among them, identify themselves as members of villages that they have never seen, but that they nonetheless can describe in meticulous detail.[16]

The specific policies of the Egyptian military administration in the Gaza Strip between 1948 and 1967 reinforced these "traditional" social

[14] Rosemary Sayigh, *Palestinians: From Peasants to Revolutionaries*, with an introduction by Noam Chomsky (London: Zed Books, 1979), 10–53.

[15] Roy perhaps overstates the contrast with the West Bank. As we have seen in the discussion of Thawra Camp in the Bethlehem area, patriarchal authority patterns remain very much intact as does the distinction between fallāḥī (peasant) and *būrjuwāzī* (bourgeois) as the primary imagined distinction between camp and town. Still, Roy's point is well taken as far as the far greater degree of accessibility to urban settings and international contacts and influences in the West Bank—at least until the imposition of the separation wall and cantonization of villages and towns during the ongoing al-Aqsa Intifada. Gaza, by comparison, has been much more isolated, geographically; since the start of Israel's occupation in 1967, it has also been encircled by high fences and checkpoints. The combined effect has led to a turning inward, socially. Sara Roy, *The Gaza Strip*, 23–24.

[16] Ibid., 19.

arrangements by preventing resettlement of the refugees within Egypt—an option that many refugees were anyway predisposed to reject, initially expecting imminent repatriation to their villages and towns. Similarly, Israeli policies after 1967 sought to prevent or undermine nationalist consciousness and organizations by empowering village elites (the *mukhtār*, pl. *makhātīr*, village elders, and *shaykh*, pl. *shuyūkh*, elders or religious leaders) as mediators and bureaucratically categorizing Palestinians according to ethnic, regional, and religious identities (e.g., as Druze, Bedouin, Christians, Muslims, and so on).[17] Moreover, in both Gaza and the West Bank after 1967, but especially in Gaza, Israel pursued policies, known euphemistically as "Open Bridges," that facilitated Palestinian access to employment in Israel while simultaneously preventing meaningful, independent economic development of the Occupied Palestinian Territories. Indeed, these policies actually had the cumulative effect, more by default than by design, of "de-developing" the Palestinian economy.[18] They prevented the emergence of an independent industrial sector, undermined the development of competitive domestic agriculture, and rendered the labor market almost completely dependent on

[17] For a detailed discussion of these policies as they were enacted among the Arab Palestinian minority that remained in the areas that became Israel after 1948, see David Mark Neuhaus, "Between Quiescence and Arousal: The Political Functions of Religion: A Case Study of the Arab Minority in Israel, 1948–1990" (Ph.D. diss., Hebrew University [Jerusalem], 1991). Sara Roy briefly discusses the same phenomenon in Gaza after 1967 in *The Gaza Strip*, 106–107. For an analysis of these policies in the West Bank, especially the effort to create the "Village Leagues," see Salim Tamari, "In League with Zion: Israel's Search for a Native Pillar," *Journal of Palestine Studies* 12, no. 4 (Summer 1983): 41–56.

[18] The term "de-development" is one that Sara Roy has coined to describe a dynamic process through which an economy is actively dismantled and, in the process, made dependent on more powerful and developed external markets. De-development describes Gaza's situation as it evolved under Israeli occupation practices that sought to dominate territory while simultaneously exploiting the labor of, and refusing any responsibility for, the people living on that territory. In the de-development model, the objectives of economic planning policies are driven not by economic rationality but by colonialist political considerations. In Israel's case, the Zionist concern for "land over people," that is, territorial expansion minus demographic integration, has provided the overriding political impulse for the policies of the occupation. Israel structured its relationship with Gaza so as to exploit its cheap labor while simultaneously separating the Palestinian populace from Israel, legally and politically. The extended collective revolt that began with the first Intifada effectively undermined this policy: the persisting violent resistance has caused Israel to react punitively by, among other measures, drastically scaling back the number of Gazan workers allowed into Israel. Israel has since unilaterally redeployed its military and removed its settlers from the Gaza Strip. It maintains control of a northern swath of territory as a "security zone" and continues to make armed incursions to assassinate Palestinian guerrilla leaders and "clear" areas from which Palestinian fighters have fired missiles into Israeli towns. Gazans remain effectively sealed in on all sides by Israel's fences, walls, naval patrols, and border controls. For a more detailed discussion of these issues, Sara Roy, *The Gaza Strip*, 117–134.

day wage labor in Israel. Between 1970 and 1988, there was a near 400 percent increase—from 22,800 to 109,400—in the number of Palestinian laborers working in Israel. By 1988, approximately 38 percent of all Gazans relied on jobs in Israel, mostly in the service, construction, and agricultural sectors.[19] This employment generated 42 percent of the Strip's GNP by 1987. Roy observes that "as early as 1970, furthermore, wages earned in Israel were 110 percent higher than those obtained in the Gaza Strip."[20] The kinds of jobs that were available were low-skilled service, construction, and agricultural day employment. Trained professionals, if they were able, emigrated to the Gulf states, the Soviet Bloc countries, Europe, or the United States. The combined effect was to structure Gaza's economy as a dependent annex that provided a vast pool of semiskilled and unskilled labor for Israel, primarily, but also the Gulf region.[21]

Jobs in Israel, although poorly paid by Israeli standards, were coveted by Gazans. Abu Jamil, my primary connection to the Asdudi family, worked at times at construction sites in and around Tel Aviv; the prolonged closures during and after the Gulf War of 1990–91, however, placed this employment option increasingly beyond his reach. Caught between an asphyxiated local economy that choked off any chance to build a business in appliance repair and arbitrary Israeli measures of collective punishment, Abu Jamil became demoralized, forced more and more to rely on handouts from U.N.R.W.A, the United Nations agency set up in 1949 to deal with the Palestinian refugee crisis, and what little support was available to him through family and friends. He was not alone: during and after the 1990–91Gulf War, when Israel imposed total closures in a bid definitively to crush the first Intifada and ensure pacification of the Palestinian population during the war, the United Nations "was feeding an unprecedented 120,000 families in the Gaza Strip, both refugee and non-refugee"; in 1992, the figure rose to "430,000 family food parcels."[22] In 1992, Abu Jamil worked for a while as a night watchman for a new business that an acquaintance of mine, a young Palestinian entrepreneur from an old landowning family in Gaza City, started after Israel began to encourage limited local investment.[23] The job was for

[19] These figures are from the Bank of Israel. Cited in ibid., 210.

[20] Ibid., 217.

[21] Ibid., 217ff.

[22] Ibid., 312.

[23] This policy, the product of a 1990 Ministry of Defense report authored by Ezra Sadan, sought to promote Palestinian industrial capacities as an extension of Israel's markets. Much like the industrial parks that have been built on the Mexican side of the U.S.-Mexico border, these projects sought to exploit Gaza's huge and relatively cheap labor market. Ibid., 326ff.

various reasons short-lived, and Abu Jamil, becoming ever more demoralized, remained unemployed or underemployed and dependent on the United Nations for survival until the arrival of the Palestinian National Authority in 1994.

Inheriting an economy from Israel that lacked any ability to absorb the thousands of unemployed in Gaza, and needing to forge popular support against Hamas and other competitors, the P.N.A., soon after its installation, began extending large-scale patronage principally through the creation of a bloated bureaucracy, including multiple, overlapping police and security apparatuses. Roy notes that by the late 1990s the P.N.A.'s public-sector salaries in the West Bank and Gaza amounted to "14 percent of GDP, which is more than twice the average for developing countries. In 1998, the wage bill neared $470 million or close to 55 percent of current expenditure. . . . In 2000, the P.A. [i.e., the Palestinian National Authority] acknowledged that the public payroll [was] expected to consume 60 percent of the $1 billion dollar budget."[24] Abu Jamil, his older brother, and his cousin all worked in P.N.A. security apparatuses and public works projects of one sort or another during the Oslo period.

Prior to Oslo, Israel's occupation policies compounded the Strip's near total reliance on employment in the Israeli economy by providing only minimal levels of state-based social welfare. This welfare was oriented toward cultivating or enforcing collaboration with the military regime, a practice that intensified during the first Intifada of the late 1980s and early 1990s. Socially, the effect was to reinforce family networks, and thus patriarchal authority structures, as the default resource for individual survival, especially in periods of prolonged closure that prevented travel to day jobs in Israel. Political factions supplemented these networks by providing charity, enhanced networking beyond the neighborhood and clan, and access, via *wāsṭa* (Palestinian colloquial: "connections"), to educational opportunities in U.N.R.W.A. training centers and universities. In the West Bank but especially in Gaza's sprawling camps, where the population had organized itself according to pre-1948 village and clan-based solidarities, faction and family functioned as extensions of one another. Membership in one often coincided with integration into the other such that a specific family would become known as having X or Y faction loyalty. Yet even if a particular family was known to be predominantly aligned with one given faction, this fact did not preclude the possibility of other solidarities. Because of Gaza's contested political terrain, families sometimes contained multiple, diverging ideological orientations, as was the case with the Asdudis.

[24] Ibid., 370.

As the existence of faction structures indicates, Gazan society possessed not only a familial-patriarchal substratum but also had developed parallel institutions and networks based on occupational and party-political modes of solidarity. The development, however attenuated, of professional associations, trade unions, women's movements, student organizations, and so forth coincided with the diversification of social spheres that accompanied massive proletarianization and urbanization, especially after 1967; it also dovetailed with the emergence of a nationalist resistance movement, embodied in the P.L.O., a kind of state-in-exile, that organized collective resistance against Israel through hierarchical, bureaucratic structures even as it co-opted the authority figures and adopted the symbols of the peasant past in an effort to ground the new nationalist solidarity in the inherited memories and values of the fallāḥī-refugee community.

The formation of the P.L.O. factions, as well as their competitors, the Muslim Brotherhood and its successor organizations, in the Gaza Strip began during the 1948 war and the subsequent Egyptian occupation. Muslim Brotherhood volunteer units fought against Zionist forces in Gaza but were forcibly disbanded by the Egyptian military following the signing of the Egyptian-Israeli General Armistice Agreement on February 24, 1949. The Egyptian government then set up a military administration in Gaza "impos[ing] harsh and total control over Gaza's civil and security affairs," including curfews every night.[25] The Egyptian military governor controlled appointments to all positions within the public administration and regulated all commercial and social functions. Egyptian officers and civilian nationals dominated the upper echelons of the administration and filled appointments in the health, business, and education sectors. The refugees were entirely excluded from these structures. Declared "stateless," they were denied passports and forced to apply for military permits whenever they wished to leave the Gaza Strip. The Egyptian military also banned all independent Palestinian political organizations. Consequently, many of these groups, including the Muslim Brotherhood, went underground to organize violent incursions across the armistice lines. These independently organized attacks, combined with large-scale Israeli retaliation and provocation raids, spurred the Egyptian military to carry out sweeping arrests of Palestinian activists and to impose even harsher controls on political and social organizations.[26]

The political situation in Gaza changed significantly with the rise of Jamal ʿAbd al-Nasir following the "Free Officers" coup in 1952 and the trilateral invasion of Egypt by France, Britain, and Israel four years later

[25] Ibid., 66.

[26] See ibid., 66, 69. See also for further background Abd al-Fattah Muhammad El-Awaisi, *The Muslim Brothers and the Palestine Question, 1928–1947* (London: Tauris Academic Studies, 1998).

in response to Nasir's closing of the Tiran Straits and nationalization of the Suez Canal. The experience of the 1956 Suez War and Israel's subsequent brief occupation of the Gaza Strip brought forth a new generation of Palestinian political leaders who formed the Fatah movement. Nasir actively nurtured Palestinian guerrilla organizations during the period leading up to the Suez War both as a way to project his claim to leadership of nascent pan-Arabism and to maintain pressure on Israel through a proxy force that would prevent a direct engagement of the Egyptian army. Nasir had become convinced of the need to strengthen his options for such pressure after two deliberatively provocative large-scale Israeli incursions into Gaza—the first in August 1953 in al-Burayj Camp, killing some fifty Palestinians, and the second against an Egyptian military encampment on February 28, 1955, that killed thirty-nine people.[27]

The formation of the guerrilla groups and the experience of fighting the Israelis during 1956–57 provided Fatah's founders with their two guiding objectives: independent Palestinian action to liberate the homeland and armed struggle. While Nasir supported this new Palestinian nationalism, he also sought to subordinate it to his needs by encouraging other Palestinian entities to come into existence under his direct tutelage. In 1958, for instance, he supported the creation of the Palestinian National Union (*al-ittiḥād al-qawmī al-filasṭīnī*). The P.N.U. was an appendage of the Arab Socialist Union—an organization founded the previous year to forge pan-Arab alliances under Egyptian control. Nasir also fostered the creation in Gaza of the Palestine Students Organization (1963) and the General Federation of Trade Unions (1964). The most important development, however, was the establishment of the Palestine Liberation Organization, the P.L.O., under the auspices of the Egyptian-dominated Arab League in January 1964. Meant as a mechanism of Arab state control of Palestinian national aspirations, the P.L.O. nonetheless came to provide the framework for an independent Palestinian movement that took the form of a state-in-exile. A key dimension of this process was the development, with Egyptian sponsorship, of Palestine Liberation Army units in the Gaza Strip. Although equipped only with light weapons, the P.L.A. became a central mobilization vehicle of the P.L.O. following the takeover by Fatah in 1968–69.[28]

[27] Sara Roy, *The Gaza Strip*, 69. On the deliberate and provocative nature of Israel's attacks, Roy cites Avi Shlaim, *Conflicting Approaches to Israel's Relations with the Arabs: Ben-Gurion and Sharett, 1953–1956*, Working Paper #27 (Washington, DC: International Security Studies Program, the Wilson Center, September 23, 1981), 6–14.

[28] Sara Roy, *The Gaza Strip*, 69–71. See also Yezid Sayigh, *Armed Struggle and the Search for State: The Palestinian National Movement, 1949–1993* (Oxford: Oxford University Press, 1997), 112–119, and Helena Cobban, *The Palestinian Liberation Organisation: People, Power and Politics* (Cambridge: Cambridge University Press, 1984), 21–35.

The emergence of Fatah and the P.L.O. as the dominant expression of Palestinian collective identity corresponded with a concomitant withdrawal and reduction of Muslim Brotherhood structures in Gaza. These formations and their associated cultural-political orientations did not disappear but rather went into abeyance, largely because of the sustained Egyptian crackdown on Islamist activism from the mid-1950s onward. The situation changed in the early 1970s. While Israel's victory in the 1967 war catalyzed Fatah's self-assertion as an independent actor on the regional Arab stage, it also spurred Islamist revitalization, principally through renewed cultural and social initiatives. The leaders of this revivification were young activists who had studied in Egyptian universities during the late 1960s and 1970s and who, in the course of their studies, had come into contact with the radical offshoots of the Muslim Brotherhood. Nasir had died by this point, and his successor, Anwar Sadat, in a bid to isolate the old guard, began cultivating the Muslim Brotherhood as a counter to Nasir's supporters. Once back in Gaza, the rising generation of Palestinian Islamists, the late Shaykh Ahmad Yasin principal among them, revitalized the old Muslim Brotherhood formations, creating new frameworks such as the Islamic Collective. Israel encouraged this revitalization by issuing permits to Islamist organizations and supporting mosque-building projects while simultaneously targeting P.L.O. activists for arrest and expulsion. The severe Israeli crackdown on the armed uprisings of 1969–72 had made sustained "armed struggle" increasingly untenable, forcing P.L.O. supporters as well to shift toward social, cultural, and political activism. Consequently, both a revitalized Islamist sociopolitical milieu and a P.L.O.-led secular-nationalist one came into existence in the Gaza Strip at roughly the same time. While the P.L.O. became the dominant expression of the collective aspirations of the Palestinian people in Gaza and the West Bank and elsewhere, the Islamic Collective and the other Islamist organizations, especially in Gaza, created an alternative constituency based in a growing network of charitable associations, mosques, labor unions, student groups, and professional associations.[29]

One final dimension of Gaza's historical experience requires discussion, namely, the dynamics of violence that have been the inevitable consequence of occupation. Palestinian violence has received much attention in the U.S. and European press. Gaza, especially, has been the focus of

[29] These issues have also been discussed in greater detail in chapters 2 and 3. Among other references cited therein, Milton-Edwards, *Islamic Politics in Palestine* 73–143; Hroub, *Hamas*, 29–36; Ziad Abu-Amr, *Islamic Fundamentalism in the West Bank and Gaza Strip* (Bloomington and Indianapolis, IN: Indiana University Press, 1994), 10–22; Sayigh, *Armed Struggle and the Search for State*, 607–613; Joost R. Hiltermann, *Behind the Intifada: Labor and Women's Movements in the Occupied Territories* (Princeton, NJ: Princeton University Press, 1991), 3–16 and subsequent chapters.

this scrutiny. It was in Gaza that the first Intifada of the late 1980s and early 1990s began. Gaza was the place from which militant Palestinian Islamism in the form of Hamas and Islamic Jihad first emerged. And it has been from Gaza that many of the "human bombers," the majority of them associated with Hamas and Islamic Jihad, have originated.[30] What often goes unremarked, however, is how the Israeli occupation in Gaza and the West Bank itself constituted a structure of controlled violence that operated through multiple modalities, some of them visible but many others less accessible to immediate observation. From the moment of its installation in 1967, the occupation functioned to enact the Zionist formula of "land over people," that is, the principle of annexing territory while isolating and containing the non-Jewish, Arab populations that previously had inhabited that land. In the Gaza Strip, between 1967 and 1990, Israel controlled approximately 58 percent of the total land area primarily through direct seizure.[31] By the start of the Oslo Process, sixteen Jewish-only settlements had access to 35 percent of this confiscated territory. By radically reducing the land area available to Palestinian settlement, Israel's policies severely intensified Palestinian population density in the Strip. By 1993, "there were 85 times as many people per dunam among Arabs than among Jews."[32] (One square mile is equivalent to approximately 261 dunams.) Put differently, by the mid-1990s, there were 5,929 Palestinians for every mile squared (overall) in Gaza—among the greatest densities of population worldwide; the figure for Israeli settlers in the Strip was 282 per square mile.[33] In addition to direct land control, the Israeli occupation also placed severe limits on Palestinian use of natural resources, especially water, redirecting the bulk of these resources to Israeli use. Buttressing these aggressive practices was an extensive apparatus of bureaucratic and legal controls. Between 1967 and 1993, the Israeli military issued approximately one thousand orders that served as the primary legal structure in the Occupied Palestinian Territories. The bureaucratic procedures through which these orders were implemented sought to control every dimension of Palestinian life. They functioned to maintain Palestinian demographic separation, blocking Palestinian settlement within Israel's pre-1967 armistice boundaries, and to encourage dependence by making permits for everything from housing construction to water use, registering a birth, taking high school exit exams, travel, and so on a matter of accepting and cooperating with

[30] On my choice of the phrase "human bombers," Ivan Strenski, "Sacrifice, Gift and the Social Logic of Muslim 'Human Bombers,'" *Terrorism and Political Violence* 15, no. 3 (Autumn 2003): 1–34.

[31] Sara Roy, *The Gaza Strip*, 175.

[32] Ibid., 176.

[33] Ibid., 178.

the occupation. An arrest record would immediately become a road-block to attaining the permits necessary for building a life.[34]

From the very beginning of the occupation, Palestinians mounted various types of resistance, ranging from different modes of nonviolent non-operation (e.g., tax refusal, commercial strikes, boycotts, sit-ins, demonstrations, prison hunger strikes) to violent insurgency. In Gaza, there were three major outbreaks of mass uprising and armed revolt: the period immediately following the 1967 war, the first Uprising of the late 1980s and early 1990s, and the most recent al-Aqsa Intifada, which began at the end of 2000. In each instance, Israel had to shift from bureaucratic modes of control to overt direct repression. The use of violent repression was usually successful. In the early 1970s, army units under the direction of Ariel Sharon effectively smashed Palestinian guerrilla activity with house-to-house searches, mass arrest campaigns, bulldozing camp homes to create wide boulevards for easy access by tanks and other heavy armaments, and so on. Many of these same tactics were employed twenty years later with the outbreak of the first Intifada. Israel has responded to the much more violent al-Aqsa Uprising by using overwhelming force: Apache attack helicopters, fighter-bomber jets, wholesale demolition of homes, especially in Gaza's Rafah refugee camp, mass arrests, assassinations, and so on. As of September 2005, Israel has adjusted its posture by removing its settlements and redeploying its army to Gaza's borders. Declaring its occupation unilaterally ended, Israel nevertheless maintains military control over Gaza from a close distance. Its forces continue to attack Palestinian armed groups at will, and it maintains a near complete closure of the Strip.

As I have argued in this book, each wave of violence and repression has resulted in the mobilization of a new generation of leaders who have revived and reoriented Palestinian nationalism. In Gaza, these generational processes have interacted with the forces that have perpetuated familial-patriarchal structures, fostered the emergence of competing Islamist and secular-nationalist formations, and reinforced the Strip's relative isolation and economic dependence on Israel. The remainder of this chapter explores this multilayered interaction at ground level through the close analysis of the life histories, attitudes, and relationships of the

[34] Ibid., 22 (on military orders) and 162–175 (on water policies). For more documentation and discussion of these occupation practices, Baruch Kimmerling and Joel Migdal, *Palestinians: The Making of a People* (Cambridge, MA: Harvard University Press, 1993, 1994), 240–242, and Ilan Pappe, *A History of Modern Palestine: One Land, Two Peoples* (Cambridge: Cambridge University Press, 2004), 196–200. Also, Amira Hass's moving firsthand narrative of life in Gaza under Israel's occupation and the conditions of uprising, *Drinking the Sea at Gaza: Days and Nights in a Land under Siege*, trans. Elana Wesley and Maxine Kaufman-Lacusta (New York: Metropolitan Books, 1996, 1999).

members of one particular refugee family. This highly concentrated focus on a single family unit in one location enables a detailed case-study analysis that sheds light on how the larger processes discussed above have shaped individual patterns of political mobilization and identity, and, conversely, how individual appropriations of Islamist and secular-nationalist symbols, discourse, and narrative have created new hybrid orientations. My close-to-the-ground analysis complicates the accepted picture of Gaza. It does so by presenting a picture of "retraditionalization" that, while significantly shaped by post-Intifada Islamization, does not track in lockstep fashion with, and indeed often diverges from or resists, Islamist conceptions of collective and individual identity. These alternative appropriations of traditionalizing orientations merge in various ways with the well-worn themes of multisectarian P.L.O. nationalism but also redirect these "secularist" orientations along new paths.

THE ASDUDIS: SOCIAL BACKGROUNDS AND PATHS OF POLITICAL MOBLIZATION

Of all the Asdudis, I am closest to the middle brother, Abu Jamil. My relationship with Abu Jamil began in July 1987 at a volunteer youth work camp run by the Palestinian Communist Party in Nazareth. As his bus was preparing to leave the camp, he invited me to return with him to visit his family in Karama. I accepted and soon found myself rocketing down Israel's coastal highway at midnight. Two hours later, we crossed Gaza's Erez checkpoint—an ad hoc border-crossing outpost. (This outpost would later be replaced, after the signing of the Oslo Accords, by a major border installation. The new structure would funnel Palestinian workers past identity checks through fenced-off corridors and turnstiles and then to waiting buses. Foreign nationals would be processed through a separate, modern-looking passport control facility on the other side of a high wall that kept the Palestinian section out of view. By contrast, the checkpoint we traversed in 1987 seemed little more than a rudimentary roadblock manned by a small detachment of soldiers—a symbol of the "Open Bridges" policy that fostered Palestinian access to employment in Israel while enforcing the demographic separation of Palestinians within segregated, policed zones like the Gaza Strip.)

After pausing momentarily for an inspection of papers, we plunged through the checkpoint and plummeted down the Strip's main artery, arriving in the center of Karama's main market. The Intifada memorial had not yet been built; the Uprising would not begin for another four months. Dusty and exhausted from the day's work, Abu Jamil and I descended from the bus and proceeded to march double time through the deserted square and down the road toward the camp's southern section. After half an hour, we passed the rock-strewn soccer field and turned up the rutted road leading to Abu Jamil's home. We came to a house with old refrigerators parked in front of the door. Three men lounging on mats in a pool of light across the road called out to us incoherently. "They're high (*masāṭīl*)," Abu Jamil whispered, ". . . always like this, every evening." We walked between the refrigerators into the dwelling. Abu Jamil brought me a chair and asked if I wanted a *dishdāsha* (an ankle-length tailored tunic) to change into. A tall, rail-thin man with a bushy beard appeared. "This is my older brother, Latif," Abu Jamil told me. Latif smiled warmly, shook my hand, and sat next to me. Reaching for a pack of Farids, he took out a lean, white cigarette, tapped it against the box, and lit it with the glowing ember of an expiring butt wedged between the yellowing fingers of his right hand. We sat in the doorway looking out at the loungers across the road.

Latif pulled on the fresh Farid, coughed softly, and began socializing me into refugee identity. "We are not from here," he told me firmly. "We are from Sumud . . . it's a village near al-Asdud [Ashdod]."[35] Dynamited and then bulldozed after the 1948 war, the site would have been visible off the coastal highway on the descent from Nazareth to Gaza. Latif's father had been a married tenant farmer with a son in 1948 when he took his family to shelter behind the Egyptian lines. He went back to the village clandestinely with other men to check on his home and fields but eventually had to return to the Strip as the Zionists consolidated their gains. "The Arab regimes didn't fight," Latif lamented bitterly. "They had a secret agreement with Israel to partition Palestine."[36] He went on to tell me that his father remarried in 1960, twelve years after his first wife died. The second wife was the mother of Latif and his two younger brothers. Their older half-brother from the first marriage moved to Saudi Arabia to become an Arabic teacher after working in the Egyptian civil administration for several years during the 1960s.

The 1967 war was a central event for both Latif and his paternal first cousin/brother-in-law Abu Qays, the former Fatah guerrilla and police captain described in the earlier discussion of the Fathawi milieu in chapter 2. In an interview in December 1999, Latif recounted how the Egyptian army had "run away," how his father had raised a white flag over their dwelling along with all the other neighbors, and how resistance to the Israeli occupation had developed in 1969 soon after Fatah and the

[35] Sumud is a fictional name. The name of the original village has been obscured to protect the identity of my friends.

[36] For the history of Jordan-Israel collaboration, see Avi Shlaim, *Collusion across the Jordan: King Abdullah, the Zionist Movement, and the Partition of Palestine* (New York: Columbia University Press, 1988).

P.L.O. began organizing operations. In the ensuing years, the Asdudi family developed a strong connection to the Fatah movement. Abu Qays, for instance, left his family at age twelve in the confusion following the 1967 war to join "the revolution" in Jordan. He signed up with Fatah and fought in one of its armed units against the Hashimite Kingdom's army in Black September (the Jordanian Civil War of 1970), commanded a guerrilla cell in Lebanon, and was captured and detained in the Israeli Ansar prison camp for several months after the 1982 war. Abu Qays was then expelled to Algeria and Libya but returned eventually to Lebanon to rejoin his family in the ʿAyn al-Hulwa Refugee Camp. He came to Karama in 1995 to become a police commander in Yasir ʿArafat's Palestinian National Authority. He and his family lived on the second floor of Latif's home for five years until the completion of new condominiums for P.L.O. returnees in the Madinat al-Zahra housing complex fifteen minutes north of Karama just off the shore road.

Latif also had a long-standing connection with Fatah. In 1979, at the age of nineteen, he went to Jordan to search for work as a new, U.N.R.W.A.-trained electrician. There he developed contacts through his family with Fatah operatives. He told me he shuttled messages and information for the movement to and from the Occupied Palestinian Territories during the post-Beirut period when Fatah was attempting to organize inside the West Bank and Gaza Strip. Latif returned to Gaza in June 1986 after being told by a relative who was a ranking Fatah activist that it would be better for him to go home to take care of his elderly father, mother, and two teenage brothers rather than join the movement in Lebanon. Later, during the Intifada, he worked for Fatah in "counterintelligence," observing and identifying people in the camp suspected of feeding information clandestinely to the Israeli military.

Latif remained loyal to Fatah, and the movement reciprocated. After the installation of the Palestinian National Authority, he was made head of maintenance in one of the new tax-free industrial zones set up to attract foreign investment.[37] He got the job through Fatah connections. "The economy's been bad and I got tired of hustling up jobs," he told me in 1999, "so I got in touch with some of the people I worked with in the Intifada and told them I was interested in finding better work." He smiled and said, "They owed me." Within a couple of months, he was sitting behind a desk in the free-trade zone sending workers on assignments. "It's coffee and tea, tea and coffee all day long," Latif told me with a laugh. Latif's job gave him enough off-duty time to supplement his income moonlighting as an electrician.

Latif's wife, Imm Muhammad, was a secondary-level science teacher

[37] For more on these zones, see Sara Roy, *The Gaza Strip*, 357–359.

in Karama's U.N.R.W.A. Girls' School, and, like her husband, aligned politically with Fatah. Her salary meant that she and Latif could build a two-story home to the west of the original camp boundaries. The home had four bathrooms, two in "Turkish" style and two in *ifranjī* ("Frankish," or Western) style. The family remodeled the kitchen and living/dining areas in the summer of 2000, borrowing money to do so. They also invested in a computer with Internet service for their kids—nine in total, ranging in age in 1999–2000 from three to sixteen. Abu Jamil criticized his brother and his wife for what seemed like extravagance by camp standards. "I love my brother, but the only thing he cares about is making everyone think he's middle-class," he said. "He should be paying off his debts, not taking out more loans." Along with the financial pragmatism, there was a hint of envy in Abu Jamil's criticism. Abu Jamil's family was barely managing to survive on his paltry police salary. Yet Abu Jamil was not completely wrong about his brother's social aspirations. I took a photograph of Latif after interviewing him in December 1999. He posed in shirtsleeves, a pen in his front pocket, holding a phone to his ear like a bureaucrat at his desk. Latif had spoken to me in his interview about how he and his wife wanted to send their kids to college and do everything they could to make the latest technology available to them such as the computer, Internet, and CD-ROM educational materials. Latif and his wife were indeed breaking with the collective ethos of refugee identity—an ethos that had upheld the suffering of poverty and dispossession and the collective struggle for restitution as virtues and as a claim on the future. The Oslo Peace Process, however, had momentarily made other futures appear possible. Latif and his family seemed to be choosing one of these alternative paths, physically leaving the camp to occupy a new two-story home, the mark of those who had left the ranks of the disinherited peasant-turned-proletariat classes to join the new middle-class bureaucrats of the Palestinian National Authority.

In contrast to Latif, Abu Jamil had only rarely traveled beyond the borders of the Gaza Strip into Israel and had never experienced any society outside this context, not even the Jordanian or Egyptian ones. His political mobilization also took a different turn. Instead of Fatah, he became associated, at the age of eighteen, with the Communist Party and then the Popular Front for the Liberation of Palestine. His connection to these groups developed through trade union organizers and faction stalwarts in Karama Camp and at the U.N.R.W.A. vocational school in Gaza City, where he trained to become an electrician and refrigerator repair specialist. His integration into these structures was less the result of studying Marx and Lenin than it was of becoming connected to networks in which his friends and schoolmates were already involved. Abu Jamil's older brother Latif put it this way:

> **Latif:** . . . The older guys would approach younger guys, and in this way they would get followers. You didn't study a faction's ideology and then make a decision. Rather, you might develop friendships with some guys with a certain faction connection—maybe some guy has a father or older brother who is tied into a faction and he and his friends help him out in secret activities and in this way they begin to organize the younger guys. . . .
>
> *So, Abu Jamil didn't study their ideas . . . ?*
>
> **Latif:** He did study them when he became more politically aware, but not at first. The majority were like this.

Latif's comments revealed the extent to which integration into factions was often a function of family and neighborhood friendship ties. Faction ideology was a strictly secondary consideration, an add-on that came later. Joining a faction was like joining a club: it was a way of locating oneself, socially, a place where one's friends were. It was also a way to mobilize resources: the faction network could help with getting into a training program, getting connected to a job, getting aid for one's family during a stint in prison, and so on. This instrumental aspect—or, rather, its failure to work on his behalf—became a source of resentment for Abu Jamil during the Uprising and then after it.

Abu Jamil never became a fully active member of either the Communist Party or the Popular Front for the Liberation of Palestine. During the first Intifada, he claimed to have become an "independent." In July 1988, the Israeli military consigned him to the infamous Ketziot Prison in the Negev Desert for three months. An informer working with the military apparently caught him on videotape throwing stones in a demonstration. This was used against him in his hearing before a military tribunal. As was true in all the other detention centers, detainees in the Negev prison organized themselves according to faction affiliation. Abu Jamil initially indicated that he was with the Popular Front for the Liberation of Palestine, but eventually he separated himself out, claiming to be independent. He had begun to look cynically on all the factions. "I was in for three months," he said, "and when my wife came to visit she told me that none of those Popular Front guys ever come around with assistance for her and the kids." All the factions were hypocritical, he said. They talked about fighting for the oppressed and the nation, but when it came to helping the truly needy, they offered empty slogans. The promise of aid was a tool to get members; principles, it seemed to Abu Jamil, counted for nothing.

Following the arrival of the Palestinian National Authority in 1994, Abu Jamil landed work in the maintenance department of the central Gaza City headquarters of the Preventative Security Forces (*quwwat al-amn al-wiqā'ī*), one of the dozen P.N.A. security apparatuses established during the Oslo Peace Process. He got the job largely through the *wasṭa* (connections) of his paternal cousin, the P.L.O. fighter who returned to Gaza from Lebanon in 1995. Abu Jamil's steady paycheck ($390 a month in 1999–2000) allowed him to dream of one day building, like his brother Latif, a small house outside the suffocating squalor of the camp confines. The job also restored his self-esteem as a breadwinner and bestowed a degree of status within and outside the camp. Reflecting the fundamental role of the patriarchal family structure and its values in the formation and expression of his identity, he repeatedly declined to allow his wife to work outside the home, even though she possessed a certificate in physical education from the U.N.R.W.A. teachers' college in Ramallah. "Who would take care of the kids?" he replied, laughing, when I proposed the idea of letting her get a job so as to increase the family's income and thereby make it possible to move out of the cramped breeze-block structure they inhabited. During the first Intifada, Abu Jamil remained unemployed for months. The family survived on U.N. rations and the kinship network. The experience was humiliating at times. He once wept in front of me in 1991, just after the first Gulf War, recounting how, when he was sweeping out the rooms of their dwelling to help his wife, his son asked why he was doing women's work.[38]

Landing a Palestinian National Authority job restored Abu Jamil's pride: it not only again made viable his self-conception as a family head and provider but also bestowed a sense of social prestige relative to the urban middle classes of Gaza City. This became apparent when he met me, dressed in military fatigues, at the Erez border in October 1999 on my first visit back to Gaza in more than three years. I asked him why he was wearing his uniform off duty; he told me, "We get more respect this way." We got into his beat-up Delta, the first car he had ever owned, a sign of his improved fortunes and new status, and drove into Rimal, the middle-class section of Gaza City, to visit a friend. Once in Rimal, we stopped along the way to ask directions from an older woman dressed in an expensive Western-style suit. The woman became nervous as we approached. "Did you see how she was afraid of me at first?" remarked Abu Jamil. "That's what I mean when I say the uniform gives us more respect."

[38] During the war, Israel imposed a total curfew and closure on the Gaza Strip. The impact was devastating: unemployment skyrocketed, families massively depleted what little savings they had (usually in the form of a woman's wedding jewelry), and malnutrition began to appear among children. For more, Sara Roy, *The Gaza Strip*, 309–312.

The prestige of the uniform and his steady income not only reestablished Abu Jamil's self-esteem but also affected his politics, at least on the surface. Once, soon after being hired in 1996, he and I were standing in a camp alley talking with one of his old Popular Front buddies. The friend spoke bitterly about the Palestinian National Authority's crackdown on opposition groups (the Popular Front opposed Oslo) and blamed ʿArafat for the patronage and corruption he perceived developing in the Authority. Abu Jamil interjected forcefully, saying, "Don't criticize Abu ʿAmmar [ʿArafat's nom de guerre] like that in front of me." Three years later, however, Abu Jamil's views had changed, at least in private. In October 1999, he and Latif drove me through the wealthy Rimal section of Gaza City. As we passed through the neighborhood, the two brothers pointed out the new multistory apartment buildings and spacious seaside villas that the members of the P.L.O. elite, outsiders and insiders, had built since 1994. The ostentatious display led the brothers to ask a question that I encountered numerous times throughout Gaza and the West Bank: where was all the money going? A few months later, behind closed doors and out of earshot of others, Abu Jamil again expressed distrust of, and disillusionment with, the Palestinian National Authority. "If there's any more fighting," he told me, "I'm staying put. Why should I lay down my life when I know these guys will sell it for a few million dollars and a worthless treaty that won't bring a better future for my kids?" Abu Jamil's brother, Latif, expressed similar sentiments. "It's the dogs around ʿArafat," he said. "They're the problem."[39] Many people in the camp resented the Palestinian National Authority and the elite that controlled it, Abu Jamil told me, and so he kept his head down. "I go from work to

[39] Latif elaborated on this, saying: "People sacrificed in the Intifada so that they could have a livelihood and some security at night. They didn't fight so that someone could come and steal from them, to impose high taxes and steal the community's wealth. . . . This is a crime, a disaster. I think if the Sulta [the Palestinian National Authority] does not discipline these thieves the people will rise up and do the job themselves. Our people are living below the poverty line . . . including the government employee. The people who have come from outside, on the other hand, are living the good life. In one of the import-export agencies, I've heard that 200,000 shekels pass through their hands monthly. If it went toward public distribution (*al-tawzīʿ al-ʿāmm*) then you'd find changes and improvements, right?" Latif absolved ʿArafat from responsibility for the perceived corruption. ʿArafat was clean, in Latif's mind, but he was tired and insulated from knowledge of the dubious practices of his officials: "The people around him are garbage. I speak truthfully. They're garbage. The bad thing about the Sulta is the administration, only. As a person, a president, a national symbol, we respect [ʿArafat] a lot." The tendency was widespread among Fatah supporters to absolve ʿArafat personally of the corruption in the Palestinian National Authority. Laetitia Bucaille documents similar attitudes in her study of younger Fatah activists in the Nablus area in the West Bank, for instance. Laetitia Bucaille, *Growing Up Palestinian: Israeli Occupation and the Intifada Generation*, trans. Anthony Roberts (Princeton, NJ: Princeton University Press, 2004), 54.

my home and back without stopping to talk to anyone," he said. "When I hear a group of guys talking about the Palestinian National Authority, I walk away. I don't want anyone accusing me of turning anyone in if the security forces pick someone up later. My relations with everyone are good, thank god."

Abu Jamil and Latif's youngest brother, ʿAbd al-Muʾmin, shared this bitterness and disillusionment about the Palestinian National Authority. Unlike his brothers, whose concerns were with a lack of fairness in the distribution of wealth and honor within the post-Oslo system as it was emerging, ʿAbd al-Muʾmin stood outside the structure as an opponent. A Hamas sympathizer, his concern was with the stifling of religious expression: "It isn't safe to be too openly pious in these times," he told me. ʿAbd al-Muʾmin's remarks reflected the insecurity generated by the Palestinian National Authority's repression of Hamas. ʿArafat struck the first blow in November 1994 when he resurrected Fatah's former Intifada militias to carry out shows of strength against Hamas and Islamic Jihad in Gaza City. The campaign followed a spate of embarrassing Hamas and Jihad operations in Israel a month earlier—including the kidnapping of an Israeli soldier and a series of deadly human bombings. The operations not only demonstrated the continuing strength and independence of the Islamist movements but also revealed ʿArafat's vulnerabilities. Committed to the Oslo Process, ʿArafat found himself having to enforce Israeli and American security dictates with very little to show in the way of tangible and steady territorial gains leading to meaningful statehood.[40]

ʿAbd al-Muʾmin was a polarizing force in his Fatah/P.L.O.-leaning family, illustrating at a microcosmic level the dynamics of the Islamist-secularist generational split and its effects on the wider society. I first met ʿAbd al-Muʾmin during my initial visit to Karama Camp in July 1987. He was still in secondary school at the time. I was quartered in his room for the night and noticed Qurʾanic commentaries piled high on his desk next to his schoolbooks. The next day, he peppered me with questions about why Christians had falsified their scriptures, a charge that had featured centrally in the anti-Christian polemic of Muslim writers during the medieval period. Despite his interest in religion, ʿAbd al-Muʾmin chose to enroll in the scientific stream in high school. He got good marks and was able to take some university-level courses in computer science after the end of the Intifada. By the end of the 1990s, he had managed, with some friends, to start an Internet computing center. He had also become married by that point. I never was able to meet his wife. Abu Jamil

[40] For more on the 1994 clashes see Usher, "The Debut of the Palestinian Authority," 68–72.

told me that she had insisted on building a cement wall down the center of the small breeze-block compound that had been the childhood home of the brothers.[41] She apparently wore the scarf and long coat in addition to a mask called *niqāb* that covered her face from below her eyes to below her chin.

The particular direction of ʿAbd al-Mu'min's political mobilization reflected a process of integration into an already existing Islamist milieu. He had become predisposed to move in this direction during his childhood. During a conversation in October 1999, he told me he became pious at an early age. His father was in his late sixties or early seventies when ʿAbd al-Mu'min was born. The elderly father would sit on his lamb's wool all day and pray. ʿAbd al-Mu'min would watch him and sometimes joined in the prayers around the time he entered kindergarten. On Fridays, his father would ask him if he wanted to go with him to the mosque, and most of the time he would go. He would walk between his father and his father's friend, he told me: two old men with a boy between them. When he got older and was in school, he would do all his prayers in the mosque, rain or shine. He told me that he also started reading and hated watching TV. He would read the Qur'an and *aḥādīth* (handed down accounts of what the Prophet Muhammad said and did). Today, he admitted, he was not as attentive to daily prayer and study. He did his prayers automatically at work, right there in his office. If he were really serious, he told me, he would go to the mosque. "They say piety [*taqwā*] is like the tide of the sea," he told me: "at some stages it is strong and high, at others it is weak and low. *In shā' allāh* [should it be in god's will] I will return to stronger piety."

Latif confirmed his brother's narrative separately in my interview with him in December 1999. He explicitly connected ʿAbd al-Mu'min's development as an Islamist to early involvement with the mosques:

Latif: Like I told you, my father was an old man by the time ʿAbd al-Mu'min was born. And, an old man always needs a little boy to take his arm and go places with him. My father would always go to the mosque to pray . . . the older men always did this. Now, who at home was around my father the most at that time? ʿAbd al-Mu'min. He would come from the kindergarten and go to the mosque with my father. . . . This was how he began to carry the Islamic ideology. He met people there who influenced him. . . . I tried to dissuade him from going in that direction, at first.

But, he didn't listen.

[41] ʿAbd al-Mu'min and Abu Jamil shared the home with their families. The cement wall was a powerful statement of separation and rejection, in Abu Jamil's eyes.

Latif: No, he didn't, and I couldn't convince him. He was young and stupid. But, today, after he started working, got married, and started having kids, he has begun to simply try to fulfill what our lord requires of us . . . if he's near a mosque, he'll go and pray and then go home.

As with Abu Jamil, ʿAbd al-Mu'min's "direction" took form through older individuals and local camp institutions, especially the mosques. In both Latif's and ʿAbd al-Mu'min's accounts, there appeared to be a seamless continuity between the "simple" piety of their father's generation and the Islamist movements of which the younger son soon became an associate. The Islamists apotheosized this piety even as they advanced a more "sophisticated," book-centered version of it as part of their effort to "return" Palestinian society to what they saw as a more pristine and authentic form of solidarity. By the time ʿAbd al-Mu'min began attending mosque with his elderly father in the late 1970s and 1980s, al-Mujammaʿ al-Islami (the Islamic Collective), Hamas's immediate precursor, had started actively attempting to mold camp and town life in line with this more book-centered piety through mosque-based social and educational programs,[42] building up a network of activists and institutions, in the process. ʿAbd al-Mu'min came into contact with these groups in the mosques, initially. Later he would be among the young Intifada activists who embraced Hamas when it made its appearance in early 1988. He would, along with his brother Abu Jamil, spend a period of time in detention in the Negev Desert. Unlike his brother, he passed this time within the Islamist section of the prison population. His apparent subsequent withdrawal from activism during the Oslo period—to which Latif referred when he described his younger brother as more concerned with raising a family and simply fulfilling his ritual duties as any other pious Muslim would—reflected the narrowing of the political space of Hamas and Islamic Jihad in the face of the Palestinian National Authority crackdown. While Latif's life-course explanation for the changes in his brother's behavior is certainly plausible, it is also the case that Islamist activism had become increasingly costly in the post-Oslo period: Recall ʿAbd al-Mu'min's comments about the dangers of appearing to be too pious in public.

The rise of the Mujammaʿ and Hamas was marked often by violent confrontation with Fatah for control of professional associations, universities, and various camp institutions.[43] The conflict and its repercussions played

[42] Milton-Edwards, *Islamic Politics in Palestine*, 104–116; Jean-François Legrain, "A Defining Moment: Palestinian Islamic Fundamentalism," in *Islamic Fundamentalisms and the Gulf Crisis*, ed. James Piscatori (Chicago: Fundamentalism Project, American Academy of Arts and Sciences, 1991), 70–87.

[43] For a more detailed narrative of Mujammaʿ/Hamas-Fatah tensions in Gaza and their later development during and after the first Intifada, see Milton-Edwards, *Islamic Politics in Palestine*, 84–93, 97–116, 124–143; Abu-Amr, *Islamic Fundamentalism in the West Bank and Gaza Strip*, 1–52; and Hass, *Drinking the Sea at Gaza*, 72–93.

out at the level of families. In the case of the Asdudis, ʿAbd al-Muʾmin's ideological turn injected tension into his relations with his brothers by bringing into question certain basic social and political assumptions that had underpinned their life, and the life of their wider society, since 1967.

CONCEPTIONS OF THE COLLECTIVE ORDER

ʿAbd al-Muʾmin's Islamism

ʿAbd al-Muʾmin's conception of social order echoed basic themes in Muslim Brotherhood and Hamas ideology. Particularly pertinent in the context of post-Oslo disillusionment was his concern with refounding society through a reform of the individual soul and social relations within the family. Such reorientation required a root-and-branch transformation of Muslim religious leadership. Since the turn of the twentieth century, lay Islamist intellectuals had charged the "traditional" religious scholars and notables, the *ʿulamāʾ*, with betrayal of the core values of Islam.[44] The scholars had allowed foreign influences (Greek philosophy, Jewish and Christian myths) and superstitious saint worship to creep into the religion. They had also failed their duties as guardians of Muslim honor by preaching quiescence toward repressive, Westernizing regimes that manipulated Islam for self-interested ends rather than upholding the divine injunctions as embodied in the Islamic code, the sharīʿa. A revival of Islam hence necessitated a break with, or radical reform of, the ʿulamāʾ-controlled institutions. Islamists, in particular, wished to replace the ʿulamāʾ ethic of *taqlīd* (imitation, or perpetuation of custom and precedent as the basis of the application of the sharīʿa to new situations—i.e., *fiqh*) in favor of a stripped-down Qurʾan-based order similar to the one that supposedly prevailed during the first generation of Muslims.

In addition to reforming the taqlīd-based ethic, a return to a true Qurʾanic orientation would also, in the minds of Islamists, counteract the secularizing effects that European colonialism had introduced and that the global political and economic structures continued to reinforce. Islamists felt their societies were under a relentless siege. "We are com-

[44] See the following for writings and general overviews of some of the main Islamist and Muslim reformist intellectuals on these issues: Ibrahim M. Abu-Rabiʿ, *Intellectual Origins of Islamic Resurgence in the Modern Arab World* (Albany, NY: SUNY Press, 1996); Sayyid Qutb, *Maʿalim fi al-Tariq* [Signposts along the Path] (Beirut and Cairo: Dar al-Shuruq, n.d.); John L. Esposito, *The Islamic Threat: Myth or Reality*? 3rd edition (New York: Oxford University Press, 1999), 129–139; John L. Esposito, *Women in Muslim Family Law* (Syracuse, NY: Syracuse University Press, 1982), 102–134; Denny, *An Introduction to Islam*, 315–378; and Ayatollah Ruhollah Khomeini, "The Form of Islamic Government," in *Islam and Revolution: Writings and Declarations of Imam Khomeini*, trans and ed. Hamid Algar (Berkeley, CA: Mizan Press, 1980), 55–125.

pletely vulnerable and open before the West," an Islamic Jihad activist in Bethlehem told me. Islamist intellectuals diagnosed this vulnerability as the result of a fundamental failure of governments and civil society to implement the sharīʿa fully. The solution went beyond reverting to the sharīʿa as the law of the land, however. A real and effective revival of Islam required a corresponding inner transformation of the spirit. Without a proper internal reorientation, any attempt to implement the divine ordinance would run the risk of becoming a cover for the pursuit of self-interest, as was the case in the past.

Contemporary Muslim societies, as the argument went, lacked both the sharīʿa and the necessary corresponding inner attitude of piety. These absences were the root of their weaknesses, sufferings, and failures. In the Palestinian case, this critique became a theodicy explaining the triumph of Zionism. The Zionists were victorious because Palestinians and Arabs in general had ceased to be true Muslims. Had they held to pristine Islam, they would have remained united and steadfast in their resistance. Instead, self-interested Western-leaning regimes and movements had cut deals with Israel. Since the signing of the Oslo Accords, the P.L.O. had joined the ranks of these corrupt governments. The Palestinians, as a result, had become divided; only a return to Islam would reunite them and make them ultimately victorious.

These themes of corruption and a need for a radical religious refounding of society emerged in a three-hour evening discussion I had with ʿAbd al-Mu'min in October 1999. Our conversation explored the tension between the actual pluralism of Palestinian society and the Islamist vision of a singular, Qur'an-based order; the failure, and its consequences, of Muslims to adhere to such a vision; and how it was possible to determine who was and was not a true Muslim. Beyond illustrating the logic of the Islamist theodicy, the discussion cast light on the polarizing effects that ʿAbd al-Mu'min's views generated within his family.

The discussion took place on a Friday evening in late October 1999 in the upstairs apartment of Latif's two-story home. At the time, Abu Qays (the paternal first cousin) and his family were living in this apartment. In a room next to the one in which we gathered on that evening, Abu Qays had hung a large framed photograph of Yasir ʿArafat in thick, black, rectangular-framed glasses, signing the 1988 Palestinian Declaration of Independence.[45] In the room in which we held our evening discussion, he had placed framed Qur'anic passages in glittery gold and silver calligraphy. One of the passages was from the apocalyptic "Surat al-Zalzala"

[45] The declaration, which took place in Algiers during the Palestinian National Council meeting, affirmed democratic rights and protections for all individuals and groups regardless of religious identity, gender, or ethnicity. At the same time, it reaffirmed patriarchal

(the Chapter of the Earthquake). There was also an elaborate tree diagram showing the progression of prophets beginning with Abraham at the base and branching in different directions. Moses and Jesus were in bold, but Muhammad's name was especially highlighted at the end of the longest extension.

During our conversation, my wife and I sat at the head of a wide circle with Abu Qays, Abu Jamil, Latif, their wives, and their children. We were nine adults and twenty-two children, in all. A television set with satellite programming blinked and droned in the corner. ʿAbd al-Mu'min arrived soon after we had sat down. He was freshly showered, clean shaven, and dressed in pressed pants and a buttondown oxford shirt. A chrome-colored pen hung from the edge of his shirt pocket. He removed his shoes at the door and then shook hands with his brothers, nephews, cousin, and me. He also kissed each adult male on both cheeks. He did not shake hands with any of the women but did acknowledge them by waving and saying, *"al-salāmu ʿalaykum"* (literally, "Peace be upon you all"). Latif's eldest son had been sitting next to me and was told to move for ʿAbd al-Mu'min. After kneeling down beside me, he apologized for not coming earlier. "Friday after the prayers is the only time I have all week to get caught up on my sleep," he said.

The conversation that ensued after ʿAbd al-Mu'min had taken his seat ranged across a variety of themes: why I had still not become a Muslim despite all of my studies; the problem of social diversity; the Qur'an and how to interpret it. Most pertinent was ʿAbd al-Mu'min's diagnosis of the Palestinian problem. His comments followed our discussion of how multiple perspectives existed in any given society and that this diversity had implications for the interpretation of texts. For ʿAbd al-Mu'min, social diversity and diverging interpretations signified replacement of obedience to god and the divine revelation with the pursuit of self-interest. Echoing ideas held by Muslims for centuries, he explained that while god had indeed created a diverse world, humans nevertheless were born Muslims and only later diverged under the influence of cultures that had gone astray. Islam was our natural state, and it was to this state that god called us to return. Christians and Jews were a case in point: god sent

---

notions of women as "guardian[s] of sustenance and life, keeper[s] of our people's perennial flame." Women's groups have leaned heavily on the more progressive dimensions of this document in advancing arguments for a gender-blind secular law based on universal human rights. For an insightful discussion of these issues, see Rema Hammami and Penny Johnson, "Equality with a Difference: Gender and Citizenship in Transitional Palestine," *Social Politics* (Fall 1999): 320–322. Hamammi and Johnson quote from the translation of the "Proclamation of the Independent Palestinian State," as provided in the appendices of Zachary Lockman and Joel Beinin, *Intifada: The Palestinian Uprising against Israeli Occupation* (Boston, MA: South End Press/MERIP, 1989), 399.

prophets who conveyed the divine commands to these two groups, but their followers distorted the messages over the years to justify selfish political ends.[46] Human diversity, hence, was the logical result of rebellion and ingratitude toward god. The Qur'an arrived to set matters straight. It reinstated the original divine dispensation, remaining pristine in form and content since the day it was handed down to Muhammad. While humans, by virtue of their social diversity, possessed varying interests and perspectives, the Qur'anic text nevertheless was clear in setting out basic principles that were beyond discussion. There could be no differences in opinion, when it came to its interpretation. The problem remained, however, that most Muslims failed to live lives grounded in true adherence to the Qur'an and its ethic. Like the Christians and Jews, they had fallen prey to false ideologies in the pursuit of selfish ends.

This neglect of Islam was the root of Palestinian weakness and suffering. If Palestinians had been true Muslims, ʿAbd al-Mu'min said, then they would have been powerful and "this disaster of Israel" would never have happened. But very few Palestinians really knew what Islam was, really practiced it. Sounding a stock Islamist refrain, he said they had tried communism and capitalism but not Islam. He contrasted this situation with the condition of converts like Cat Stevens, the British folksinger who became a Muslim and took the name of Yusuf Islam. Stevens represented the virtues of a true believer:

> [He] tried everything—Buddhism, Christianity—but in the end he only found peace in Islam. He is very strong in his Islam. This is always the case with people who choose Islam consciously, unlike those who are born into it and are Muslims by convention.

We could see many examples of this phenomenon in history, ʿAbd al-Mu'min told me. There were many converts in Europe during medieval times. They were zealous for the religion, more so than the other Muslims. But, I asked, how was it possible to know who was or was not a true Muslim? ʿAbd al-Mu'min responded by saying that fidelity to the faith became apparent in practice: "There are basic principles in Islam—prayer, fasting, the pilgrimage, charitable giving, saying the *shahāda* [the 'testimony' that 'there is no deity save god, and Muhammad is the

[46] This was a version of the idea of *taḥrīf* (alteration) or *inḥirāf* (deviation) that figured in medieval disputations and polemics between Muslim and Christian scholars. For careful analyses of these issues, see Jane Dammen McAuliffe, *Qur'ānic Christians: An Analysis of Classical and Modern Exegesis* (New York: Cambridge University Press, 1991), and Norman Daniel, *Islam and the West: The Making of an Image* (Edinburgh, Scotland: Edinburgh University Press, 1960; reprint, Oxford: One World Publications, 1993).

message-bearer of god']. We can know if someone is practicing Islam from what they do every day."

For ʿAbd al-Mu'min, the example of dedicated converts, modern and medieval, threw the current state of Palestinian society into sharp relief. Palestinians, like the once-searching Cat Stevens, had either become lost in foreign ideologies, communism and capitalism, for instance, or they had become "Muslims by convention" who went along with the fast or prayed now and then because this was "custom and tradition" (ʿāda wa taqlīd). This lack of conscious, zealous adherence to Islam had resulted in social weakness leading to defeat at the hands of Israel. It followed, thus, that reversal of this situation required a return to Islamic principles and practices.

But genuine revival depended not just on an external implementation and enforcement of sharīʿa legislation but even more so on an internal, metanoic transformation.[47] ʿAbd al-Mu'min explained this process of inner change as a struggle of the will against the forces of vanity and distraction as personified in Iblis (the devil, Satan). One had to tame evil (*sharr*) and orient the heart toward goodness (*khayr*) through disciplined pious practice; but one also had to be vigilant, since pride stood ready to turn practice into vain boasting. He cited a *ḥadīth* (a recorded saying about what the Prophet Muhammad said and did) that described how some rich people spent their money "in the path of god" (*fī sabīl illāh*—i.e., to support good works, charity, the *jihād*, etc.). On Judgment Day, they would boast of their piety and point to their spending as proof; but god would say, "You have given your money only so that you could say you were pious, not because you truly were pious." So they would go directly to "the Fire" (*al-nār*). ʿAbd al-Mu'min went on to comment that

[47] According to Max Weber, a metanoic transformation is an internal change or conversion of the heart, which then must issue in outward behavior that conforms with a given set of norms (the sharīʿa, for instance). In such manner, an individual becomes a charismatically qualified member of a society or brotherhood of inner-worldly ascetics that prizes inner change as an aspect of conformity to external codes of conduct. An Islamic analogue of metanoia lies in the concept of *taqwā*. Among Muslim thinkers, however, taqwā ("god consciousness" or "fear of god") is more the result of piety than its prior condition. This view parallels the Aristotelian concept of "practices of virtue"—modes of habit formation that seek the cultivation of specific inner orientations. For more on these issues, see Max Weber, *Economy and Society: An Outline of Interpretive Sociology, Volume Two*, ed. Guenther Roth and Claus Wittich (Berkeley, CA: University of California Press, 1978), 1115–1117, and Hans Wehr, *A Dictionary of Modern Written Arabic*, ed. J. Milton Cowan (Wiesbaden: Otto Harrassowitz, 1966, 1971, 1974; reprint, Libraire du Liban, May 1980), 95. On taqwā as an aspect of the ideal disposition of a believer, see Toshihiko Izutsu, *Ethico-Religious Concepts in the Qur'ān* (Montreal: McGill University Press, 1966), 195–199. On the Aristotelian dimensions of taqwā, see Saba Mahmood, *Politics of Piety: The Islamic Revival and the Feminist Subject* (Princeton, NJ: Princeton University Press, 2005), 27–29.

Iblis (the devil) worked in this insidious psychological way, sowing self-serving justifications within a person's heart. He would take every opportunity to distort the works of religion and the intentions underlying them. The only way to prevent this from happening was by strengthening one's spiritual relation with god. God had created the body and the spirit. The body was weak, however. "All of its chemical elements would come to, let's say one thousand dollar, at the most," he said, "but the spirit has no price; it alone endures." One could learn to strengthen the spirit, he told me. Just as one learned *sharr* (evil) one also could learn *khayr* (good). It was a matter of practice, of performing the prayers and doing so with a sincere intention (*niyya*). If one tried to be sincere and was disciplined in one's practice, he said, god would see this and remember it on the Last Day.

The theme of inner transformation, metanoia, had long been an emphasis in Muslim Brotherhood ideology by way of Sufism. Hasan al-Banna, the founder of the Brotherhood movement in Egypt, and an erstwhile Sufi, preached the necessity of reforming "the heart, soul, and spirit of the individual" as the first step in returning Muslims to their authentic identity. This theme had been a trademark of Sufi theories, stretching back to the medieval period, which described the path of the soul's ascent into the presence of god. Banna politicized the concept by making inner change the essential preliminary task in the struggle against British colonial rule. "Imagine a man," wrote al-Banna, "who washed himself ritually in quiet and prayed with humility and fasted with sincerity and paid the poor tax dutifully and made the pilgrimage in fear of god and then learned in doing this that he had to do good toward people and that nothing was to issue from him except good and that happiness lay not in entering into the legal disputes of the scholars [the ʿulamāʾ] but in simply conveying what was required of him as it was required of the Prophet and his Companions. . . . What would a man like this lack? Nothing! Rather, he would gain peace of heart, purity of conscience . . . patience in adversity, and freedom from the worry born of straitened circumstances."[48] Such a man would also become the foundation for a new society. "What do we find in the house of a Muslim truly practicing Islam?" continued al-Banna. "We find a united family living in happiness." And what if such men became rulers? What would we find in their nations? Al-Banna answered by recounting how ʿUmar ibn al-Khattab, the Muslim conqueror of Jerusalem, wept when he learned of the suffering of his people.[49] A real Muslim ruler, as ʿUmar demonstrated, would

[48] Hasan al-Banna, *Nazarat fi islah al-nafs wa al-mujtamaʿ* [Views on the Reformation of the Soul and Society] (Cairo: Maktabat al-Iʿtisam, 1980), 60–61.

[49] Ibid., 57–60.

feel the weight of responsibility for his society because he was god-conscious. And the people would follow him wholeheartedly because the ruler was an irreproachable model and guarantor of Islam. The model was patrimonial, conjuring images of a brotherhood under the leadership of a wise and beneficent patriarch, or a tested Sufi guide, who exemplified the virtues of Islam through his own ascetic self-discipline, becoming worthy of the trust of the faithful in the process. Islam united ruler and ruled in mutual love through a common attitude of *taqwā* (piety) that was both internally present and outwardly manifested in acts of worship and charity.

ʿAbd al-Mu'min drew similar conclusions. The transformation of hearts would produce a unified Palestinian society capable of reversing the historic defeats and current corruption, he implied. Such solidarity was the test of an authentic metanoia among believers and citizens. He referred to his own family. If Latif and he and all their friends were truly pious, they would find a really strong bond forming among them. They would never go to sleep before visiting one another to find out each other's news. They would share whatever resources they had with one another, especially in times of hardship. Unfortunately, such solidarity was utterly absent. The conditions that came into existence with the Oslo Accords and the Sulta (the Palestinian National Authority) made the open expression of piety dangerous and the pursuit of selfish ends profitable. Moreover, the pressures of daily life prevented people from carrying out their religious duties to the fullest extent. His own busyness prevented him from performing the five daily prayers in the mosque. All this conspired to create a myopic concern with self at the expense of the solidarity of the *umma* (the universal community of Muslims).

Ironically, ʿAbd al-Mu'min made these comments about his brothers and friends immediately after performing the *ʿishā'* (evening) prayer, in which all the males of the family present in the room—with the notable exception of Abu Jamil—had participated. This act had ritually instituted and symbolically expressed a basic religious unity that seemed to contradict everything ʿAbd al-Mu'min was now saying about a lack of Islamic commitment and solidarity in his family and the larger society. Earlier, when he got up to pray, Latif, Abu Qays, and the older boys rose with him. In the adjacent room where the men had chosen to do their prostrations, I could hear ʿAbd al-Mu'min leading the prayer, chanting short Qur'anic chapters and the set invocations of praise and blessing in a fast, lyrical clip, punctuating the syllables in full-throated exclamation and subsiding with each *rakʿa* (cycle of prostration). I got up and walked to the bathroom, which was next to the ad hoc prayer room. I glanced through the open door as I walked past and saw ʿAbd al-Mu'min kneeling. Lined up behind him in two parallel ranks were Latif and Abu Qays along with their sons. They copied ʿAbd al-Mu'min's motions, kneeling and straightening in tandem. The group was facing the wall on which Abu Qays had hung a photograph of Yasir ʿArafat signing the 1988 Declaration of Independence. They had made a mosque of the room, and ʿAbd al-Mu'min was serving as their *imām* (prayer leader). When I returned, Abu Jamil's wife stood up and asked where she could do ablutions for the prayer.

What did ʿAbd al-Mu'min mean when he implied that he and his brothers and their friends failed to give evidence of Islam in their daily lives, that they were somehow not as unified as this act of prayer would have seemed to show? Clues to this underlying lack of concord lay with his two brothers, Abu Jamil and Latif. Abu Jamil had remained seated in front of the TV during my conversation with his younger brother and then absented himself from the prayer. At one point, he left the room entirely to sit outside. He had little time for displays of piety and could barely tolerate being in the same space with his brother as he held forth on the topic of worship and the consequences of failing to live by god's commands. Latif, for his part, had just started to pray again after a very long lapse. When I asked him about this change in a later phone conversation, he said, "What can I do? One gets older and starts thinking of his lord." Piety in his case seemed tied to a life-course expectation that as men became older they would become more "serious," upholding community norms and participating in its institutions. He told me that he was not very regular in his observance though he was trying to go to mosque on Fridays. His wife, who was very pious and something of a self-taught expert on fiqh (jurisprudence) and Qur'an, had been giving him a hard time about his lack of discipline. After they had returned from praying behind ʿAbd al-Mu'min, I asked Latif and Abu Qays what the imām's sermon had addressed earlier that day in the mosque. They laughed, saying they could not remember. The brothers and their cousin, it seemed, were not all of one mind about the demands of the divine, after all.

Abu Jamil and "Traditionalist Nationalism"

Abu Jamil's negative attitude toward his brother had developed gradually. During my first visit in July 1987, he described his brother as pious (*mutadayyin*), a "shaykh," sympathetic to the Muslim Brotherhood (Al-Ikhwan al-Muslimin), but there was no noticeable gap between the two brothers at the time. Abu Jamil did, however, express clear distaste for the Ikhwan. During that first visit, he pointed out a group of five Muslim Brothers walking in a tight formation through the camp. Each man was wearing a white dishdāsha (an ankle-length tunic), white skullcap, and long beard. Some had sticks. Abu Jamil found the spectacle distasteful. These guys, he alleged, had gone around beating people they considered to be violating the standards of Islamic morality. His good-natured, hashish-smoking, and alcohol-drinking neighbor across the road had been one of their victims.

The tension increased between Abu Jamil and ʿAbd al-Mu'min after their respective marriages. As is accepted practice, the wives came to live with the brothers in the original family home. ʿAbd al-Mu'min's new wife apparently dressed head-to-toe in black and insisted that her husband build a concrete wall down the middle of the al-Asdudi dwelling so that she could have complete privacy. Brilliantly exploiting traditional and Qur'anic arguments regarding the necessity of segregating potentially marriageable individuals (the notion of *maḥram*), she was able through these measures to impose a relatively large degree of independence from her husband's family within what were, by any measure, already extremely cramped quarters. The move generated strong feelings of alienation and anger in Abu Jamil. The resentment deepened over the years. In 1999, he complained that ʿAbd al-Mu'min's wife "won't even shake our hands or let her kids play with our kids." Except for obligatory feast day visits, the brothers almost never saw each other except in passing. And even on feast days, Abu Jamil told me, ʿAbd al-Mu'min "spends the majority of time with his wife's family." In Abu Jamil's eyes, ʿAbd al-Mu'min was more concerned with his own self-interest than he was with supporting his brothers. Abu Jamil claimed that his brother's in-laws had Hamas connections and had helped ʿAbd al-Mu'min, through these ties, to open his computer center. While Abu Jamil had taken classes at the center for free, he nevertheless remained resentful. From his perspective, his brother was yet another example of the self-seeking ethos that he believed had taken root in the camp during the past decade. ʿAbd al-Mu'min and Hamas, generally, in Abu Jamil's view, failed to live up to their lofty proclamations about brotherhood and sharing in times of hardship because, like all the other factions, they made assistance contingent on movement loyalty and personal connections rather than the ethic of general reciprocity and plain need.[50]

[50] It is a tricky business separating out the factors that led to the seeming rift between ʿAbd al-Mu'min and Abu Jamil. The primary causes appear to be the domestic social order that ʿAbd al-Mu'min's wife imposed on the larger household as well as the envy and resentment that Abu Jamil felt toward his younger brother's business and professional successes. The new wife's actions represented a break with accepted practice. As Rosemary Sayigh observed in her ethnographic studies of Palestinian refugee communities in Lebanon, "there is no sex segregation of house space [among Palestinians, as opposed to Egyptian or Algerian peasants, i.e.], it being treated as an open social meeting ground between kin and

Abu Jamil contrasted his brother with his best friend Muhammad, an irreverent man in his early thirties who enjoyed a good party. Muhammad, his father, and his brothers operated a small sewing workshop that assembled clothing for the Israeli and local markets. We would often end up visiting the workshop during my visits to Karama. On several of these occasions, Abu Jamil took care of electrical problems that the workshop was having. Muhammad repaid these favors by making clothing for Abu Jamil and his family. The type of relationship that existed between the two friends became clearer to me when, on one of my visits, Abu Jamil picked out two winter jackets for my wife and me. I protested, but he explained that he and Muhammad did things for each other; the coats would cost him nothing more than a few more favors for his friend. Several months later, before the start of school in September 2000, I found Abu Jamil's children dressed in new blue shirts and blue jeans. "Muhammad made the clothes," Abu Jamil told me. "He also knows my measurements and my wife's sizes and will make us clothing without even asking."

---

neighbors, not as a private domestic preserve" (Rosemary Sayigh, *Palestinians*, 21). Many, if not most, Gazans did practice some form of gender segregation in the home, especially when hosting visitors from outside the immediate family circle. However, in line with Sayigh's point, among the Asdudis (with the notable exception of ʿAbd al-Mu'min) and most other homes I visited in Karama, husbands, wives, uncles, aunts, brothers, sisters, daughters, sons, parents, and grandparents would usually gather together in the same room for evening visiting. By creating literal and symbolic walls, ʿAbd al-Mu'min's wife radically altered this established form of sociability among the Asdudis. Islamization in this instance represented the rejection of a traditional social pattern in favor of a new religious ideal that trumped the force of received practices by appealing to a "higher," more "authentic" source of legitimacy (i.e., the Qur'an and *aḥādīth* as interpreted through Islamist lenses). Interestingly, in this case, a woman exploited religious discourse and practice, as reconstituted by the Islamists, to achieve a degree of independence from her husband's family and thereby create an autonomous domestic space of her own. Abu Jamil's resentment toward his brother and his family perhaps echoed anger resulting from the disruption of the long-established economy of familial interaction. Abu Jamil had to contend directly with this disruption because he shared the original al-Asdudi compound with his brother's family. His resentment flowed perhaps from the fact that he could no longer have the "normal" exchange of visits and favors that undergirded family relations and sustained individuals in a context of material scarcity. Abu Jamil viewed his brother as engaging in a type of treason by replacing the deeper claims and bonds of family for a sectarian religious solidarity. His brother had clearly benefited from this replacement by receiving support from his in-laws and Hamas colleagues. The problem, for Abu Jamil, was not so much that his brother had benefited but that he had failed to make his comparative wealth available to his family of origin through the economy of familial exchange. What ʿAbd al-Mu'min did do, however, was to preach about Islamic morality to his brothers and their families. Abu Jamil's comments, described further on in this chapter, that true religion resided in spontaneous acts of generosity toward others and not in pious posturing, thus constituted an indirect reproach of his brother's preaching and concomitant breaking of the accepted patterns of familial sociability.

Abu Jamil once described the difference between the relationship he had with Muhammad and the one he had with ʿAbd al-Mu'min as a contrast between two types of morality. He captured the distinction in the categorically opposed notions of *ṣāḥib al-maṣlaḥa* (someone who pursues a friendship for personal gain; a "user") and *ṣāḥib al-ṣuḥba* (a true friend). The ṣāḥib al-maṣlaḥa was someone who posed as a friend but was really interested in extracting a service without providing compensation. He or she was a person who made friendship or family solidarity contingent on receiving assistance. As a self-employed electrician and refrigerator repair specialist, Abu Jamil had to deal repeatedly with neighbors, friends, and relatives who tried to avoid paying for his services by exploiting the commonly accepted understanding that family, friends, and neighbors did favors for each other without expecting any recompense. This was especially the case during the Intifada, when the Israeli military tightly restricted the flow of Gazan labor, thereby causing camp economies to nose-dive. The resulting scarcity strained neighborhood and friendship bonds. The arrival of the Palestinian National Authority eased the stress somewhat by providing patronage jobs. Still, at the time of my fieldwork in 1999–2000, intense scarcity persisted. Employment in Israel had not returned to its pre-Intifada levels, and the P.N.A., inheriting the legacy of twenty-seven years of "de-development" under the Israeli occupation, had not been able to provide an industrial base capable of absorbing Gaza's vast camp proletariat. In such a context, individuals had to exploit connections and the good graces of neighbors and friends to secure their livelihoods.

Abu Jamil was as subject to these externally imposed constraints and their consequences for camp dynamics as the people he accused of being self-seeking and exploitative. The distinction he drew between ṣāḥib al-maṣlaḥa and ṣāḥib al-ṣuḥba had less to do with exchanging favors than with the quality of the relationship. Abu Jamil desired a sense of general reciprocity. True friendship and family solidarity depended, for him, on seemingly spontaneous, mutual acts of generosity. Muhammad and his brothers and employees at the workshop embodied this spirit. Unlike ʿAbd al-Mu'min, who, according to Abu Jamil, showed up on his doorstep only if he needed help with a broken appliance, his friends at the shop were interested in having him as their companion. Abu Jamil admitted that there was maṣlaḥa (self-interest) in his friendship with Muhammad and the rest of the guys, but there was a difference: He did electrical work for them without asking for a *girsh* (a piaster, or penny) in return. They, in turn, made jackets every winter for his wife and kids. The men performed these services for each other apparently without thinking twice about it. The ṣāḥib al-ṣuḥba did favors, thus, with no thought of compensation. But, of course, compensation did take place; it was essential to maintaining the sense of reciprocity that undergirded the ṣāḥib al-ṣuḥba relation. If return did not occur, then the friendship would become one-sided and deteriorate into the parasitic dynamic that Abu Jamil attributed to the ṣāḥib al-maṣlaḥa. Providing was thus as important as receiving, and the two had to be mutual and seemingly spontaneous for a relationship to have noble-heartedness (*karāma*).

Abu Jamil invoked the values of mutuality and noble-heartedness in expressing his attitude toward religion (al-dīn). "I believe that true religion lies in one's actions toward others [*muʿāmala*—a term that also, in fiqh manuals, refers to the rules of conduct among believers]," he told me. "You're not more of a human being just because you grow your beard long." His wife took issue with this statement, saying that prayer and fasting were the essence of religion. Abu Jamil responded: "Maybe I will begin praying, who knows; but if this happens I will make a full commitment to it. One should not do such things lightly." There had to be consistency, that is, between one's outer practices and the inner spirit that motivated them. Without this consistency there was only hypocrisy.[51] The point here was that real religion, its inner spirit, resided fundamentally in the quality of one's attitudes and actions toward others and not in overt acts of piety. Real religion was noble-heartedness—the very quality that resided in and animated the spontaneous acts of generosity of the ṣāḥib al-ṣuḥba. If this dimension was absent, then prayer and fasting meant little. ʿAbd al-Mu'min had made a similar point earlier in relating the ḥadīth about the man who boasted of his charitable giving. This man, contrary to his expectations, would end up spending eternity in hell. True piety made no display. Rather, it issued spontaneously from an ingrained consciousness of god and his requirements.[52] Yet, ironically, from Abu Jamil's perspective, ʿAbd al-Mu'min was as culpable of vanity as the man in the ḥadīth.

In contrast to his brother's explicitly religious framework, Abu Jamil rooted collective morality in the values of general reciprocity as enshrined in the ʿādāt wa taqālīd (customs and traditions). These values

[51] The remarks echoed a fairly common understanding among my respondents about the commitment required for religious practices. Intisar in chapter 2 wrestled with achieving consistency between her inner pious dispositions and her outer practices. She was considering putting on the ḥijāb to become more consistent, morally. Husayn in the same chapter said he would oppose his wife if she should ever decide to stop wearing the ḥijāb. If one committed oneself to something like the ḥijāb or prayer, then one had to continue with it. It was a serious matter to embark on the path of piety, and this fact was what Abu Jamil was getting at when he said that if he ever started praying he would do so in every respect, that is, he would conform to all the requirements of religion. One should not pray or fast if one was not ready to do this. Hypocrisy was the price of ill-considered piety.

[52] Doing charity in secret is also a Qur'anic concern. See, for instance, Q 2:271.

connected refugee identity with the peasant (fallāḥī) past, the true source of authenticity for Abu Jamil.[53] Captured in the concept of karāma, they encompassed the virtues of courage, quick wits, noble-heartedness, honor, duty to family and neighbors, mutuality, graciousness, and modesty—especially female modesty. Many of these qualities embodied themselves for Abu Jamil in an uncle who had come to serve for him as a surrogate father and family patriarch. Abu Jamil regularly visited this uncle both as an expression of filial deference to an elder and because he enjoyed listening to the old man's stories of outwitting the British during the Mandate period. The uncle was also fond of commenting irreverently and acerbically about the hypocrisy of "the men of religion" (*rijāl al-dīn*)—something that also appealed to Abu Jamil. To be a real man was, for Abu Jamil, to be like this uncle—to possess his courage and wits, his sharp and sagacious insights into the behavior of others, and his graciousness.

The uncle dressed in the baggy drawstring pants that villagers of his generation used to work in. Over this garment, he wore a white dishdāsha (ankle-length tunic) and a white skullcap. He sported a clipped white beard that partly hid the scar he had received during surgery to remove a tumor from the corner of his mouth. He spent evenings sitting with visitors on thin mats and cushions in the open-air patio of his meticulously kept three-room, U.N.-built dwelling—a structure that dated back to the period immediately following the 1948 war. He kept a brass pot full of bitter Bedouin-style coffee warming on hot coals in an aluminum *chānūn*,[54] or brazier.

I visited this uncle several times over the years with Abu Jamil. Once in July 2000, Abu Jamil, Latif, and I sat cross-legged on mats arranged

[53] The peasant past figured centrally in stock P.L.O. and Hamas symbolism. The kūfiyya (checkered head scarf that farmers wore) and dabka ("traditional" line dance), for instance, often were prominent features of any P.L.O. or Hamas rally. Yasir ʿArafat always appeared in public with a black and white kūfiyya draped around his head and shoulders in a manner that suggested the shape of historic Mandate Palestine. Women in nationalist poster art were often shown wearing the embroidered thawb dresses that older refugee women from the 1948 era dressed in. Hamas iconography also displayed young male activists (*shabāb*) with the kūfiyya wrapped entirely around their heads in the manner that became common among the *mulaththamīn* ("masked" street fighters who set up barricades and threw stones at army patrols). Women were portrayed in the newer white ḥijāb scarf pulled tightly around their faces. In invoking the ʿādāt wa taqālīd, thus, Abu Jamil's discourse implied a long-established set of symbols and narratives that had structured the Palestinian sense of collective national identity since the rise of Fatah and the P.L.O. in the late 1960s and 1970s. He pointedly revived these meanings in an effort to reassert a type of nonsectarian, anti-Islamist solidarity that remained authentically nationalist.

[54] Palestinian rural dialects transform the "*ka*" into "*cha*." Hence, "*kānūn*" becomes "*chānūn*" in village colloquial.

at right angles with the uncle and three of his sons visiting from ʿAmman, Jordan. After one of the uncle's stories about getting the better of some British soldiers during Mandate days, the conversation turned to family members who had fallen down on duties of caring for elders and reciprocating visits. Abu Jamil brought up a cousin who had consistently refused his invitations to come to lunch. "Does he think he is more hospitable and noble than I am [*akram minī*]?" asked Abu Jamil indignantly. The other men agreed this was unbecoming behavior and offered the explanation that the cousin was complicated (*muʿaqqad*), always keeping things to himself, never revealing his real motives. One of the ʿAmman cousins then related a story about a relative who refused to help his dying father while he was in the hospital. He would not visit or tend to him. One of the father's former neighbors saw what was happening and began caring for the man, even cleaning him up after he became incontinent. The only time the son came to visit the father was to inquire about the will. The father threw the son out of his room. The story led the group to reflect on the loss of values in today's world. "People only care about getting ahead," rued the uncle.

Embedded within this idea that the contemporary world had lost sight of what really mattered was a conception of society divided between the keepers of tradition and the purveyors of modern ways. Modernity, in this view, was individualistic, exploitative, and corrosive of the ethic of reciprocity and loyalty that had held camp residents together. How this was so became clearer for me in a conversation I had with Abu Jamil on the phenomenon of middle-class and wealthy Palestinians keeping Sri Lankan and Filipina maids. Maids used to be unheard of until the arrival of the P.L.O. elites from outside. Abu Jamil claimed that "those rich people who came from the Gulf countries and other places were the ones who brought [the maids] . . . we are peasants [fallāḥīn]. Our values are different." People in the camp cared about what people said. If someone from the camp were to hire a maid, people would start saying that he had middle-class pretensions and that he did not want to be like the rest of the community. Even one's wife would not agree to have a maid. The house was a wife's responsibility, and she would not want anyone else taking her place. She might also become jealous. She would see the maid talking to her husband every day. Such interaction was unavoidable. The maid lived with the family, so the husband would have to have a relationship. But the customs and traditions (the ʿādāt wa taqālīd) did not allow people in the camp to do this. Maybe if someone improved his situation and left the camp for the city, then maybe he might get a maid; but then he would no longer be part of the camp. The colonels and generals who came back from the Gulf countries to staff the Palestinian National Authority's upper echelons had maids. But the camp was different. Its values were more conservative. This difference could be seen in how people dressed. Women in other places, Abu Jamil observed, wore short sleeves and short skirts and did not cover their hair all the way. In the camp women did not feel comfortable going out in short dresses or without a scarf on. People (*al-nās*) would talk about them if they behaved in such a manner.[55]

The ability to hire a maid and attire one's wife in the latest Western fashions, then, marked socioeconomic class differences; but they also became signifiers of diverging moralities. A camp resident would not hire a maid, because it would subvert the wife's traditional position as homemaker, produce domestic strife, and create questions in the community about one's fidelity and honor as a husband.[56] Hiring a maid also signaled a turning of one's back on one's origins. Rich people did not work with their hands. They got others to do menial labor. Those others came from camps or camplike places such as Sri Lanka or the Philippines. As Abu Jamil put it in commenting on the differences that separated the two of us: "Your hands are smooth, Loren. You are from the city. But, we have rough hands." As a refugee, hiring a maid (or any other type of "bourgeois" behavior) would be seen as a betrayal of the basic values of the "customs and traditions" that defined collective life in the camp. It was pretentious and ultimately destructive of social solidarity to attempt to cross over, to be something other than what one was born into.

Yet, in the post-Oslo period, many camp residents, including Abu Jamil's brother Latif, were attempting to leave the camp behind and to remake themselves into members of the emerging bureaucratic and professional middle classes. Abu Jamil, himself, was proud of his salaried position in one of the Palestinian National Authority security services and dreamed of building a house beyond the camp confines. Such transitions and desires undermined the long-standing refugee narrative of

[55] Men were also bound by codes of modesty. They generally never wore short pants or tank tops around the camp except if they were doing heavy labor or sitting on the beach.

[56] Abu Jamil and other married Muslim men I knew, however, teased their wives by threatening to take second wives—a practice that Islamic law permitted. This was understood as kidding, especially since economic circumstances made the threats nothing more than hypothetical possibilities. Nevertheless, the joking amounted to reassertions of male privilege and power. I noticed that Christian men also joked with their wives in similar manner. Polygamy, as everyone in these settings well understood, was forbidden for Christians. The joking thus played on the understood sectarian differences between Muslims and Christians. At the same time, however, it contained the veiled threat of infidelity—of fooling around, of having an affair—and thus, as with Muslim men, Christian husbands used kidding about second wives as a way to remind their spouses of male privilege and power in the marital relation. This power rested fundamentally on a woman's economic dependence on her husband. Threats of infidelity and second marriages dramatized this dependence by showing the possibility of husbands withdrawing or weakening their economic support of their wives.

return to the villages that were lost in 1948. They signaled a fundamental break, as well, with the fallāḥī identity that undergirded this narrative. In places like Thawra and Karama, debates raged about the dangers of "normalization" under the Oslo regime: should refugees maintain camp solidarity to achieve the demands of return and restitution, or should they embrace the emerging opportunities to move out and move on? People like Abu Jamil stood on the border. They lacked the means to leave, and they resented those who did possess such resources. Forced to stay, they apotheosized their predicament, casting it as fidelity to the authentic values of the nation (its fallāḥī "customs and traditions," i.e.) and its core refugee constituency.

At another level, however, Abu Jamil's emphasis on "customs and traditions" reflected the synchronic generational split between secular nationalists and Islamists that had formed in the first Intifada and then grown during the post-Oslo period. Rather than the liberal secularism found in Thawra Camp, Abu Jamil, despite his association with leftist groups before and during the Uprising, expressed a type of pluralist nationalism that paralleled the *muḥāfiẓ* (conservative) orientation of Fathawis such as Husayn in chapter 2. The muḥāfiẓ upheld the customs and traditions as the common cultural bond that united all Palestinians regardless of their particular subnational identities. Islam, in this view, was but one of several cultural tributaries to the nation. Abu Jamil shared this basic perspective but differed from it in the degree to which he privileged the ʿādāt wa taqālīd over the formal requirements of religion. In the context of the strong Islamist presence in Gaza, the traditions and customs provided him with a culturally authenticated ground on which to mark out an alternative moral space. Islamists helped to create this parallel dimension by, as ʿAbd al-Mu'min demonstrated, insisting on distinctions between the truly pious and everyone else. In dividing society in this way, they opened themselves up to charges of hypocrisy. "Religion is how you treat others," Abu Jamil told me. Its essence lay in the ethic of general reciprocity that the ʿādāt wa taqālīd embodied. Although the Islamists claimed to uphold this same ethic, their actual behavior, in Abu Jamil's view, was no better than that of any other political faction. Like the others, they made aid contingent on movement membership and loyalty. They, in other words, epitomized the ethic of the ṣāḥib al-maṣlaḥa—the individual who pursued friendships to achieve instrumental ends.

There was some overlap, however, between the Islamists and Abu Jamil's brand of traditionalism. The basic patriarchal arrangement of society was never in dispute between them, for example. The issue was, rather, how to order and express the values of that arrangement. For Abu Jamil, formal and overt religious identity and practice was far less important than adherence to values embedded within karāma (generosity, noble-heartedness) and the ṣāḥib al-ṣuḥba (the friend who provided aid without explicit expectation of compensation—the ethic of general reciprocity). While this orientation was not exactly a secularist one, there was a latent multisectarianism embedded within its de-emphasis of formal adherence to religion. Abu Jamil commented, in this regard, that whether a person was a Muslim or not was of no significance to him; what really mattered was whether an individual's behavior expressed karāma and ṣuḥba. Abu Jamil in effect elided sectarian religious identity by desacralizing and generalizing the values of the patriarchal substratum. "Real religion" resided at this more fundamental level.

Abu Jamil's stance, finally, coincided with his needs and interests as a self-proclaimed political "independent" who nevertheless relied heavily on Palestinian National Authority patronage. By appealing to an ethic rooted in the general reciprocity of "traditional" peasant (fallāḥī) life, he was able to remain a "general nationalist" while avoiding allying himself explicitly with one faction over another. Others around him had concluded from his P.N.A. job that he supported Fatah and its policies. As disillusionment grew with the P.N.A. and the Oslo peace process, such associations became more awkward and uncomfortable. He sought to counter these perceptions by emphasizing his refugee solidarity, at the core of which was a commitment to the ʿādāt wa taqālīd. Unlike the maid-owning generals and ministers who controlled the P.N.A., unlike the self-serving factions that sought to influence or resist the P.N.A., and unlike the self-promoters who curried the favor of others to move up the ladder of social status, he remained a regular guy just trying to get by. In a Gazan society divided deeply by class, religion, and politics, fidelity to the "customs and traditions" provided a zone of relative neutrality and alternative authenticity.

Islam without the Islamists: Latif, Imm Muhammad, and Abu Qays

In contrast to Abu Jamil's anti-Islamist traditionalism, his older brother Latif, his wife, and the cousin, Abu Qays, exemplified an orientation that simultaneously accommodated certain elements of Islamist discourse and practice while rejecting the idea that Islamists were the true bearers of the national will. The attitude strongly paralleled the muḥāfiẓ orientation detailed in chapter 2. The accommodating dimension appeared in the way Latif and Abu Qays lined up with their sons behind ʿAbd al-Mu'min to observe the evening prayer described earlier. It also emerged in their use of Islamist-like arguments, especially ones that enlisted science to prove Qur'anic assertions. During my visits to Karama, I would often end up in long discussions about Islam, Christianity, and science with Latif, his wife, and Abu Qays. What they had to say in these conversations about the Qur'an, sharīʿa, and an Islamic state revealed the extent to which Islamist-like concepts and practices had shaped their moral and political perspectives.

One such discussion that took place during my October 1999 visit featured Latif's wife, Imm Muhammad, as a main interlocutor. A science teacher at the Karama School for Girls, Imm Muhammad, who was in her midthirties, often stayed at the school after classes to meet with a group of other female teachers who read and debated the Qur'an, the interpretive literature related to the Qur'an (the *tafāsīr*), and points of sharīʿa and fiqh. Latif explained that she did this for her own benefit. Her group was not part of any Islamist organization, he assured me. Imm Muhammad wore a scarf (ḥijāb) and coat (jilbāb) in the style that Islamist activism had made ubiquitous. Yet she would always shake my hand in greeting. She had sharp, intelligent eyes and spoke in quick-fire staccato. She pounced on points of debate, rapidly countering the assertions of others with her own arguments and examples. She was the moral backbone of the family, overseeing the religious education of her nine children and working on her husband to become more observant in his prayers and fasting. She often joked about catching Latif sneaking snacks during the Ramadan fast.

Imm Muhammad enjoyed engaging me on religious topics. She instigated our October 1999 conversation by bringing up the subject of how Mary and Jesus were portrayed in the New Testament versus the Qur'an. The discussion inevitably led into the question of the relative authority of the two scriptures. In the process, her brother, Abu Qays, appealed to scientific discoveries that appeared to prove the veracity of Qur'anic statements. Latif followed suit, arguing that modern desalinization technology confirmed a Qur'anic passage about the transformation of saltwater into freshwater. Imm Muhammad stood up while we were talking and got a *muṣḥaf* (a copy of the Qur'an) and started thumbing quickly through the pages. She stopped and began reading out loud the chapter on the creation of humans from mud. When she finished, she remarked: "Modern science has demonstrated this very thing: that we evolved in stages from the earth." I replied: "But, this is Darwin's idea." She shot back: "The Qur'an came before his theory, and the theory confirms what the Qur'an says!" Abu Qays then read passages from the Qur'an that described the balls of fire that the angels threw at the *jinn* (phantoms who can intervene for good and ill in human lives) every time they tried to scale the heavens to learn the creator's secrets. He commented that this passage referred to comets, which science only discovered several hundred

Figure 8. Islam without the Islamists. Titled "The Intifada," this 1993 painting by an anonymous 15-years-old girl from the Rafah Refugee Camp in the Gaza Strip illustrates the increasing incorporation of religious signifiers with Fathawi nationalist iconography. The imagery is replete with standard nationalist themes: the rocks that were thrown at Israeli soldiers by young street activists, the victory signs, the young men clad in the black and white checkered *kūfiyyāt* (sing, *kūfiyya*) that had long served as a Fathawi nationalist symbol, and the portrait of the young "martyr." What is novel in this collage of images is the depiction of the two young women dressed in white *ḥijāb* scarves. It is this last image that indexes the generational shift that occurred in the first Intifada.

years later. "There is much in the Qur'an that human knowledge has yet to understand," he said.[57]

The demonstration of Qur'anic veracity by appeal to science had long been a feature of Salafist thought, the intellectual tradition that provided the conceptual basis for both the modernist and the fundamentalist religious trends in Islam during the twentieth century. Such ideas had come to shape the religious attitudes of the wider Muslim publics. The influence of the modernists remained generally limited to the intellectual elite of the upper middle classes; fundamentalists, by contrast, were far more effective in mobilizing constituencies and spreading their ideas by creating charities, youth groups, study groups, and political movements and parties.[58] Among Palestinians, groups such as the Muslim Brotherhood, the Islamic Collective, Islamic Jihad, and Hamas were the primary carriers of Salafist-type thought. By the late 1990s, their ideas cut across class and faction distinctions. Latif, Imm Muhammad, and Abu Qays were longtime Fatah supporters; yet in their appeal to science to back up the Qur'an, they echoed themes found commonly in the discourse of Islamist activists.

Most striking, however, was how the Islamist theodicy—the explanation for Palestinian failures and Israeli successes—had seeped into the way Latif, Imm Muhammad, and Abu Qays analyzed the historical and contemporary predicament of Palestinian society. When I asked Abu Qays about a Qur'anic passage he had placed on a wall in his home, he explained: "This is 'Surat al-Zalzala' (the Chapter of the Earthquake). It tells us what will happen on the Last Day. I put it up to keep us humble

---

Figure 8. (*Continued*)
Secular-nationalist female activists of the 1970s and early 1980s—women like Layla Khalid—sometimes appeared in photos with the checkered kūfiyya thrown loosely over their shoulders and hair, but often they dispensed with head coverings altogether. In this painting, the attire of the two women marks them as virtuous adherents of Islam as defined by Islamist symbols and practice. The scarves sanction the inclusion of the two women in nationalist activism, but it is Islamist signifiers—the white scarves pinned tightly under the chin—that provide the parameters of this inclusion. The Association of Artists—Gaza Strip.

[57] For the references to the story of the angels hurling fire at the *jinn*, see the following Qur'anic passages—37:6–10; 72:8–10.

[58] For discussions of Salafism and its embodiment in modernist and fundamentalist tendencies, Esposito, *The Islamic Threat*, 52–59; Albert Hourani, *Arabic Thought in the Liberal Age* (Oxford: Oxford University Press, 1970); and Mansoor Moaddel and Kamran Talattof, eds., *Modernist and Fundamentalist Debates in Islam: A Reader* (New York: Palgrave MacMillan, 2000).

and to remind us of our final destiny and our final hope . . . that the Jews will not in the end prevail, god will." He then took the copy of the Qur'an and read from "Surat al-Isra'" (Chapter of the Ascension, also known as "Surat Bani Isra'il," the Chapter of the People of Israel). The text he recited described god giving the Israelites multiple opportunities to follow divine guidance and the Israelites constantly violating these strictures and becoming repressive rulers. God promised, the passages proclaimed, to punish the Israelites again and again for their transgressions. Assuming an identity between the group described in the text and the modern Jewish state, Abu Qays concluded his reading, commenting that "Israel cannot avoid the Last Day no matter how powerful it thinks it is right now." Such ideas were core themes in Hamas's ideology,[59] but they had now entered into the more general political discourse of Palestinians across the factional spectrum. This seepage was particularly striking in the case of Abu Qays. He had spent his entire adult life as a Fatah guerrilla commander in Jordan, Lebanon, and Tunis. He expressed a basic P.L.O. pluralist nationalism. He possessed an Arabic translation of the Bible and a Greek Orthodox prayer manual he had picked up in Lebanon. He talked of the necessity of establishing a secular state to accommodate the different religious communities, including Jews, in the Palestinian nation. Yet, as his comments on the Last Day showed, he had absorbed an attitude that echoed the Islamist eschatology as it had come to be expressed in Hamas's ideology. This would suggest perhaps that Abu Qays, as he adapted to the post-Intifada cultural-political terrain (marked by the secularist-Islamist split) of the Gaza Strip, had added a new layer of Islamist-like religious theory to his basic nationalist orientation.

Imm Muhammad also echoed Hamas's social and political themes, but she added a critical twist, turning the Islamist theodicy against the Islamist factions themselves. "Today," she said, "we have many parties, like Hamas. They only care about individual gain. In true Islam there are no parties, there are only believers." She elaborated on the characteristics of believers by quoting the first twenty verses of "Surat al-Baqara" (Chapter of the Cow). These opening lines dealt with belief and unbelief. The passages described unbelievers as self-deceived and confident in their ignorance and arrogance. They also portrayed god as omniscient and omnipotent in allowing unbelief to exist and even causing it by strengthening the wayward in their blindness and hard-heartedness. God made their hearts, hearing, and site impervious to faith (Q2:7). And for their unbelief they would be painfully punished (Q2:7). But god also had the power to lift unbelief if he so desired (Q2:20). Believers believed in all of

[59] These ideas come up in Hamas's charter, for example. For an English translation of the charter, see Hroub, *Hamas*, 267–291.

god's revelation, believed in the absence of tangible confirmation, and were attentive to prayer (Q2:3). When she finished reading the verses, Imm Muhammad looked up and said: "If people really followed Islam, then all our troubles would disappear and there would be order again." A part of following Islam, for Imm Muhammad, involved instituting the sharīʿa (the codified religious customary law). She insisted that the sharīʿa was perfect in its current form. It did not require adaptation or interpretation. Women had full rights under the religious law. Men, however, distorted and diminished these rights to serve their own ends; and, in this selfishness, they became examples of those who undermined true Islam.

Imm Muhammad's discussion of collective responsibility, the requirements of belief, the necessity of instituting the sharīʿa, and the failure of Palestinian society to be fully Muslim mixed Islamist-like themes with a critique of Hamas and all the other factions. She echoed, for instance, the Islamist political theodicy that explained the defeats at the hands of Israel as a collective failure to adhere to Islam. Imm Muhammad argued that a lack of faithfulness had resulted in a general moral disintegration in Karama and elsewhere in Palestinian society. If people became true believers, then the social ills would disappear and the nation would recover its strength. Everyone had failed to live up to Islam, in Imm Muhammad's view, including, ironically, the Islamists. Hamas was like any other self-serving faction. In a truly Islamic society, there would be no factions and divisions of any sort. All would be of one mind, united in observance of god's divine legislation.

Imm Muhammad's brother, the former guerrilla, Abu Qays, was equally critical of Hamas even though, as we saw above, he incorporated elements of the Islamist outlook. While supporting the idea of an Islamic state, he argued that leadership of such a political order would require someone with the moral caliber of an ʿUmar ibn al-Khattab, the second of the "Rightly Guided Caliphs" and conqueror of Jerusalem. Abu Qays illustrated his point by relating a story in which ʿUmar supposedly intervened with ʿAmr ibn al-ʿAss, the Muslim general who conquered Egypt during the initial seventh-century expansion of Islam, on behalf of a Christian whose land was about to be confiscated to build a mosque. The Christian found the incorruptible ʿUmar not in a palace but under a palm tree sleeping with his sandal under his head.[60] ʿUmar wrote a few lines on a piece of parchment and gave it to the man. The Christian returned to Egypt and showed the note to ʿAmr. The commander then immediately

[60] The description of ʿUmar here echoed accounts of Yasir ʿArafat's austere practices. ʿArafat was widely known to lead a life of few personal possessions, frugal eating habits, a simple bed, and a frenetic, Herculean daily work schedule. This reputation in large part inoculated him against charges of direct, personal corruption even as he stood accused of using money and favors to buy the loyalty of others.

ordered that the land remain with the Christian in recognition of ʿUmar's authority and wisdom.

Abu Qays concluded his story by saying that, contrary to popular assumptions in the West, a true Muslim state would be the most just in the world. The present historical moment, however, was not favorable to recreating the Islamic political system. As the brutal war in Chechnya demonstrated, the West would fight any attempt by an Islamist movement to conquer territory and establish such a state. The Islamist movements were too weak, and their leaders as self-interested as those of any other party. In a historical context like the current one, it was necessary to work from the bottom up to build an Islamic consciousness. The real work lay in raising Muslim families. But Islam also required Muslims to liberate Islamic land. Palestine was an Islamic trust (*waqf*), and all Muslims were called to engage in the jihād to liberate it.[61] Hamas had joined in this struggle and therefore was a part of the national movement. "There is no difference between Hamas and Fatah in this regard," said Abu Qays. "The only difference is in our strategy: Hamas wants to liberate Palestine all at once, all of it; while we have taken a piecemeal approach, one segment at a time."

Abu Qays blurred the distinction between Fatah and Hamas. He actually recontextualized elements of Hamas's Islamism in nationalist terms; but in doing so he also shifted Fathawi nationalism in an Islamic, if not Islamist, direction. His overarching frame remained, crucially, a multisectarian Fathawi one. His particular version of this nationalism was not per se democratic; rather it based itself on a benevolent paternalism projected through the ideal image of ʿUmar ibn al-Khattab. This outlook homologously aligned with various patrimonial models on offer in contemporary Palestinian society, for example, Shaykh Ahmad Yasin's spiritual father role in Hamas (akin to the Sufi *murshid*, or guide) and Yasir ʿArafat's carefully cultivated father-of-the-nation image that was based on, but superseded, his historic leadership of Fatah and the P.L.O.

Abu Qays described ʿArafat and the other founders of Fatah and the P.L.O. as—pace ʿUmar ibn al-Khattab—wise, incorruptible, and courageous nationalists. While the Islamists had finally come on board during the Intifada, their leaders lacked the depth of experience and record of sacrifice and suffering that the historic founders of the Palestinian National Liberation Movement (Fatah) possessed. ʿArafat and his generation alone were worthy of trust by virtue of their proven past. Hence, even though he appeared to have taken on elements of the Islamist outlook, Abu Qays remained a P.L.O. nationalist, one whose identity had

[61] This is a main theme in Hamas statements. For more on this, see the English translation of the Hamas charter in Hroub, *Hamas*, 267–291.

been formed in the main as a guerrilla fighter in the diaspora. In generational terms, he represented an "old guard" consciousness, a classic Fathawi pragmatism that subordinated particular solidarities to the national movement. Though younger, and though shaped by the particular histories of the inside, Imm Muhammad and Latif shared this same basic orientation. The extent to which all three individuals expressed Islamist-like attitudes reflected both the impact of Islamist activism on the general cultural-political terrain of Gaza and the capacity of classic Fathawism to pragmatically absorb diverging ideological viewpoints within its basic form of nationalism. In adapting in this manner, however, the ethos of Fathawism appeared to shift, at least among my interlocutors, in a quasi-Islamist direction.

CONCLUSION

The case presented in this chapter illustrates how sociomoral milieus and generational tendencies and interactions combined to produce a complex dynamic of retraditionalization in Karama Camp. Despite its proletarianization and exposure to Israel, the sociomoral ethos of Karama remained firmly rooted in patriarchal family formations. Patriarchal structures, too, persisted in Thawra Camp in the West Bank, but Thawra residents had greater contact with professionalizing milieus and forces (secular liberal-arts universities, the socially diverse urban settings of the Bethlehem-Jerusalem corridor, greater and easier access to Israel, etc.). Karama—situated as it was in the middle of the Gaza Strip, which was itself surrounded on all sides either by the Mediterranean Sea or by a heavily patrolled security fence—was much more isolated and self-contained. Still, the arrival of the Palestinian National Authority had spurred some initial status transformation. Latif and Abu Jamil had found employment in P.N.A. structures; their salaries were enabling them to move out, or at least dream of moving out, of the camp confines and into the emerging middle-class echelons comprising of state employees. ʿAbd al-Mu'min, for his part, had started his own computing center. Yet despite their partial movements toward professional middle-class existence, the primary orientations of these three men remained defined by the patriarchal "customs and traditions" of Karama's fallāḥī past. Their conceptions of social honor revolved primarily around the provider/protector role that men were expected to play. Even in Latif's family, in which the wife worked as a public employee and was the most dominant personality, the female still carried the burden of domestic labor while the male remained the head, at least in title.

Given the basic patriarchal substratum of the generally proletarianized and very partially professionalized milieu of Karama, the generational tensions between secular nationalists and Islamists in the camp, as reflected among the Asdudis, took the shape of a cultural-political struggle to define the character and contours of the male-dominated, family-centered social order. The secular nationalists (Latif, Abu Qays, Imm Muhammad, and Abu Jamil) conceived of the nation as an extended family or clan under the headship of the father of the nation, Yasir ʿArafat. They subdivided among themselves—largely in response to the impact of Islamization—on the extent to which they viewed this national family as primarily Muslim and in need of grounding in the sharīʿa. Abu Jamil de-emphasized the religious sectarian aspect, stressing instead a sense of intersectarian collective unity based on the ʿādāt wa taqālīd, while the others argued the case of Islam even as they remained critical of the Islamists for being divisive, hypocritical, and naive.

The Islamist movements, by contrast, collectively put themselves forward as the one group that had not compromised on core values and concerns. Their appeal to Islam was central to this claim. They defined the liberation of Palestine as a struggle to free land that god had bequeathed to Muslims and had made holy through the Prophet's ascension into heaven from the Noble Sanctuary (al-Haram al-Sharif) in Jerusalem. The fight for Palestine was, hence, simultaneously a national and a religious duty. By sacrificing for Palestine, one was also sacrificing for god. In demonstrating this twofold commitment, the Islamist of the family, ʿAbd al-Mu'min, challenged the P.L.O.'s claim to be the authentic expression of the Palestinian nation. He also challenged the P.L.O./Fathawi vision of the nation as an extended family. For him, the nation was truly Muslim, and only true Muslims could adequately and effectively represent Palestinian aspirations. For true Muslims to exist, however, there needed to be a fundamental internal (metanoic) transformation in the hearts of believers, a transformation that would accord with the demands of sharīʿa and jihād. The path to liberation, thus, lay in the discipline of prayer, education, and missionary activism to transform others who had gone in for wrongheaded ideologies or an unthinking tradition. It also lay in a return to the jihād when the time was right. For now, in a context in which opponents of the peace process were being actively repressed, it was wiser to focus on self-reform. In adopting this stance, ʿAbd al-Mu'min came into parallel with Mujahida's position, as characterized by the notion of "*al-jihād fī sabīl al-nafs*" (the jihād for the sake of the soul, i.e.) in chapter 3. This position represented a revivification of the culturalist strategies that had typified the activism of the Muslim Brotherhood and the Islamic Collective that preceded the emergence of Hamas. These tendencies never really disappeared but rather had become subsumed under the organizations that focused on charity work within the milieus that supported Hamas and Islamic Jihad. In the post-Oslo situation, a context in which the P.N.A. actively repressed Islamist militancy, nonpolitical missionary and charity work and an attendant stress on cultivating personal piety became a default option for individuals seeking, like ʿAbd al-Mu'min, to maintain ideological consistency.

The tension and interaction embodied in the relationship of ʿAbd al-Mu'min and his brothers and cousin reflected in microcosm the broader generational dynamics that had taken hold in Palestinian society since the first Intifada. In particular, it showed how the two major generational formations—Islamist and P.L.O. nationalist—that had emerged during the Uprising of the late 1980s and early 1990s coincided with the appearance of contrasting sociopolitical affiliations and orientations at the ground level. The interaction among individuals with these diverging affiliations, however, had surprising consequences. Embedded within shared family and neighborhood structures, individuals negotiated and contested the inherited narratives of Islam, the "customs and traditions" of the fallāḥī past, and the collective national struggle to produce variations and hybridizations, in the process creating new, blended ideological and social orientations. Viewed from this ground-level perspective, Islamism and secular nationalism in Gaza were two sides of an interactive cultural-political dialectic that generated multiple, contrasting syntheses of religion, nationalism, and traditionalism. As the experience of the Asdudis has revealed, Islamization provoked counterretrievals of "tradition" (al-ʿādāt wa taqālīd) and rearticulations of other solidarities that either harked back to the familial bonds and general reciprocity of peasant/refugee life or selectively adapted Islamist claims to buttress basic P.L.O. nationalism. The result was a retraditionalization process that moved in three directions: Islamist religious revivification, Islamist-Fathawi hybridization, and "moral-familial" revitalization.[62]

[62] The term "moral familism" refers to the centrality of the family as the basic unit of solidarity in peasant village societies. The ethos and worldview of such societies flowed from the priority placed on loyalty to the ḥumūla (clan) and its patriarchal head (an elder male). Rosemary Sayigh, *Palestinians*, 20–25.

Epilogue

After more than six years of intense violence that has utterly devastated the West Bank and Gaza Strip, it appears that the vectors of change traced in the preceding pages will continue to develop and perhaps move in new directions under volatile conditions. The competition between Hamas and Fatah persists and has deepened. After the death of Yasir ʿArafat, the second-ever Palestinian presidential election temporarily reaffirmed the dominance of Fatah as ʿArafat's successor, Mahmud ʿAbbas (nom de guerre, "Abu Mazen"), took approximately 62 percent of the 70 percent of votes cast from among the pool of registered voters.[1] ʿAbbas interpreted his victory as a popular affirmation for an ending of the armed Intifada in favor of a nonviolent campaign against the occupation and a return to negotiations with Israel. At the same time, results from later municipal-level elections indicated majority support for Hamas candidates in Gaza and significant backing for Islamist-leaning ones in the West Bank. On January 26, 2006, Hamas achieved an overwhelming victory in elections for the Palestinian Legislative Council, ending Fatah's forty-year dominance of Palestinian politics. Violent clashes between Hamas supporters and Fatah loyalists, many of whom feared losing patronage positions in the Palestinian National Authority, broke out in the immediate aftermath of the elections. Younger Fatah activists also began to stage large demonstrations demanding the resignation of the old-guard Fatah leadership. Israel meanwhile indicated its refusal to have anything to do with a Hamas-led government, threatening to end all transfers of tax revenue to the Palestinian National Authority. Similar threats to cut off aid echoed in European capitals and Washington, DC. In response, Hamas oscilliated between attempting to soften its rhetoric of nonrecognition of Israel with talk of a long-term truce (hudna) in exchange for Israel's withdrawal to the pre-1967 boundaries

[1] At the last minute, fearing a low turnout might hurt Abu Mazen's claim to a mandate, Fatah operatives appeared to pressure election workers into allowing unregistered individuals to vote using only their identity cards, thus raising fears of potential double voting. Some analysts, as a result, significantly downgraded the estimates of actual voter turnout at below 50 percent, concluding that most Palestinians voted to stay home. For the official election statistics and statements on voting irregularities, see the documents of the Palestinian Central Elections Commission at http://www.elections.ps/english.aspx. See also ʿAli Abunimah, "Media Grossly Overestimate Palestinian Voter Turnout," *Electronic Intifada* (January 10, 2005), http://electronicintifada.net/v2/article3508.shtml, for a critique of the election results and irregularities. Abunimah places actual voter turnout at approximately 46.7%.

and issuing threats of its own to seek funding elsewhere in the Arab and Islamic world. Israel, all bluster aside, appeared set to continue the policy of unilateralism that Ariel Sharon—who had a few weeks earlier suffered a massive stroke that terminated his political life—had spearheaded by redeploying the Israeli military and settlers out of the Gaza Strip in September 2005 and building the so-called separation wall in the West Bank. The Hamas victory simply provided more cover for this policy by enabling Israel to repeat its insistence that it had "no partner for peace."

What these various developments mean for the long term is far from clear. Although Hamas and its allies appear to be ascendant, they will continue to confront a fissured society. It is not certain at all whether the Islamists will be able to create a new political umbrella that can replace the Fatah-led P.L.O. and its brand of multisectarian nationalism. Given the fundamental pluralism of Palestinian society, Hamas most likely will have to conform to multisectarianism even as it attempts to recast Palestinian nationalism in Islamist-oriented terms. While they clearly desire a reform of their internal political situation, Palestinians, as a whole, remain divided and ambivalent about the ends and means of their collective struggle. They have voted Hamas into power and yet in every opinion poll they indicate overwhelming desire for a negotiated two-state solution and a democratic political system. This ambivalence reflects the continuing effects of the first Intifada and the subsequent but now moribund Oslo Process.

At the end of the 1990s, with Oslo stalemated and in crisis, the political divisions among Palestinians deepened. Two questions lay at the center of the debate within and between the main Islamist and secularist factions: Would negotiations with Israel really lead to the desired ends? Or would it be necessary to resort, again, to armed resistance? As the voices presented in this book demonstrate, activists on both sides of the secularist-Islamist divide, especially the younger generation of leaders who had arisen during and after the first Intifada, felt that a revived uprising, one that would be much more violent, would indeed be necessary in the face of intensified Israeli settlement construction throughout the Occupied Palestinian Territories and what appeared to be the Israeli bottom line of granting only a truncated, territorially noncontiguous form of partial sovereignty in the West Bank and Gaza Strip with nominal, symbolic presence in Jerusalem. Such a prospect fell far short of the stated goals of the first Uprising. The apparent willingness of Fatah's senior, "outside" leadership to go along with the unfolding final scenario further heightened the feeling among Fatah's "new guard" that they should take matters into their own hands both to guarantee the realization of nationalist goals and to impose greater influence on decision making at the highest levels. There was also the need to respond to the persisting Islamist challenge. The Islamists had continued to reject the Oslo Process, periodically illustrating their capacity to act independently by carrying out spectacular "martyr operations" against Israeli civilian and military targets. Fatah, as a whole, and the new guard that sought to inherit leadership of Fatah, in particular, needed to maintain an armed option in the event of the collapse of the peace process if only to prevent Hamas and the Islamic Jihad from asserting control of any new revived revolt.

But the armed option was not unproblematic for any faction, Islamist or secular nationalist. What guarantee was there for a war-weary population that violence would succeed? Palestinians had been jubilant at the sight of withdrawing Israeli troops and the arrival of Palestinian police to take their place in the early days of the Palestinian National Authority. The elections for the Legislative Council and presidency in 1996, moreover, drew a very high voter turnout; the results, heavily in favor of Yasir ʿArafat and the Fatah slate of candidates, seemed to vindicate the decision to go down the Oslo path. In the wake of the elections, the opponents of Oslo, principally the Islamists, who had boycotted the poll, found themselves marginalized and needing, at least momentarily, to reassess their strategic direction. That moment did not last long for a host of reasons, among them Israeli foot-dragging on agreed-upon land transfers; the intensified settlement building; continued restrictions on travel between Palestinian towns; ongoing raids, arrests, and assassinations of Palestinian "militants"; Islamist-led bombings in Israeli cities; and the widely held perception that the Palestinian National Authority had become corrupt. Life under the Oslo regime, though marginally better than direct occupation by the Israeli military (which still controlled major swaths of the West Bank—the zones demarcated under the Oslo security agreements as Areas B and C, e.g.), was thus a far cry from the settled, independent national existence that Palestinians had hoped for. By the time then Likud Party chairman and soon-to-be Israeli prime minister Ariel Sharon made his infamous tour of al-Haram al-Sharif (the Noble Sanctuary, known also as the Temple Mount), both the Israeli military and the Palestinian political factions were primed for a return to full-throttle armed violence.[2]

[2] On Palestinian and Israeli preparations for a possible return to all-out violence, see Deborah Sontag, "In Mock Palestinian Hill Town, Israeli Troops Prepare for Worst," *New York Times*, June 24, 2000, and John F. Burns, "Palestinian Summer Camp Offers the Games of War," *New York Times*, August 3, 2000. Both articles are available through the archive service at http://www.nytimes.com.

Alongside the issue of whether to reignite the uprising as an alternative to negotiations, the Oslo Process, as an exercise in state building, however fraught with uncertainty and contradiction, also generated fundamental questions about what kind of state and society Palestinians wanted. Was the Palestinian National Authority under Yasir ʿArafat's personal, neopatrimonial rule really the desired form, or was some other model required? What was that other model? A secular democracy that relegated religion to the private sphere? A multiconfessional one that incorporated elements of religious regulation into the Basic Law? An Islamically oriented democratic system that affirmed social and political pluralism within the limits of sharīʿa? Or a version of personal/patriarchal rule grounded in a deeply engrained sharīʿa piety of the leader and his followers alike?

This debate was not so much an instrumental one, with leaders and followers changing ideological frames at will for reasons of political expediency. Rather, at least among my interlocutors, it reflected a more thoroughgoing set of transformations and tensions within the structures and ethos of Palestinian nationalism, generally. These changes began during the 1980s, gained steam with the first Intifada, and remained dynamic through the period of the Oslo Peace Process. The main force propelling these changes, I have argued, has been the synchronic cultural-political division within the generation of Islamist and secular-nationalist activists who came of age during the first Intifada. Having grown up under occupation, the young activists of the first Uprising experienced the mass revolt as a revolutionary moment requiring radically altered approaches. Youth took to the streets to protest and engage Israeli soldiers in stone-throwing encounters that often ended in arrests, injuries, and deaths. The trope of the *shahīd* (the Islamic religious term for one who dies "in the path of God," i.e., in advocating or defending the faith) began to define the horizon of aspiration of these new activists. A collective ethos of revolt and voluntary self-sacrifice for the nation took root. It was precisely in response to the emergence of this ethos that senior Muslim Brotherhood leaders abandoned their "culturalist" approach and entered directly into the fray with a new organizational structure and militant frame embodied in Hamas. The emergence of this new, retooled Islamist movement, along with the Islamic Jihad, subsequently institutionalized a synchronic division within the Intifada generation, setting in motion the secularist-Islamist dialectic that this book has explored in depth.

To describe as "Islamization" the transformation that this dialectic produced would be too simplistic. If there is anything to conclude from the preceding chapters, it is that Palestinian identities are not easily reducible to the simple dichotomy of Islamist versus secular nationalist. The generational dialectic has produced multiple, diverging trajectories of identity. Among many of the individuals featured in the preceding pages, the lines dividing Islamists and secular nationalists had become porous, blurred, and redrawn. Recall, for instance, how some of my Islamist interviewees reconceptualized jihād as electoral activism that aimed at shaping the institutions of the emerging state. Individuals like Abu Hasan forged cross-factional ties and, in so doing, redefined the Islamist option as a broad umbrella under which an oppositional, issues-based politics could be mobilized across the political and social spectrum. Interestingly, Abu Hasan's rethinking had led him to criticize the more authoritarian variants of Islamism, particularly those that desired to reactivate the caliphate as a form of personal-patriarchal political order. Against such wishes, he asserted the need for a democratic system shaped by and congruent with core Islamic religious principles that affirmed religious and cultural pluralism and consultation (*shūrā*).

Where does someone like Abu Hasan fall on the Islamist/secular-nationalist continuum? Certainly, he is committed to realizing the Islamist aim of a sharīʿa-oriented polity; but the means he advocates imply a basic acceptance of secular-liberal premises regarding the source of political authority ("the people" and not the divine, e.g.) and the notion of secular-democratic citizenship (as opposed to conceptions of political membership that structure rights and status on the basis of religious identity). He is not entirely consistent on this point, as he desires to make the sharīʿa the foundation of the Basic Law while providing limited autonomy to religious minorities to follow their own customs—a type of modified medieval *millet* system. Still, his insistence on the need for democratic process would seem to imply acceptance of the equality of individuals under a single legal standard regardless of religious affiliation. Abu Hasan, it should be pointed out, is also committed to the very secular notion of a territorially bounded Palestinian nation-state, an idea at odds, prima facie, with the concept of a transnational *umma* (worldwide Islamic community). Taken as a whole, Abu Hasan's stance reflects a secularization of Islamist tendencies. This secularizing orientation—in the sense of accepting the framework of electoral politics and a territorially bounded nation-state—will continue to evolve and perhaps become predominant in the Islamist milieu should Israel continue to withdraw from territory, unilaterally or through negotiations. Evidence of this evolution is already discernible in the aftermath of Hamas's spectacular victory in the January 2006 Palestinian Legislative Council elections. Responsible now for governance, Hamas will need to find a way to placate and possibly integrate oppositional Fatah elements as well as ensure the continued flow of aid from abroad. These pressures could very well force a tempering of militancy and accommodation of political and religious pluralism—that is, as long as isolation of a Hamas-led government by external powers does not provoke a return to radicalism.

Just as there was a secularization of Islamist orientations among some of my Hamas and Islamic Jihad interlocutors, most notably Abu Hasan, so there had also been a discernible selective integration of Islamist themes among secular-nationalist activists, especially Fathawis. We have seen how some Fathawi interviewees adopted Islamist theodicies that explained the failure to overcome Israel as the result of a falling away from piety; their conclusions mirrored Islamist ones, too: the road back from the brink had to trace its course through a renewed commitment to Islam, but not necessarily in the manner that the Islamist movements might have intended. For these individuals, the key distinction lay between *muḥāfiẓ* ("conservative," connoting "moderate") Islam, the true Islam in their view, and the *mutashaddid* ("strict," connoting "radical fundamentalist") variations that had distorted the religion.

The embrace of "moderate Islam" had begun to manifest itself even in leftist circles, to the consternation of Marxist-nationalist stalwarts. Individuals like Hamdi, the former Communist Party activist in Thawra Camp who adopted a more pious lifestyle after an encounter with a Hamas-leaning work colleague, elided the boundary between Islamic and leftist values. Hamdi argued that the Communists of Thawra embodied the essence of Islam in their respect for the *ʿādāt wa taqālīd* (customs and traditions) and basic conventions of reciprocity and decency. For other former "leftists" like Abu Jamil in Gaza, true religion resided not so much in Islam, per se, but in a personal patriarchal ethos characterized by individual generosity, general reciprocity, and respect for the ʿādāt wa taqālīd that had structured the *fallāḥī* ("peasant") world of the pre-1948 past and its proletarianized, refugee present. Yet a third approach affirmed religion while nevertheless insisting on a general secularity. Sabr, the Fatah activist in the Bethlehem area who was planning to study international relations in the United States, gave voice to this perspective by arguing that Islam was a matter of personal practice and interpretation. While she prayed and fasted and was careful, as a single woman, to have her brother accompany her to meetings with me, for instance, she refused the scarf (*ḥijāb*) and other gendered markers of piety that had become associated with Islamism, opting for a modest "Western style" of dress. Religion was to be a matter of individual practice and never legislated from above by the state. She feared that should the line between personal morality and public secularity be erased, Palestinian society would follow the path of Taliban Afghanistan or post-1979 Iran. Both routes augured poorly for women, she said. She proposed instead to revive a *qawmī* (pan-Arab) nationalism that affirmed Islamic cultural traditions as a general national heritage, leaving its particular instantiations to individual appropriation and practice.

One consequence of the Islamist/secular-nationalist dialectic for my secular-nationalist interviewees, thus, was a revitalized traditionalism as a type of counter-Islamism. This traditionalizing of the secular-nationalist milieu, at least as it appeared among my interviewees, reflected the long-standing emphasis within Fathawi/P.L.O. nationalism on symbols drawn from the peasant and Arab past; at the same time, however, the explicit incorporation and reinterpretation of Islamic discourse and practice in terms of traditional/national values produced novel variations of the protean Fathawi nationalism. Among my interviewees, there was a re-casting of mainstream secular nationalism in a manner that responded to and integrated the discourse of Islam, albeit in the altered and diverging registers of muḥāfiẓ moderation, qawmī nationalism, or peasant traditionalism or "moral familism" (as figured, for instance, in the discourse of the ʿādāt wa taqālīd).

That Fathawi nationalism would incorporate elements of Islamic religion as part of its conception of the *secular* state is nothing new in the Middle East. National movements and states throughout the region have long attempted, to one degree or another, to integrate and domesticate religious symbols, discourses, and structures for purposes of legitimization. In the process, they have engaged in a larger project that has typified late modernity, as a whole, which is the construction of "religion" and "the religious" as a bounded sphere of bureaucratic control alongside other regulated spheres within the territorially limited space of the nation-state. In the Palestinian case, we have seen how both Islamists and secular nationalists—as figured, for example, in the "democratic Islamism" of someone like Abu Hasan and the muḥāfiẓ multiconfessionalism of Husayn and Abu ʿAdnan (the Christian Fatah leader in Bethlehem)—have begun to converge on an acceptance, at least provisionally, of such a construction of "religion" vis-à-vis the secular, even if the placement of the boundary between the two remains a highly contested issue between the groups. In such a convergence lie the seeds of new political formations that could emerge from the fragmentation of the old movements (Fatah, Hamas, etc.). While dissolution and reorganization have not yet fully occurred, a revived state-building process could very well definitively force apart the present secular-nationalist and Islamist coalitions, creating opportunities for new cross-faction alliances in the struggle to determine the shape and orientation of the emerging nation-state.[3]

Such an eventuality could also generate attempts to prevent boundary

[3] Bruce Lawrence, *Shattering the Myth: Islam beyond Violence* (Princeton, NJ: Princeton University Press, 1998), for case studies of different approaches taken by nation-states with majority Muslim population to the incorporation/domestication of Islamic symbols and regulatory customs. Also, John L. Esposito, *The Islamic Threat: Myth or Reality?* 3rd edition (New York: Oxford University Press, 1999), especially 74–127; Dale F. Eickelman and James Piscatori, *Muslim Politics* (Princeton, NJ: Princeton University Press, 1996), 18–21, and chapters 3, 4, and 5; and the final chapter on Islamic modernist reform in early

blurring and reinforce key ideological distinctions. Indications of this type of response became manifest among some of my Islamist interviewees, taking two distinct forms: power-oriented and piety-oriented. The clearest example of the power-centered approach was Ibn Fadlallah—the Islamic Jihad activist who was expelled to southern Lebanon in 1992 and while there engaged with, and drew inspiration from, Iranian and Lebanese Shiʿa activists. Ibn Fadlallah argued for a revival of a militant, armed jihād to revitalize the national struggle against Israel. The inspirational example set by Hussayn at Karbala in the seventh century and his modern-day incarnation, the Hizbullah, provided the model for the refounding of the Palestinian national movement, the key features of which would be selflessness, sacrifice, and courage in the face of overwhelming odds—features that stood in sharp contrast to the self-seeking behavior of a seemingly corrupt Fatah/Palestinian National Authority leadership. Unique among my respondents, Ibn Fadlallah articulated a revitalized pan-Islamism that creatively integrated the themes of Shiʿa revivalism with those of Palestinian nationalism.

After the outbreak of the new round of violence in the closing months of 2000, Palestinian activists explicitly invoked the example of Hizbullah's successful guerrilla campaign against Israel in southern Lebanon. Hizbullah flags appeared in mass demonstrations in the Occupied Palestinian Territories, and Hizbullah itself extolled the uprising in its radio and television broadcasts. The attempt to emulate Hizbullah's model, however, has yet to prove successful. If victory for the armed struggle is ever claimed—and Hamas made such a claim in the aftermath of Israel's unilateral redeployment out of its forward positions in the Gaza Strip—it

---

twentieth-century Egypt in Talal Asad, *Formations of the Secular: Christianity, Islam, Modernity* (Stanford, CA: Stanford University Press, 2003). Saba Mahmood, *Politics of Piety: The Islamic Revival and the Feminist Subject* (Princeton, NJ: Princeton University Press, 2005), 73–78, discusses the implications of state intervention for female *daʿwa* activists. Mahmood notes, perceptively, that simply because the Egyptian state, in an effort to mobilize Islam for purposes of political legitimization and control, has integrated sharīʿa precepts into its personal status law, regulates the training and licensing of mosque preachers and teachers, controls the major center of Islamic learning, al-Azhar University, and so on, does not mean that it is not really secular in its orientation. There is, she observes, no one single model of secularism, no one mode of marking off the realm of the religious so as to produce and extend the taken-for-granted domain of the secular. Moreover, even in the so-called West, the line between the religious and the secular is always being negotiated: the religious continues to intervene and shape the secular in multiple ways and to varying degrees just as it does in modern Muslim-majority nation-states. Hence, I would add, the question of secularity and religion is not one that divides neatly along "civilizational" boundaries, with Muslim-majority societies being more "religious" than Western ones. Rather, the question has to do with the modalities of the secular-religious dynamic as they manifest themselves in varying forms and directions in different national settings.

will be a pyrrhic one. Israeli repression has been massive and brutal. Activists at every level, including top Islamist leaders such as Hamas founder Shaykh Ahmad Yasin and the prominent Hamas spokesman Dr. ʿAbd al-ʿAziz al-Rantisi, have been methodically assassinated. Mass sweeps have imprisoned thousands of young men. Checkpoints and the new, massive wall under construction along the entire length of the West Bank and East Jerusalem have cut off contact between Palestinian towns and villages. Prolonged closures have ruined the economy. Thousands of Palestinians now live below the internationally stipulated poverty line of $2.10 per day. Entire neighborhoods, especially in Gaza's Rafah Refugee Camp, have been leveled by the Israeli military's gigantic armored Caterpillar bulldozers in an effort to create free-fire zones and punish individual families and entire communities for supporting the uprising. At the time of this writing, the violence has produced no diplomatic gains and indeed has isolated the Palestinian leadership. Yet, in the absence of substantive negotiations, the harsh crackdown, economic immiseration, and ceaseless rounds of tit-for-tat attack and retaliation have engendered a culture of resentment, resistance, and violence in which the apotheosis of the shahīd (one who, through the sacrifice of his or her life, bears witness on behalf of god and the violated, suffering nation) has come to define yet again—in a society stripped of stability, "normalcy," and alternative life courses—the life aspirations of many of the young.[4]

Notwithstanding the high levels of resentment and readiness for violent self-sacrificial action among the youth, multiple polls taken since 2001 suggest that the majority of Palestinians still desire a return to negotiations; and the electoral victory of Mahmud ʿAbbas, who has proclaimed the need to end the armed uprising and restart negotiations, seems to confirm this desire among the populace—at least among those who voted—to fashion a new direction.[5] Yet the armed activists in the

[4] Nasra Hassan, "Letter from Gaza: An Arsenal of Believers—Talking to the 'Human Bombs,'" *New Yorker*, November 19, 2001, explores the culture of the shahīd early during the latest round of violence through interviews with Hamas and Islamic Jihad operatives. Article posted at http://www.newyorker.com/fact/content/?011119fa_FACT1. Lamis Andoni, "Searching for Answers: Gaza's Suicide Bombers," *Journal of Palestine Studies* 26, no. 4 (Summer 1997): 33–45, traces the story of two friends who were among the first Hamas bombers to strike after the signing of the Oslo Declaration of Principles in 1993. These two men were politicized as Fatah activists during the first Intifada but then, after becoming disillusioned soon after the installation of the Palestinian National Authority, were drawn into Islamist radicalism.

[5] P.C.P.S.R. exit polls show that those who voted for Abu Mazen in the recent presidential election did so in support of restarting negotiations with Israel and ending the armed Intifada. The same polls indicate that Hamas's victories in local elections were due to the perception of Islamist candidates as incorruptible. For these data and the numerous polls since 2001 indicating majority support for a return to negotiations, see the Palestinian Centre for Policy and Survey Research index at http://www.pcpsr.org/survey/index.html.

various Islamist and secular-nationalist militias will not be so easily sidelined; nor will the shahīd culture that frames and legitimizes militancy and facilitates recruitment to armed groups be easily transformed. The Islamists, in particular, have gained much credibility through their demonstrated willingness to fight and die for nationalist and religious principles. Moreover, Fatah's "new-guard" activists, particularly those who have been leading the various militias that comprise the amorphous Fatah-associated al-Aqsa Martyrs Brigades, will be loath to return to the status quo ante. ʿAbbas, who, during his election campaign, appeared in the company of al-Aqsa fighters, must show that any new negotiations will produce what Oslo could not: statehood in the entire West Bank, Gaza Strip, and East Jerusalem. Similar pressures will confront Hamas, as well, now that it has gained control of the Palestinian Legislative Council. Faced with the need to secure external funding for P.N.A. ministries, Hamas will be forced to tone down its rhetoric of armed insurrection and engage in the diplomatic process. The extent to which Israel, Europe, and the United States are willing to deal with an Islamist-led P.N.A., however, remains to be seen. Meanwhile, Fatah will most likely continue to fragment along diachronic generational lines, especially if the old-guard leadership resists relinquishing control of the movement.

Should new negotiations begin and Palestinian state formation restart, it is possible that some Islamists will reject "politics," choosing instead a "piety-oriented" response that seeks to prevent the dilution of religious solidarity by withdrawing into an Islamist subculture while simultaneously reviving the cultural struggle against secularism within the wider society. Two of my interlocutors, Mujahida, the Bethlehem-area female Islamic Jihad activist, and ʿAbd al-Muʾmin, the younger Asdudi brother who was a Gaza Hamas supporter, exemplified this reflex. As armed activism became increasingly less tenable during the Oslo period, these two individuals came to believe that only a thoroughgoing metanoic transformation of hearts—a cultural jihād that aimed at the reorientation of inner dispositions through the disciplining of outer comportment—would achieve a true and lasting commitment to Islam in the society at large. Such commitment was, for these two, the sine qua non of liberation at every level—psychologically and culturally, in removing inauthentic forms of consciousness imposed by the West, and politically in relation to Israel and the West, generally. Imm Muhammad, Latif's Fatah-leaning wife in Karama Camp in Gaza, felt a similar need for a metanoic change of this sort; but, she argued, the Islamist factions would never be the vehicle for this kind of deep inner transformation, because they were no better than any other political movement (i.e., they used religion in the service of politics and in so doing debased and distorted Islam). Thus, ironically, the general critique of politics from the standpoint of piety—

one that transcends faction boundaries—snagged the Islamists themselves within its net. Such an antipolitics of piety could very well continue to erode faction legitimacy across the spectrum should the current stalemate continue or should renewed state-building revive the perceptions of corruption within the Palestinian National Authority and the parties that lead or cooperate with it, including Islamist ones.[6]

A revived antisecularist cultural struggle among Islamists, as envisioned by Mujahida and ʿAbd al-Muʾmin, for instance, could concomitantly produce a secularist countermovement to resist Islamization. This possibility was already emerging among some of my "liberal" Popular Front interlocutors. For these individuals, it was paramount—during this period when the core institutions of the nation-state were taking form—to create the conditions for the flourishing of diverse forms of individuality and community. Doing so required the building of a democratic system that preserved the secularity of the public sphere while protecting the private domain from the encroachments of any particular group. Advancing Islamization was now the primary threat to achieving these ends. In the event of Islamists taking power, what would happen, they asked, to secular Muslims, like themselves, who did not pray, fast, or abstain from alcohol? Their response to the perceived Islamist threat was, like that of their Islamist competitors, to try to shift the cultural equation in their favor. Former secular leftists in Thawra withdrew from faction activism to start social centers that projected "liberal" values—the mixing of the sexes in educational and cultural activities, for example—and attracted new support through the extension of services.

Among female secular activists concerned with the problem of sharīʿa and "personal status law," debate centered on whether to try to reinterpret the sharīʿa in line with "progressive" values or whether steadfastly to refuse to give any ground to religious custom and practice within the emerging legal framework of the state-to-be. Advocates of the latter approach insisted on the need for open encounter and confrontation with Islamists and, even more important, with those in the secular-nationalist camp who were ready to compromise on the question of women's equality by allowing personal status law to be based on sharīʿa prescriptions. These activists pointed to the failure of the secular-nationalist leadership to stop the forceful imposition of the head scarf on "uncovered" women in Gaza in the early days of the first Intifada as a case in point, demonstrating what happens when compromise is made on "cultural" ques-

[6] Saba Mahmood observes similar types of criticism leveled by piety-oriented activists against the politically active, power-centered Islamist groups. See also her excellent discussion of how the *daʿwa* concept became reinterpreted among key twentieth-century intellectuals committed to the revival of Islamic institutions as an alternative to secular European ideas and practices. Mahmood, *Politics of Piety*, 40–78.

tions. This secularist collapse on the scarf question indexed a larger failure to grasp and vigorously contest the wider Islamizing shift underway in Gaza at the time. The need now, it was argued, was to focus on women's equality, enshrined in a secular personal-status law, as the core element in the struggle to create a liberal democratic society. These debates will only intensify now that Hamas has achieved majority power in the Palestinian Legislative Council.

What will finally emerge as the dominant expression of Palestinian political identity remains unclear. Much depends on whether Israel, by far the more powerful external actor, sufficiently meets basic Palestinian demands for sovereignty. If the Hamas-controlled Palestinian National Authority can broker a peace settlement that ends Israel's occupation and brings into existence meaningful Palestinian statehood in the entirety, or near entirety, of the West Bank, Gaza Strip, and East Jerusalem, then, because surveys indicate a broad desire for such an outcome, it will reap the benefit of wide popular support and the legitimacy that would come with it. To achieve this end, Islamist forces will most likely have to moderate their political rhetoric and strategies. Of course, if Israel persists in a policy of violent repression and settlement and wall construction, then the dynamic of armed resistance and further radicalization could well unfold on all sides as the Palestinian political and social order descends yet again into collapse.

Either scenario—state building and Islamist moderation or continued repression and militancy—will shift the Islamist-secularist dynamic in various directions but not eradicate it. At this point, even as the balance has shifted, neither side of the dialectic is yet strong enough to overcome or absorb the other. A return to state building will once again bring to the fore the fundamental questions of the legal and cultural foundation of the emerging polity. An Islamist-secularist cultural-political struggle may then ensue at the parliamentary and civil society levels. Continued occupation, on the other hand, may simply perpetuate the "politics of atrocity"[7] in which, in the absence of a viable Palestinian state, militias associated with the factions compete for prestige, popularity, and power amongst their ranks and in the wider society through the performance of ever more violent acts that provoke even more violent Israeli retaliations.

Whatever direction events take, Islamism will remain a vibrant and multifaceted dimension of Palestinian society. Islamists are now a dominant force that can no longer be ignored or dismissed. Islamist social service networks have engendered trust and respect, especially in the absence

[7] The phrase is Graham Usher's; see "The Politics of Atrocity," chap. in *Dispatches from Palestine: The Rise and Fall of the Oslo Peace Process* (London: Pluto Press, 1999), 83–87.

of comparable Palestinian National Authority institutions. And Islamist symbols, discourses, and practices have become widely disseminated across the factional spectrum, significantly reframing what it means to be a Palestinian. This fact needs simply to be grasped and accepted.

But it is not an unalloyed fact. Palestinian identity in its various Islamist and secularist variants is, as the preceding pages have shown, highly fluid, hybrid and multiplex, open to diverse horizons. How these horizons evolve, and which ones become dominant, will depend in large part on how powerful outsiders—Israel, the United States, the other Arab countries—respond to the Palestinians and the continuing predicament of alienation, dislocation, dispossession, and statelessness that has so violently stamped the outlines of their collective life. To be sure, Palestinians, too, through the inner dialectics of their culture and politics, will shape whatever future emerges for them; but they will do so in relation to Israeli hegemony, the putative U.S. "war on terrorism," and the shifting regional power balance in the wake of the political cataclysms in Iraq and Lebanon.

If regional and international powers desire Palestinian moderation, if only to achieve stability in one critical corner of the Middle East, then they will need to create the conditions for a viable, territorially contiguous Palestinian state, and they will need to do so immediately. In the absence of such a state, in the face of yet more promises deferred, the brutal litany of bombings, ambushes, assassinations, and home demolitions could well continue, producing yet another discontented generation that will forge a new radicalism to overcome the perennial failure of the elders. Indeed, this future has already come to pass in the last six and a half years of unrelenting violence.

But this eventuality, now realized in the present, was not, and is not, inevitable. Meaningful statehood could induce a very different generational trajectory that consigns militancy to the elders and recasts the present as a civil struggle, Islamist and secularist, to define the character of the state, confront the challenges of governance, and grapple with coexistence with Israel and Israelis. It is not too late to achieve this future. The way forward will require imagination and the will to intervene against unilateral "solutions" that seek to shore up the current untenable status quo of Israeli domination and Palestinian immiseration. Above all else, it will require knowledge and empathy on the part of outsiders of the diverse, often contradictory responses of Palestinians to the immense external forces and unresolved inner tensions that have so powerfully shaped their collective national experience. Islamism is now as much a part of the Palestinian political landscape as is P.L.O. secular nationalism. It has taken up the torch of nationalist militancy that the P.L.O. once carried in its decades-long effort to ignite and sustain the "revolution." Whether this new "religious" form of Palestinian national revolt moderates depends on the willingness of Israel and the international community to deal with a Hamas-led Palestinian National Authority and enable the emergence, through meaningful negotiations, of a viable Palestinian state—one that equitably resolves the core questions of territorial boundaries, refugee repatriation, and the status of Jerusalem.

References

Abu-Amr, Ziad. *Islamic Fundamentalism in the West Bank and Gaza: Muslim Brotherhood and Islamic Jihad*. Bloomington and Indianapolis, IN: Indiana University Press, 1994.

Abu-Manneh, Butrus. "The Husaynis: The Rise of a Notable Family in 18th Century Palestine." Chap. in *Palestine in the Late Ottoman Period: Political, Social, and Economic Transformation*. Edited by David Kushner. Leiden: E. J. Brill, 1986.

Abunimah, ʿAli. "Media Grossly Overestimate Palestinian Voter Turnout." *Electronic Intifada*, January 10, 2005, http://electronicintifada.net/v2/article3508.shtml.

Abu-Rabiʿ, Ibrahim M. *Intellectual Origins of Islamic Resurgence in the Modern Arab World*. Albany, NY: SUNY Press, 1996.

Ahmed, Leila. *Women and Gender in Islam*. New Haven, CT: Yale University Press, 1992.

Ajami, Fouad. *The Vanished Imam: Musa al Sadr and the Shia of Lebanon*. Ithaca, NY: Cornell University Press, 1986.

Amireh, Amal. "Between Complicity and Subversion: Body Politics in Palestinian National Narrative." *South Atlantic Quarterly* 102, no. 4 (Fall 2003): 747–772.

Andoni, Lamis. "Searching for Answers: Gaza's Suicide Bombers." *Journal of Palestine Studies* 26, no. 4 (Summer 1997): 33–45.

Asad, Talal. *Formations of the Secular: Christianity, Islam, Modernity*. Stanford, CA: Stanford University Press, 2003.

El-Awaisi, Abd al-Fattah Muhammad. *The Muslim Brothers and the Palestine Question, 1928–1947*. London: Tauris Academic Studies, 1998.

Al-Banna, Hasan. *Mudhakkirat al-daʿwa wa al-daʿiya*. [Remembrances of the Summons and of the One Who Issues It]. Beirut: al-Maktab al-Islami, 1947, 1966, 1974, 1979.

———. *Nazarat fi islah al-nafs wa al-mujtamaʿ*. [Views on the Reformation of the Soul and Society]. Cairo: Maktabat al-Iʿtisam,1980.

Bayat, Asaf. "Revolution without Movement, Movement without Revolution: Comparing Islamic Activism in Iran and Egypt." *Comparative Studies in Society and History* 40, no. 1 (January 1998): 136–169.

Brown, L. Carl. *Religion and State: The Muslim Approach to Politics*. New York: Columbia University Press, 2000.

Btselem. "Separation Barrier." http://www.btselem.org/english/Separation_Barrier/Index.asp.

Bucaille, Laetitia. *Growing Up Palestinian: Israeli Occupation and the Intifada Generation*. Translated by Anthony Roberts. Princeton, NJ: Princeton University Press, 2004.

Burns, John F. "Palestinian Summer Camp Offers the Games of War." *New York Times*, August 3, 2000, http://www.nytimes.com.

Chomsky, Noam. *The Fateful Triangle: The United States, Israel, and the Palestinians*. Boston, MA: South End Press, 1983.

Cobban, Helena. *The Palestinian Liberation Organisation: People, Power and Politics*. Cambridge: Cambridge University Press, 1984.

Cook, David. *Understanding Jihad*. Berkeley, CA: University of California Press, 2005.

Cork, Dan. "Information Brief, Number 79: The Palestinian Economy Post-Oslo: Unsustainable Development." Washington, DC: Center for Policy Analysis on Palestine, July 11, 2001, http://www.palestinecenter.org/cpap/pubs/20010711ib.html.

Daniel, Norman. *Islam and the West: The Making of an Image*. Edinburgh, Scotland: Edinburgh University Press, 1960; reprint, Oxford: One World Publications, 1993.

Dellios, Hugh. "Clashes Choke Palestinian Economy: Israeli Blockades Restrict Flow of Workers, Goods." *Chicago Tribune*, December 12, 2000, sec. 1, p. 3.

Denny, Frederick Mathewson. *An Introduction to Islam*, 3rd edition. Upper Saddle River, NJ: Pearson Prentice Hall, 1994, 2006.

Dolphin, Ray. *The West Bank Wall: Unmaking Palestine*. London: Pluto Press, 2006.

Dunham, Charlotte. "Generation Units and the Life Course: A Sociological Perspective on Youth and the Anti-war Movement." *Journal of Political and Military Sociology* 26, no. 2 (Winter 1998): 137–155.

Eickelman, Dale F., and James Piscatori. *Muslim Politics*. Princeton, NJ: Princeton University Press, 1996.

Emirbayer, Mustafa, and Jeff Godwin. "Network Analysis, Culture, and the Problem of Agency." *American Journal of Sociology* 99, no. 6 (May 1994): 1411–1454.

Esacove, Anne W. "Dialogic Framing: The Framing/Counterframing of 'Partial-Birth' Abortion." *Sociological Inquiry* 74, no. 1 (February 2004): 70–101.

Esposito, John L. *The Islamic Threat: Myth or Reality?* 3rd edition. New York: Oxford University Press, 1999.

———. *Women in Muslim Family Law*. Syracuse, NY: Syracuse University Press, 1982.

Esposito, John L., and Azzam Tamimi, eds. *Islam and Secularism in the Middle East*. New York: New York University Press, 2000.

Euben, Roxanne. *Enemy in the Mirror: Islamic Fundamentalism and the Limits of Modern Rationalism, a Work of Comparative Political Theory*. Princeton, NJ: Princeton University Press, 1999.

Friedman, Gil. "Popular Trust and Distrust in Palestinian Politicians and Factions." Jerusalem: Jerusalem Media and Communications Center, August 2000, http://www.jmcc.org/research/reports/study1.htm#intro.

Gaffney, Patrick D. *The Prophet's Pulpit: Islamic Preaching in Contemporary Egypt*. Berkeley, CA: University of California Press, 1994.

Gramsci, Antonio. *The Antonio Gramsci Reader: Selected Writings, 1916–1935*. Edited by David Forgacs. London: Lawrence and Wishart, 1986 and 1999.

Haddad, Robert M. *Syrian Christians in Muslim Society: An Interpretation.* Princeton, NJ: Princeton University Press, 1970.

Haddad, Yvonne Y. "Sayyid Qutb: Ideologue of Islamic Revival." In *Voices of Resurgent Islam*. Edited by John L. Esposito. New York: Oxford University Press, 1983.

Halper, Jeff. "The Key to Peace: Dismantling the Matrix of Control." Jerusalem: March 2000. http://www.icahd.org/eng/articles.asp?menu=6&submenu=3.

Hammami, Rema. "Women, the Hijab, and the Intifada." *MERIP* 164/165 (May–August 1990): 24–31.

Hammami, Rema, and Penny Johnson. "Equality with a Difference: Gender and Citizenship in Transitional Palestine." *Social Politics* 6, no. 3 (Fall 1999): 314–343.

Hammer, Joshua. *A Season in Bethlehem: Unholy War in a Sacred Place*. New York: Free Press, 2003.

Hass, Amira. *Drinking the Sea at Gaza: Days and Nights in a Land under Siege.* Translated by Elana Wesley and Maxine Kaufman-Lacusta. New York: Metropolitan Books, Henry Holt and Co., 1996, 1999.

Hassan, Nasra. "Letter from Gaza: An Arsenal of Believers—Talking to the 'Human Bombs.'" *New Yorker*, November 19, 2001, http://www.newyorker.com/fact/content/?011119fa_FACT1.

Hilal, Jamil. "The Effect of the Oslo Agreement on the Palestinian Political System." In *After Oslo: New Realities, Old Problems*. Edited by George Giacaman and Dag Jørund Lønning. London: Pluto Press, 1998.

———. *Al-nizam al-siyasi al-filastini ba'da Oslo: Dirasa tahliliyya naqdiyya.* [The Palestinian Political System after Oslo: An Analytical Study]. Beirut: Institute for Palestinian Studies, 1998.

Hiltermann, Joost R. *Behind the Intifada: Labor and Women's Movements in the Occupied Territories*. Princeton, NJ: Princeton University Press, 1991.

Hodgson, Marshall. *The Venture of Islam: Conscience and History in a World Civilization*. Vol. 1, *The Classical Age of Islam*. Chicago: University of Chicago Press, 1974.

Hourani, Albert. *Arabic Thought in the Liberal Age*. Oxford: Oxford University Press, 1970.

———. *A History of the Arab Peoples*. Cambridge, MA: Harvard University Press, 1991.

———. "Ottoman Reform and the Politics of Notables." Chap. in *Beginnings of Modernization in the Middle East: The Nineteenth Century*. Edited by William R. Polk and Richard L. Chambers. Chicago: University of Chicago Press, 1968.

Hroub, Khaled. *Hamas: Political Thought and Practice*. Washington, DC: Institute for Palestine Studies, 2000.

Husayn, 'Abd al-Baqi Muhammad. *Sayyid Qutb: hayatuhu wa adabu*. [Sayyid Qutb: His Life and Literature]. Al-Mansura, Egypt: Dar al-Wafa', 1986.

International Court of Justice. "Advisory Opinion: Legal Consequences of the Construction of a Wall in the Occupied Palestinian Territory," http://www.icj-cij.org/icjwww/ipresscom/ipress2004/ipresscom2004-28_mwp_20040709.htm.

"Israeli Supreme Court Judgment Regarding the Security Fence" (HCJ 2056/04). http://www.jewishvirtuallibrary.org/jsource/Peace/fencesct.html and http://www.israelemb.org/articles/2004/June/2004063002.htm.

Izutsu, Toshiko. *Ethico-Religious Concepts in the Qur'ān*. Montreal: McGill University Press, 1966.

Jerusalem Media and Communications Center. "Report on Today's Incidents," September 28, 1996.

Kane, Anne E. "Theorizing Meaning Construction in Social Movements: Symbolic Structures and Interpretation during the Irish Land War, 1879–1882." *Sociological Theory* 15, no. 3 (November 1997): 249–276.

Kazziha, Walid W. *Revolutionary Transformation in the Arab World: Habash and His Comrades from Nationalism to Marxism*. New York: St. Martin's Press, 1975.

Kelsay, John. *Islam and War: A Study in Comparative Ethics*. Louisville, KY: Westminster/John Knox Press, 1993.

Kepel, Giles. *Muslim Extremism in Egypt: The Prophet and the Pharaoh*. Trans. Jon Rothschild. Berkeley, CA: University of California Press, 1985.

Khadduri, Majid. *War and Peace in the Law of Islam*. Baltimore: The Johns Hopkins University Press, 1955.

Khalidi, Rashid. *Palestinian Identity: The Construction of Modern National Consciousness*. New York: Columbia University Press, 1997.

Khalidi, Walid. *Dayr Yasin: al-jumʿa, 9 nisan/abril 1948*. [Dayr Yasin: Friday, 9 April 1948]. Beirut: Mu'assasat al-Dirasat al-Filastiniyya, 1999.

Khalifeh, Sahar. "Comments by Five Women Activists: Siham Abdullah, Amal Kharisha Barghouthi, Rita Giacaman, May Mistakmel Nassar, Amal Wahdan." Translated by Nagla El-Bassiouni. In *Palestinian Women of Gaza and the West Bank*. Edited by Suha Sabbagh. Bloomington and Indianapolis, IN: Indiana University Press, 1998.

Khawaja, Marwan. "Resource Mobilization, Hardship, and Popular Collective Action in the West Bank." *Social Forces* 73, no. 1 (September 1994): 191–220.

Khomeini, Ruhollah. *Islam and Revolution: Writings and Declarations of Imam Khomeini*. Translated and edited by Hamid Algar. Berkeley, CA: Mizan Press, 1980.

Kimmerling, Baruch, and Joel S. Migdal. *Palestinians: The Making of a People*. Cambridge, MA: Harvard University Press, 1993, 1994.

Kupferschmidt, Uri M. *The Supreme Muslim Council: Islam under the British Mandate for Palestine*. Leiden: E. J. Brill, 1987.

Al-Kurd, Mustafa. *Awlad Filastin*. [Children of Palestine]. Jerusalem, 1988. Sound cassette.

Lachman, Shai. "Arab Rebellion and Terrorism in Palestine, 1929–39: The Case of Sheikh Izz al-Din al-Qassam and His Movement." In *Zionism and Arabism in Palestine and Israel*. Edited by Elie Kedourie and Sylvia G. Haim. London: Frank Cass, 1982.

Lawrence, Bruce B. *Shattering the Myth: Islam beyond Violence*. Princeton, NJ: Princeton University Press, 1998.

Legrain, Jean-François. "A Defining Moment: Palestinian Islamic Fundamentalism." In *Islamic Fundamentalisms and the Gulf Crisis*. Edited by

James Piscatori. Chicago: Fundamentalism Project, American Academy of Arts and Sciences, 1991.

Lesch, Ann Mosely. *Arab Politics in Palestine, 1917–1939: The Frustration of a Nationalist Movement*. Ithaca, NY: Cornell University Press, 1979.

Lia, Brynjar. *The Society of the Muslim Brothers in Egypt: The Rise of an Islamic Mass Movement, 1928–1942*. Foreword by Jamal al-Banna. Reading, UK: Ithaca Press, 1998.

Lings, Martin. *Muhammad: His Life Based on the Earliest Sources*. London: Unwin Hyman, 1983, 1986, 1988.

Lockman, Zachary, and Joel Beinin. *Intifada: The Palestinian Uprising against Israeli Occupation*. Boston, MA: South End Press/MERIP, 1989.

Mahmood, Saba. *Politics of Piety: The Islamic Revival and the Feminist Subject*. Princeton, NJ: Princeton University Press, 2005.

Manna',ʿAdil. *Aʿlam filastin fi awakhir al-ʿahd al-ʿUthmani, 1800–1918*. [The Distinguished Personalities of Palestine of the Late Ottoman Period, 1800–1918]. Jerusalem: Jamʿiyat al-Dirasat al-ʿArabiyya, 1986.

Mannheim, Karl. "The Problem of Generations." Chap. in *Essays on the Sociology of Knowledge*. Edited by Paul Kecskemeti. London: Routledge & Kegan Paul, 1952.

Mansour, Camille. "The Palestinian-Israeli Peace Negotiations: An Overview and Assessment." *Journal of Palestine Studies* 22, no. 3 (Spring 1993): 5–31.

Mattar, Phillip. *The Mufti of Jerusalem: Al-Hajj Amin al-Husayni and the Palestinian National Movement*. New York: Columbia University Press, 1988.

McAuliffe, Jane Dammen. *Qur'ānic Christians: An Analysis of Classical and Modern Exegesis*. New York: Cambridge University Press, 1991.

Mernisi, Fatima. *Beyond the Veil: Male-Female Dynamics in Modern Muslim Society, Revised Edition*. Bloomington and Indianapolis, IN: Indiana University Press, 1975, 1987.

Milton-Edwards, Beverley. *Islamic Politics in Palestine*. London: Tauris Academic Studies, 1996.

Mir, Mustansir. "*Jihad* in Islam." In *The Jihad and Its Times*. Edited by Jadia Dajani-Shakeel and Ronald A. Messeir. Ann Arbor, MI: University of Michigan, Center for Near Eastern and North African Studies, 1991.

Mishal, Shaul, and Avraham Sela. *The Palestinian Hamas: Vision, Violence, and Coexistence*. New York: Columbia University Press, 2000.

Mitchell, Richard P. *The Society of the Muslim Brothers*. Foreword by John O. Voll. Oxford: Oxford University Press, 1969, 1993.

Moaddel, Mansoor, and Kamran Talattof, eds. *Modernist and Fundamentalist Debates in Islam: A Reader*. New York: Palgrave MacMillan, 2000.

Momen, Moojan. *An Introduction to Shiʿi Islam: The History and Doctrines of Twelver Shiʿism*. New Haven, CT: Yale University Press, 1985.

Moussalli, Ahmed S. *Radical Islamic Fundamentalism: The Ideological and Political Discourse of Sayyid Qutb*. Beirut: American University of Beirut Press, 1992.

Muslih, Muhammad Y. *The Origins of Palestinian Nationalism*. New York: Columbia University Press, 1988.

Neuhaus, David Mark. "Between Quiescence and Arousal: The Political Functions of Religion: A Case Study of the Arab Minority in Israel, 1948–1990." Ph.D. diss., Hebrew University (Jerusalem), 1991.

Nüsse, Andrea. *Muslim Palestine: The Ideology of Hamas*. Amsterdam: Harwood Academic Publishers, 1998; reprint, London: Routledge Curzon, 2002.

Online Newshour. "Middle East Background Reports," September 26–30, 1996, http://www.pbs.org/newshour/bb/middle_east/middle_east-pre2001 .html.

Palestinian Central Bureau of Statistics. *Population, Housing, and Establishment Census—1997, Final Results, Population Report, Bethlehem Governorate, First Part*. Ramallah, Palestine: PCBS, May 1999.

———. *Population, Housing, and Establishment Census—1997, Final Results, Population Report, Gaza Strip, First Part*. Ramallah, Palestine: PCBS, May 1999.

Pappe, Ilan. *A History of Modern Palestine: One Land, Two Peoples*. Cambridge: Cambridge University Press, 2004.

Peteet, Julie. "Male Gender and Rituals of Resistance in the Palestinian *Intifada*: A Cultural Politics of Violence." *American Ethnologist* 21, no. 1 (1994): 31–49.

Peters, Rudolph. *Islam and Colonialism: The Doctrine of Jihad in Modern History*. The Hague: Mouton Publishers, 1979.

———, trans. and ed. *Jihad in Mediaeval and Modern Islam: The Chapter on Jihad from Averroes' Legal Handbook 'Bidāyat al-mudjtahid' and the Treatise 'Koran and Fighting' by the Late Shaykh-al-Azhar, Mahmūd Shaltūt*. Leiden: E. J. Brill, 1977.

Pickthall, Mohammed Marmaduke. *The Meaning of the Glorious Koran*. New York: Penguin Books, n.d.

Porath, Yohoshua. *The Emergence of the Palestinian-Arab National Movement, 1918–1929*. London: Frank Cass, 1974.

———. *The Palestinian-Arab National Movement, 1929–1939: From Riots to Rebellion*. London: Frank Cass, 1977.

Quandt, William B., Fuad Jabber, and Ann Mosely Lesch. *The Politics of Palestinian Nationalism*. Berkeley, CA: University of California Press, 1973.

Al-qur'an al-karim. [The Glorious Qur'an]. Saudi Arabia: Majma' al-Malik Fahd li-Tiba'at al-Mushaf al-Sharif, n.d.

Qutb, Sayyid. *Al-'adala al-ijtima'iyya fi al-islam*. [Social Justice in Islam]. Beirut and Cairo: Dar al-Shuruq, 1975.

———. *Hadha al-din*. [This Religion]. Beirut and Cairo: Dar al-Shuruq, 1986.

———. *Ma'alim fi al-tariq* [Signposts along the Path]. Beirut and Cairo: Dar al-Shuruq, n.d.

Riesebrodt, Martin. *Pious Passion: The Emergence of Modern Fundamentalism in the United States and Iran*. Translated by Don Reneau. Berkeley, CA: University of California Press, 1993.

Robinson, Glenn E. "Hamas and the Islamist Mobilization." Chap. in *Building a Palestinian State: The Incomplete Revolution*. Bloomington and Indianapolis, IN: Indiana University Press, 1997.

Rosenfeld, Maya. "Power Structure, Agency, and Family in a Palestinian Refugee Camp." *International Journal of Middle East Studies* 34, no. 3 (August 2002): 519–551.
Roy, Olivier. *The Failure of Political Islam*. Translated by Carol Volk. Cambridge, MA: Harvard University Press, 1994.
Roy, Sara. *The Gaza Strip: The Political Economy of De-development*. Washington, DC: Institute for Palestine Studies, 1995; reprint, 2001.
Rubin, Barry. *Revolution until Victory? The Politics and History of the PLO*. Cambridge, MA: Harvard University Press, 1994.
Saad-Ghorayeb, Amal. *Hizbu'llah: Politics and Religion*. London: Pluto Press, 2002.
Sachedina, Abdulaziz A. "The Development of Jihad in Islamic Revelation and History." In *Cross, Crescent, and Sword: The Justification and Limitation of War in Western and Islamic Traditions*. Edited by James Turner Johnson and John Kelsay. New York: Greenwood Press, 1990.
Said, Edward W. *After the Last Sky: Palestinian Lives*. With photographs by Jean Mohr. New York: Pantheon Books, 1985, 1986; reprint, New York: Columbia University Press, 1998.
Sayigh, Rosemary. *Palestinians: From Peasants to Revolutionaries*. With an introduction by Noam Chomsky. London: Zed Books, 1979.
Sayigh, Yezid. *Armed Struggle and the Search for State: The Palestinian National Movement, 1949–1993*. Oxford: Oxford University Press, 1997.
Schiff, Ze'ev, and Ehud Ya'ari. *Intifada: The Palestinian Uprising—Israel's Third Front*. Edited and translated by Ina Friedman. New York: Simon and Schuster, 1989, 1990.
Schimmel, Annemarie. *Mystical Dimensions of Islam*. Chapel Hill, NC: University of North Carolina Press, 1975.
Schleifer, Abdullah. "Izz al-Din al-Qassam: Preacher and *Mujahid*." In *Struggle and Survival in the Modern Middle East*. Edited by Edmund Burke, III. Berkeley, CA: University of California Press, 1993.
Schoch, Bernd. *The Islamic Movement: A Challenge for Palestinian State-Building*. Jerusalem: PASSIA, 1999.
Schuman, Howard, and Jacqueline Scott. "Generations and Collective Memories." *American Sociological Review* 54 (June 1989): 359–381.
Sewell, William H., Jr. "Historical Events as Transformations of Structures: Inventing Revolution at the Bastille." *Theory and Society* 25, no. 6 (December 1996): 841–881.
———. "A Theory of Structure: Duality, Agency, and Transformation." *American Journal of Sociology* 98, no. 1 (July 1992): 1–29.
Shepard, William E. "Sayyid Qutb's Doctrine of *jāhiliyya*." *International Journal of Middle East Studies* 4, no. 35 (November 2003): 521–545.
Shikaki, Khalil. "Old Guard, Young Guard: The Palestinian Authority and the Peace Process at a Crossroads." Ramallah, Palestine: Palestinian Centre for Policy and Survey Research, November 1, 2001, http://www.amin.org/eng/khalil_shikaki/2001/00nov2001.html.
———. "Palestinians Divided." *Foreign Affairs* (January/February 2002): 89–105.

Shlaim, Avi. *Collusion across the Jordan: King Abdullah, the Zionist Movement, and the Partition of Palestine*. New York: Columbia University Press, 1988.

———. "Prelude to the Accord: Likud, Labor, and the Palestinians." *Journal of Palestine Studies* 23, no. 2 (Winter 1994): 5–19.

Simmel, Georg. "The Web of Group-Affiliation." Chap. in *Conflict and the Web of Group-Affiliations*. Translated by Reinhard Bendix. New York: Free Press, 1955.

Snow, David A., and Susan E. Marshall. "Cultural Imperialism, Social Movements, and the Islamic Revival." *Research in Social Movements, Conflicts and Change* 7 (1984): 131–152.

Sontag, Deborah. "In Mock Palestinian Hill Town, Israeli Troops Prepare for Worst." *New York Times*, June 24, 2000, http://www.nytimes.com.

Strenski, Ivan. "Sacrifice, Gift and the Social Logic of Muslim 'Human Bombers.'" *Terrorism and Political Violence* 15, no. 3 (Autumn 2003): 1–34.

Swedenburg, Ted. *Memories of Revolt: The 1936–1939 Rebellion and the Palestinian National Past*. Minneapolis: University of Minnesota Press, 1995.

Swidler, Ann. "Culture in Action: Symbols and Strategies." *American Sociological Review* 51 (April 1986): 273–286.

Tamari, Salim. "In League with Zion: Israel's Search for a Native Pillar." *Journal of Palestine Studies* 12, no. 4 (Summer 1983): 41–56.

———. "Left in Limbo: Leninist Heritage and Islamist Challenge." *MERIP* (November–December 1992): 16–21.

Toth, James. "Islamism in Southern Egypt: A Case Study of a Radical Religious Movement." *International Journal of Middle East Studies* 4, no. 35 (November 2003): 547–572.

Tucker, Judith E. "The Arab Family in History: 'Otherness' and the Study of the Family." In *Arab Women: Old Boundaries, New Frontiers*. Edited by Judith E. Tucker. Bloomington and Indianapolis, IN: Indiana University Press, 1993.

Turner, Bryan S. "Strategic Generations: Historical Change, Literary Expression, and Generational Politics." In *Generational Consciousness, Narrative, and Politics*. Edited by June Edmunds and Bryan S. Turner. Lanham, MD: Rowman & Littlefield Publishers, 2002.

United Nations Development Program. "UNDP Calls for Immediate Action to Address Emergency Needs of Palestinian Communities Affected by Israeli Separation Wall." Jerusalem: August 5, 2003. http://www.papp.undp.org/undp_papp/pr/wall.htm.

United Nations Office of the Special Coordinator in the Occupied Territories. "The Impact on the Palestinian Economy of Confrontations, Mobility Restrictions and Border Closures, 1 October 2000–31 January 2001." New York: February 2001, http://domino.un.org/unispal.nsf/0/edadfb71ec0f110085256c3a0066fd23?OpenDocument; http://www.arts.mcgill.ca/mepp/unsco/unfront.html.

United Nations Security Council. *UNSCR Resolution 1073* (1996), http://www.palestine-UN.org/news/oct96_r1073.html.

Usher, Graham. "The Debut of the Palestinian Authority." Chap. in *Palestine in Crisis: The Struggle for Peace and Political Independence after Oslo*. London: Pluto Press, 1995, 1997.

———. "Fatah, Hamas, and the Crisis of Oslo: Interviews with Marwan Barghouti and Ibrahim Ghoshah." Chap. in *Palestine in Crisis: The Struggle for Peace and Political Independence after Oslo*. London: Pluto Press, 1995, 1997.

———. "The Intifada This Time." *Al-Ahram Weekly On-Line*, October 31, 2000, http://weekly.ahram.org.eg/2000/506/re1.htm.

———. "The Islamist Challenge." Chap. in *Palestine in Crisis: The Struggle for Peace and Political Independence after Oslo*. London: Pluto Press, 1995, 1997.

———. "The Meaning of Sheikh Yassin." Chap. in *Dispatches from Palestine: The Rise and Fall of the Oslo Peace Process*. London: Pluto Press, 1999.

———. "The Politics of Atrocity." Chap. in *Dispatches from Palestine: The Rise and Fall of the Oslo Peace Process*. London: Pluto Press, 1999.

———. "What Kind of Nation? The Rise of Hamas in the Occupied Territories." Chap. in *Dispatches from Palestine: The Rise and Fall of the Oslo Peace Process*. London: Pluto Press, 1999.

Weber, Max. *Ancient Judaism*. Translated and edited by Hans H. Gerth and Don Martindale. New York: Free Press, 1952.

———. *Economy and Society: An Outline of Interpretive Sociology, Volumes One and Two*. Edited by Guenther Roth and Claus Wittich. Berkeley, CA: University of California Press, 1968, 1978.

———. "Politics as a Vocation." Chap. in *From Max Weber: Essays in Sociology*. New York: Free Press, 1946.

Wehr, Hans. *A Dictionary of Modern Written Arabic*. Edited by J. Milton Cowan. Wiesbaden: Otto Harrassowitz, 1966, 1971, 1974; reprint, Libraire du Liban, May 1980.

Wiktorowicz, Quintan, ed. *Islamic Activism: A Social Movement Theory Approach*. Bloomington, IN: Indiana University Press, 2004.

Index